THE RIGHT WING INDIVIDUALIST
TRADITION IN AMERICA

The Right Wing Individualist Tradition in America

Advisory Editors:
Dr. Murray N. Rothbard,
Polytechnic Institute of Brooklyn
Jerome Tuccille,
New School for Social Research

LET'S ABOLISH GOVERNMENT

Lysander Spooner

Arno Press & The New York Times
New York • 1972

Reprint Edition 1972 by Arno Press Inc.

LC# 73-172232
ISBN 0-405-00441-9

The Right Wing Individualist Tradition in America
ISBN for complete set: 0-405-00410-9
See last pages of this volume for titles.

Manufactured in the United States of America

CONTENTS

AN ESSAY ON THE TRIAL BY JURY

A LETTER TO GROVER CLEVELAND, ON HIS FALSE INAUGURAL ADDRESS, THE USURPATIONS AND CRIMES OF LAWMAKERS AND JUDGES, AND THE CONSEQUENT POVERTY, IGNORANCE, AND SERVITUDE OF THE PEOPLE

NO TREASON: The Constitution of No Authority, and A LETTER TO THOMAS F. BAYARD

AN ESSAY

ON THE

TRIAL BY JURY.

BY LYSANDER SPOONER.

BOSTON:
JOHN P. JEWETT AND COMPANY.
CLEVELAND, OHIO:
JEWETT, PROCTOR & WORTHINGTON.
1852.

Entered according to Act of Congress, in the year 1852, by
LYSANDER SPOONER,
In the Clerk's Office of the District Court of Massachusetts.

NOTICE TO ENGLISH PUBLISHERS.

The author claims the copyright of this book in England, on Common Law principles, without regard to acts of parliament; and if the main principle of the book itself be true, viz., that no legislation, in conflict with the Common Law, is of any validity, his claim is a legal one. He forbids any one to reprint the book without his consent.

Stereotyped by
HOBART & ROBBINS;
New England Type and Stereotype Foundery,
BOSTON.

NOTE.

This volume, it is presumed by the author, gives what will generally be considered satisfactory evidence,— though not all the evidence,— of what the Common Law trial by jury really is. In a future volume, if it should be called for, it is designed to corroborate the grounds taken in this; give a concise view of the English constitution; show the unconstitutional character of the existing government in England, and the unconstitutional means by which the trial by jury has been broken down in practice; prove that, neither in England nor the United States, have legislatures ever been invested by the people with any authority to impair the powers, change the oaths, or (with few exceptions) abridge the jurisdiction, of juries, or select jurors on any other than Common Law principles; and, consequently, that, in both countries, legislation is still constitutionally subordinate to the discretion and consciences of Common Law juries, in all cases, both civil and criminal, in which juries sit. The same volume will probably also discuss several political and legal questions, which will naturally assume importance if the trial by jury should be reëstablished.

CONTENTS.

		PAGE
CHAPTER I.	THE RIGHT OF JURIES TO JUDGE OF THE JUSTICE OF LAWS, ...	5
	SECTION 1, ...	5
	SECTION 2, ...	11
CHAPTER II.	THE TRIAL BY JURY, AS DEFINED BY MAGNA CARTA, ...	20
	SECTION 1. *The History of Magna Carta,* . . .	20
	SECTION 2. *The Language of Magna Carta,* . .	25
CHAPTER III.	ADDITIONAL PROOFS OF THE RIGHTS AND DUTIES OF JURORS, ...	51
	SECTION 1. *Weakness of the Regal Authority,* . .	51
	SECTION 2. *The Ancient Common Law Juries were mere Courts of Conscience,*	68
	SECTION 3. *The Oaths of Jurors,*	85
	SECTION 4. *The Right of Jurors to fix the Sentence,*	91
	SECTION 5. *The Oaths of Judges,*	98
	SECTION 6. *The Coronation Oath,*	102
CHAPTER IV.	THE RIGHTS AND DUTIES OF JURIES IN CIVIL SUITS, ...	110
CHAPTER V.	OBJECTIONS ANSWERED, ...	128
CHAPTER VI.	JURIES OF THE PRESENT DAY ILLEGAL, .	142
CHAPTER VII.	ILLEGAL JUDGES, ...	157
CHAPTER VIII.	THE FREE ADMINISTRATION OF JUSTICE, .	172
CHAPTER IX.	THE CRIMINAL INTENT, ...	178
CHAPTER X.	MORAL CONSIDERATIONS FOR JURORS, . .	189
CHAPTER XI.	AUTHORITY OF MAGNA CARTA, ...	192
CHAPTER XII.	LIMITATIONS IMPOSED UPON THE MAJORITY BY THE TRIAL BY JURY, ...	206
APPENDIX — TAXATION, ...		222

TRIAL BY JURY.

CHAPTER I.

THE RIGHT OF JURIES TO JUDGE OF THE JUSTICE OF LAWS.

SECTION I.

For more than six hundred years — that is, since Magna Carta, in 1215 — there has been no clearer principle of English or American constitutional law, than that, in criminal cases, it is not only the right and duty of juries to judge what are the facts, what is the law, and what was the moral intent of the accused; *but that it is also their right, and their primary and paramount duty, to judge of the justice of the law, and to hold all laws invalid, that are, in their opinion, unjust or oppressive, and all persons guiltless in violating, or resisting the execution of, such laws.*

Unless such be the right and duty of jurors, it is plain that, instead of juries being a "palladium of liberty" — a barrier against the tyranny and oppression of the government — they are really mere tools in its hands, for carrying into execution any injustice and oppression it may desire to have executed.

But for their right to judge of the law, *and the justice of the law*, juries would be no protection to an accused person, *even as to matters of fact;* for, if the government can dictate to a jury any law whatever, in a criminal case, it can certainly dictate to them the laws of evidence. That is, it can dictate what evidence is admissible, and what inadmissible, *and also what force or weight is to be given to the evidence admitted.* And if the government can thus dictate to a jury the laws of evidence, it can not only make it necessary for them to convict on a partial exhibition of the evidence rightfully pertaining to the case, but it can even require them

1*

to convict on any evidence whatever that it pleases to offer them.

That the rights and duties of jurors must necessarily be such as are here claimed for them, will be evident when it is considered what the trial by jury is, and what is its object.

"*The trial by jury,*" then, is a "*trial by the country*" — that is, *by the people — as distinguished from a trial by the government.*

It was anciently called "trial *per pais*" — that is, "trial by the country." And now, in every criminal trial, the jury are told that the accused "has, for trial, put himself upon the *country;* which *country* you (the jury) are."

The object of this trial "by the country," or by the people, in preference to a trial by the government, is to guard against every species of oppression by the government. In order to effect this end, it is indispensable that the people, or "the country," judge of and determine their own liberties against the government; instead of the government's judging of and determining its own powers over the people. How is it possible that juries can do anything to protect the liberties of the people against the government, if they are not allowed to determine what those liberties are?

Any government, that is its own judge of, and determines authoritatively for the people, what are its own powers over the people, is an absolute government of course. It has all the powers that it chooses to exercise. There is no other — or at least no more accurate — definition of a despotism than this.

On the other hand, any people, that judge of, and determine authoritatively for the government, what are their own liberties against the government, of course retain all the liberties they wish to enjoy. *And this is freedom.* At least, it is freedom *to them;* because, although it may be theoretically imperfect, it, nevertheless, corresponds to *their* highest notions of freedom.

To secure this right of the people to judge of their own liberties against the government, the jurors are taken, (or must be, to make them lawful jurors,) from the body of the people, *by lot*, or by some process that precludes any previous knowledge, choice, or selection of them, on the part of the government.

This is done to prevent the government's constituting a jury of its own partisans or friends; in other words, to prevent the government's *packing* a jury, with a view to maintain its own laws, and accomplish its own purposes.

It is supposed that, if twelve men be taken, *by lot*, from the mass of the people, without the possibility of any previous knowledge, choice, or selection of them, on the part of the government, the jury will be a fair epitome of "the country" at large, and not merely of the party or faction that sustain the measures of the government; that substantially all classes of opinions, prevailing among the people, will be represented in the jury; and especially that the opponents of the government, (if the government have any opponents,) will be represented there, as well as its friends; that the classes, who are oppressed by the laws of the government, (if any are thus oppressed,) will have their representatives in the jury, as well as those classes, who take sides with the oppressor — that is, with the government.

It is fairly presumable that such a tribunal will agree to no conviction except such as *substantially the whole country* would agree to, if they were present, taking part in the trial. A trial by such a tribunal is, therefore, in effect, "a trial by the country." In its results it probably comes as near to a trial by the whole country, as any trial that it is practicable to have, without too great inconvenience and expense. And as unanimity is required for a conviction, it follows that no one can be convicted, except for the violation of such laws as substantially the *whole* country wish to have maintained. The government can enforce none of its laws, (by punishing offenders, through the verdicts of juries,) except such as substantially the whole people wish to have enforced. The government, therefore, consistently with the trial by jury, can exercise no powers over the people, (or, what is the same thing, over the accused person, who represents the rights of the people,) except such as substantially the whole people of the country consent that it may exercise. In such a trial, therefore, "the country," or the people, judge of and determine their own liberties against the government, instead of the government's judging of and determining its own powers over the people.

But all this "trial by the country" would be no trial at all "by the country," but only a trial by the government, if the government could either declare who may, and who may not, be jurors, or could dictate to the jury anything whatever, either of law or evidence, that is of the essence of the trial.

If the government may decide who may, and who may not, be jurors, it will of course select only its partisans, and those friendly to its measures. It may not only prescribe who may, and who may not, be eligible to be drawn as jurors; but it may also question each person drawn as a juror, as to his sentiments in regard to the particular law involved in each trial, before suffering him to be sworn on the panel; and exclude him if he be found unfavorable to the maintenance of such a law.*

So, also, if the government may dictate to the jury *what laws they are to enforce,* it is no longer a " trial by the country,"

---

* To show that this supposition is not an extravagant one, it may be mentioned that courts have repeatedly questioned jurors to ascertain whether they were prejudiced *against the government* — that is, whether they were in favor of, or opposed to, such laws of the government as were to be put in issue in the then pending trial. This was done (in 1851) in the United States District Court for the District of Massachusetts, by Peleg Sprague, the United States district judge, in empanelling three several juries for the trials of Scott, Hayden, and Morris, charged with having aided in the rescue of a fugitive slave from the custody of the United States deputy marshal. This judge caused the following question to be propounded to all the jurors separately; and those who answered unfavorably for the purposes of the government, were excluded from the panel.

"Do you hold any opinions upon the subject of the Fugitive Slave Law, so called, which will induce you to refuse to convict a person indicted under it, if the facts set forth in the indictment, *and constituting the offence,* are proved against him, and the court direct you that the law is constitutional?"

The reason of this question was, that "the Fugitive Slave Law, so called," was so obnoxious to a large portion of the people, as to render a conviction under it hopeless, if the jurors were taken indiscriminately from among the people.

A similar question was soon afterwards propounded to the persons drawn as jurors in the United States *Circuit* Court for the District of Massachusetts, by Benjamin R. Curtis, one of the Justices of the Supreme Court of the United States, in empanelling a jury for the trial of the aforesaid Morris on the charge before mentioned; and those who did not answer the question favorably for the government were again excluded from the panel.

It has also been an habitual practice with the Supreme Court of Massachusetts, in empanelling juries for the trial of *capital* offences, to inquire of the persons drawn as jurors whether they had any conscientious scruples against finding verdicts of guilty

but a trial by the government; because the jury then try the accused, not by any standard of their own — not by their own judgments of their rightful liberties — but by a standard dictated to them by the government. And the standard, thus dictated by the government, becomes the measure of the people's liberties. If the government dictate the standard of trial, it of course dictates the results of the trial. And such a trial is no trial by the country, but only a trial by the government; and in it the government determines what are its own powers over the people, instead of the people's determining what are their own liberties against the government. In short, if the jury have no right to judge of the justice of a law of the government, they plainly can do nothing to protect the people against the oppressions of the government; for there are no oppressions which the government may not authorize by law.

The jury are also to judge whether the laws are rightly expounded to them by the court. Unless they judge on this point, they do nothing to protect their liberties against the oppressions that are capable of being practised under cover of a corrupt exposition of the laws. If the judiciary can authoritatively dictate to a jury any exposition of the law, they can dictate to them the law itself, and such laws as they please; because laws are, in practice, one thing or another, according as they are expounded.

---

in such cases; that is, whether they had any conscientious scruples against sustaining the law prescribing death as the punishment of the crime to be tried; and to exclude from the panel all who answered in the affirmative.

The only principle upon which these questions are asked, is this — that no man shall be allowed to serve as juror, unless he be ready to enforce any enactment of the government, however cruel or tyrannical it may be.

What is such a jury good for, as a protection against the tyranny of the government? A jury like that is palpably nothing but a mere tool of oppression in the hands of the government. A trial by such a jury is really a trial by the government itself — and not a trial by the country — because it is a trial only by men specially selected by the government for their readiness to enforce its own tyrannical measures.

If that be the true principle of the trial by jury, the trial is utterly worthless as a security to liberty. The Czar might, with perfect safety to his authority, introduce the trial by jury into Russia, if he could but be permitted to select his jurors from those who were ready to maintain his laws, without regard to their injustice.

This example is sufficient to show that the very pith of the trial by jury, as a safeguard to liberty, consists in the jurors being taken indiscriminately from the whole people, and in their right to hold invalid all laws which they think unjust.

The jury must also judge whether there really be any such law, (be it good or bad,) as the accused is charged with having transgressed. Unless they judge on this point, the people are liable to have their liberties taken from them by brute force, without any law at all.

The jury must also judge of the laws of evidence. If the government can dictate to a jury the laws of evidence, it can not only shut out any evidence it pleases, tending to vindicate the accused, but it can require that any evidence whatever, that it pleases to offer, be held as conclusive proof of any offence whatever which the government chooses to allege.

It is manifest, therefore, that the jury must judge of and try the whole case, and every part and parcel of the case, free of any dictation or authority on the part of the government. They must judge of the existence of the law; of the true exposition of the law; *of the justice of the law;* and of the admissibility and weight of all the evidence offered; otherwise the government will have everything its own way; the jury will be mere puppets in the hands of the government; and the trial will be, in reality, a trial by the government, and not a "trial by the country." By such trials the government will determine its own powers over the people, instead of the people's determining their own liberties against the government; and it will be an entire delusion to talk, as for centuries we have done, of the trial by jury, as a "palladium of liberty," or as any protection to the people against the oppression and tyranny of the government.

The question, then, between trial by jury, as thus described, and trial by the government, is simply a question between liberty and despotism. The authority to judge what are the powers of the government, and what the liberties of the people, must necessarily be vested in one or the other of the parties themselves — the government, or the people; because there is no third party to whom it can be entrusted. If the authority be vested in the government, the government is absolute, and the people have no liberties except such as the government sees fit to indulge them with. If, on the other hand, that authority be vested in the people, then the people have all liberties, (as against the government,) except such as substantially the whole people (through a jury) choose to disclaim; and the government can exercise no power except such as substantially the whole people (through a jury) consent that it may exercise.

SECTION II.

The force and justice of the preceding argument cannot be evaded by saying that the government is chosen by the people; that, in theory, it represents the people; that it is designed to do the will of the people; that its members are all sworn to observe the fundamental or constitutional law instituted by the people; that its acts are therefore entitled to be considered the acts of the people; and that to allow a jury, representing the people, to invalidate the acts of the government, would therefore be arraying the people against themselves.

There are two answers to such an argument.

One answer is, that, in a representative government, there is no absurdity or contradiction, nor any arraying of the people against themselves, in requiring that the statutes or enactments of the government shall pass the ordeal of any number of separate tribunals, before it shall be determined that they are to have the force of laws. Our American constitutions have provided five of these separate tribunals, to wit, representatives, senate, executive,* jury, and judges; and have made it necessary that each enactment shall pass the ordeal of all these separate tribunals, before its authority can be established by the punishment of those who choose to transgress it. And there is no more absurdity or inconsistency in making a jury one of these several tribunals, than there is in making the representatives, or the senate, or the executive, or the judges, one of them. There is no more absurdity in giving a jury a veto upon the laws, than there is in giving a veto to each of these other tribunals. The people are no more arrayed against themselves, when a jury puts its veto upon a statute, which the other tribunals have sanctioned, than they are when the

---

* The executive has a qualified veto upon the passage of laws, in most of our governments, and an absolute veto, in all of them, upon the execution of any laws which he deems unconstitutional; because his oath to support the constitution (as he understands it) forbids him to execute any law that he deems unconstitutional.

same veto is exercised by the representatives, the senate, the executive, or the judges.

But another answer to the argument that the people are arrayed against themselves, when a jury hold an enactment of the government invalid, is, that the government, and all the departments of the government, *are merely the servants and agents of the people;* not invested with arbitrary or absolute authority to bind the people, but required to submit all their enactments to the judgment of a tribunal more fairly representing the whole people, before they carry them into execution, by punishing any individual for transgressing them. If the government were not thus required to submit their enactments to the judgment of "the country," before executing them upon individuals — if, in other words, the people had reserved to themselves no veto upon the acts of the government, the government, instead of being a mere servant and agent of the people, would be an absolute despot over the people. It would have all power in its own hands; because the power to *punish* carries all other powers with it. A power that can, of itself, and by its own authority, punish disobedience, can compel obedience and submission, and is above all responsibility for the character of its laws. In short, it is a despotism.

And it is of no consequence to inquire how a government came by this power to punish, whether by prescription, by inheritance, by usurpation, or by delegation from the people? *If it have now but got it,* the government is absolute.

It is plain, therefore, that if the people have invested the government with power to make laws that absolutely bind the people, and to punish the people for transgressing those laws, the people have surrendered their liberties unreservedly into the hands of the government.

It is of no avail to say, in answer to this view of the case, that in surrendering their liberties into the hands of the government, the people took an oath from the government, that it would exercise its power within certain constitutional limits; for when did oaths ever restrain a government that was otherwise unrestrained? Or when did a government fail to determine that all its acts were within the constitutional and authorized limits of its power, if it were permitted to determine that question for itself?

Neither is it of any avail to say, that, if the government abuse its power, and enact unjust and oppressive laws, the government may be changed by the influence of discussion, and the exercise of the right of suffrage. Discussion can do nothing to prevent the enactment, or procure the repeal, of unjust laws, unless it be understood that the discussion is to be followed by resistance. Tyrants care nothing for discussions that are to end only in discussion. Discussions, which do not interfere with the enforcement of their laws, are but idle wind to them. Suffrage is equally powerless and unreliable. It can be exercised only periodically; and the tyranny must at least be borne until the time for suffrage comes. Besides, when the suffrage is exercised, it gives no guaranty for the repeal of existing laws that are oppressive, and no security against the enactment of new ones that are equally so. The second body of legislators are liable and likely to be just as tyrannical as the first. If it be said that the second body may be chosen for their integrity, the answer is, that the first were chosen for that very reason, and yet proved tyrants. The second will be exposed to the same temptations as the first, and will be just as likely to prove tyrannical. Who ever heard that succeeding legislatures were, on the whole, more honest than those that preceded them? What is there in the nature of men or things to make them so? If it be said that the first body were chosen from motives of injustice, that fact proves that there is a portion of society who desire to establish injustice; and if they were powerful or artful enough to procure the election of their instruments to compose the first legislature, they will be likely to be powerful or artful enough to procure the election of the same or similar instruments to compose the second. The right of suffrage, therefore, and even a change of legislators, guarantees no change of legislation — certainly no change for the better. Even if a change for the better actually comes, it comes too late, because it comes only after more or less injustice has been irreparably done.

But, at best, the right of suffrage can be exercised only periodically; and between the periods the legislators are wholly irresponsible. No despot was ever more entirely irresponsible than are republican legislators during the period for which they are chosen. They can neither be removed from their office, nor called to account while in their office, nor punished after they leave their office, be their tyranny what it may. Moreover, the judicial and executive departments of the government are equally irresponsible *to the people*, and are only responsible, (by impeachment, and dependence for their salaries), to these irresponsible legislators. This dependence of the judiciary and executive upon the legislature is a guaranty that they will always sanction and execute its laws, whether just or unjust. Thus the legislators hold the whole power of the government in their hands, and are at the same time utterly irresponsible for the manner in which they use it.

If, now, this government, (the three branches thus really united in one), can determine the validity of, and enforce, its own laws, it is, for the time being, entirely absolute, and wholly irresponsible to the people.

But this is not all. These legislators, and this government, so irresponsible while in power, can perpetuate their power at pleasure, if they can determine what legislation is authoritative upon the people, and can enforce obedience to it; for they can not only declare their power perpetual, but they can enforce submission to all legislation that is necessary to secure its perpetuity. They can, for example, prohibit all discussion of the rightfulness of their authority; forbid the use of the suffrage; prevent the election of any successors; disarm, plunder, imprison, and even kill all who refuse submission. If, therefore, the government (all departments united) be absolute for a day — that is, if it can, for a day, enforce obedience to its own laws — it can, in that day, secure its power for all time — like the queen, who wished to reign but for a day, but in that day caused the king, her husband, to be slain, and usurped his throne.

Nor will it avail to say that such acts would be unconstitutional, and that unconstitutional acts may be lawfully resisted; for everything a government pleases to do will, of course, be determined to be constitutional, if the government itself be permitted to determine the question of the constitutionality of its own acts. Those who are capable of tyranny, are capable of perjury to sustain it.

The conclusion, therefore, is, that any government, that can, *for a day*, enforce its own laws, without appealing to the people, (or to a tribunal fairly representing the people,) for their consent, is, in theory, an absolute government, irresponsible to the people, and can perpetuate its power at pleasure.

The trial by jury is based upon a recognition of this principle, and therefore forbids the government to execute any of its laws, by punishing violators, in any case whatever, without first getting the consent of "the country," or the people, through a jury. In this way, the people, at all times, hold their liberties in their own hands, and never surrender them, even for a moment, into the hands of the government.

The trial by jury, then, gives to any and every individual the liberty, at any time, to disregard or resist any law whatever of the government, if he be willing to submit to the decision of a jury, the questions, whether the law be intrinsically just and obligatory? and whether his conduct, in disregarding or resisting it, were right in itself? And any law, which does not, in such trial, obtain the unanimous sanction of twelve men, taken at random from the people, and judging according to the standard of justice in their own minds, free from all dictation and authority of the government, may be transgressed and resisted with impunity, by whomsoever pleases to transgress or resist it.*

The trial by jury authorizes all this, or it is a sham and a hoax, utterly worthless for protecting the people against oppression. If it do not authorize an individual to resist the first and least act of injustice or tyranny, on the part of the government, it does not authorize him to resist the last and the greatest. If it do not authorize individuals to nip tyranny in the bud, it does not authorize them to cut it down when its branches are filled with the ripe fruits of plunder and oppression.

Those who deny the right of a jury to protect an individual in resisting an unjust law of the government, deny him all

---

* And if there be so much as a reasonable *doubt* of the justice of the laws, the benefit of that doubt must be given to the defendant, and not to the government. So that the government must keep its laws *clearly* within the limits of justice, if it would ask a jury to enforce them.

legal defence whatsoever against oppression. The right of revolution, which tyrants, in mockery, accord to mankind, is no *legal* right *under* a government; it is only a *natural* right to overturn a government. The government itself never acknowledges this right. And the right is practically established only when and because the government no longer exists to call it in question. The right, therefore, can be exercised with impunity, only when it is exercised victoriously. All *unsuccessful* attempts at revolution, however justifiable in themselves, are punished as treason, if the government be permitted to judge of the treason. The government itself never admits the injustice of its laws, as a legal defence for those who have attempted a revolution, and failed. The right of revolution, therefore, is a right of no practical value, except for those who are stronger than the government. So long, therefore, as the oppressions of a government are kept within such limits as simply not to exasperate against it a power greater than its own, the right of revolution cannot be appealed to, and is therefore inapplicable to the case. This affords a wide field for tyranny; and if a jury cannot *here* intervene, the oppressed are utterly defenceless.

It is manifest that the only security against the tyranny of the government lies in forcible resistance to the execution of the injustice; because the injustice will certainly be executed, *unless it be forcibly resisted.* And if it be but suffered to be executed, it must then be borne; for the government never makes compensation for its own wrongs.

Since, then, this forcible resistance to the injustice of the government is the only possible means of preserving liberty, it is indispensable to all *legal* liberty that this *resistance* should be *legalized.* It is perfectly self-evident that where there is no *legal* right to resist the oppression of the government, there can be no *legal* liberty. And here it is all-important to notice, that, *practically speaking*, there can be no *legal* right to resist the oppressions of the government, unless there be some *legal* tribunal, other than the government, and wholly independent of, and *above*, the government, to judge between the government and those who resist its oppressions; in other words, to judge what laws of the government are to be obeyed, and what may be resisted and held for nought. The only tribunal known to our laws, for this purpose, is a jury. If a jury have not the right to judge between the government and those who disobey its laws, and resist its oppressions, the government is absolute, and the people, *legally speaking*, are slaves. Like many other slaves they may have sufficient courage and strength to keep their masters somewhat in check; but they are nevertheless *known to the law* only as slaves.

That this right of resistance was recognized as a common law right, when the ancient and genuine trial by jury was in force, is not only proved by the nature of the trial itself, but is acknowledged by history.*

This right of resistance is recognized by the constitution of the United States, as a strictly legal and constitutional right. It is so recognized, first by the provision that "the trial of all crimes, except in cases of impeachment, shall be by jury"— that is, by the country — and not by the government; secondly, by the provision that "the right of the people to keep and bear arms shall not be infringed." This constitutional security for "the right to keep and bear arms," implies the right to use them — as much as a constitutional security for the right to buy and keep food would have implied the right to eat it. The constitution, therefore, takes it for granted that

---

* *Hallam* says, "The relation established between a lord and his vassal by the feudal tenure, far from containing principles of any servile and implicit obedience, permitted the compact to be dissolved in case of its violation by either party. This extended as much to the sovereign as to inferior lords. * * If a vassal was aggrieved, and if justice was denied him, he sent a defiance, that is, a renunciation of fealty to the king, and was entitled to enforce redress at the point of his sword. It then became a contest of strength as between two independent potentates, and was terminated by treaty, advantageous or otherwise, according to the fortune of war. * * There remained the original principle, that allegiance depended conditionally upon good treatment, and that an appeal might be *lawfully* made to arms against an oppressive government. Nor was this, we may be sure, left for extreme necessity, or thought to require a long-enduring forbearance. In modern times, a king, compelled by his subjects' swords to abandon any pretension, would be supposed to have ceased to reign ; and the express recognition of such a right as that of insurrection has been justly deemed inconsistent with the majesty of law. But ruder ages had ruder sentiments. Force was necessary to repel force ; and men accustomed to see the king's authority defied by a private riot, were not much shocked when it was resisted in defence of public freedom." — 3 *Middle Ages,* 240-2.

the people will judge of the conduct of the government, and that, as they have the right, they will also have the sense, to use arms, whenever the necessity of the case justifies it. And it is a sufficient and *legal* defence for a person accused of using arms against the government, if he can show, to the satisfaction of a jury, *or even any one of a jury*, that the law he resisted was an unjust one.

In the American *State* constitutions also, this right of resistance to the oppressions of the government is recognized, in various ways, as a natural, legal, and constitutional right. In the first place, it is so recognized by provisions establishing the trial by jury; thus requiring that accused persons shall be tried by "the country," instead of the government. In the second place, it is recognized by many of them, as, for example, those of Massachusetts, Maine, Vermont, Connecticut, Pennsylvania, Ohio, Indiana, Michigan, Kentucky, Tennessee, Arkansas, Mississippi, Alabama, and Florida, by provisions expressly declaring that the people shall have the right to bear arms. In many of them also, as, for example, those of Maine, New Hampshire, Vermont, Massachusetts, New Jersey, Pennsylvania, Delaware, Ohio, Indiana, Illinois, Florida, Iowa, and Arkansas, by provisions, in their bills of rights, declaring that men have a natural, inherent, and inalienable right of "*defending* their lives and liberties." This, of course, means that they have a right to defend them against any injustice *on the part of the government*, and not merely on the part of private individuals; because the object of all bills of rights is to assert the rights of individuals and the people, *as against the government*, and not as against private persons. It would be a matter of ridiculous supererogation to assert, in a constitution of government, the natural right of men to defend their lives and liberties against private trespassers.

Many of these bills of rights also assert the natural right of all men to protect their property — that is, to protect it *against the government.* It would be unnecessary and silly indeed to assert, in a constitution of government, the natural right of individuals to protect their property against thieves and robbers.

The constitutions of New Hampshire and Tennessee also declare that "The doctrine of non-resistance against arbitrary power and oppression is absurd, slavish, and destructive of the good and happiness of mankind."

The legal effect of these constitutional recognitions of the right of individuals to defend their property, liberties, and lives, against the government, is to legalize resistance to all injustice and oppression, of every name and nature whatsoever, on the part of the government.

But for this right of resistance, on the part of the people, all governments would become tyrannical to a degree of which few people are aware. Constitutions are utterly worthless to restrain the tyranny of governments, unless it be understood that the people will, by force, compel the government to keep within the constitutional limits. Practically speaking, no government knows any limits to its power, except the endurance of the people. But that the people are stronger than the government, and will resist in extreme cases, our governments would be little or nothing else than organized systems of plunder and oppression. All, or nearly all, the advantage there is in fixing any constitutional limits to the power of a government, is simply to give notice to the government of the point at which it will meet with resistance. If the people are then as good as their word, they may keep the government within the bounds they have set for it; otherwise it will disregard them — as is proved by the example of all our American governments, in which the constitutions have all become obsolete, at the moment of their adoption, for nearly or quite all purposes except the appointment of officers, who at once become practically absolute, except so far as they are restrained by the fear of popular resistance.

The bounds set to the power of the government, by the trial by jury, as will hereafter be shown, are these — that the government shall never touch the property, person, or natural or civil rights of an individual, against his consent, (except for the purpose of bringing them before a jury for trial,) unless in pursuance and *execution* of a judgment, or decree, rendered by a jury in each individual case, upon such evidence, and such law, as are satisfactory to their own understandings and consciences, irrespective of all legislation of the government.

CHAPTER II.

THE TRIAL BY JURY, AS DEFINED BY MAGNA CARTA.

THAT the trial by jury is all that has been claimed for it in the preceding chapter, is proved both by the history and the language of the Great Charter of English Liberties, to which we are to look for a true definition of the trial by jury, and of which the guaranty for that trial is the vital, and most memorable, part.

SECTION I.

The History of Magna Carta.

In order to judge of the object and meaning of that chapter of Magna Carta which secures the trial by jury, it is to be borne in mind that, at the time of Magna Carta, the king (with exceptions immaterial to this discussion, but which will appear hereafter) was, constitutionally, the entire government; the sole *legislative, judicial,* and executive power of the nation. The executive and judicial officers were merely his servants, appointed by him, and removable at his pleasure. In addition to this, " the king himself often sat in his court, which always attended his person. He there heard causes, and pronounced judgment; and though he was assisted by the advice of other members, it is not to be imagined that a decision could be obtained contrary to his inclination or opinion."* Judges were in those days, and afterwards, such abject servants of the king, that " we find that King Edward I. (1272 to 1307) fined and imprisoned his judges, in the same manner as Alfred the Great, among the Saxons, had done before him, by the sole exercise of his authority."†

---

* 1 Hume, Appendix 2.   † Crabbe's History of the English Law, 236.

Parliament, so far as there was a parliament, was a mere *council* of the king.* It assembled only at the pleasure of the king; sat only during his pleasure; and when sitting had no power, so far as *general* legislation was concerned, beyond that of simply *advising* the king. The only legislation to which their assent was constitutionally necessary, was demands for money and military services for *extraordinary* occasions. Even Magna Carta itself makes no provisions whatever for any parliaments, except when the king should want means to carry on war, or to meet some other *extraordinary* necessity.† He had no need of parliaments to raise taxes for the *ordinary* purposes of government; for his revenues from the rents of the crown lands and other sources, were ample for all except extraordinary occasions. Parliaments, too, when assembled, consisted only of bishops, barons, and other great men of the kingdom, unless the king chose to invite others.‡ There was no House of Commons at that time, and the people had no right to be heard, unless as petitioners.§

---

* *Coke* says, "The king of England is armed with divers councils, one whereof is called *commune concilium*, (the common council,) and that is the court of parliament, and so it is *legally* called in writs and judicial proceedings *commune concilium regni Angliæ*, (the common council of the kingdom of England.) And another is called *magnum concilium*, (great council;) this is sometimes applied to the upper house of parliament, and sometimes, out of parliament time, to the peers of the realm, lords of parliament, who are called *magnum concilium regis*, (the great council of the king;) * * Thirdly, (as every man knoweth,) the king hath a privy council for matters of state. * * The fourth council of the king are his judges for law matters."

1 *Coke's Institutes*, 110 a.

† The Great Charter of Henry III., (1216 and 1225,) confirmed by Edward I., (1297,) makes no provision whatever for, or mention of, a parliament, unless the provision, (Ch. 37,) that "Escuage, (a military contribution,) from henceforth shall be taken like as it was wont to be in the time of King Henry our grandfather," mean that a parliament shall be summoned for that purpose.

‡ The Magna Carta of John, (Ch. 17 and 18,) defines those who were entitled to be summoned to parliament, to wit, "The Archbishops, Bishops, Abbots, Earls, and Great Barons of the Realm, * * and all others who hold of us *in chief*." Those who held land of the king *in chief* included none below the rank of knights.

§ The parliaments of that time were, doubtless, such as Carlyle describes them, when he says, "The parliament was at first a most simple assemblage, quite cognate to the situation; that Red William, or whoever had taken on him the terrible task of being King of England, was wont to invite, oftenest about Christmas time, his subordinate Kinglets, Barons as he called them, to give him the pleasure of their company for a week or two; there, in earnest conference all morning, in freer talk over Christmas

Even when laws were made at the time of a parliament, they were made in the name of the king alone. Sometimes it was inserted in the laws, that they were made with the *consent* or *advice* of the bishops, barons, and others assembled; but often this was omitted. Their consent or advice was evidently a matter of no legal importance to the enactment or validity of the laws, but only inserted, when inserted at all, with a view of obtaining a more willing submission to them on the part of the people. The style of enactment generally was, either " *The King wills and commands,*" or some other form significant of the sole legislative authority of the king. The king could pass laws at any time when it pleased him. The presence of a parliament was wholly unnecessary. Hume says, "It is asserted by Sir Harry Spelman, as an undoubted fact, that, during the reigns of the Norman princes, every order of the king, issued with the consent of his privy council, had the full force of law." * And other authorities abundantly corroborate this assertion.†

The king was, therefore, constitutionally the government; and the only legal limitation upon his power seems to have been simply the *Common Law*, usually called "*the law of the land*," which he was bound by oath to maintain; (which oath had about the same practical value as similar oaths have always had.) This "law of the land" seems not to have been regarded at all by many of the kings, except so far as they found it convenient to do so, or were constrained to observe it by the fear of arousing resistance. But as all people are slow in making resistance, oppression and usurpation often reached a great height; and, in the case of John, they had become so intolerable as to enlist the nation almost universally against him; and he was reduced to the necessity of complying with any terms the barons saw fit to dictate to him.

It was under these circumstances, that the Great Charter of

---

cheer all evening, in some big royal hall of Westminster, Winchester, or wherever it might be, with log fires, huge rounds of roast and boiled, not lacking malmsey and other generous liquor, they took counsel concerning the arduous matters of the kingdom."

* Hume, Appendix 2.
† This point will be more fully established hereafter.

English Liberties was granted. The barons of England, sustained by the common people, having their king in their power, compelled him, as the price of his throne, to pledge himself that he would punish no freeman for a violation of any of his laws, unless with the consent of the peers — that is, the equals — of the accused.

The question here arises, Whether the barons and people intended that those peers (the jury) should be mere puppets in the hands of the king, exercising no opinion of their own as to the intrinsic merits of the accusations they should try, or the *justice* of the laws they should be called on to enforce? Whether those haughty and victorious barons, when they had their tyrant king at their feet, gave back to him his throne, with full power to enact any tyrannical laws he might please, reserving only to a jury ("the country") the contemptible and servile privilege of ascertaining, (under the dictation of the king, or his judges, as to the laws of evidence), the simple *fact* whether those laws had been transgressed? Was this the only restraint, which, when they had all power in their hands, they placed upon the tyranny of a king, whose oppressions they had risen in arms to resist? Was it to obtain such a charter as that, that the whole nation had united, as it were, like one man, against their king? Was it on such a charter that they intended to rely, for all future time, for the security of their liberties? No. They were engaged in no such senseless work as that. On the contrary, when they required him to renounce forever the power to punish any freeman, unless by the consent of his peers, they intended those peers should judge of, and try, the whole case on its merits, independently of all arbitrary legislation, or judicial authority, on the part of the king. In this way they took the liberties of each individual — and thus the liberties of the whole people — entirely out of the hands of the king, and out of the power of his laws, and placed them in the keeping of the people themselves. And this it was that made the trial by jury the palladium of their liberties.

The trial by jury, be it observed, was the only real barrier interposed by them against absolute despotism. Could this trial, then, have been such an entire farce as it necessarily must have been, if the jury had had no power to judge of the justice of the laws the people were required to obey? Did it not rather imply that the jury were to judge independently and fearlessly as to everything involved in the charge, and especially as to its intrinsic justice, and thereon give their decision, (unbiased by any legislation of the king,) whether the accused might be punished? The reason of the thing, no less than the historical celebrity of the events, as securing the liberties of the people, and the veneration with which the trial by jury has continued to be regarded, notwithstanding its essence and vitality have been almost entirely extracted from it in practice, would settle the question, if other evidences had left the matter in doubt.

Besides, if his laws were to be authoritative with the jury, why should John indignantly refuse, as at first he did, to grant the charter, (and finally grant it only when brought to the last extremity,) on the ground that it deprived him of all power, and left him only the name of a king? *He* evidently understood that the juries were to veto his laws, and paralyze his power, at discretion, by forming their own opinions as to the true character of the offences they were to try, and the laws they were to be called on to enforce; and that "*the king wills and commands*" was to have no weight with them contrary to their own judgments of what was intrinsically right.*

The barons and people having obtained by the charter all the liberties they had demanded of the king, it was further

---

* It is plain that the king and all his partisans looked upon the charter as utterly prostrating the king's legislative supremacy before the discretion of juries. When the schedule of liberties demanded by the barons was shown to him, (of which the trial by jury was the most important, because it was the only one that protected all the rest,) "the king, falling into a violent passion, asked, *Why the barons did not with these exactions demand his kingdom?* * * and *with a solemn oath protested, that he would never grant such liberties as would make himself a slave.*" * * But afterwards, "seeing himself deserted, and fearing they would seize his castles, he sent the Earl of Pembroke and other faithful messengers to them, to let them know *he would grant them the laws and liberties they desired.*" * * But after the charter had been granted, "the king's mercenary soldiers, desiring war more than peace, were by their leaders continually whispering in his ears, *that he was now no longer king, but the scorn of other princes; and that it was more eligible to be no king, than such a one as he.*" * * He applied "to the

provided by the charter itself that twenty-five barons should be appointed by the barons, out of their number, to keep special vigilance in the kingdom to see that the charter was observed, with authority to make war upon the king in case of its violation. The king also, by the charter, so far absolved all the people of the kingdom from their allegiance to him, as to authorize and require them to swear to obey the twenty-five barons, in case they should make war upon the king for infringement of the charter. It was then thought by the barons and people, that something substantial had been done for the security of their liberties.

This charter, in its most essential features, and without any abatement as to the trial by jury, has since been confirmed more than thirty times; and the people of England have always had a traditionary idea that it was of some value as a guaranty against oppression. Yet that idea has been an entire delusion, unless the jury have had the right to judge of the justice of the laws they were called on to enforce.

SECTION II.

The Language of Magna Carta.

The language of the Great Charter establishes the same point that is established by its history, viz., that it is the right and duty of the jury to judge of the justice of the laws.

Pope, that he might by his apostolic authority make void what the barons had done. * * At Rome he met with what success he could desire, where all the transactions with the barons were fully represented to the Pope, and the Charter of Liberties shown to him, in writing; which, when he had carefully perused, he, with a furious look, cried out, *What! Do the barons of England endeavor to dethrone a king, who has taken upon him the Holy Cross, and is under the protection of the Apostolic See; and would they force him to transfer the dominions of the Roman Church to others? By St. Peter, this injury must not pass unpunished.* Then debating the matter with the cardinals, he, by a definitive sentence, damned and cassated forever the Charter of Liberties, and sent the king a bull containing that sentence at large." — *Echard's History of England*, p. 106-7.

These things show that the nature and effect of the charter were well understood by the king and his friends; that they all agreed that he was effectually stripped of power. *Yet the legislative power had not been taken from him; but only the power to enforce his laws, unless juries should freely consent to their enforcement.*

The chapter guaranteeing the trial by jury is in these words:

"Nullus liber homo capiatur, vel imprisonetur, aut disseisetur, aut utlagetur, aut exuletur, aut aliquo modo destruatur; nec super eum ibimus, nec super eum mittemus, nisi per legale judicium parium suorum, vel per legem terræ."*

The corresponding chapter in the Great Charter, granted by Henry III., (1225,) and confirmed by Edward I., (1297,) (which charter is now considered the basis of the English laws and constitution,) is in nearly the same words, as follows:

"Nullus liber homo capiatur, vel imprisonetur, aut disseisetur de libero tenemento, vel libertatibus, vel liberis consuetudinibus suis, aut utlagetur, aut exuletur, aut aliquo modo destruatur, nec super eum ibimus, nec super eum mittemus, nisi per legale judicium parium suorum, vel per legem terræ."

The most common translation of these words, at the present day, is as follows:

"No freeman shall be arrested, or imprisoned, or deprived of his freehold, or his liberties, or free customs, or outlawed, or exiled, or in any manner destroyed, *nor will we (the king) pass upon him, nor condemn him*, unless by the judgment of his peers, or the law of the land."

"*Nec super eum ibimus, nec super eum mittemus.*"

There has been much confusion and doubt as to the true meaning of the words, "*nec super eum ibimus, nec super eum mittemus.*" The more common rendering has been, "*nor will we pass upon him, nor condemn him.*" But some have translated them to mean, "*nor will we pass upon him, nor commit him to prison.*" Coke gives still a different rendering, to the effect that "No man shall be condemned at the king's suit, either before the king in his bench, nor before any other commissioner or judge whatsoever."†

But all these translations are clearly erroneous. In the first

---

* The laws were, at that time, all written in Latin.

† "No man shall be condemned at the king's suit, either before the king in his bench, where pleas are *coram rege*, (before the king,) (and so are the words *nec super eum ibimus*, to be understood,) nor before any other commissioner or judge whatsoever, and so are the words *nec super eum mittemus*, to be understood, but by the judgment of his peers, that is, equals, or according to the law of the land." — 2 *Coke's Inst.*, 46.

place, "*nor will we pass upon him,*" — meaning thereby to decide upon his guilt or innocence *judicially* — is not a correct rendering of the words, "*nec super eum ibimus.*" There is nothing whatever, in these latter words, that indicates *judicial* action or opinion at all. The words, in their common signification, describe *physical* action alone. And the true translation of them, as will hereafter be seen, is, "*nor will we proceed against him,*" *executively.*

In the second place, the rendering, "*nor will we condemn him,*" bears little or no analogy to any common, or even uncommon, signification of the words "*nec super eum mittemus.*" There is nothing in these latter words that indicates *judicial* action or decision. Their common signification, like that of the words *nec super eum ibimus,* describes *physical* action alone. "*Nor will we send upon (or against) him,*" would be the most obvious translation, and, as we shall hereafter see, such is the true translation.

But although these words describe *physical* action, on the part of the king, as distinguished from judicial, they nevertheless do not mean, as one of the translations has it, "*nor will we commit him to prison;*" for that would be a mere repetition of what had been already declared by the words "*nec imprisonetur.*" Besides, there is nothing about prisons in the words "*nec super eum mittemus;*" nothing about sending *him* anywhere; but only about sending (something or somebody) *upon* him, or *against* him — that is, *executively.*

Coke's rendering is, if possible, the most absurd and gratuitous of all. What is there in the words, "*nec super eum mittemus,*" that can be made to mean "*nor shall he be condemned before any other commissioner or judge whatsoever?*" Clearly there is nothing. The whole rendering is a sheer fabrication. And the whole object of it is to give color for the exercise of a *judicial* power, by the king, or his judges, which is nowhere given them.

Neither the words, "*nec super eum ibimus, nec super eum mittemus,*" nor any other words in the whole chapter, authorize, provide for, describe, or suggest, any *judicial* action whatever, on the part either of the king, or of his judges, or of anybody, *except the peers, or jury.* There is nothing about the king's *judges* at all. And there is nothing whatever, in the whole chapter, *so far as relates to the action of the king*, that describes or suggests anything but *executive* action.*

But that all these translations are certainly erroneous, is proved by a temporary charter, granted by John a short time previous to the Great Charter, for the purpose of giving an opportunity for conference, arbitration, and reconciliation between him and his barons. It was to have force until the matters in controversy between them could be submitted to the Pope, and to other persons to be chosen, some by the king, and some by the barons. The words of the charter are as follows:

"Sciatis nos concessisse baronibus nostris qui contra nos sunt quod nec eos nec homines suos capiemus, nec disseisiemus *nec super eos per vim vel per arma ibimus* nisi per legem regni nostri vel per judicium parium suorum in curia nostra donec consideratio facta fuerit," &c., &c.

That is, "Know that we have granted to our barons who are opposed to us, that we will neither arrest them nor their men, nor disseize them, *nor will we proceed against them by force or by arms*, unless by the law of our kingdom, or by the judgment of their peers in our court, until consideration shall be had," &c., &c.

A copy of this charter is given in a note in Blackstone's Introduction to the Charters.†

Mr. Christian speaks of this charter as settling the true meaning of the corresponding clause of Magna Carta, on the principle that laws and charters on the same subject are to be construed with reference to each other. See 3 *Christian's Blackstone*, 41, *note*.

---

* Perhaps the assertion in the text should be made with this qualification — that the words "*per legem terræ*," (according to the law of the land,) and the words "*per legale judicium parium suorum*," (according to the *legal* judgment of his peers,) imply that the king, before proceeding to any *executive* action, will take notice of "the law of the land," and of the *legality* of the judgment of the peers, and will *execute* upon the prisoner nothing except what the law of the land authorizes, and no judgments of the peers, except *legal* ones. With this qualification, the assertion in the text is strictly correct — that there is nothing in the whole chapter that grants to the king, or his judges, any *judicial* power at all. The chapter only describes and *limits* his *executive* power.

† See Blackstone's Law Tracts, page 294, Oxford Edition.

The true meaning of the words, *nec super eum ibimus, nec super eum mittemus*, is also proved by the "*Articles of the Great Charter of Liberties*," demanded of the king by the barons, and agreed to by the king, under seal, a few days before the date of the Charter, and from which the Charter was framed.* Here the words used are these:

"Ne corpus liberi hominis capiatur nec imprisonetur nec disseisetur nec utlagetur nec exuletur nec aliquo modo destruatur *nec rex eat vel mittat super eum vi* nisi per judicium parium suorum vel per legem terræ."

That is, "The body of a freeman shall not be arrested, nor imprisoned, nor disseized, nor outlawed, nor exiled, nor in any manner destroyed, *nor shall the king proceed or send (any one) against him* WITH FORCE, unless by the judgment of his peers, or the law of the land."

The true translation of the words *nec super eum ibimus, nec super eum mittemus*, in Magna Carta, is thus made certain, as follows, "*nor will we (the king) proceed against him, nor send (any one) against him* WITH FORCE OR ARMS."†

It is evident that the difference between the true and false translations of the words, *nec super eum ibimus, nec super eum mittemus*, is of the highest legal importance, inasmuch as the true translation, *nor will we (the king) proceed against him, nor send (any one) against him by force or arms*, represents the king only in an *executive* character, *carrying the judgment of the peers and "the law of the land" into execution*; whereas the false translation, *nor will we pass upon him, nor condemn him*, gives color for the exercise of a *judicial* power, on the

---

* These Articles of the Charter are given in Blackstone's collection of Charters, and are also printed with the *Statutes of the Realm*. Also in Wilkins' Laws of the Anglo-Saxons, p. 356.

† Lingard says, "The words, '*We will not destroy him, nor will we go upon him, nor will we send upon him*,' have been very differently expounded by different legal authorities. Their real meaning may be learned from John himself, who the next year promised by his letters patent . . . nec super eos *per vim vel per arma* ibimus, nisi per legem regni nostri, vel per judicium parium suorum in curia nostra, (nor will we go upon them *by force or by arms*, unless by the law of our kingdom, or the judgment of their peers in our court.) Pat. 16 Johan, apud Drad. 11, app. no. 124. He had hitherto been in the habit of *going* with an armed force, or *sending* an armed force on the lands, and against the castles, of all whom he knew or suspected to be his secret enemies, without observing any form of law."— 3 Lingard, 47 note.

part of the king, to which the king had no right, but which, according to the true translation, belongs wholly to the jury.

"*Per legale judicium parium suorum.*"

The foregoing interpretation is corroborated, (if it were not already too plain to be susceptible of corroboration,) by the true interpretation of the phrase "*per legale judicium parium suorum.*"

In giving this interpretation, I leave out, for the present, the word *legale*, which will be defined afterwards.

The true meaning of the phrase, *per judicium parium suorum*, is, *according to the sentence of his peers.* The word *judicium, judgment,* has a technical meaning in the law, signifying the decree rendered in the decision of a cause. In civil suits this decision is called a *judgment;* in chancery proceedings it is called a *decree;* in criminal actions it is called a *sentence*, or *judgment,* indifferently. Thus, in a criminal suit, "a motion in arrest of *judgment,*" means a motion in arrest of *sentence.**

In cases of sentence, therefore, in criminal suits, the words *sentence* and *judgment* are synonymous terms. They are, to this day, commonly used in law books as synonymous terms. And the phrase *per judicium parium suorum*, therefore, implies that the jury are to fix the sentence.

The word *per* means *according to.* Otherwise there is no sense in the phrase *per judicium parium suorum.* There

---

* "*Judgment, judicium.* * * The sentence of the law, pronounced by the court, upon the matter contained in the record." — 3 *Blackstone*, 395. *Jacob's Law Dictionary. Tomlin's do.*

"*Judgment* is the decision or sentence of the law, given by a court of justice or other competent tribunal, as the result of the proceedings instituted therein, for the redress of an injury." — *Bouvier's Law Dict.*

"*Judgment, judicium.* * * Sentence of a judge against a criminal. * * Determination, decision in general." — *Bailey's Dict.*

"*Judgment.* * * In a legal sense, a sentence or decision pronounced by authority of a king, or other power, either by their own mouth, or by that of their judges and officers, whom they appoint to administer justice in their stead." — *Chambers' Dict.*

"*Judgment.* * * In law, the sentence or doom pronounced in any case, civil or criminal, by the judge or court by which it is tried." — *Webster's Dict.*

Sometimes the punishment itself is called *judicium, judgment;* or, rather, it *was* at the time of Magna Carta. For example, in a statute passed fifty-one years after

would be no sense in saying that a king might imprison, disseize, outlaw, exile, or otherwise punish a man, or proceed against him, or send any one against him, *by force or arms, by* a judgment of his peers; but there is sense in saying that the king may imprison, disseize, and punish a man, or proceed against him, or send any one against him, by force or arms, *according to* a judgment, or *sentence,* of his peers; because in that case the king would be merely carrying the sentence or judgment of the peers into execution.

The word *per*, in the phrase "*per* judicium parium suorum," of course means precisely what it does in the next phrase, "*per* legem terræ;" where it obviously means *according to*, and not *by*, as it is usually translated. There would be no sense in saying that the king might proceed against a man by force or arms, *by* the law of the land; but there is sense in saying that he may proceed against him, by force or arms, *according to* the law of the land; because the king would then be acting only as an executive officer, carrying the law of the land into execution. Indeed, the true meaning of the word *by*, as used in similar cases now, always is *according to;* as, for example, when we say a thing was done by the government, or by the executive, *by law*, we mean only that it was done by them *according to law ;* that is, that they merely executed the law.

Or, if we say that the word *by* signifies *by authority of*, the result will still be the same; for nothing can be done *by authority of* law, except what the law itself authorizes or directs

---

Magna Carta, it was said that a baker, for default in the weight of his bread, "debeat amerciari vel subire *judicium* pillorie;" that is, ought to be amerced, or suffer the punishment, or judgment, of the pillory. Also that a brewer, for "selling ale contrary to the assize," "debeat amerciari, vel pati *judicium* tumbrelli"; that is, ought to be amerced, or suffer the punishment, or judgment, of the tumbrel. — 51 *Henry* 3, *St.* 6. (1266.)

Also the "*Statutes of uncertain date,*" (but supposed to be prior to Edward III., or 1326,) provide, in chapters 6, 7, and 10, for "*judgment* of the pillory." — *See* 1 *Ruffhead's Statutes,* 187, 188. 1 *Statutes of the Realm,* 203.

Blackstone, in his chapter "Of *Judgment*, and its Consequences," says, "*Judgment* (unless any matter be offered in arrest thereof) follows upon conviction; being the pronouncing of that punishment which is expressly ordained by law." — *Blackstone's Analysis of the Laws of England,* Book 4, Ch. 29, Sec. 1. *Blackstone's Law Tracts,* 126.

Coke says, "*Judicium* . . the judgment is the guide and direction of the execution." 3 *Inst.* 210.

to be done; that is, nothing can be done by authority of law, except simply to carry the law itself into execution. So nothing could be done *by authority of* the sentence of the peers, or *by authority of* "the law of the land," except what the sentence of the peers, or the law of the land, themselves authorized or directed to be done; nothing, in short, but to carry the sentence of the peers, or the law of the land, themselves into execution.

Doing a thing *by* law, or *according to* law, is only carrying the law into execution. And punishing a man *by*, or *according to*, the sentence or judgment of his peers, is only carrying that sentence or judgment into execution.

If these reasons could leave any doubt that the word *per* is to be translated *according to*, that doubt would be removed by the terms of an antecedent guaranty for the trial by jury, granted by the Emperor Conrad, of Germany,* two hundred years before Magna Carta. Blackstone cites it as follows:— (3 *Blackstone*, 350.)

"Nemo beneficium suum perdat, nisi *secundum* consuetudinem antecessorum nostrorum, et judicium parium suorum." That is, No one shall lose his estate,† unless *according to* ("*secundum*") the custom (or law) of our ancestors, and (*according to*) the sentence (or judgment) of his peers.

The evidence is therefore conclusive that the phrase *per judicium parium suorum* means *according to the sentence of his peers;* thus implying that the jury, and not the government, are to fix the sentence.

If any additional proof were wanted that juries were to fix the sentence, it would be found in the following provisions of Magna Carta, viz.:

"A freeman shall not be amerced for a small crime, (*delicto*,) but according to the degree of the crime; and for a great crime in proportion to the magnitude of it, saving to him his *contene-*

---

* This precedent from Germany is good authority, because the trial by jury was in use, in the northern nations of Europe generally, long before Magna Carta, and probably from time immemorial; and the Saxons and Normans were familiar with it before they settled in England.

† *Beneficium* was the legal name of an estate held by a feudal tenure. See Spelman's Glossary.

ment;* and after the same manner a merchant, saving to him his merchandise. And a villein shall be amerced after the same manner, saving to him his waynage,† if he fall under our mercy; *and none of the aforesaid amercements shall be imposed, (or assessed, ponatur,) but by the oath of honest men of the neighborhood. Earls and Barons shall not be amerced but by their peers,* and according to the degree of their crime." ‡

Pecuniary punishments were the most common punishments at that day, and the foregoing provisions of Magna Carta show that the amount of those punishments was to be fixed by the jury.

Fines went to the king, and were a source of revenue; and if the amounts of the fines had been left to be fixed by the king, he would have had a pecuniary temptation to impose unreasonable and oppressive ones. So, also, in regard to other punishments than fines. If it were left to the king to fix the punishment, he might often have motives to inflict cruel and oppressive ones. As it was the object of the trial by jury to protect the people against all possible oppression from the king, it was necessary that the jury, and not the king, should fix the punishments. §

"*Legale.*"

The word "*legale,*" in the phrase "*per legale judicium*

---

* *Contenement* of a freeman was the means of living in the condition of a freeman.

† *Waynage* was a villein's plough-tackle and carts.

‡ Tomlin says, "The ancient practice was, when any such fine was imposed, to inquire by a jury *quantum inde regi dare valeat per annum, salva sustentatione sua et uxoris et liberorum suorum,* (how much is he able to give to the king per annum, saving his own maintenance, and that of his wife and children). And since the disuse of such inquest, it is never usual to assess a larger fine than a man is able to pay, without touching the implements of his livelihood; but to inflict corporal punishment, or a limited imprisonment, instead of such a fine as might amount to imprisonment for life. And this is the reason why fines in the king's courts are frequently denominated ransoms, because the penalty must otherwise fall upon a man's person, unless it be redeemed or ransomed by a pecuniary fine." — *Tomlin's Law Dict., word Fine.*

§ Because juries were to fix the sentence, it must not be supposed that the king was *obliged* to carry the sentence into execution; *but only that he could not go beyond the sentence.* He might pardon, or he might acquit on grounds of law, notwithstanding the sentence; but he could not punish beyond the extent of the sentence. Magna Carta does not prescribe that the king *shall punish* according to the sentence of the peers; but only that he shall not punish "*unless according to*" that *sentence.* He may acquit or pardon, notwithstanding their sentence or judgment; but he cannot punish, except according to their judgment.

parium suorum," doubtless means two things. 1. That the sentence must be given in a legal manner; that is, by the legal number of jurors, legally empanelled and sworn to try the cause; and that they give their judgment or sentence after a legal trial, both in form and substance, has been had. 2. That the sentence shall be for a legal cause or offence. If, therefore, a jury should convict and sentence a man, either without giving him a legal trial, or for an act that was not really and legally criminal, the sentence itself would not be legal; and consequently this clause forbids the king to carry such a sentence into execution; for the clause guarantees that he will execute no judgment or sentence, except it be *legale judicium,* a legal sentence. Whether a sentence be a legal one, would have to be ascertained by the king or his judges, on appeal, or might be judged of informally by the king himself.

The word *"legale"* clearly did not mean that the *judicium parium suorum* (judgment of his peers) should be a sentence which any law (of the king) should *require* the peers to pronounce; for in that case the sentence would not be the sentence of the peers, but only the sentence of the law, (that is, of the king); and the peers would be only a mouthpiece of the law, (that is, of the king,) in uttering it.

"*Per legem terræ.*"

One other phrase remains to be explained, viz., "*per legem terræ,*" "*by the law of the land.*"

All writers agree that this means the *common law.* Thus, Sir Matthew Hale says:

"The common law is sometimes called, by way of eminence, *lex terræ,* as in the statute of *Magna Carta,* chap. 29, where certainly the common law is principally intended by those words, *aut per legem terræ;* as appears by the exposition thereof in several subsequent statutes; and particularly in the statute of 28 Edward III., chap. 3, which is but an exposition and explanation of that statute. Sometimes it is called *lex Angliæ,* as in the statute of Merton, cap. 9, "*Nolumus leges Angliæ mutari,*" &c., (We will that the laws of England be not changed). Sometimes it is called *lex et consuetudo regni* (the law and custom of the kingdom); as in all commissions of oyer and terminer; and in the statutes of 18 Edward I., cap. —, and *de quo warranto,* and divers others. But most commonly it is called the Common Law, or the Common Law of England; as in the statute *Articuli super Chartas*, cap. 15, in the statute 25 Edward III., cap. 5, (4,) and infinite more records and statutes." — 1 *Hale's History of the Common Law*, 128.

This common law, or "law of the land," *the king was sworn to maintain.* This fact is recognized by a statute made at Westminster, in 1346, by Edward III., which commences in this manner:

"Edward, by the Grace of God, &c., &c., to the Sheriff of Stafford, Greeting: Because that by divers complaints made to us, we have perceived that *the law of the land, which we by oath are bound to maintain,*" &c. — *St.* 20 *Edward III.*

The foregoing authorities are cited to show to the unprofessional reader, what is well known to the profession, that *legem terræ, the law of the land,* mentioned in Magna Carta, was the common, ancient, fundamental law of the land, which the kings were bound by oath to observe; *and that it did not include any statutes or laws enacted by the king himself, the legislative power of the nation.*

If the term *legem terræ* had included laws enacted by the king himself, the whole chapter of Magna Carta, now under discussion, would have amounted to nothing as a protection to liberty; because it would have imposed no restraint whatever upon the power of the king. The king could make laws at any time, and such ones as he pleased. He could, therefore, have done anything he pleased, *by the law of the land,* as well as in any other way, if his own laws had been "*the law of the land.*" If his own laws had been "the law of the land," within the meaning of that term as used in Magna Carta, this chapter of Magna Carta would have been sheer nonsense, inasmuch as the whole purport of it would have been simply that "no man shall be arrested, imprisoned, or deprived of his freehold, or his liberties, or free customs, or outlawed, or exiled, or in any manner destroyed (by the king); nor shall the king proceed against him, nor send any one against him with force and arms, unless by the judgment of his peers, *or unless the king shall please to do so.*"

This chapter of Magna Carta would, therefore, have imposed not the slightest restraint upon the power of the king, or afforded the slightest protection to the liberties of the people, if the laws of the king had been embraced in the term *legem terræ*. But if *legem terræ* was the common law, which the king was sworn to maintain, then a real restriction was laid upon his power, and a real guaranty given to the people for their liberties.

Such, then, being the meaning of *legem terræ*, the fact is established that Magna Carta took an accused person entirely out of the hands of the legislative power, that is, of the king; and placed him in the power and under the protection of his peers, and the common law alone; that, in short, Magna Carta suffered no man to be punished for violating any enactment of the legislative power, unless the peers or equals of the accused freely consented to it, or the common law authorized it; that the legislative power, *of itself*, was wholly incompetent to *require* the conviction or punishment of a man for any offence whatever.

Whether Magna Carta allowed of any other trial than by jury.

The question here arises, whether "*legem terræ*" did not allow of some other mode of trial than that by jury.

The answer is, that, at the time of Magna Carta, it is not probable, (for the reasons given in the note,) that *legem terræ* authorized, in criminal cases, any other trial than the trial by jury; but, if it did, it certainly authorized none but the trial by battle, the trial by ordeal, and the trial by compurgators. These were the only modes of trial, except by jury, that had been known in England, in criminal cases, for some centuries previous to Magna Carta. All of them had become nearly extinct at the time of Magna Carta, and it is not probable that they were included in "*legem terræ*," as that term is used in that instrument. But if they were included in it, they have now been long obsolete, and were such as neither this nor any future age will ever return to.* For all practical purposes of

---

* *The trial by battle* was one in which the accused challenged his accuser to single combat, and staked the question of his guilt or innocence on the result of the duel. This trial was introduced into England by the Normans, within one hundred and fifty years before Magna Carta. It was not very often resorted to even by the Normans

the present day, therefore, it may be asserted that Magna Carta allows no trial whatever but trial by jury.

Whether Magna Carta allowed sentence to be fixed otherwise than by the jury.

Still another question arises on the words *legem terræ*, viz., whether, in cases where the question of guilt was determined by the jury, the amount of *punishment* may not have been fixed by *legem terræ*, the Common Law, instead of its being fixed by the jury.

I think we have no evidence whatever that, at the time of Magna Carta, or indeed at any other time, *lex terræ*, the com-

---

themselves; probably never by the Anglo-Saxons, unless in their controversies with the Normans. It was strongly discouraged by some of the Norman princes, particularly by Henry II., by whom the trial by jury was especially favored. It is probable that the trial by battle, so far as it prevailed at all in England, was rather tolerated as a matter of chivalry, than authorized as a matter of law. At any rate, it is not likely that it was included in the "*legem terræ*" of Magna Carta, although such duels have occasionally occurred since that time, and have, by some, been supposed to be lawful. I apprehend that nothing can be properly said to be a part of *lex terræ*, unless it can be shown either to have been of Saxon origin, or to have been recognized by Magna Carta.

The trial by ordeal was of various kinds. In one ordeal the accused was required to take hot iron in his hand; in another to walk blindfold among red-hot ploughshares; in another to thrust his arm into boiling water; in another to be thrown, with his hands and feet bound, into cold water; in another to swallow the *morsel of execration;* in the confidence that his guilt or innocence would be miraculously made known. This mode of trial was nearly extinct at the time of Magna Carta, and it is not likely that it was included in "*legem terræ*," as that term is used in that instrument. This idea is corroborated by the fact that the trial by ordeal was specially prohibited only four years after Magna Carta, "by act of Parliament in 3 Henry III., according to Sir Edward Coke, or rather by an order of the king in council." — 3 *Blackstone* 345, *note.*

I apprehend that this trial was never forced upon accused persons, but was only allowed to them, *as an appeal to God,* from the judgment of a jury.*

The trial by compurgators was one in which, if the accused could bring twelve of his neighbors, who would make oath that they believed him innocent, he was held to be so. It is probable that this trial was really the trial by jury, or was allowed as an appeal from a jury. It is wholly improbable that two different modes of trial, so nearly resembling each other as this and the trial by jury do, should prevail at the same time, and among a rude people, whose judicial proceedings would naturally be of the simplest kind. But if this trial really were any other than the trial by jury, it must have been nearly or quite extinct at the time of Magna Carta; and there is no probability that it was included in "*legem terræ.*"

* Hallam says, " It appears as if the ordeal were permitted to persons already convicted by the verdict of a jury."— 2 *Middle Ages,* 446, *note.*

mon law, fixed the punishment in cases where the question of guilt was tried by a jury; or, indeed, that it did in any other case. Doubtless certain punishments were common and usual for certain offences; but I do not think it can be shown that the *common law*, the *lex terræ*, which the king was sworn to maintain, required any one specific punishment, or any precise amount of punishment, for any one specific offence. If such a thing be claimed, it must be shown, for it cannot be presumed. In fact, the contrary must be presumed, because, in the nature of things, the amount of punishment proper to be inflicted in any particular case, is a matter requiring the exercise of discretion at the time, in order to adapt it to the moral quality of the offence, which is different in each case, varying with the mental and moral constitutions of the offenders, and the circumstances of temptation or provocation. And Magna Carta recognizes this principle distinctly, as has before been shown, in providing that freemen, merchants, and villeins, " shall not be amerced for a small crime, but according to the degree of the crime; and for a great crime in proportion to the magnitude of it;" and that " none of the aforesaid amercements shall be imposed (or assessed) but by the oaths of honest men of the neighborhood;" and that " earls and barons shall not be amerced but by their peers, and according to the quality of the offence."

All this implies that the moral quality of the offence was to be judged of at the trial, and that the punishment was to be fixed by the discretion of the peers, or jury, and not by any such unvarying rule as a common law rule would be.

I think, therefore, it must be conceded that, in all cases, tried by a jury, Magna Carta intended that the punishment should be fixed by the jury, and not by the common law, for these several reasons.

1. It is uncertain whether the *common law* fixed the punishment of any offence whatever.

2. The words "*per judicium parium suorum*," *according to the sentence of his peers*, imply that the jury fixed the sentence in *some* cases tried by them; and if they fixed the sentence in some cases, it must be presumed they did in all, unless the contrary be clearly shown.

3. The express provisions of Magna Carta, before adverted to, that no amercements, or fines, should be imposed upon freemen, merchants, or villeins, "but by the oath of honest men of the neighborhood," and "according to the degree of the crime," and that "earls and barons should not be amerced but by their peers, and according to the quality of the offence," *proves* that, at least, there was no common law fixing the amount of *fines*, or, if there were, that it was to be no longer in force. And if there was no common law fixing the amount of *fines*, or if it was to be no longer in force, it is reasonable to infer, (in the absence of all evidence to the contrary,) either that the common law did not fix the amount of any other punishment, or that it was to be no longer in force for that purpose.*

Under the Saxon laws, fines, payable to the injured party, seem to have been the common punishments for all offences. Even murder was punishable by a fine payable to the relatives of the deceased. The murder of the king even was punishable

---

* Coke attempts to show that there is a distinction between amercements and fines — admitting that amercements must be fixed by one's peers, but claiming that fines may be fixed by the government. (2 *Inst.* 27, 8 *Coke's Reports* 38.) But there seems to have been no ground whatever for supposing that any such distinction existed at the time of Magna Carta. If there were any such distinction in the time of Coke, it had doubtless grown up within the four centuries that had elapsed since Magna Carta, and is to be set down as one of the numberless inventions of government for getting rid of the restraints of Magna Carta, and for taking men out of the protection of their peers, and subjecting them to such punishments as the government chooses to inflict.

The first statute of Westminster, passed sixty years after Magna Carta, treats the fine and amercement as synonymous, as follows:

"Forasmuch as *the common fine and amercement* of the whole county in Eyre of the justices for false judgments, or for other trespass, is unjustly assessed by sheriffs and baretors in the shires, * * it is provided, and the king wills, that from henceforth such sums shall be assessed before the justices in Eyre, afore their departure, *by the oath of knights and other honest men,*" &c. — 3 *Edward I., Ch.* 18. (1275.)

And in many other statutes passed after Magna Carta, the terms *fine* and *amercement* seem to be used indifferently, in prescribing the punishments for offences. As late as 1461, (246 years after Magna Carta,) the statute 1 *Edward IV., Ch.* 2, speaks of "*fines, ransoms, and amerciaments*" as being levied upon criminals, as if they were the common punishments of offences.

St. 2 and 3 *Philip and Mary, Ch.* 8, uses the terms, "*fines, forfeitures, and amerciaments*" five times. (1555.)

St. 5 *Elizabeth, Ch.* 13, *Sec.* 10, uses the terms "*fines, forfeitures, and amerciaments.*"

That amercements were fines, or pecuniary punishments, inflicted for offences, is proved by the following statutes, (all supposed to have been passed within one hundred

by fine. When a criminal was unable to pay his fine, his relatives often paid it for him. But if it were not paid, he was put out of the protection of the law, and the injured parties, (or, in the case of murder, the kindred of the deceased,) were allowed to inflict such punishment as they pleased. And if the relatives of the criminal protected him, it was lawful to take vengeance on them also. Afterwards the custom grew up of exacting fines also to the king as a punishment for offences.* And this latter was, doubtless, the usual punishment at the time of Magna Carta, as is evidenced by the fact that for many years immediately following Magna Carta, nearly or quite all statutes that prescribed any punishment at all, prescribed that the offender should "be grievously amerced," or "pay a great fine to the king," or a "grievous ransom," — with the alternative in some cases (perhaps *understood* in all) of imprisonment, banishment, or outlawry, in case of non-payment.†

---

and fifteen years after Magna Carta,) which speak of amercements as a species of "*judgment*," or punishment, and as being inflicted for the same offences as other "judgments."

Thus one statute declares that a baker, for default in the weight of his bread, "ought to be *amerced*, or suffer the *judgment* of the pillory ;" and that a brewer, for "selling ale contrary to the assize," "ought to be *amerced*, or suffer the *judgment* of the tumbrel." — 51 *Henry III., St.* 6. (1266.)

Among the "*Statutes of Uncertain Date*," but supposed to be prior to Edward III., (1326,) are the following:

Chap. 6 provides that "if a brewer break the assize, (fixing the price of ale,) the first, second, and third time, he shall be *amerced ;* but the fourth time he shall suffer *judgment* of the pillory without redemption."

Chap. 7 provides that "a butcher that selleth swine's flesh measled, or flesh dead of the murrain, or that buyeth flesh of Jews, and selleth the same unto Christians, after he shall be convict thereof, for the first time he shall be grievously *amerced ;* the second time he shall suffer *judgment* of the pillory ; and the third time he shall be imprisoned and make *fine ;* and the fourth time he shall forswear the town."

Chap. 10, a statute against *forestalling*, provides that,

"He that is convict thereof, the first time shall be *amerced*, and shall lose the thing so bought, and that according to the custom of the town ; he that is convicted the second time shall have *judgment* of the pillory ; at the third time he shall be imprisoned and make *fine ;* the fourth time he shall abjure the town. And this *judgment* shall be given upon all manner of forestallers, and likewise upon them that have given them counsel, help, or favor." — 1 *Ruffhead's Statutes,* 187, 188. 1 *Statutes of the Realm,* 203.

* 1 Hume, Appendix, 1.

† Blackstone says, "Our ancient Saxon laws nominally punished theft with death, if above the value of twelve pence ; but the criminal was permitted to redeem his life

Judging, therefore, from the special provisions in Magna Carta, requiring *fines*, or amercements, to be imposed only by juries, (without mentioning any other punishments;) judging, also, from the statutes which immediately followed Magna Carta, it is probable that the Saxon custom of punishing all, or nearly all, offences by *fines*, (with the alternative to the criminal of being imprisoned, banished, or outlawed, and exposed to private vengeance, in case of non-payment,) continued until the time of Magna Carta; and that in providing expressly that *fines* should be fixed by the juries, Magna Carta provided for nearly or quite all the punishments that were expected to be inflicted; that if there were to be any others, they were to be fixed by the juries; and consequently that nothing was left to be fixed by "*legem terræ.*"

But whether the common law fixed the punishment of any offences, or not, is a matter of little or no practical importance at this day; because we have no idea of going back to any common law punishments of six hundred years ago, if, indeed, there were any such at that time. It is enough for us to know — *and this is what it is material for us to know* — that the jury fixed the punishments, in all cases, unless they were fixed by the *common law;* that Magna Carta allowed

---

by a pecuniary ransom, as among their ancestors, the Germans, by a stated number of cattle. But in the ninth year of Henry the First, (1109,) this power of redemption was taken away, and all persons guilty of larceny above the value of twelve pence were directed to be hanged, which law continues in force to this day." — 4 *Blackstone*, 238.

I give this statement of Blackstone, because the latter clause may seem to militate with the idea, which the former clause corroborates, viz., that at the time of Magna Carta, fines were the usual punishments of offences. But I think there is no probability that a law so unreasonable in itself, (unreasonable even after making all allowance for the difference in the value of money,) and so contrary to immemorial custom, could or did obtain any general or speedy acquiescence among a people who cared little for the authority of kings.

Maddox, writing of the period from William the Conqueror to John, says:

"The amercements in criminal and common pleas, which were wont to be imposed during this first period and afterwards, were of so many several sorts, that it is not easy to place them under distinct heads. Let them, for method's sake, be reduced to the heads following: Amercements for or by reason of murders and manslaughters, for misdemeanors, for disseisins, for recreancy, for breach of assize, for defaults, for non-appearance, for false judgment, and for not making suit, or hue and cry. To them may be added miscellaneous amercements, for trespasses of divers kinds." — 1 *Maddox' History of the Exchequer*, 542.

no punishments to be prescribed by statute — that is, by the legislative power — nor in any other manner by the king, or his judges, in any case whatever; and, consequently, that all statutes prescribing particular punishments for particular offences, or giving the king's judges any authority to fix punishments, were void.

If the power to fix punishments had been left in the hands of the king, it would have given him a power of oppression, which was liable to be greatly abused; which there was no occasion to leave with him; and which would have been incongruous with the whole object of this chapter of Magna Carta; which object was to take all discretionary or arbitrary power over individuals entirely out of the hands of the king, and his laws, and entrust it only to the common law, and the peers, or jury — that is, the people.

What lex terræ did authorize.

But here the question arises, What then did "*legem terræ*" authorize the king, (that is, the government,) to do in the case of an accused person, if it neither authorized any other trial than that by jury, nor any other punishments than those fixed by juries?

The answer is, that, owing to the darkness of history on the point, it is probably wholly impossible, at this day, to state, *with any certainty or precision*, anything whatever that the *legem terræ* of Magna Carta did authorize the king, (that is, the government,) to do, (if, indeed, it authorized him to do anything,) in the case of criminals, *other than to have them tried and sentenced by their peers, for common law crimes;* and to carry that sentence into execution.

The trial by jury was a part of *legem terræ*, and we have the means of knowing what the trial by jury was. The fact that the jury were to fix the sentence, implies that they were to *try* the accused; otherwise they could not know what sentence, or whether any sentence, ought to be inflicted upon him. Hence it follows that the jury were to judge of everything involved in the trial; that is, they were to judge of the nature of the offence, of the admissibility and weight of testimony, and of everything else whatsoever that was of the essence of the trial. If anything whatever could be dictated to them, either of law or evidence, the sentence would not be theirs, but would be dictated to them by the power that dictated to them the law or evidence. The trial and sentence, then, were wholly in the hands of the jury.

We also have sufficient evidence of the nature of the oath administered to jurors in criminal cases. It was simply, that they *would neither convict the innocent, nor acquit the guilty.* This was the oath in the Saxon times, and probably continued to be until Magna Carta.

We also know that, in case of *conviction*, the sentence of the jury was not necessarily final; that the accused had the right of appeal to the king and his judges, and to demand either a new trial, or an acquittal, if the trial or conviction had been against law.

So much, therefore, of the *legem terræ* of Magna Carta, we know with reasonable certainty.

We also know that Magna Carta provides that " No bailiff (*balivus*) shall hereafter put any man to his law, (put him on trial,) on his single testimony, without credible witnesses brought to support it." Coke thinks "that under this word *balivus*, in this act, is comprehended every justice, minister of the king, steward of the king, steward and bailiff." (2 Inst. 44.) And in support of this idea he quotes from a very ancient law book, called the Mirror of Justices, written in the time of Edward I., within a century after Magna Carta. But whether this were really a common law principle, or whether the provision grew out of that jealousy of the government which, at the time of Magna Carta, had reached its height, cannot perhaps now be determined.

We also know that, by Magna Carta, amercements, or fines, could not be imposed to the ruin of the criminal; that, in the case of a freeman, his *contenement*, or means of subsisting in the condition of a freeman, must be saved to him; that, in the case of a merchant, his merchandise must be spared; and in the case of a villein, his *waynage*, or plough-tackle and carts. This also is likely to have been a principle of the common law, inasmuch as, in that rude age, when the means of getting employment as laborers were not what they are now, the man and his family would probably have been liable to starvation, if these means of subsistence had been taken from him.

We also know, *generally*, that, at the time of Magna Carta, *all acts intrinsically criminal*, all trespasses against persons and property, were crimes, according to *lex terræ*, or the common law.

Beyond the points now given, we hardly know anything, probably nothing *with certainty*, as to what the "*legem terræ*" of *Magna Carta* did authorize, in regard to crimes. There is hardly anything extant that can give us any real light on the subject.

It would seem, however, that there were, even at that day, some common law principles governing arrests; and some common law forms and rules as to holding a man for trial, (by bail or imprisonment;) putting him on trial, such as by indictment or complaint; summoning and empanelling jurors, &c., &c. Whatever these common law principles were, Magna Carta requires them to be observed; for Magna Carta provides for the whole proceedings, commencing with the arrest, ("no freeman shall be *arrested*," &c.,) and ending with the execution of the sentence. And it provides that nothing shall be done, by the government, from beginning to end, unless according to the sentence of the peers, or "*legem terræ*," the common law. The trial by peers was a part of *legem terræ*, and we have seen that the peers must necessarily have governed the whole proceedings at the trial. But all the proceedings for arresting the man, and bringing him to trial, must have been had before the case could come under the cognizance of the peers, and they must, therefore, have been governed by other rules than the discretion of the peers. We may *conjecture*, although we cannot perhaps know with much certainty, that the *lex terræ*, or common law, governing these other proceedings, was somewhat similar to the common law principles, on the same points, at the present day. Such seem to be the opinions of Coke, who says that the phrase *nisi per legem terræ* means *unless by due process of law*.

Thus, he says:

"*Nisi per legem terræ. But by the law of the land.* For

the true sense and exposition of these words, see the statute of 37 Edw. III., cap. 8, where the words, *by the law of the land*, are rendered *without due process of law;* for there it is said. though it be contained in the Great Charter, that no man be taken, imprisoned, or put out of his freehold, *without process of the law; that is, by indictment or presentment of good and lawful men, where such deeds be done in due manner, or by writ original of the common law.*

"Without being brought in to answer but by due process of the common law.

"No man be put to answer without presentment before justices, or thing of record, or by due process, or by writ original, *according to the old law of the land." — 2 Inst.* 50.

The foregoing interpretations of the words *nisi per legem terræ* are corroborated by the following statutes, enacted in the next century after Magna Carta.

"That no man, from henceforth, shall be attached by any accusation, nor forejudged of life or limb, nor his land, tenements, goods, nor chattels, seized into the king's hands, against the form of the Great Charter, *and the law of the land."* — *St.* 5 *Edward III., Ch.* 9. (1331.)

"Whereas it is contained in the Great Charter of the franchises of England, that none shall be imprisoned, nor put out of his freehold, nor of his franchises, nor free customs, *unless it be by the law of the land;* it is accorded, assented, and established, that from henceforth none shall be taken by petition, or suggestion made to our lord the king, or to his council, *unless it be by indictment or presentment of good and lawful people of the same neighborhood where such deeds be done in due manner, or by process made by writ original at the common law;* nor that none be put out of his franchises, nor of his freehold, *unless he be duly brought into answer, and forejudged of the same by the course of the law;* and if anything be done against the same, it shall be redressed and holden for none." — *St.* 25 *Edward III., Ch.* 4. (1350.)

"That no man, of what estate or condition that he be, shall be put out of land or tenement, nor taken, nor imprisoned, nor disinherited, nor put to death, without being brought in answer *by due process of law." — St.* 28 *Edward III., Ch.* 3. (1354.)

"That no man be put to answer without presentment before justices, or matter of record, or by due process and writ original, according to the *old law of the land.* And if anything from henceforth be done to the contrary, it shall be void in law, and holden for error." — *St.* 42 *Edward III., Ch.* 3. (1368.)

The foregoing interpretation of the words *nisi per legem terræ* — that is, *by due process of law* — including indictment, &c., has been adopted as the true one by modern writers and courts; as, for example, by Kent, (2 *Comm.* 13,) Story, (3 *Comm.* 661,) and the Supreme Court of New York, (19 *Wendell*, 676; 4 *Hill*, 146.)

The fifth amendment to the constitution of the United States seems to have been framed on the same idea, inasmuch as it provides that "no person shall be deprived of life, liberty, or property, *without due process of law.*"*

Whether the word VEL *should be rendered by* OR, *or by* AND.

Having thus given the meanings, or rather the applications, which the words *vel per legem terræ* will reasonably, and perhaps must necessarily, bear, it is proper to suggest, that it has been supposed by some that the word *vel*, instead of being rendered by *or*, as it usually is, ought to be rendered by *and*, inasmuch as the word *vel* is often used for *et*, and the whole phrase *nisi per judicium parium suorum, vel per legem terræ,* (which would then read, unless by the sentence of his peers, *and* the law of the land,) would convey a more intelligible and harmonious meaning than it otherwise does.

Blackstone suggests that this may be the true reading. (*Charters*, p. 41.) Also Mr. Hallam, who says:

"Nisi per legale judicium parium suorum, *vel* per legem terræ. Several explanations have been offered of the alternative clause; which some have referred to judgment by default, or demurrer; others to the process of attachment for contempt. Certainly there are many legal procedures besides trial by jury, through which a party's goods or person may be taken. But one may doubt whether these were in contemplation of the framers of Magna Carta. In an entry of the Charter of 1217 by a contemporary hand, preserved in the Town-clerk's office in London, called Liber Custumarum et Regum antiquarum, a various reading, *et* per legem terræ, occurs. *Blackstone's Charters*, p. 42 (41.) And the word *vel* is so frequently used for *et*, that I am not wholly free from a suspicion that it

---

* Coke, in his exposition of the words *legem terræ*, gives quite in detail the principles of the common law governing *arrests ;* and takes it for granted that the words "*nisi per legem terræ*" are applicable to arrests, as well as to the indictment, &c. — 2 *Inst.*, 51, 52.

was so intended in this place. The meaning will be, that no person shall be disseized, &c., except upon a lawful cause of action, found by the verdict of a jury. This really seems as good as any of the disjunctive interpretations; but I do not offer it with much confidence." — 2 *Hallam's Middle Ages*, *Ch.* 8, *Part* 2, p. 449, *note.**

---

* I cite the above extract from Mr. Hallam solely for the sake of his authority for rendering the word *vel* by *and;* and not by any means for the purpose of indorsing the opinion he suggests, that *legem terræ* authorized " judgments by default or demurrer," *without the intervention of a jury.* He seems to imagine that *lex terræ*, the common law, at the time of Magna Carta, included everything, even to the practice of courts, that is, *at this day,* called by the name of *Common Law;* whereas much of what is *now* called Common Law has grown up, by usurpation, since the time of Magna Carta, in palpable violation of the authority of that charter. He says, " Certainly there are many legal procedures, besides *trial* by jury, through which a party's goods or person may be taken." Of course there are *now* many such ways, in which a party's goods or person *are* taken, besides by the judgment of a jury ; but the question is, whether such takings are not in violation of Magna Carta.

He seems to think that, in cases of "judgment by default or demurrer," there is no need of a jury, and thence to infer that *legem terræ* may not have required a jury in those cases. But this opinion is founded on the erroneous idea that juries are required only for determining contested *facts*, and not for judging of the law. In case of default, the plaintiff must present a *prima facie* case before he is entitled to a judgment ; and Magna Carta, (supposing it to require a jury trial in civil cases, as Mr. Hallam assumes that it does,) as much requires that this *prima facie* case, both law and fact, be made out to the satisfaction of a jury, as it does that a contested case shall be.

As for a demurrer, the jury must try a demurrer (having the advice and assistance of the court, of course) as much as any other matter of law arising in a case.

Mr. Hallam evidently thinks there is no use for a jury, except where there is a "*trial* " — meaning thereby a contest on matters of *fact*. His language is, that " there are many legal procedures, besides *trial* by jury, through which a party's goods or person may be taken." Now Magna Carta says nothing of *trial* by jury; but only of the *judgment*, or sentence, of a jury. It is only *by inference* that we come to the conclusion that there must be a *trial* by jury. Since the jury alone can give the *judgment*, or *sentence*, we *infer* that they must *try* the case; because otherwise they would be incompetent, and would have no moral right, to give *judgment*. They must, therefore, examine the grounds, (both of law and fact,) or rather *try* the grounds, of every action whatsoever, whether it be decided on "default, demurrer," or otherwise, and render their judgment, or sentence, thereon, before any judgment can be a legal one, on which " to take a party's goods or person." In short, the principle of Magna Carta is, that no judgment can be valid *against a party's goods or person*, (not even a judgment for costs,) except a judgment rendered by a jury. Of course a jury must try every question, both of law and fact, that is involved in the rendering of that judgment. They are to have the assistance and advice of the judges, so far as they desire them; but the judgment itself must be theirs, and not the judgment of the court.

As to "process of attachment for contempt," it is of course lawful for a judge, in his character of a peace officer, to issue a warrant for the arrest of a man guilty of a contempt, as he would for the arrest of any other offender, and hold him to bail, (or, in default of bail, commit him to prison,) to answer for his offence before a jury. Or he

48   TRIAL BY JURY.

The idea that the word *vel* should be rendered by *and*, is corroborated, if not absolutely confirmed, by the following passage in Blackstone, which has before been cited. Speaking of the trial by jury, as established by Magna Carta, he calls it,

"A privilege which is couched in almost the same words

---

may order him into custody without a warrant when the offence is committed in the judge's presence. But there is no reason why a judge should have the power of *punishing* for contempt, any more than for any other offence. And it is one of the most dangerous powers a judge can have, because it gives him absolute authority in a court of justice, and enables him to tyrannize as he pleases over parties, counsel, witnesses, and jurors. If a judge have power to punish for contempt, and to determine for himself what is a contempt, the whole administration of justice (or injustice, if he choose to make it so) is in his hands. And all the rights of jurors, witnesses, counsel, and parties, are held subject to his pleasure, and can be exercised only agreeably to his will. He can of course control the entire proceedings in, and consequently the decision of, every cause, by restraining and punishing every one, whether party, counsel, witness, or juror, who presumes to offer anything contrary to his pleasure.

This arbitrary power, which has been usurped and exercised by judges to punish for contempt, has undoubtedly had much to do in subduing counsel into those servile, obsequious, and cowardly habits, which so universally prevail among them, and which have not only cost so many clients their rights, but have also cost the people so many of their liberties.

If any *summary* punishment for contempt be ever necessary, (as it probably is not,) beyond exclusion for the time being from the court-room, (which should be done, not as a punishment, but for self-protection, and the preservation of order,) the judgment for it should be given by the jury, (where the trial is before a jury,) and not by the court, for the jury, and not the court, are really the judges. For the same reason, exclusion from the court-room should be ordered only by the jury, in cases when the trial is before a jury, because they, being the real judges and triers of the cause, are entitled, if anybody, to the control of the court-room. In appeal courts, where no juries sit, it may be necessary — not as a punishment, but for self-protection, and the maintenance of order — that the court should exercise the power of excluding a person, for the time being, from the court-room; but there is no reason why they should proceed to sentence him as a criminal, without his being tried by a jury.

If the people wish to have their rights respected and protected in courts of justice, it is manifestly of the last importance that they jealously guard the liberty of parties, counsel, witnesses, and jurors, against all arbitrary power on the part of the court.

Certainly Mr. Hallam may very well say that "one may doubt whether these (the several cases he has mentioned) were in contemplation of the framers of Magna Carta" — that is, as exceptions to the rule requiring that all judgments, that are to be enforced "*against a party's goods or person*," be rendered by a jury.

Again, Mr. Hallam says, if the word *vel* be rendered by *and*, "the meaning will be, that no person shall be disseized, &c., *except upon a lawful cause of action*." This is true; but it does not follow that any cause of action, founded on *statute only*, is therefore a "*lawful* cause of action," within the meaning of *legem terræ*, or the Common Law. Within the meaning of the *legem terræ* of Magna Carta, nothing but a *common law* cause of action is a "*lawful*" one.

with that of the Emperor Conrad two hundred years before: 'nemo beneficium suum perdat, nisi secundum consuetudinem antecessorum nostrorum, *et* judicium parium suorum.'" (No one shall lose his estate unless according to the custom of our ancestors, *and* the judgment of his peers.) — 3 *Blackstone*, 350.

If the word *vel* be rendered by *and*, (as I think it must be, at least in some cases,) this chapter of Magna Carta will then read that no freeman shall be arrested or punished, "unless according to the sentence of his peers, *and* the law of the land."

The difference between this reading and the other is important. In the one case, there would be, at first view, some color of ground for saying that a man might be punished in either of two ways, viz., according to the sentence of his peers, *or* according to the law of the land. In the other case, it requires both the sentence of his peers *and* the law of the land (common law) to authorize his punishment.

If this latter reading be adopted, the provision would seem to exclude all trials except trial by jury, and all causes of action except those of the *common law*.

But I apprehend the word *vel* must be rendered both by *and*, and by *or;* that in cases of a *judgment*, it should be rendered by *and*, so as to require the concurrence both of "the judgment of the peers *and* the law of the land," to authorize the king to make execution upon a party's goods or person; but that in cases of arrest and imprisonment, simply for the purpose of bringing a man to trial, *vel* should be rendered by *or*, because there can have been no judgment of a jury in such a case, and "the law of the land" must therefore necessarily be the only guide to, and restraint upon, the king. If this guide and restraint were taken away, the king would be invested with an arbitrary and most dangerous power in making arrests, and confining in prison, under pretence of an intention to bring to trial.

Having thus examined the language of this chapter of Magna Carta, so far as it relates to criminal cases, its legal import may be stated as follows, viz.:

No freeman shall be arrested, or imprisoned, or deprived of his freehold, or his liberties, or free customs, or be outlawed, or exiled, or in any manner destroyed, (harmed,) nor will we (the king) proceed against him, nor send any one against him, by force or arms, unless according to (that is, in execution of) the sentence of his peers, *and* (or *or*, as the case may require) the Common Law of England, (as it was at the time of Magna Carta, in 1215.)

CHAPTER III.

ADDITIONAL PROOFS OF THE RIGHTS AND DUTIES OF JURORS.

IF any evidence, extraneous to the history and language of Magna Carta, were needed to prove that, by that chapter which guaranties the trial by jury, all was meant that has now been ascribed to it, *and that the legislation of the king was to be of no authority with the jury beyond what they chose to allow to it*, and that the juries were to limit the punishments to be inflicted, we should find that evidence in various sources, such as the laws, customs, and characters of their ancestors on the continent, and of the northern Europeans generally; in the legislation and customs that immediately succeeded Magna Carta; in the oaths that have at different times been administered to jurors, &c., &c. This evidence can be exhibited here but partially. To give it all would require too much space and labor.

SECTION I.

Weakness of the Regal Authority.

Hughes, in his preface to his translation of Horne's "*Mirror of Justices*," (a book written in the time of Edward I., 1272 to 1307,) giving a concise view of the laws of England generally, says:

"Although in the Saxon's time I find the usual words of the acts then to have been *edictum*, (edict,) *constitutio*, (statute,) little mention being made of the commons, yet I further find that, *tum demum leges vim et vigorem habuerunt, cum fuerunt non modo institutæ sed firmatæ approbatione communitatis.*" (The laws had force and vigor only when they were not only enacted, but confirmed by the approval of the community.)

The *Mirror of Justices* itself also says, (ch. 1, sec. 3,) in speaking " *Of the first Constitutions of the Ancient Kings:*"

"Many ordinances were made by many kings, until the time of the king that now is (Edward I.); the which ordinances were abused, *or not used by many, nor very current,* because they were not put in writing, and certainly published." — *Mirror of Justices*, p. 6.

Hallam says:

"The Franks, Lombards, and Saxons seem alike to have been jealous of judicial authority; and averse to surrendering what concerned every man's private right, out of the hands of his neighbors and equals." — 1 *Middle Ages,* 271.

The "judicial authority," here spoken of, was the authority of the kings, (who at that time united the office of both legislators and judges,) and not of a separate department of government, called the judiciary, like what has existed in more modern times.*

Hume says:

"The government of the Germans, and that of all the northern nations, who established themselves on the ruins of Rome, was always extremely free; and those fierce people, accustomed to independence and inured to arms, *were more guided by persuasion than authority, in the submission which they paid to their princes.* The military despotism, which had taken place in the Roman empire, and which, previously to the irruption of those conquerors, had sunk the genius of men, and destroyed every noble principle of science and virtue, was unable to resist the vigorous efforts of a free people, and Europe, as from a new epoch, rekindled her ancient spirit, and shook off the base servitude to arbitrary will and authority under which she had so long labored. The free constitutions then established, however impaired by the encroachments of succeeding princes, still preserve an air of independence and legal administration, which distinguished the European nations; and if that part of the globe maintain sentiments

---

* Hale says:

"The trial by jury of twelve men was the *usual* trial among the Normans, in most suits; especially in assizes, *et juris utrum.*" — 1 *Hale's History of the Common Law,* 219. This was in Normandy, *before* the conquest of England by the Normans. *See Ditto,* p. 218.

Crabbe says:

"It cannot be denied that the practice of submitting causes to the decision of twelve men was universal among all the northern tribes (of Europe) from the very remotest antiquity." — *Crabbe's History of the English Law,* p. 32.

of liberty, honor, equity, and valor, superior to the rest of mankind, it owes these advantages chiefly to the seeds implanted by those generous barbarians.

"The Saxons, who subdued Britain, as they enjoyed great liberty in their own country, obstinately retained that invaluable possession in their new settlement; and they imported into this island the same principles of independence, which they had inherited from their ancestors. The chieftains, (for such they were, more than kings or princes,) who commanded them in those military expeditions, still possessed a very limited authority; and as the Saxons exterminated, rather than subdued the ancient inhabitants, they were, indeed, transplanted into a new territory, but preserved unaltered all their civil and military institutions. The language was pure Saxon; even the names of places, which often remain while the tongue entirely changes, were almost all affixed by the conquerors; the manners and customs were wholly German; and the same picture of a fierce and bold liberty, which is drawn by the masterly pen of Tacitus, will suit those founders of the English government. The king, so far from being invested with arbitrary power, was only considered as the first among the citizens; his authority depended more on his personal qualities than on his station; he was even so far on a level with the people, that a stated price was fixed for his head, and a legal fine was levied upon his murderer, which though proportionate to his station, and superior to that paid for the life of a subject, was a sensible mark of his subordination to the community." — 1 *Hume, Appendix,* 1.

Stuart says:

"The Saxons brought along with them into Britain their own customs, language, and civil institutions. Free in Germany, they renounced not their independence, when they had conquered. Proud from victory, and with their swords in their hands, would they surrender their liberties to a private man? Would temporary leaders, limited in their powers, and unprovided in resources, ever think to usurp an authority over warriors, who considered themselves as their equals, were impatient of control, and attached with devoted zeal to their privileges? Or, would they find leisure to form resolutions, or opportunities to put them in practice, amidst the tumult and confusion of those fierce and bloody wars, which their nations first waged with the Britons, and then engaged in among themselves? Sufficiently flattered in leading the armies of their countrymen, the ambition of commanders could as little suggest such designs, as the liberty of the people could submit to them. The conquerors of Britain retained their independence; and this island saw itself again in that free state in which the Roman arms had discovered it.

"The same firmness of character, and generosity of manners, which, in general, distinguished the Germans, were possessed in an eminent degree by the Saxons; and while we endeavor to unfold their political institutions, we must perpetually turn our observation to that masterly picture in which the Roman historian has described these nations. In the woods of Germany shall we find the principles which directed the state of land, in the different kingdoms of Europe; and there shall we find the foundation of those ranks of men, and of those civil arrangements, which the barbarians everywhere established; and which the English alone have had the good fortune, or the spirit, to preserve." — *Stuart on the Constitution of England*, p. 59-61.

"Kings they (the Germans) respected as the first magistrates of the state; but the authority possessed by them was narrow and limited." — *Ditto*, p. 134.

"Did he, (the king,) at any time, relax his activity and martial ardor, did he employ his abilities to the prejudice of his nation, or fancy he was superior to the laws; the same power which raised him to honor, humbled and degraded him. The customs and councils of his country pointed out to him his duty; and if he infringed on the former, or disobeyed the latter, a fierce people set aside his authority. * * *

"His long hair was the only ornament he affected, and to be foremost to attack an enemy was his chief distinction. Engaged in every hazardous expedition, he was a stranger to repose; and, rivalled by half the heroes of his tribe, he could obtain little power. Anxious and watchful for the public interest, he felt every moment his dependence, and gave proofs of his submission.

"He attended the general assembly of his nation, and was allowed the privilege to harangue it first; but the arts of persuasion, though known and respected by a rude people, were unequally opposed to the prejudices and passions of men." — *Ditto*, p. 135-6.

"*The authority of a Saxon monarch was not more considerable. The Saxons submitted not to the arbitrary rule of princes. They administered an oath to their sovereigns, which bound them to acknowledge the laws, and to defend the rights of the church and people; and if they forgot this obligation, they forfeited their office.* In both countries, a price was affixed on kings, a fine expiated their murder, as well as that of the meanest citizen; and the smallest violation of ancient usage, or the least step towards tyranny, was always dangerous, and often fatal to them." — *Ditto*, p. 139–40.

"They were not allowed to impose taxes on the kingdom." — *Ditto*, p. 146.

"Like the German monarchs, they deliberated in the general assembly of the nation ; *but their legislative authority was not much respected ;* and their assent was considered in no better light than as a form. This, however, was their chief prerogative; and they employed it to acquire an ascendant in the state. To art and insinuation they turned, as their only resource, and flattered a people whom they could not awe; but address, and the abilities to persuade, were a weak compensation for the absence of real power.

"They declared war, it is said, and made peace. In both cases, however, they acted as the instruments of the state, and put in execution the resolutions which its councils had decreed. If, indeed, an enemy had invaded the kingdom, and its glory and its safety were concerned, the great lords took the field at the call of their sovereign. But had a sovereign declared war against a neighboring state, without requiring their advice, or if he meant to revenge by arms an insult offered to him by a subject, a haughty and independent nobility refused their assistance. These they considered as the quarrels of the king, and not of the nation; and in all such emergencies he could only be assisted by his retainers and dependents." — *Ditto*, p. 147–8.

"Nor must we imagine that the Saxon, any more than the German monarchs, succeeded each other in a lineal descent,* or that they disposed of the crown at their pleasure. In both countries, the free election of the people filled the throne; and their choice was the only rule by which princes reigned. The succession, accordingly, of their kings was often broken and interrupted, and their depositions were frequent and groundless. The will of a prince whom they had long respected, and the favor they naturally transferred to his descendant, made them often advance him to the royal dignity; but the crown of his ancestor he considered as the gift of the people, and neither expected nor claimed it as a right." — *Ditto*, p. 151–3.

In Germany "It was the business of the great to command in war, and in peace they distributed justice. * * *

---

* "The people, who in every general council or assembly could oppose and dethrone their sovereigns, were in little dread of their encroachments on their liberties ; and kings, who found sufficient employment in keeping possession of their crowns, would not likely attack the more important privileges of their subjects."

"The *princes* in Germany were *earls* in England. The great contended in both countries in the number of their retainers, and in that splendor and magnificence which are so alluring to a rude people; and though they joined to set bounds to regal power, they were often animated against each other with the fiercest hatred. To a proud and impatient nobility it seemed little and unsuiting to give or accept compositions for the injuries they committed or received; and their vassals adopting their resentment and passions, war and bloodshed alone could terminate their quarrels. What necessarily resulted from their situation in society, was continued as a *privilege;* and the great, in both countries, made war, of their private authority, on their enemies. The Saxon earls even carried their arms against their sovereigns; and, surrounded with retainers, or secure in fortresses and castles, they despised their resentment, and defied their power.

"The judges of the people, they presided in both countries in courts of law.* The particular districts over which they exerted their authority were marked out in Germany by the council of the state; and in England their jurisdiction extended over the fiefs and other territories they possessed. All causes, both civil and criminal, were tried before them; and they judged, except in cases of the utmost importance, without appeal. They were even allowed to grant pardon to criminals, and to correct by their clemency the rigors of justice. Nor did the sovereign exercise any authority in their lands. In these his officers formed no courts, and his *writ* was disregarded. * * *

"They had officers, as well as the king, who collected their revenues, and added to their greatness; and the inhabitants of their lands they distinguished by the name of *subjects.*

"But to attend the general assembly of their nation was the chief prerogative of the German and Saxon princes; and as they consulted the interest of their country, and deliberated concerning matters of state, so in the *king's court,* of which also they were members, they assisted to pronounce judgment in the complaints and appeals which were lodged in it."— *Ditto,* p. 158 to 165.

Henry says:

"Nothing can be more evident than this important truth; that our Anglo-Saxon kings were not absolute monarchs; but

---

* This office was afterwards committed to sheriffs. But even while the court was held by the lord, "*the Lord was not judge, but the Pares (peers) only.*"— *Gilbert on the Court of Exchequer,* 61-2.

that their powers and prerogatives were limited by the laws and customs of the country. Our Saxon ancestors had been governed by limited monarchs in their native seats on the continent; and there is not the least appearance or probability that they relinquished their liberties, and submitted to absolute government in their new settlements in this island. It is not to be imagined that men, whose reigning passion was the love of liberty, would willingly resign it; and their new sovereigns, who had been their fellow-soldiers, had certainly no power to compel them to such a resignation." — 3 *Henry's History of Great Britain*, 358.

Mackintosh says: "The Saxon chiefs, who were called kings, originally acquired power by the same natural causes which have gradually, and everywhere, raised a few men above their fellows. They were, doubtless, more experienced, more skilful, more brave, or more beautiful, than those who followed them. * * A king was powerful in war by the lustre of his arms, and the obvious necessity of obedience. His influence in peace fluctuated with his personal character. In the progress of usage his power became more fixed and more limited. * * It would be very unreasonable to suppose that the northern Germans who had conquered England, had so far changed their characteristic habits from the age of Tacitus, that the victors became slaves, and that their generals were converted into tyrants." — *Mackintosh's Hist. of England*, Ch. 2. 45 *Lardner's Cab. Cyc.*, 73–4.

Rapin, in his discourse on the "Origin and Nature of the English Constitution," says:

"There are but two things the Saxons did not think proper to trust their kings with; for being of like passions with other men, they might very possibly abuse them; namely, the power of changing the laws enacted by consent of king and people; and the power of raising taxes at pleasure. From these two articles sprung numberless branches concerning the liberty and property of the subject, which the king cannot touch, without breaking the constitution, and they are the distinguishing character of the English monarchy. The prerogatives of the crown, and the rights and privileges of the people, flowing from the two fore-mentioned articles, are the ground of all the laws that from time to time have been made by unanimous consent of king and people. The English government consists in the strict union of the king's prerogatives with the people's liberties. * * But when kings arose, as some there were, that aimed at absolute power, by changing the old, and making new laws, at pleasure; by imposing illegal taxes on the people; this excellent government being, in a manner, dissolved by these destructive measures, confusion and civil wars ensued, which some very wrongfully ascribe to the fickle and restless temper of the English." — *Rapin's Preface to his History of England.*

Hallam says that among the Saxons, " the royal authority was weak." — 2 *Middle Ages,* 403.

But although the king himself had so little authority, that it cannot be supposed for a moment that his laws were regarded as imperative by the people, it has nevertheless been claimed, in modern times, by some who seem determined to find or make a precedent for the present legislative authority of parliament, that his laws were authoritative, *when assented to* by the *Witena-gemote*, or assembly of wise men — that is, the bishops and barons. But this assembly evidently had no legislative power whatever. The king would occasionally invite the bishops and barons to meet him for consultation on public affairs, *simply as a council*, and not as a legislative body. Such as saw fit to attend, did so. If they were agreed upon what ought to be done, the king would pass a law accordingly, and the barons and bishops would then return and inform the people orally what laws had been passed, and use their influence with them to induce them to conform to the law of the king, and the recommendation of the council. And the people no doubt were much more likely to accept a law of the king, if it had been approved by this council, than if it had not. But it was still only a law of the king, which they obeyed or disregarded according to their own notions of expediency. The numbers who usually attended this council were too small to admit of the supposition that they had any legislative authority whatever, to impose laws upon the people against their will.

Lingard says :

" It was necessary that the king should obtain the assent of these (the members of the Witena-gemotes) to all legislative enactments; *because, without their acquiescence and support, it was impossible to carry them into execution.* To many charters (laws) we have the signatures of the *Witan.* *They seldom exceed thirty in number; they never amount to sixty.*" — 1 *Lingard,* 486.

It is ridiculous to suppose that the assent of such an assembly gave any *authority* to the laws of the king, or had any influence in securing obedience to them, otherwise than by way of persuasion. If this body had had any real legislative authority, such as is accorded to legislative bodies of the present day, they would have made themselves at once the most conspicuous portion of the government, and would have left behind them abundant evidence of their power, instead of the evidence simply of their assent to a few laws passed by the king.

More than this. If this body had had any real legislative authority, they would have constituted an aristocracy, having, in conjunction with the king, absolute power over the people. Assembling voluntarily, merely on the invitation of the king; deputed by nobody but themselves; representing nobody but themselves; responsible to nobody but themselves; their legislative authority, if they had had any, would of necessity have made the government the government of an aristocracy merely, *and the people slaves, of course.* And this would necessarily have been the picture that history would have given us of the Anglo-Saxon government, *and of Anglo-Saxon liberty.*

The fact that the people had no representation in this assembly, and the further fact that, through their juries alone, they nevertheless maintained that noble freedom, the very tradition of which (after the substance of the thing itself has ceased to exist) has constituted the greatest pride and glory of the nation to this day, *prove* that this assembly exercised no authority which juries of the people acknowledged, except at their own discretion.*

---

* The opinion expressed in the text, that the Witan had no legislative authority, is corroborated by the following authorities :

"From the fact that the new laws passed by the king and the Witan were laid before the shire-mote, (county court,) we should be almost justified in the inference that a second sanction was necessary before they could have the effect of law in that particular county." — *Dunham's Middle Ages*, Sec. 2, B. 2, Ch. 1. 57 *Lardner's Cab. Cyc.*, 53.

The "*second sanction*" required to give the legislation of the king and Witan the effect of law, was undoubtedly, I think, *as a general thing, the sanction of a jury.* I know of no evidence whatever that laws were ever submitted to popular vote in the county courts, as this author seems to suppose possible. Another mode, sometimes re-

There is not a more palpable truth, in the history of the Anglo-Saxon government, than that stated in the Introduction to Gilbert's History of the Common Pleas,* viz., *"that the County and Hundred Courts,"* (to which should have been added the other courts in which juries sat, the courts-baron and court-leet,) *"in those times were the real and only Parliaments of the kingdom."* And why were they the real and only parliaments of the kingdom? Solely because, as will be hereafter shown, the juries in those courts tried causes on their intrinsic merits, according to their own ideas of justice, irrespective of the laws agreed upon by kings, priests, and barons; and whatever principles they uniformly, or perhaps generally, enforced, *and none others*, became practically the law of the land as matter of course.†

Finally, on this point. Conclusive proof that the legislation of the king was of little or no authority, is found in the fact *that the kings enacted so few laws*. If their laws had been received as authoritative, in the manner that legislative enactments are at this day, they would have been making laws continually. Yet the codes of the most celebrated kings are very small, and were little more than compilations of immemorial customs. The code of Alfred would not fill twelve

---

sorted to for obtaining the sanction of the people to the laws of the Witan, was, it seems, to persuade the people themselves to swear to observe them. Mackintosh says:

"The preambles of the laws (of the Witan) speak of the infinite number of *liegemen* who attended, as only applauding the measures of the assembly. But this applause was neither so unimportant to the success of the measures, nor so precisely distinguished from a share in legislation, as those who read history with a modern eye might imagine. It appears that under Athelstan expedients were resorted to, to obtain a consent to the law from great bodies of the people in their districts, which their numbers rendered impossible in a national assembly. That monarch appears to have sent commissioners to hold *shire-gemotes* or county meetings, where they proclaimed the laws made by the king and his counsellors, which, being acknowledged and sworn to at these *folk-motes* (meetings of the people) became, by their assent, completely binding on the whole nation." — *Mackintosh's Hist. of England*, Ch. 2. 45 *Lardner's Cab. Cyc.*, 75.

* Page 31.

† Hallam says, "It was, however, to the county court that an English freeman chiefly looked for the maintenance of his civil rights." — 2 *Middle Ages*, 392.

Also, "This (the county court) was the great constitutional judicature in all questions of civil right." — *Ditto*, 395.

Also, "The liberties of these Anglo-Saxon thanes were chiefly secured, next to their swords and their free spirits, by the inestimable right of deciding civil and criminal suits in their own county courts." — *Ditto*, 399.

pages of the statute book of Massachusetts, and was little or nothing else than a compilation of the laws of Moses, and the Saxon customs, evidently collected from considerations of convenience, rather than enacted on the principle of authority. The code of Edward the Confessor would not fill twenty pages of the statute book of Massachusetts, and, says Blackstone, "seems to have been no more than a new edition, or fresh promulgation of Alfred's code, or *dome-book*, with such additions and improvements as the experience of a century and a half suggested." — 1 *Blackstone*, 66.*

---

* " Alfred may, in one sense, be called the founder of these laws, (the Saxon,) for until his time they were an *unwritten* code, but he expressly says, '*that I, Alfred, collected the good laws of our forefathers into one code, and also I wrote them down*' — which is a decisive fact in the history of our laws well worth noting." — *Introduction to Gilbert's History of the Common Pleas*, p. 2, *note*.

Kelham says, "Let us consult our own lawyers and historians, and they will tell us * * that Alfred, Edgar, and Edward the Confessor, were the great *compilers and restorers* of the English Laws." — *Kelham's Preliminary Discourse to the Laws of William the Conqueror*, p. 12. *Appendix to Kelham's Dictionary of the Norman Language*.

"He (Alfred) also, like another Theodosius, *collected the various customs* that he found dispersed in the kingdom, and reduced and digested them into one uniform system, or code of laws, in his *som-bec*, or *liber judicialis* (judicial book). This he *compiled* for the use of the court baron, hundred and county court, the court-leet and sheriff's tourn, tribunals which he established for the trial of all causes, civil and criminal, in the very districts wherein the complaints arose." — 4 *Blackstone*, 411.

Alfred himself says, "Hence I, King Alfred, gathered these together, and commanded many of those to be written down which our forefathers observed — those which I liked — and those which I did not like, by the advice of my Witan, I threw aside. For I durst not venture to set down in writing over many of my own, since I knew not what among them would please those that should come after us. But those which I met with either of the days of me, my kinsman, or of Offa, King of Mercia, or of Æthelbert, who was the first of the English who received baptism — those which appeared to me the justest — I have here collected, and abandoned the others. Then I, Alfred, King of the West Saxons, showed these to all my Witan, and they then said that they were all willing to observe them." — *Laws of Alfred, translated by R. Price, prefixed to Mackintosh's History of England*, vol. 1. 45 *Lardner's Cab. Cyc.*

"King Edward * * projected and begun what his grandson, King Edward the Confessor, afterwards completed, viz., one uniform digest or body of laws to be observed throughout the whole kingdom, *being probably no more than a revival of King Alfred's code*, with some improvements suggested by necessity and experience, particularly the incorporating some of the British, or, rather, Mercian *customs*, and also *such of the Danish* (customs) as were reasonable and approved, into the *West Saxon Lage*, which was still the ground-work of the whole. And this appears to be the best supported and most plausible conjecture, (for certainty is not to be expected,) of the rise and original of that admirable system of maxims and unwritten customs which is now known by the

The Code of William the Conqueror * would fill less than seven pages of the statute book of Massachusetts; and most of the laws contained in it are taken from the laws of the preceding kings, and especially of Edward the Confessor (whose laws William swore to observe); but few of his own being added.

The codes of the other Saxon and Norman kings were, as a general rule, less voluminous even than these that have been named; and probably did not exceed them in originality.† The Norman princes, from William the Conqueror to John, I think without exception, bound themselves, and, in order to maintain their thrones, were obliged to bind themselves, to observe the ancient laws and customs, in other words, the "*lex terræ*," or "*common law*" of the kingdom. Even Magna Carta contains hardly anything other than this same "*common law*," with some new securities for its observance.

---

name of the *common law*, as extending its authority universally over all the realm, and which is doubtless of Saxon parentage." — 4 *Blackstone*, 412.

"By the *Lex Terræ* and *Lex Regni* is understood the laws of Edward the Confessor, confirmed and enlarged as they were by William the Conqueror; and this Constitution or Code of Laws is what even to this day are called '*The Common Law of the Land.*'" — *Introduction to Gilbert's History of the Common Pleas*, p. 22, note.

* Not the conqueror of the English people, (as the friends of liberty maintain,) but only of Harold the usurper. — See *Hale's History of the Common Law*, ch. 5.

† For all these codes see Wilkins' Laws of the Anglo-Saxons.

"Being regulations adapted to existing institutions, the Anglo-Saxon statutes are concise and technical, alluding to the law which was then living and in vigor, rather than defining it. The same clauses and chapters are often repeated word for word, in the statutes of subsequent kings, showing that enactments which bear the appearance of novelty are merely declaratory. Consequently the appearance of a law, seemingly for the first time, is by no means to be considered as a proof that the matter which it contains is new; nor can we trace the progress of the Anglo-Saxon institutions with any degree of certainty, by following the dates of the statutes in which we find them first noticed. All arguments founded on the apparent chronology of the subjects included in the laws, are liable to great fallacies. Furthermore, a considerable portion of the Anglo-Saxon law was never recorded in writing. There can be no doubt but that the rules of inheritance were well established and defined; yet we have not a single law, and hardly a single document from which the course of the descent of land can be inferred. * * Positive proof cannot be obtained of the commencement of any institution, because the first written law relating to it may posssibly be merely confirmatory or declaratory; neither can the non-existence of any institution be inferred from the absence of direct evidence. Written laws were modified and controlled by customs of which no trace can be discovered, until after the lapse of centuries, although those usages must have been in constant vigor during the long interval of silence." — 1 *Palgrave's Rise and Progress of the English Commonwealth*, 58-9.

How is this abstinence from legislation, on the part of the ancient kings, to be accounted for, except on the supposition that the people would accept, and juries enforce, few or no new laws enacted by their kings? Plainly it can be accounted for in no other way. In fact, all history informs us that anciently the attempts of the kings to introduce or establish new laws, met with determined resistance from the people, and generally resulted in failure. "*Nolumus Leges Angliæ mutari,*" (we will that the laws of England be not changed,) was a determined principle with the Anglo-Saxons, from which they seldom departed, up to the time of Magna Carta, and indeed until long after.*

SECTION II.

The Ancient Common Law Juries were mere Courts of Conscience.

But it is in the administration of justice, or of law, that the freedom or subjection of a people is tested. If this administration be in accordance with the arbitrary will of the legislator — that is, if his will, as it appears in his statutes, be the highest rule of decision known to the judicial tribunals, — the government is a despotism, and the people are slaves. If, on the other hand, the rule of decision be those principles of natural equity and justice, which constitute, or at least are embodied in, the general conscience of mankind, the people are free in just so far as that conscience is enlightened.

That the authority of the king was of little weight with the *judicial tribunals*, must necessarily be inferred from the fact already stated, that his authority over the *people* was but weak. If the authority of his laws had been paramount in the judicial tribunals, it would have been paramount with the people, of course; because they would have had no alternative

---

* Rapin says, "The customs now practised in England are, for the most part, the same as the Anglo-Saxons brought with them from Germany." — *Rapin's Dissertation on the Government of the Anglo-Saxons*, vol. 2, Oct. Ed., p. 138. *See Kelham's Discourse before named.*

but submission. The fact, then, that his laws were *not* authoritative with the people, is proof that they were *not* authoritative with the tribunals — in other words, that they were not, as matter of course, enforced by the tribunals.

But we have additional evidence that, up to the time of Magna Carta, the laws of the king were not binding upon the judicial tribunals; and if they were not binding before that time, they certainly were not afterwards, as has already been shown from Magna Carta itself. It is manifest from all the accounts we have of the courts in which juries sat, prior to Magna Carta, such as the court-baron, the hundred court, the court-leet, and the county court, *that they were mere courts of conscience, and that the juries were the judges, deciding causes according to their own notions of equity, and not according to any laws of the king, unless they thought them just.*

These courts, it must be considered, were very numerous, and held very frequent sessions. There were probably seven, eight, or nine hundred courts *a month*, in the kingdom; the object being, as Blackstone says, "*to bring justice home to every man's door.*" (3 *Blackstone*, 30.) The number of the *county* courts, of course, corresponded to the number of counties, (36.) The *court-leet* was the criminal court for a district less than a county. The *hundred court* was the court for one of those districts anciently called a *hundred*, because, at the time of their first organization for judicial purposes, they comprised (as is supposed) but a hundred families.* The court-baron was the court for a single manor, and there was a court for every manor in the kingdom. All these courts were holden as often as once in three or five weeks; the county court once a month. The king's judges were present at none of these courts; the only officers in attendance being sheriffs, bailiffs, and stewards, merely ministerial, and not judicial, officers; doubtless incompetent, and, if not incompetent, untrustworthy, for giving the juries any reliable information in matters of law, beyond what was already known to the jurors themselves.

---

* Hallam says, "The county of Sussex contains sixty-five ('hundreds'); that of Dorset forty-three; while Yorkshire has only twenty-six; and Lancashire but six." — 2 *Middle Ages*, 391.

And yet these were the courts, in which was done all the judicial business, both civil and criminal, of the nation, except appeals, and some of the more important and difficult cases.* It is plain that the juries, in these courts, must, of necessity, have been the sole judges of all matters of law whatsoever; because there was no one present, but sheriffs, bailiffs, and stewards, to give them any instructions; and surely it will not be pretended that the jurors were bound to take their law from such sources as these.

In the second place, it is manifest that the principles of law, by which the juries determined causes, were, as a general rule, nothing else than their own ideas of natural equity, *and not any laws of the king;* because but few laws were enacted, and many of those were not written, but only agreed upon in council.† Of those that were written, few copies only were made, (printing being then unknown,) and not enough to supply all, or any considerable number, of these numerous courts. Beside and beyond all this, few or none of the jurors could have read the laws, if they had been written; because few or none of the common people could, at that time, read. Not only were the common people unable to read their own language, but, at the time of Magna Carta, the laws were written in Latin, a language that could be read by few persons except the priests, who were also the lawyers of the nation. Mackintosh says, "the first act of the House of Commons composed and recorded in the English tongue," was in 1415, two centuries after Magna Carta.‡ Up to this time, and for some seventy years later, the laws were generally written

---

* Excepting also matters pertaining to the collection of the revenue, which were determined in the king's court of exchequer. But even in this court it was the law "*that none be amerced but by his peers.*" — *Mirror of Justices*, 49.

† "For the English laws, *although not written,* may, as it should seem, and that without any absurdity, be termed *laws,* (since this itself is law — that which pleases the prince has the force of law,) I mean those laws which it is evident were promulgated by the advice of the nobles and the authority of the prince, concerning doubts to be settled in their assembly. For if from the mere want of writing only, they should not be considered laws, then, unquestionably, writing would seem to confer more authority upon laws themselves, than either the equity of the persons constituting, or the reason of those framing them." — *Glanville's Preface,* p. 38. (Glanville was chief justice of Henry II., 1180.) 2 *Turner's History of the Anglo-Saxons,* 280.

‡ Mackintosh's History of England, ch. 3. Lardner's Cabinet Cyclopædia, 266.

either in Latin or French; both languages incapable of being read by the common people, as well Normans as Saxons; and one of them, the Latin, not only incapable of being read by them, but of being even understood when it was heard by them.

To suppose that the people were bound to obey, and juries to enforce, laws, many of which were unwritten, none of which *they* could read, and the larger part of which (those written in Latin) they could not translate, or understand when they heard them read, is equivalent to supposing the nation sunk in the most degrading slavery, instead of enjoying a liberty of their own choosing.

Their knowledge of the laws passed by the king was, of course, derived only from oral information; and "*the good laws,*" as some of them were called, in contradistinction to others — those which the people at large esteemed to be good laws — were doubtless enforced by the juries, and the others, as a general thing, disregarded.*

That such was the nature of judicial proceedings, and of the power of juries, up to the time of Magna Carta, is further shown by the following authorities.

"The sheriffs and bailiffs caused the free tenants of their bailiwics to meet at their counties and hundreds; *at which justice was so done, that every one so judged his neighbor by such judgment as a man could not elsewhere receive in the like cases*, until such times as the customs of the realm were put in writing, and certainly published.

"And although a freeman commonly was not to serve (as a juror or judge) without his assent, nevertheless it was assented unto that free tenants should meet together in the counties and hundreds, and lords courts, if they were not specially exempted to do such suits, *and there judged their neighbors.*" — *Mirror of Justices*, p. 7, 8.

---

* If the laws of the king were received as authoritative by the juries, what occasion was there for his appointing special commissioners for the trial of offences, without the intervention of a jury, as he frequently did, in manifest and acknowledged violation of Magna Carta, and "the law of the land?" These appointments were undoubtedly made for no other reason than that the juries were not sufficiently subservient, but judged according to their own notions of right, instead of the will of the king — whether the latter were expressed in his statutes, or by his judges.

Gilbert, in his treatise on the Constitution of England, says:

"In the county courts, if the debt was above forty shillings, there issued a *justicies* (a commission) to the sheriff, to enable him to hold such a plea, *where the suitors (jurors) are judges of the law and fact.*" — *Gilbert's Cases in Law and Equity, &c., &c.,* 456.

All the ancient writs, given in Glanville, for summoning jurors, indicate that the jurors judged of everything, *on their consciences only.* The writs are in this form:

"Summon twelve free and legal men (or sometimes twelve knights) to be in court, *prepared upon their oaths to declare whether A or B have the greater right to the land (or other thing) in question.*" See Writs in Beames' Glanville, p. 54 to 70, and 233–306 to 332.

Crabbe, speaking of the time of Henry I., (1100 to 1135,) recognizes the fact that the jurors were the judges. He says:

"By one law, every one was to be tried by his peers, who were of the same neighborhood as himself. * * By another law, *the judges, for so the jury were called,* were to be chosen by the party impleaded, after the manner of the Danish *nembas;* by which, probably, is to be understood that the defendant had the liberty of taking exceptions to, or challenging the jury, as it was afterwards called." — *Crabbe's History of the English Law,* p. 55.

Reeve says:

"The great court for *civil* business was the *county court;* held once every four weeks. Here the sheriff presided; *but the suitors of the court, as they were called, that is, the freemen or landholders of the county, were the judges;* and the sheriff was to execute the judgment. * * *

"The *hundred court* was held before *some bailiff;* the *leet* before the lord of the manor's *steward.* † * *

"Out of the county court was derived an inferior court of *civil* jurisdiction, called the *court-baron.* This was held from three weeks to three weeks, *and was in every respect like the county court;*" (*that is, the jurors were judges in it;*) "only the lord to whom this franchise was granted, *or his steward,*

---

† Of course, Mr. Reeve means to be understood that, in the hundred court, and court-leet, *the jurors were the judges,* as he declares them to have been in the county court; otherwise the "bailiff" or "steward" must have been judge.

presided instead of the sheriff." — 1 *Reeve's History of the English Law,* p. 7.

Chief Baron Gilbert says:

"Besides the tenants of the king, which held *per baroniam,* (by the right of a baron,) and did suit and service (served as judges) at his own court; and the burghers and tenants in ancient demesne, that did suit and service (served as jurors or judges) in their own court in person, and in the king's by proxy, there was also a set of freeholders, that did suit and service (served as jurors) at the county court. These were such as anciently held of the lord of the county, and by the escheats of earldoms had fallen to the king; or such as were granted out by service to hold of the king, but with particular reservation to do suit and service (serve as jurors) before the king's bailiff; *because it was necessary the sheriff, or bailiff of the king, should have suitors (jurors) at the county court, that the business might be despatched. These suitors are the pares (peers) of the county court, and indeed the judges of it; as the pares (peers) were the judges in every court-baron;* and therefore the king's bailiff having a court before him, there must be *pares or judges, for the sheriff himself is not a judge;* and though the style of the court is *Curia prima Comitatus E. C. Milit.' vicecom' Comitat' præd' Tent' apud B.,* &c. (First Court of the county, E. C. knight, sheriff of the aforesaid county, held at B., &c.); by which it appears that the court was the sheriff's; *yet, by the old feudal constitutions, the lord was not judge, but the pares (peers) only;* so that, even in a *justicies,* which was a commission to the sheriff to hold plea of more than was allowed by the natural jurisdiction of a county court, *the pares (peers, jurors) only were judges, and not the sheriff;* because it was to hold plea in the same manner as they used to do in that (the lord's) court." — *Gilbert on the Court of Exchequer,* ch. 5, p. 61–2.

"It is a distinguishing feature of the feudal system, to make civil jurisdiction necessarily, and criminal jurisdiction ordinarily, coëxtensive with tenure; and accordingly there is inseparably incident to every manor a court-baron (curia baronum), *being a court in which the freeholders of the manor are the sole judges,* but in which the lord, by himself, or more commonly by his steward, presides." — *Political Dictionary,* word *Manor.*

The same work, speaking of the *county* court, says: "*The judges were the freeholders who did suit to the court.*" See word *Courts.*

"In the case of freeholders attending as suitors, the county court or court-baron, (as in the case of the ancient tenants *per baroniam* attending Parliament,) *the suitors are the judges of the court, both for law and for fact*, and the sheriff or the under sheriff in the county court, and the lord or his steward in the court-baron, are only presiding officers, *with no judicial authority.*" — *Political Dictionary*, word *Suit*.

"COURT, (curtis, curia aula); the space enclosed by the walls of a feudal residence, in which the followers of a lord used to assemble in the middle ages, to administer justice, and decide respecting affairs of common interest, &c. It was next used for those who stood in immediate connexion with the lord and master, the *pares curiæ*, (peers of the court,) the limited portion of the general assembly, to which was entrusted the pronouncing of judgment," &c.—*Encyclopedia Americana*, word *Court*.

"In court-barons or county courts *the steward was not judge, but the pares (peers, jurors)*; nor was the speaker in the House of Lords judge, but the barons only." — *Gilbert on the Court of Exchequer*, ch. 3, p. 42.

Crabbe, speaking of the Saxon times, says:

"The sheriff presided at the *hundred court*, * * and sometimes sat in the place of the alderman (earl) in the *county court*." — *Crabbe*, 23.

The sheriff afterwards became the sole presiding officer of the county court.

Sir Thomas Smith, Secretary of State to Queen Elizabeth, writing more than three hundred years after Magna Carta, in describing the difference between the *Civil* Law and the English Law, says:

"*Judex* is of us called Judge, but our fashion is so divers, that they which give the deadly stroke, and either condemn or acquit the man for guilty or not guilty, *are not called judges, but the twelve men. And the same order as well in civil matters and pecuniary, as in matters criminal.*" — *Smith's Commonwealth of England*, ch. 9, p. 53, Edition of 1621.

Court-Leet. "That the *leet* is the most ancient court in the land for *criminal* matters, (the court-baron being of no less antiquity in *civil*,) has been pronounced by the highest legal authority. * * Lord Mansfield states that this court was coeval with the establishment of the Saxons here, and its activity marked very visibly both among the Saxons and Danes. * * The leet is a court of record for the cognizance of criminal matters, or pleas of the crown; and necessarily belongs to the king; though a subject, usually the lord of the manor, may be, and is, entitled to the profits, consisting of the essoign pence, fines, and amerciaments.

"*It is held before the steward, or was, in ancient times, before the bailiff, of the lord.*" — *Tomlin's Law Dict.*, word *Court-Leet.*

Of course the jury were the judges in this court, where only a "steward" or "bailiff" of a manor presided.

"No cause of consequence was determined without the king's writ; for even in the county courts, of the debts, which were above forty shillings, there issued a *Justicies* (commission) to the sheriff, to enable him to hold such plea, *where the suitors are judges of the law and fact.*" — *Gilbert's History of the Common Pleas, Introduction,* p. 19.

"'This position'" (that "the matter of law was decided by the King's Justices, but the matter of fact by the *pares*") "*is wholly incompatible with the common law, for the Jurata (jury) were the sole judges both of the law and the fact.*" — *Gilbert's History of the Common Pleas,* p. 70, *note.*

"We come now to the challenge; and of old *the suitors in court, who were judges,* could not be challenged; nor by the feudal law could the *pares* be even challenged, *Pares qui ordinariam jurisdictionem habent recusari non possunt;* (the peers who have ordinary jurisdiction cannot be rejected;) "*but those suitors who are judges of the court,* could not be challenged; and the reason is, that there are several qualifications required by the writ, viz., that they be *liberos et legales homines de vincineto* (free and legal men of the neighborhood) of the place laid in the declaration," &c., &c. — *Ditto,* p. 93.

"*Ad questionem juris non respondent Juratores.*" (To the question of law the jurors do not answer.) "The Annotist says, that this is indeed a maxim in the Civil-Law Jurisprudence, *but it does not bind an English jury, for by the common law of the land the jury are judges as well of the matter of law, as of the fact,* with this difference only, that the (a Saxon word) or judge on the bench is to give them no assistance in determining the matter of *fact,* but if they have any doubt among themselves relating to matter of *law,* they may then request him to explain it to them, which when he hath done, and they are thus become well informed, they, and they only, become competent judges of the matter of *law.* And this is the province of the judge on the bench, namely, to show, or *teach* the law, but not to take upon him the trial of the delinquent, either in matter of fact or in matter of law." (Here various Saxon laws are quoted.) "In neither of these fundamental laws is there the least word, hint, or idea, that the earl or alderman (that is to say, the *Prepositus* (presiding officer) of the court, which is tantamount to *the judge on the bench*) is to take upon him to judge the delinquent in any sense whatever, the sole purport of his office is to *teach* the secular or worldly law." — *Ditto*, p. 57, *note*.

"The administration of justice was carefully provided for; it was not the caprice of their lord, *but the sentence of their peers, that they obeyed. Each was the judge of his equals, and each by his equals was judged*." — *Introd. to Gilbert on Tenures*, p. 12.

Hallam says: "A respectable class of free socagers, having, in general, full rights of alienating their lands, and holding them probably at a small certain rent from the lord of the manor, frequently occur in Domes-day Book. * * They undoubtedly were suitors to the court-baron of the lord, to whose *soc*, or right of justice, they belonged. *They were consequently judges in civil causes, determined before the manorial tribunal.*" — 2 *Middle Ages*, 481.

Stephens adopts as correct the following quotations from Blackstone:

"The *Court-Baron* is a court incident to every manor in the kingdom, to be holden by the steward within the said manor." * * It "*is a court of common law, and it is the court before the freeholders who owe suit and service to the manor,*" (are bound to serve as jurors in the courts of the manor,) "*the steward being rather the registrar than the judge.* * * The freeholders' court was composed of the lord's tenants, who were the *pares* (equals) of each other, and were bound by their feudal tenure to assist their lord in the dispensation of domestic justice. This was formerly held every three weeks; *and its most important business was to determine, by writ of right, all controversies relating to the right of lands within the manor.*" — 3 *Stephens' Commentaries*, 392–3. 3 *Blackstone*, 32–3.

"A *Hundred Court* is only a larger court-baron, being held for all the inhabitants of a particular hundred, instead of a manor. *The free suitors (jurors) are here also the judges, and the steward the register.*" — 3 *Stephens*, 394. 3 *Blackstone*, 33.

"The *County Court* is a court incident to the jurisdiction of the sheriff. * * *The freeholders of the county are the real judges in this court, and the sheriff is the ministerial officer.*" — 3 *Stephens*, 395–6. 3 *Blackstone*, 35–6.

Blackstone describes these courts, as courts "*wherein injuries were redressed in an easy and expeditious manner, by the suffrage of neighbors and friends.*" — *3 Blackstone*, 30.

"When we read of a certain number of *freemen* chosen by the parties to decide in a dispute — all bound by oath to vote *in foro conscientia* — and that *their* decision, *not the will of the judge presiding, ended the suit*, we at once perceive that a great improvement has been made in the old form of compurgation — an improvement which impartial observation can have no hesitation to pronounce as identical in its main features with the trial by jury." — *Dunham's Middle Ages*, Sec. 2, B. 2, Ch. 1.   57 *Lardner's Cab. Cyc.*, 60.

"The bishop and the earl, or, in his absence, the gerefa, (sheriff,) and sometimes both the earl and the gerefa, presided at the *schyre-mote* (county court); the gerefa (sheriff) usually alone presided at the *mote* (meeting or court) of the hundred. In the cities and towns which were not within any peculiar jurisdiction, there was held, at regular stated intervals, a *burgh mote*, (borough court,) for the administration of justice, at which a gerefa, or a magistrate appointed by the king, presided." — *Spence's Origin of the Laws and Political Institutions of Modern Europe*, p. 444.

"The right of the plaintiff and defendant, and of the prosecutor and criminal, *to challenge the judices*, (judges,) *or assessors*,* *appointed to try the cause in civil matters, and to decide upon the guilt or innocence of the accused in criminal matters*, is recognized in the treatise called the Laws of Henry the First; but I cannot discover, from the Anglo-Saxon laws or histories, that before the Conquest the parties had any general right of challenge; *indeed, had such right existed, the injunctions to all persons standing in the situation of judges (jurors) to do right according to their conscience*, would scarcely have been so frequently and anxiously repeated." — *Spence*, 456.

Hale says:

"The administration of the common justice of the kingdom seems to be wholly dispensed in the county courts, hundred courts, and courts-baron; except some of the greater crimes reformed by the laws of King Henry I., and that part thereof which was sometimes taken up by the *Justitiarius Angliæ*.

---

* The jurors were sometimes called "assessors," because they assessed, or determined the amount of fines and amercements to be imposed.

This doubtless bred great inconvenience, uncertainty, and variety in the laws, viz.:

"*First, by the ignorance of the judges, which were the freeholders of the county.* * *

"Thirdly, a third inconvenience was, that all the business of any moment was carried by parties and factions. *For the freeholders being generally the judges,* and conversing one among another, *and being as it were the chief judges, not only of the fact, but of the law;* every man that had a suit there, sped according as he could make parties." — 1 *Hale's History of the Common Law*, p. 246.

"In all these tribunals," (county court, hundred court, &c.,) "*the judges were the free tenants,* owing suit to the court, and afterwards called its peers." — 1 *Lingard's History of England*, 488.

Henry calls the twelve jurors "assessors," and says:

"These assessors, *who were in reality judges,* took a solemn oath, that they would faithfully discharge the duties of their office, and not suffer an innocent man to be condemned, nor any guilty person to be acquitted." — 3 *Henry's History of Great Britain*, 346.

Tyrrell says:

"Alfred cantoned his kingdom, first into *Trihings* and *Lathes,* as they are still called in Kent and other places, consisting of three or four Hundreds; *in which, the freeholders being judges,* such causes were brought as could not be determined in the Hundred court." — *Tyrrell's Introduction to the History of England*, p. 80.

Of the *Hundred Court* he says:

"In this court anciently, *one of the principal inhabitants, called the alderman, together with the barons of the Hundred* * —*id est the freeholders* — *was judge.*" — *Ditto*, p. 80.

Also he says:

"By a law of Edward the Elder, 'Every sheriff shall con-

---

* "The barons of the Hundred" were the freeholders. Hallam says : "The word *baro,* originally meaning only a man, was of very large significance, and is not unfrequently applied to common freeholders, as in the phrase *court-baron.*" — 3 *Middle Ages,* 14–15.

Blackstone says : "The *court-baron* * * is a court of common law, and it is the court of the barons, by which name the freeholders were sometimes anciently called ; for that it is held before the freeholders who owe suit and service to the manor." — 3 *Blackstone,* 33.

vene the people once a month, and do equal right to all, putting an end to controversies at times appointed.'" — *Ditto,* p. 86.

"A statute, emphatically termed the 'Grand Assize,' enabled the defendant, if he thought proper, to abide by the testimony of the twelve good and lawful knights, chosen by four others of the vicinage, *and whose oaths gave a final decision to the contested claim.*" — 1 *Palgrave's Rise and Progress of the English Commonwealth,* 261.

"From the moment when the crown became accustomed to the 'Inquest,' a restraint was imposed upon every branch of the prerogative. *The king could never be informed of his rights, but through the medium of the people.* Every 'extent' by which he claimed the profits and advantages resulting from the casualties of tenure, every process by which he repressed the usurpations of the baronage, depended upon the 'good men and true' who were impanelled to 'pass' between the subject and the sovereign; and the thunder of the Exchequer at Westminster might be silenced by the honesty, the firmness, or the obstinacy, of one sturdy knight or yeoman in the distant shire.

Taxation was controlled in the same manner by the voice of those who were most liable to oppression. * * A jury was impanelled to adjudge the proportion due to the sovereign; and this course was not essentially varied, even after the right of granting aids to the crown was fully acknowledged to be vested in the parliament of the realm. The people taxed themselves; and the collection of the grants was checked and controlled, and, perhaps, in many instances evaded, by these virtual representatives of the community.

The principle of the jury was, therefore, not confined to its mere application as a mode of trying contested facts, whether in civil or criminal cases; and, both in its form and in its consequences, it had a very material influence upon the general constitution of the realm. * * The main-spring of the machinery of remedial justice existed in the franchise of the lower and lowest orders of the political hierarchy. Without the suffrage of the yeoman, the burgess, and the churl, the sovereign could not exercise the most important and most essential function of royalty; from them he received the power of life and death; he could not wield the sword of justice until the humblest of his subjects placed the weapon in his hand." — 1 *Palgrave's Rise and Progress of the English Constitution,* 274–7.

Coke says, "The court of the county is no court of record,* *and the suitors are the judges thereof."* — 4 *Inst.*, 266.

Also, "The court of the Hundred is no court of record, *and the suitors be thereof judges."* — 4 *Inst.*, 267.

Also, "The court-baron is a court incident to every manor, and is not of record, *and the suitors be thereof judges."* — 4 *Inst.*, 268.

Also, "The court of ancient demesne is in the nature of a court-baron, *wherein the suitors are judges*, and is no court of record." — 4 *Inst.*, 269.

Millar says, "Some authors have thought that jurymen were originally *compurgators*, called by a defendant to swear that they believed him innocent of the facts with which he was charged. . . But . . compurgators were merely witnesses; *jurymen were, in reality, judges.* The former were called to confirm the oath of the party by swearing, according to their belief, that he had told the truth, (in his oath of purgation;) *the latter were appointed to try, by witnesses, and by all other means of proof, whether he was innocent or guilty.* . . Juries were accustomed to ascertain the truth of facts, by the defendant's oath of purgation, together with that of his compurgators. . . Both of them (jurymen and compurgators) were obliged to swear that they would *tell the truth.* . . According to the simple idea of our forefathers, guilt or innocence was regarded as a mere matter of fact; and it was thought that no man, who knew the real circumstances of a case, could be at a loss to determine whether the culprit ought to be condemned or acquitted." — 1 *Millar's Hist. View of Eng. Gov.*, ch. 12, p. 332-4.

Also, "The same form of procedure, which took place in the administration of justice among the vassals of a barony, was gradually extended to the courts held in the *trading towns."* — *Same*, p. 335.

Also, "The same regulations, concerning the distribution of justice by the intervention of juries, . . *were introduced into the baron courts of the king*, as into those of the nobility, or such of his subjects as retained their allodial property." — *Same*, p. 337.

Also, "This tribunal" (the *aula regis*, or king's court, afterwards divided into the courts of King's Bench, Common

---

* The ancient jury courts kept no records, because those who composed the courts could neither make nor read records. Their decisions were preserved by the memories of the jurors and other persons present.

Pleas, and Exchequer) "was properly the ordinary baron-court of the king; and, being in the same circumstances with the baron courts of the nobility, it was under the same necessity of trying causes by the intervention of a jury." — *Same,* vol. 2, p. 292.

Speaking of the times of Edward the First, (1272 to 1307,) Millar says:

"What is called the petty jury was therefore introduced into these tribunals, (the King's Bench, the Common Pleas, and the *Exchequer,*) as well as into their auxiliary courts employed to distribute justice in the circuits; and was thus rendered essentially necessary in determining causes of every sort, whether civil, criminal, or *fiscal.*" — *Same,* vol. 2, p. 293–4.

Also, "That this form of trial (by jury) obtained universally in all the feudal governments, as well as in that of England, there can be no reason to doubt. In France, in Germany, and in other European countries, where we have any accounts of the constitution and procedure of the feudal courts, it appears that lawsuits of every sort concerning the freemen or vassals of a barony, were determined by the *pares curiæ* (peers of the court;) *and that the judge took little more upon him than to regulate the method of proceeding, or to declare the verdict of the jury.*" — *Same,* vol. 1, ch. 12, p. 329.

Also, "Among the Gothic nations of modern Europe, the custom of deciding lawsuits by a jury seems to have prevailed universally; first in the allodial courts of the county, or of the hundred, and afterwards in the baron-courts of every feudal superior." — *Same,* vol. 2, p. 296.

Palgrave says that in Germany "The Graff (gerefa, sheriff) placed himself in the seat of judgment, and gave the charge to the assembled free Echevins, warning them to pronounce judgment according to right and justice." — 2 *Palgrave,* 147

Also, that, in Germany, "The Echevins were composed of the villanage, somewhat obscured in their functions by the learning of the grave civilian who was associated to them, and somewhat limited by the encroachments of modern feudality; *but they were still substantially the judges of the court.*" — *Same,* 148.

Palgrave also says, "Scotland, in like manner, had the laws of Burlaw, or Birlaw, which were made and determined by the neighbors, elected by common consent, in the Burlaw or Birlaw courts, wherein knowledge was taken of complaints between neighbor and neighbor, *which men, so chosen, were judges and arbitrators,* and called Birlaw men." — 1 *Palgrave's Rise,* &c., p. 80.

ANCIENT COMMON LAW JURIES COURTS OF CONSCIENCE. 77

But, in order to understand the common law trial by jury, as it existed prior to Magna Carta, and as it was guaranteed by that instrument, it is perhaps indispensable to understand more fully the nature of the courts in which juries sat, and the extent of the powers exercised by juries in those courts. I therefore give in a note extended extracts, on these points, from Stuart on the Constitution of England, and from Blackstone's Commentaries.*

---

* Stuart says :

"The courts, or civil arrangements, which were modelled in Germany, preserved the independence of the people; and having followed the Saxons into England, and continuing their importance, they supported the envied liberty we boast of. * *

"As a chieftain led out his retainers to the field, and governed them during war; so in peace he summoned them together, and exerted a civil jurisdiction. He was at once their captain and their judge. They constituted his court; and having inquired with him into the guilt of those of their order whom justice had accused, they assisted him to enforce his decrees.

"This court (the court-baron) was imported into England; but the innovation which conquest introduced into the fashion of the times altered somewhat its appearance. * *

"The head or lord of the manor called forth his attendants to his hall. * * He inquired into the breaches of custom, and of justice, which were committed within the precincts of his territory; and with his followers, *who sat with him as judges*, he determined in all matters of debt, and of trespass to a certain amount. He possessed a similar jurisdiction with the chieftain in Germany, and his tenants enjoyed an equal authority with the German retainers.

"But a mode of administration which intrusted so much power to the great could not long be exercised without blame or injustice. The German, guided by the candor of his mind, and entering into all his engagements with the greatest ardor, perceived not, at first, that the chieftain to whom he submitted his disputes might be swayed, in the judgments he pronounced, by partiality, prejudice, or interest ; and that the influence he maintained with his followers was too strong to be restrained by justice. Experience instructed him of his error; he acknowledged the necessity of appealing from his lord; and the court of the Hundred was erected.

"This establishment was formed both in Germany and England, by the inhabitants of a certain division, who extended their jurisdiction over the territory they occupied.* They bound themselves under a penalty to assemble at stated times; *and having elected the wisest to preside over them, they judged, not only all civil and criminal matters*, but of those also which regarded religion and the priesthood. The judicial power thus invested in the people was extensive ; they were able to preserve their rights, and attended this court in arms.

"As the communication, however, and intercourse, of the individuals of a German community began to be wider, and more general, as their dealings enlarged, and as disputes arose among the members of different hundreds, the insufficiency of these

* "It was the freemen in Germany, and the possessors of land in England, who were *suitors* (jurors) in the hundred court. These ranks of men were the same. The alteration which had happened in relation to property had invested the German freemen with land or territory."

That all these courts were mere *courts of conscience, in which the juries were sole judges, administering justice according to their own ideas of it*, is not only shown by the extracts

---

courts for the preservation of order was gradually perceived. The *shyre mote,* therefore, or *county court,* was instituted; and it formed the chief source of justice both in Germany and England.

"The powers, accordingly, which had been enjoyed by the court of the *hundred,* were considerably impaired. It decided no longer concerning capital offences; it decided not concerning matters of liberty, and the property of estates, or of slaves; its judgments, in every case, became subject to review; and it lost entirely the decision of causes, when it delayed too long to consider them.

"Every subject of claim or contention was brought, in the first instance, or by appeal, to the *county court;* and the *earl,* or *eorldorman,* who presided there, was active to put the laws in execution. He repressed the disorders which fell out within the circuit of his authority; and the least remission in his duty, or the least fraud he committed, was complained of and punished. He was elected from among the great, and was above the temptation of a bribe; but, to encourage his activity, he was presented with a share of the territory he governed, or was entitled to a proportion of the fines and profits of justice. Every man, in his district, was bound to inform him concerning criminals, and to assist him to bring them to trial; and, as in rude and violent times the poor and helpless were ready to be oppressed by the strong, he was instructed particularly to defend them.

"His court was ambulatory, and assembled only twice a year, unless the distribution of justice required that its meetings should be oftener. Every freeholder in the county was obliged to attend it; and should he refuse this service, his possessions were seized, and he was forced to find surety for his appearance. The neighboring earls held not their courts on the same day; and, what seems very singular, no judge was allowed, after meals, to exercise his office.

"The druids also, or priests, in Germany, as we had formerly occasion to remark, and the clergy in England, exercised a jurisdiction in the *hundred* and *county* courts. They instructed the people in religious duties, and in matters regarding the priesthood; and the princes, earls, or *eorldormen,* related to them the laws and customs of the community. These judges were mutually a check to each other; but it was expected that they should agree in their judgments, and should willingly unite their efforts for the public interest.*

"*But the prince or earl performed not, at all times, in person, the obligations of his office.* The enjoyment of ease and of pleasure, to which in Germany he had delivered himself over, when disengaged from war, and the mean idea he conceived of the drudgery of civil affairs, *made him often delegate to an inferior person the distribution of justice in his district.* The same sentiments were experienced by the Saxon nobility; and the service which they owed by their tenures, and the high employments they sustained, called them often from the management of their counties. The progress, too, of commerce,

---

* It would be wholly erroneous, I think, to infer from this statement of Stuart, that either the "priests, princes, earls, or *eorldormen*" exercised any authority over the jury in the trial of causes, in the way of dictating the law to them. Henry's account of this matter doubtless gives a much more accurate representation of the truth. He says that *anciently*

"The meeting (the county court) was opened with a discourse by the bishop, explaining, out of the Scriptures and ecclesiastical canons, their several duties as good Christians and members of the

already given, but is explicitly acknowledged in the following one, in which the *modern " courts of conscience "* are compared with the *ancient hundred and county courts*, and the preference

---

giving an intricacy to cases, and swelling the civil code, added to the difficulty of their office, and made them averse to its duties. *Sheriffs, therefore, or deputies, were frequently appointed to transact their business; and though these were at first under some subordination to the earls, they grew at length to be entirely independent of them. The connection of jurisdiction and territory ceasing to prevail, and the civil being separated from the ecclesiastical power, they became the sole and proper officers for the direction of justice in the counties.*

"The *hundred*, however, and *county* courts, were not equal of themselves for the purposes of jurisdiction and order. It was necessary that a court should be erected, of supreme authority, where the disputes of the great should be decided, where the disagreeing sentiments of judges should be reconciled, and where protection should be given to the people against their fraud and injustice.

"The princes accordingly, or chief nobility, in the German communities, assembled together to judge of such matters. The Saxon nobles continued this prerogative; and the king, or, in his absence, the chief *justiciary*, watched over their deliberations. But it was not on every trivial occasion that this court interested itself. In smaller concerns, justice was refused during three sessions of the *hundred*, and claimed without effect, at four courts of the county, before there could lie an appeal to it.

"So gradually were these arrangements established, and so naturally did the varying circumstances in the situation of the Germans and Anglo-Saxons direct those successive improvements which the preservation of order, and the advantage of society, called them to adopt. The admission of the people into the courts of justice preserved, among the former, that equality of ranks for which they were remarkable ; and it helped to overturn, among the latter, those envious distinctions which the feudal system tended to introduce, and prevented that venality in judges, and those arbitrary proceedings, which the growing attachment to interest, and the influence of the crown, might otherwise have occasioned." — *Stuart on the Constitution of England*, p. 222 to 245.

"In the Anglo-Saxon period, accordingly, *twelve* only were elected; and these, together with the judge, or presiding officer of the district, being sworn to regard justice, and the voice of reason, or conscience, all causes were submitted to them." — *Ditto*, p. 260.

"Before the orders of men were very nicely distinguished, the jurors were elected from the same rank. When, however, a regular subordination of orders was established, and when a knowledge of property had inspired the necessitous with envy, and the rich with contempt, *every man was tried by his equals*. The same spirit of liberty which gave rise to this regulation attended its progress. Nor could monarchs assume a more arbitrary method of proceeding. 'I will not' (said the Earl of Cornwall to his church. After this, the alderman, or one of his assessors, made a discourse on the laws of the land, and the duties of good subjects and good citizens. *When these preliminaries were over, they proceeded to try and determine, first the causes of the church, next the pleas of the crown, and last of all the controversies of private parties.*" — 3 *Henry's History of Great Britain*, 348.

This view is corroborated by *Tyrrell's Introduction to the History of England*, p. 83–84, and by *Spence's Origin of the Laws and Political Institutions of Modern Europe*, p. 447, and the note on the same page. Also by a law of Canute to this effect, *In every county let there be twice a year an assembly, whereat the bishop and the earl shall be present, the one to instruct the people in divine, the other in human, laws.* — *Wilkins*, p. 136.

given to the latter, on the ground that the duties of the jurors in the one case, and of the commissioners in the other, are the same, and that the consciences of a jury are a safer and purer

---

sovereign) 'render up my castles, nor depart the kingdom, but by judgment of my peers.' Of this institution, so wisely calculated for the preservation of liberty, all our historians have pronounced the eulogium." — *Ditto*, p. 262-3.

Blackstone says:

"The policy of our ancient constitution, as regulated and established by the great Alfred, was to bring justice home to every man's door, by constituting as many courts of judicature as there are manors and towns in the kingdom; *wherein injuries were redressed in an easy and expeditious manner, by the suffrage of neighbors and friends.* These little courts, however, communicated with others of a larger jurisdiction, and those with others of a still greater power; ascending gradually from the lowest to the supreme courts, which were respectively constituted to correct the errors of the inferior ones, and to determine such causes as, by reason of their weight and difficulty, demanded a more solemn discussion. The course of justice flowing in large streams from the king, as the fountain, to his superior courts of record; and being then subdivided into smaller channels, till the whole and every part of the kingdom were plentifully watered and refreshed. An institution that seems highly agreeable to the dictates of natural reason, as well as of more enlightened policy. * * *

"These inferior courts, at least the name and form of them, still continue in our legal constitution; but as the superior courts of record have, in practice, obtained a concurrent original jurisdiction, and as there is, besides, a power of removing plaints or actions thither from all the inferior jurisdictions; upon these accounts (among others) it has happened that these petty tribunals have fallen into decay, and almost into oblivion; whether for the better or the worse may be matter of some speculation, when we consider, on the one hand, the increase of expense and delay, and, on the other, the more able and impartial decisions that follow from this change of jurisdiction.

"The order I shall observe in discoursing on these several courts, constituted for the redress of *civil* injuries, (for with those of a jurisdiction merely *criminal* I shall not at present concern myself,*) will be by beginning with the lowest, and those whose jurisdiction, though public and generally dispersed through the kingdom, is yet (with regard to each particular court) confined to very narrow limits; and so ascending gradually to those of the most extensive and transcendent power." — 3 *Blackstone,* 30 to 32.

"The *court-baron* is a court incident to every manor in the kingdom, *to be holden by the steward within the said manor.* This court-baron is of two natures; the one is a customary court, of which we formerly spoke, appertaining entirely to the copy-holders, in which their estates are transferred by surrender and admittance, and other matters transacted relative to their tenures only. The other, of which we now speak, is a court of common law, and it is a court of the barons, by which name the freeholders were sometimes anciently called; *for that it is held by the freeholders who owe suit and service to the manor, the steward being rather the registrar than the judge.* These courts, though in their nature distinct, are frequently confounded together. *The court we are now considering, viz., the freeholders court, was composed of the lord's tenants, who were the pares* (equals)

---

* There was no distinction between the civil and criminal courrts, as to the rights or powers of juries.

tribunal than the consciences of individuals specially appointed, and holding permanent offices.

"But there is one species of courts constituted by act of Parliament, in the city of London, and other trading and populous districts, which, in their proceedings, so vary from the course of the common law, that they deserve a more particular consideration. I mean the court of requests, *or courts of conscience*, for the recovery of small debts. The first of these was established in London so early as the reign of Henry VIII., by an act of their common council; which, however, was certainly insufficient for that purpose, and illegal, till confirmed by statute 3 Jac. I., ch. 15, which has since been explained and amended by statute 14 Geo. II., ch. 10. The constitution is this: two aldermen and four commoners sit twice a week to hear all causes of debt not exceeding the value of forty shillings; which they examine in a summary way, by the oath of the parties or other witnesses, *and make such order therein as is consonant to equity and good conscience.* * * * Divers trading towns and other districts have obtained acts of Parlia-

---

of each other, and were bound by their feudal tenure to assist their lord in the dispensation of domestic justice. This was formerly held every three weeks; and its most important business is to determine, by writ of right, all controversies relating to the right of lands within the manor. It may also hold plea of any personal actions, of debt, trespass in the case, or the like, where the debt or damages do not amount to forty shillings; which is the same sum, or three marks, that bounded the jurisdiction of the ancient Gothic courts in their lowest instance, or *fierding courts*, so called because four were instituted within every superior district or hundred." — 3 *Blackstone*, 33, 34.

"A *hundred court* is only a larger court-baron, being held for all the inhabitants of a particular hundred, instead of a manor. *The free suitors are here also the judges, and the steward the registrar, as in the case of a court-baron.* It is likewise no court of record, resembling the former at all points, except that in point of territory it is of greater jurisdiction. This is said by Sir Edward Coke to have been derived out of the county court for the ease of the people, that they might have justice done to them at their own doors, without any charge or loss of time; but its institution was probably coeval with that of hundreds themselves, which were formerly observed to have been introduced, though not invented, by Alfred, being derived from the polity of the ancient Germans. The *centeni*, we may remember, were the principal inhabitants of a district composed of different villages, originally in number a *hundred*, but afterward only called by that name, and who probably gave the same denomination to the district out of which they were chosen. Cæsar speaks positively of the judicial power exercised in *their* hundred courts and courts-baron. '*Princeps regiorum atque pagorum*' (which we may fairly construe the lords of hundreds and manors) '*inter suos jus dicunt, controversias que minuunt.*' (The chiefs of the country and the villages declare the law among them, and abate controversies.) And Tacitus, who had examined their constitution still more attentively, informs us not only of the authority of the lords, but that of the *centeni*, the hundreders, or jury, *who were taken out of the common freeholders, and had themselves a share in the determination.* '*Eliguntur in conciliis et principes, qui jura per pagos vicosque reddunt, centeni*

ment, for establishing in them *courts of conscience* upon nearly the same plan as that in the city of London.

"The anxious desire that has been shown to obtain these several acts, proves clearly that the nation, in general, is truly sensible of the great inconvenience arising from the disuse of the ancient county and hundred courts, wherein causes of this small value were always formerly decided with very little trouble and expense to the parties. But it is to be feared that the general remedy, which of late hath been principally applied to this inconvenience, (the erecting these new jurisdictions,) may itself be attended in time with very ill consequences; as the method of proceeding therein is entirely in derogation of the common law; and their large discretionary powers create a petty tyranny in a set of standing commissioners; and as the disuse of the trial by jury may tend to estrange the minds of the people from that valuable prerogative of Englishmen, which has already been more than sufficiently excluded in many instances. *How much rather is it to be wished that the proceedings in the county and hundred courts could be again*

---

singulis, ex plebe comites concilium simul et auctoritas adsunt.' (The princes are chosen in the assemblies, who administer the laws throughout the towns and villages, and with each one are associated an hundred companions, taken from the people, for purposes both of counsel and authority.) This hundred court was denominated *hæreda* in the Gothic constitution. But this court, as causes are equally liable to removal from hence as from the common court-baron, and by the same writs, and may also be reviewed by writ of false judgment, is therefore fallen into equal disuse with regard to the trial of actions." — 3 *Blackstone*, 34, 35.

"The *county court* is a court incident to the jurisdiction of the *sheriff*. It is not a court of record, but may hold pleas of debt, or damages, under the value of forty shillings; over some of which causes these inferior courts have, by the express words of the statute of Gloucester, (6 Edward I., ch. 8,) a jurisdiction totally exclusive of the king's superior courts. * * The county court may also hold plea of many real actions, and of all personal actions to any amount, by virtue of a special writ, called a *justicies*, which is a writ empowering the sheriff, for the sake of despatch, to do the same justice in his county court as might otherwise be had at Westminster. *The freeholders of the county court are the real judges in this court, and the sheriff is the ministerial officer.* * * * In modern times, as proceedings are removable from hence into the king's superior courts, by writ of *pone* or *recordari*, in the same manner as from hundred courts and courts-baron, and as the same writ of false judgment may be had in nature of a writ of error, this has occasioned the same disuse of bringing actions therein." — 3 *Blackstone*, 36, 37.

"Upon the whole, we cannot but admire the wise economy and admirable provision of our ancestors in settling the distribution of justice in a method so well calculated for cheapness, expedition, and ease. By the constitution which they established, all trivial debts, and injuries of small consequence, were to be recovered or redressed in every man's own county, hundred, or perhaps parish." — 3 *Blackstone*, 59.

revived, without burdening the freeholders with too frequent and tedious attendances; and at the same time removing the delays that have insensibly crept into their proceedings, and the power that either party has of transferring at pleasure their suits to the courts at Westminster! *And we may, with satisfaction, observe, that this experiment has been actually tried, and has succeeded in the populous county of Middlesex*, which might serve as an example for others. For by statute 23 Geo. II., ch. 33, it is enacted:

1. That a special county court shall be held at least once in a month, in every hundred of the county of Middlesex, *by the county clerk*.

2. *That twelve freeholders of that hundred, qualified to serve on juries, and struck by the sheriff, shall be summoned to appear at such court by rotation;* so as none shall be summoned oftener than once a year.

3. That in all causes not exceeding the value of forty shillings, *the county clerk and twelve suitors (jurors) shall proceed in a summary way*, examining the parties and witnesses on oath, without the formal process anciently used; *and shall make such order therein as they shall judge agreeable to conscience.*" — 3 *Blackstone*, 81–83.

What are these but courts of conscience? And yet Blackstone tells us they are a *revival of the ancient hundred and county courts*. And what does this fact prove, but that the ancient common law courts, in which juries sat, were mere courts of conscience?

It is perfectly evident that in all these courts the jurors were the judges, and determined all questions of law for themselves; because the only alternative to that supposition is, *that the jurors took their law from sheriffs, bailiffs, and stewards*, of which there is not the least evidence in history, nor the least probability in reason. It is evident, also, that they judged independently of the laws of the king, for the reasons before given, viz., that the authority of the king was held in very little esteem; and, secondly, that the laws of the king (not being printed, and the people being unable to read them if they had been printed) must have been in a great measure unknown to them, and could have been received by them only on the authority of the sheriff, bailiff, or steward. If laws were to be received by them on the authority of these officers, the latter would have imposed such laws upon the people as they pleased.

These courts, that have now been described, were continued in full power long after Magna Carta, no alteration being made in them by that instrument, *nor in the mode of administering justice in them.*

There is no evidence whatever, so far as I am aware, that the juries had any *less* power in the courts held by the king's justices, than in those held by sheriffs, bailiffs, and stewards; and there is no probability whatever that they had. All the difference between the former courts and the latter undoubtedly was, that, in the former, the juries had the benefit of the advice and assistance of the justices, which would, of course, be considered valuable in difficult cases, on account of the justices being regarded as more learned, not only in the laws of the king, but also in the common law, or "law of the land."

The conclusion, therefore, I think, inevitably must be, that neither the laws of the king, nor the instructions of his justices, had any authority over jurors beyond what the latter saw fit to accord to them. And this view is confirmed by this remark of Hallam, the truth of which all will acknowledge:

"The rules of legal decision, among a rude people, are always very simple; not serving much to guide, far less to control the feelings of natural equity." — 2 *Middle Ages*, ch. 8, part 2, p. 465.

It is evident that it was in this way, *by the free and concurrent judgments of juries, approving and enforcing certain laws and rules of conduct, corresponding to their notions of right and justice*, that the laws and customs, which, for the most part, made up the *common law*, and were called, at that day, "*the good laws, and good customs*," and "*the law of the land*," were established. How otherwise could they ever have become established, as Blackstone says they were, "*by long and immemorial usage, and by their universal reception throughout the kingdom*,"* when, as the Mirror says, "*justice was so done, that every one so judged his neighbor, by such judgment as a man could not elsewhere receive in the like cases, until such*

---

* 1 Blackstone, 63–67.

times as the customs of the realm were put in writing and certainly published?"

The fact that, in that dark age, so many of the principles of natural equity, as those then embraced in the *Common Law*, should have been so uniformly recognized and enforced by juries, as to have become established by general consent as "*the law of the land;*" and the further fact that this "law of the land" was held so sacred that even the king could not lawfully infringe or alter it, but was required to swear to maintain it, are beautiful and impressive illustrations of the truth that men's minds, even in the comparative infancy of other knowledge, have clear and coincident ideas of the elementary principles, and the paramount obligation, of justice. The same facts also prove that the common mind, and the general, or, perhaps, rather, the universal conscience, as developed in the untrammelled judgments of juries, may be safely relied upon for the preservation of individual rights in civil society; and that there is no necessity or excuse for that deluge of arbitrary legislation, with which the present age is overwhelmed, under the pretext that unless laws be *made*, the law will not be known; a pretext, by the way, almost universally used for overturning, instead of establishing, the principles of justice.

SECTION III.

The Oaths of Jurors.

The oaths that have been administered to jurors, in England, and which are their *legal* guide to their duty, *all* (so far as I have ascertained them) corroborate the idea that the jurors are to try all cases on their intrinsic merits, independently of any laws that they deem unjust or oppressive. It is probable that an oath was never administered to a jury in England, either in a civil or criminal case, to try it *according to law.*

The earliest oath that I have found prescribed by law to be administered to jurors is in the laws of Ethelred, (about the year 1015,) which require that the jurors "*shall swear, with their hands upon a holy thing, that they will condemn no man that is innocent, nor acquit any that is guilty."* — 4 *Blackstone,* 302.   2 *Turner's History of the Anglo-Saxons,* 155. *Wilkins' Laws of the Anglo-Saxons,* 117.   *Spelman's Glossary,* word *Jurata.*

Blackstone assumes that this was the oath of the *grand* jury (4 *Blackstone,* 302); but there was but one jury at the time this oath was ordained. The institution of two juries, grand and petit, took place after the Norman Conquest.

Hume, speaking of the administration of justice in the time of Alfred, says that, in every hundred,

"Twelve freeholders were chosen, who, having sworn, together with the hundreder, or presiding magistrate of that division, *to administer impartial justice,* proceeded to the examination of that cause which was submitted to their jurisdiction." — *Hume,* ch. 2.

By a law of Henry II., in 1164, it was directed that the sheriff "*faciet jurare duodecim legales homines de vicineto seu de villa, quod inde veritatem secundum conscientiam suam manifestabunt,*" (shall make twelve legal men from the neighborhood *to swear that they will make known the truth according to their conscience.*) — *Crabbe's History of the English Law,* 119.   1 *Reeves,* 87.   *Wilkins,* 321–323.

Glanville, who wrote within the half century previous to Magna Carta, says:

"Each of the knights summoned for this purpose (as jurors) ought to swear that he will neither utter that which is false, nor knowingly conceal the truth." — *Beames' Glanville,* 65.

Reeve calls the trial by jury "*the trial by twelve men sworn to speak the truth.*" — 1 *Reeve's History of the English Law,* 87.

Henry says that the jurors "took a solemn oath, that they would faithfully discharge the duties of their office, and not suffer an innocent man to be condemned, nor any guilty person to be acquitted." — 3 *Henry's Hist. of Great Britain,* 346.

The *Mirror of Justices,* (written within a century after Magna Carta,) in the chapter on the abuses of the Common Law, says:

"It is abuse to use the words, *to their knowledge,* in their oaths, to make the jurors speak upon thoughts, *since the chief words of their oaths be that they speak the truth.*" — p. 249.

Smith, writing in the time of Elizabeth, says that, in *civil* suits, the jury "be sworn to declare the truth of that issue according to the evidence, and their conscience." — *Smith's Commonwealth of England,* edition of 1621, p. 73.

In *criminal* trials, he says:

"The clerk giveth the juror an oath to go uprightly betwixt the prince and the prisoner." — *Ditto,* p. 90.*

---

* This quaint and curious book (Smith's Commonwealth of England) describes the *minutiæ* of trials, giving in detail the mode of impanelling the jury, and then the conduct of the lawyers, witnesses, and court. I give the following extracts, *tending to show that the judges impose no law upon the juries, in either civil or criminal cases, but only require them to determine the causes according to their consciences.*

In civil causes he says:

"When it is thought that it is enough pleaded before them, and the witnesses have said what they can, one of the judges, with a brief and pithy recapitulation, reciteth to the twelve in sum the arguments of the sergeants of either side, that which the witnesses have declared, and the chief points of the evidence showed in writing, and once again putteth them in mind of the issue, and sometime giveth it them in writing, delivering to them the evidence which is showed on either part, if any be, (evidence here is called writings of contracts, authentical after the manner of England, that is to say, written, sealed, and delivered,) and biddeth them go together." — p. 74.

This is the whole account given of the charge to the jury.

In criminal cases, after the witnesses have been heard, and the prisoner has said what he pleases in his defence, the book proceeds :

"When the judge hath heard them say enough, he asketh if they can say any more: If they say no, then he turneth his speech to the inquest. 'Good men, (saith he,) ye of the inquest, ye have heard what these men say against the prisoner. You have also heard what the prisoner can say for himself. *Have an eye to your oath, and to your duty, and do that which God shall put in your minds to the discharge of your consciences,* and mark well what is said.' " — p. 92.

This is the whole account given of the charge in a criminal case.

The following statement goes to confirm the same idea, that jurors in England have formerly understood it to be their right and duty to judge only according to their consciences, and not to submit to any dictation from the court, either as to law or fact.

"If having pregnant evidence, nevertheless, the twelve do acquit the malefactor, which they will do sometime, especially if they perceive either one of the justices or of the judges, or some other man, to pursue too much and too maliciously the death of the prisoner, * * the prisoner escapeth; but the twelve (are) not only rebuked by the judges, but also threatened of punishment; and many times commanded to appear in the Star-Chamber, or before the Privy Council for the matter. But this threatening chanceth oftener than the execution thereof ; *and the twelve answer with most gentle words, they did it according to their consciences,* and pray the judges to be good unto them, *they did as they thought right, and as they accorded all,* and so it passeth away for the most part." — p. 100.

The account given of the trial of a peer of the realm corroborates the same point :

"If any duke, marquis, or any other of the degrees of a baron, or above, lord of the Parliament, be appeached of treason, or any other capital crime, he is judged by his peers and equals; that is, the yeomanry doth not go upon him, but an inquest of the Lords of Parliament, and they give their voice not one for all, but each severally as they do in Parliament, being (beginning) at the youngest lord. And for judge one lord sitteth, who is constable of England for that day. The judgment once given, he breaketh his staff, and abdicateth his office. In the rest there is no difference from that above written," (that is, in the case of a freeman.) — p. 98.

Hale says:

"Then twelve, and no less, of such as are indifferent and are returned upon the principal panel, or the *tales*, are sworn to try the same according to the evidence." — 2 *Hale's History of the Common Law*, 141.

It appears from Blackstone that, even *at this day, neither in civil nor criminal cases*, are jurors in England sworn to try causes *according to law*. He says that in *civil* suits the jury are

"Sworn well and truly to *try the issue* between the parties, and a true verdict to give according to the evidence." — 3 *Blackstone*, 365.

"*The issue*" to be tried is whether A owes B anything; and if so, how much? or whether A has in his possession anything that belongs to B; or whether A has wronged B, and ought to make compensation; and if so, how much?

No statute passed by a legislature, simply as a legislature, can alter either of these "issues" in hardly any conceivable case, perhaps in none. No *unjust* law could ever alter them in any. They are all mere questions of natural justice, which legislatures have no power to alter, and with which they have no right to interfere, further than to provide for having them settled by the most competent and impartial tribunal that it is practicable to have, and then for having all just decisions enforced. And any tribunal, whether judge or jury, that attempts to try these issues, has no more moral right to be swerved from the line of justice, by the will of a legislature, than by the will of any other body of men whatever. And this oath does not require or permit a jury to be so swerved.

In criminal cases, Blackstone says the oath of the jury in England is:

"Well and truly to try, and true deliverance make, between our sovereign lord, the king, and the prisoner whom they have in charge, and a true verdict to give according to the evidence." — 4 *Blackstone*, 355.

"The issue" to be tried, in a criminal case, is "*guilty*," or "*not guilty*." The laws passed by a legislature can rarely, if ever, have anything to do with this issue. "*Guilt*" is an *intrinsic* quality of actions, and can neither be created, destroyed, nor changed by legislation. And no tribunal that attempts to try this issue can have any moral right to declare a man *guilty*, for an act that is intrinsically innocent, at the bidding of a legislature, any more than at the bidding of anybody else. And this oath does not require or permit a jury to do so.

The words, "*according to the evidence*," have doubtless been introduced into the above oaths in modern times. They are unquestionably in violation of the Common Law, and of Magna Carta, if by them be meant such evidence only as the government sees fit to allow to go to the jury. If the government can dictate the evidence, and require the jury to decide according to that evidence, it necessarily dictates the conclusion to which they must arrive. In that case the trial is really a trial by the government, and not by the jury. *The jury* cannot *try an issue*, unless *they* determine what evidence shall be admitted. The ancient oaths, it will be observed, say nothing about "*according to the evidence.*" They obviously take it for granted that the jury try the whole case; and of course that *they* decide what evidence shall be admitted. It would be intrinsically an immoral and criminal act for a jury to declare a man guilty, or to declare that one man owed money to another, unless all the evidence were admitted, which *they* thought ought to be admitted, for ascertaining the truth.*

Grand Jury. — If jurors are bound to enforce all laws passed by the legislature, it is a very remarkable fact that the oath of grand juries does not require them to be governed by the laws in finding indictments. There have been various forms of oath administered to grand jurors; but by none of them that I recollect ever to have seen, except those of the States

---

* " The present form of the jurors' oath is that they shall ' give a true verdict *according to the evidence.*' At what time this form was introduced is uncertain; but for several centuries after the Conquest, the jurors, *both in civil and criminal cases*, were sworn merely *to speak the truth.* (Glanville, lib. 2, cap. 17; Bracton, lib. 3, cap. 22; lib. 4, p. 287, 291; Britton, p. 135.) Hence their decision was accurately termed *veredictum*, or verdict, that is, ' a thing truly said '; whereas the phrase ' true verdict ' in the modern oath is not an accurate expression." — *Political Dictionary*, word *Jury*.

of Connecticut and Vermont, are they sworn to present men *according to law.* The English form, as given in the essay on Grand Juries, written near two hundred years ago, and supposed to have been written by *Lord Somers,* is as follows:

" You shall diligently inquire, and true presentment make, of all such articles, matters, and things, as shall be given you in charge, and of all other matters and things as shall come to your knowledge touching this present service. The king's council, your fellows, and your own, you shall keep secret. You shall present no person for hatred or malice; neither shall you leave any one unpresented for favor, or affection, for love or gain, or any hopes thereof; but in all things you shall present the truth, the whole truth, and nothing but the truth, to the best of your knowledge. So help you God."

This form of oath is doubtless quite ancient, for the essay says "our ancestors appointed" it. — *See Essay,* p. 33-34.

On the obligations of this oath, the essay says:

"If it be asked how, or in what manner, the (grand) juries shall inquire, the answer is ready, *according to the best of their understandings.* They only, not the judges, are sworn to search diligently to find out all treasons, &c., within their charge, and they must and ought to use their own discretion in the way and manner of their inquiry. *No directions can legally be imposed upon them by any court or judges;* an honest jury will thankfully accept good advice from judges, as their assistants; but they are bound by their oaths to present the truth, the whole truth, and nothing but the truth, to the best of their own, not the judge's, knowledge. Neither can they, without breach of that oath, resign their consciences, or blindly submit to the dictates of others; and therefore ought to receive or reject such advices, as they judge them good or bad. * * Nothing can be more plain and express than the words of the oath are to this purpose. The jurors need not search the law books, nor tumble over heaps of old records, for the explanation of them. Our greatest lawyers may from hence learn more certainly our ancient law in this case, than from all the books in their studies. The language wherein the oath is penned is known and understood by every man, and the words in it have the same signification as they have wheresoever else they are used. The judges, without assuming to themselves a legislative power, cannot put a new sense upon them, other than according to their genuine, common meaning. They cannot magisterially impose their opinions upon the jury, and make them forsake the direct words of their oath, to pursue their glosses. The grand inquest are bound to observe alike strictly every part of their oath, and to use all just and proper ways which may enable them to perform it; otherwise it were to say, that after men had sworn to inquire diligently after the truth, according to the best of their knowledge, they were bound to forsake all the natural and proper means which their understandings suggest for the discovery of it, if it be commanded by the judges." — *Lord Somers' Essay on Grand Juries*, p. 38.

What is here said so plainly and forcibly of the oath and obligations of grand juries, is equally applicable to the oath and obligations of petit juries. In both cases the simple oaths of the jurors, and not the instructions of the judges, nor the statutes of kings nor legislatures, are their legal guides to their duties.*

SECTION IV.

The Right of Juries to fix the Sentence.

The nature of the common law courts existing prior to Magna Carta, such as the county courts, the hundred courts, the court-leet, and the court-baron, all prove, what has already been proved from Magna Carta, that, in jury trials, the juries fixed the sentence; because, in those courts, there was no one but the jury who could fix it, unless it were the sheriff, bailiff, or steward; and no one will pretend that it was fixed by them. The juries unquestionably gave the "judgment" in both civil and criminal cases.

That the juries were to fix the sentence under Magna Carta, is also shown by statutes subsequent to Magna Carta.

A statute passed fifty-one years after Magna Carta, says that a baker, for default in the weight of his bread, "*debeat amerciari vel subire judicium pilloræ,*" — that is, "*ought* to be amerced, or suffer the sentence of the pillory." And that a brewer, for "selling ale, contrary to the assize," "*debeat amerciari, vel pati judicium tumbrelli;*" that is, "*ought* to be

---

* Of course, there can be no legal trial by jury, in either civil or criminal cases, where the jury are sworn to try the cases "*according to law.*"

amerced, or suffer judgment of the tumbrel." — 51 *Henry III.*, st. 6. (1266.)

If the king (the legislative power) had had authority to fix the punishments of these offences imperatively, he would naturally have said these offenders *shall* be amerced, and *shall* suffer judgment of the pillory and tumbrel, instead of thus simply expressing the opinion that they *ought* to be punished in that manner.

The statute of Westminster, passed sixty years after Magna Carta, provides that,

"No city, borough, nor town, *nor any man*, be amerced, without reasonable cause, and according to the quantity of the trespass; that is to say, every freeman saving his freehold, a merchant saving his merchandise, a villein his waynage, *and that by his or their peers.*" — 3 *Edward I.*, ch. 6. (1275.)

The same statute (ch. 18) provides further, that,

"Forasmuch as the *common fine and amercement* of the whole county in Eyre of the justices for false judgments, or for other trespass, is unjustly assessed by sheriffs and baretors in the shires, so that the sum is many times increased, and the parcels otherwise assessed than they ought to be, to the damage of the people, which be many times paid to the sheriffs and baretors, which do not acquit the payers; it is provided, and the king wills, that from henceforth such sums shall be assessed before the justices in Eyre, afore their departure, *by the oath of knights and other honest men*, upon all such as ought to pay; and the justices shall cause the parcels to be put into their estreats, which shall be delivered up unto the exchequer, and not the whole sum." — *St.* 3 *Edward I.*, ch. 18, (1275.)*

The following statute, passed in 1341, one hundred and twenty-five years after Magna Carta, providing for the trial of peers of the realm, and the king's ministers, contains a re-

---

* *Coke*, as late as 1588, admits that amercements must be fixed by the peers (8 Coke's Rep. 38, 2 Inst. 27); but he attempts, wholly without success, as it seems to me, to show a difference between fines and amercements. The statutes are very numerous, running through the three or four hundred years immediately succeeding Magna Carta, in which fines, ransoms, and amercements are spoken of as if they were the common punishments of offences, and as if they all meant the same thing. If, however, any technical difference could be made out between them, there is clearly none in principle; and the word *amercement*, as used in Magna Carta, must be taken in its most comprehensive sense.

cognition of the principle of Magna Carta, that the jury are to fix the sentence.

"Whereas before this time the peers of the land have been arrested and imprisoned, and their temporalities, lands, and tenements, goods and cattels, asseized in the king's hands, and some put to death without judgment of their peers: It is accorded and assented, that no peer of the land, officer, nor other, because of his office, nor of things touching his office, nor by other cause, shall be brought in judgment to lose his temporalities, lands, tenements, goods and cattels, nor to be arrested, nor imprisoned, outlawed, exiled, nor forejudged, nor put to answer, nor be judged, but by *award* (*sentence*) of the said peers in Parliament."—15 *Edward III.*, st. 1, sec. 2.

Section 4, of the same statute provides,

"That in every Parliament, at the third day of every Parliament, the king shall take in his hands the offices of all the ministers aforesaid," (that is, "the chancellor, treasurer, barons, and chancellor of the exchequer, the justices of the one bench and of the other, justices assigned in the country, steward and chamberlain of the king's house, keeper of the privy seal, treasurer of the wardrobe, controllers, and they that be chief deputed to abide nigh the king's son, Duke of Cornwall,") "and so they shall abide four or five days; except the offices of justices of the one place or the other, justices assigned, barons of exchequer; so always that they and all other ministers be put to answer to every complaint; and if default be found in any of the said ministers, by complaint or other manner, and of that attainted in Parliament, he shall be punished by judgment of the peers, and put out of his office, and another convenient put in his place. And upon the same our said sovereign lord the king shall do (cause) to be pronounced and made execution without delay, *according to the judgment* (*sentence*) of the said peers in the Parliament."

Here is an admission that the peers were to fix the sentence, or judgment, and the king promises to make execution "*according to*" that sentence.

And this appears to be the law, under which peers of the realm and the great officers of the crown were tried and sentenced, for four hundred years after its passage, and, for aught I know, until this day.

The first case given in Hargrave's collection of English State Trials, is that of *Alexander Nevil*, Archbishop of York,

Robert Vere, Duke of Ireland, *Michael de la Pole*, Earl of Suffolk, and *Robert Tresilian*, Lord Chief Justice of England, with several others, convicted of treason, before "the Lords of Parliament," in 1388. The sentences in these cases were adjudged by the "Lords of Parliament," in the following terms, as they are reported.

"Wherefore the said *Lords of Parliament*, there present, as judges in Parliament, in this case, *by assent of the king, pronounced their sentence*, and did adjudge the said archbishop, duke, and earl. with Robert Tresilian, so appealed, as aforesaid, to be guilty, and convicted of treason, and to be drawn and hanged, as traitors and enemies to the king and kingdom; and that their heirs should be disinherited forever, and their lands and tenements, goods and chattels, forfeited to the king, and that the temporalities of the Archbishop of York should be taken into the king's hands."

Also, in the same case, Sir *John Holt*, Sir *William Burgh*, Sir *John Cary*, Sir *Roger Fulthorpe*, and *John Locton*, "*were by the lords temporal, by the assent of the king*, adjudged to be drawn and hanged, as traitors, their heirs disinherited, and their lands and tenements, goods and chattels, to be forfeited to the king."

Also, in the same case, *John Blake*, "of council for the king," and *Thomas Uske*, under sheriff of Middlesex, having been convicted of treason,

" *The lords awarded, by assent of the king*, that they should both be hanged and drawn as traitors, as open enemies to the king and kingdom, and their heirs disinherited forever, and their lands and tenements, goods and chattels, forfeited to the king."

Also, "*Simon Burleigh*, the king's chamberlain," being convicted of treason, "*by joint consent of the king and the lords*, sentence was pronounced against the said Simon Burleigh, that he should be drawn from the town to Tyburn, and there be hanged till he be dead, and then have his head struck from his body."

Also, "*John Beauchamp*, steward of the household to the king, *James Beroverse*, and *John Salisbury*, knights, gentlemen of the privy chamber, *were in like manner condemned.*" — 1 *Hargrave's State Trials*, first case.

Here the sentences were all fixed by the peers, *with the assent of the king*. But that the king should be consulted, and his assent obtained to the sentence pronounced by the peers, does not imply any deficiency of power on their part to fix the sentence independently of the king. There are obvious reasons why they might choose to consult the king, and obtain his approbation of the sentence they were about to impose, without supposing any legal necessity for their so doing.

So far as we can gather from the reports of state trials, peers of the realm were usually sentenced by those who tried them, *with the assent of the king*. But in some instances no mention is made of the assent of the king, as in the case of "Lionel, Earl of Middlesex, Lord High Treasurer of England," in 1624, (four hundred years after Magna Carta,) where the sentence was as follows:

"This High Court of Parliament doth adjudge, that Lionel, Earl of Middlesex, now Lord Treasurer of England, shall lose all his offices which he holds in this kingdom, and shall, hereafter, be made incapable of any office, place, or employment in the state and commonwealth. That he shall be imprisoned in the tower of London, during the king's pleasure. That he shall pay unto our sovereign lord the king a fine of 50,000 pounds. That he shall never sit in Parliament any more, and that he shall never come within the verge of the court." — 2 *Howell's State Trials*, 1250.

Here was a peer of the realm, and a minister of the king, of the highest grade; and if it were ever *necessary* to obtain the assent of the king to sentences pronounced by the peers, it would unquestionably have been obtained in this instance, and his assent would have appeared in the sentence.

Lord Bacon was sentenced by the House of Lords, (1620,) *no mention being made of the assent of the king*. The sentence is in these words:

"And, therefore, this High Court doth adjudge, That the Lord Viscount St. Albans, Lord Chancellor of England, shall undergo fine and ransom of 40,000 pounds. That he shall be imprisoned in the tower during the king's pleasure. That he shall forever be incapable of any office, place, or employment in the state or commonwealth. That he shall never sit in Parliament, nor come within the verge of the court."

And when it was demanded of him, before sentence, whether it were his hand that was subscribed to his confession, and whether he would stand to it; he made the following answer, which implies that the *lords* were the ones to determine his sentence.

"My lords, it is my act, my hand, my heart. *I beseech your lordships to be merciful to a broken reed.*" — 1 *Hargrave's State Trials,* 386–7.

The sentence against Charles the First, (1648,) after reciting the grounds of his condemnation, concludes in this form:

"For all which treasons and crimes, *this court doth adjudge,* that he, the said Charles Stuart, as a tyrant, traitor, murderer, and public enemy to the good people of this nation, shall be put to death by the severing his head from his body."

The report then adds:

"This sentence being read, the president (of the court) spake as followeth: 'This sentence now read and published, is the act, sentence, judgment and resolution of the whole court.'" — 1 *Hargrave's State Trials,* 1037.

Unless it had been the received "*law of the land*" that those who tried a man should fix his sentence, it would have required an act of Parliament to fix the sentence of Charles, and his sentence would have been declared to be "*the sentence of the law,*" instead of "*the act, sentence, judgment, and resolution of the court.*"

But the report of the proceedings in "the trial of Thomas, Earl of Macclesfield, Lord High Chancellor of Great Britain, before the House of Lords, for high crimes and misdemeanors in the execution of his office," in 1725, is so full on this point, and shows so clearly that it rested wholly with the lords to fix the sentence, and that the assent of the king was wholly unnecessary, that I give the report somewhat at length.

After being found guilty, the earl addressed the *lords,* for a *mitigation of sentence,* as follows:

"'I am now to expect your lordships' judgment; and I hope that you will be pleased to consider that I have suffered no small matter already in the trial, in the expense I have been at, the fatigue, and what I have suffered otherways. * * I have paid back 10,800 pounds of the money already; I have lost my office; I have undergone the censure of both houses of Parliament, which is in itself a severe punishment,'" &c., &c.

On being interrupted, he proceeded:

"'My lords, I submit whether this be not proper in *mitigation of your lordships' sentence;* but whether it be or not, I leave myself to your lordships' justice and mercy; I am sure neither of them will be wanting, and I entirely submit.' * *

"'Then the said earl, as also the managers, were directed to withdraw; and the House (of Lords) ordered Thomas, Earl of Macclesfield, to be committed to the custody of the gentleman usher of the black rod; and then proceeded to the consideration of what *judgment*," (that is, *sentence*, for he had already been found *guilty*,) "to give upon the impeachment against the said earl." * *

"The next day, the Commons, with their speaker, being present at the bar of the House (of Lords), * * the speaker of the House of Commons said as follows:

"'My Lords, the knights, citizens, and burgesses in Parliament assembled, in the name of themselves, and of all the commons of Great Britain, did at this bar impeach Thomas, Earl of Macclesfield, of high crimes and misdemeanors, and did exhibit articles of impeachment against him, and have made good their charge. I do, therefore, in the name of the knights, citizens, and burgesses, in Parliament assembled, and of all the commons of Great Britain, demand *judgment* (*sentence*) of your lordships against Thomas, Earl of Macclesfield, for the said high crimes and misdemeanors.'

"Then the Lord Chief Justice King, Speaker of the House of Lords, said: 'Mr. Speaker, the Lords are now ready to proceed to judgment in the case by you mentioned.

"'Thomas, Earl of Macclesfield, the Lords have unanimously found you guilty of high crimes and misdemeanors, charged on you by the impeachment of the House of Commons, and do now, according to law, proceed to *judgment* against you, which I am ordered to pronounce. Their lordships' *judgment* is, and this high court doth adjudge, that you, Thomas, Earl of Macclesfield, be fined in the sum of thirty thousand pounds unto our sovereign lord the king; and that you shall be imprisoned in the tower of London, and there kept in safe custody, until you shall pay the said fine.'" — 6 *Hargrave's State Trials*, 762-3-4.

This case shows that the principle of Magna Carta, that a man should be *sentenced* only by his peers, was in force, and acted upon as law, in England, so lately as 1725, (five hundred years after Magna Carta,) so far as it applied to a *peer of the realm.*

98   TRIAL BY JURY.

But the same principle, on this point, that applies to a peer of the realm, applies to every freeman. The only difference between the two is, that the peers of the realm have had influence enough to preserve their constitutional rights; while the constitutional rights of the people have been trampled upon and rendered obsolete by the usurpation and corruption of the government and the courts.

SECTION V.

The Oaths of Judges.

As further proof that the legislation of the king, whether enacted with or without the assent and advice of his parliaments, was of no authority unless it were consistent with the *common law,* and unless juries and judges saw fit to enforce it, it may be mentioned that it is probable that no judge in England was ever sworn to observe the laws enacted either by the king alone, or by the king with the advice and assent of parliament.

The judges were sworn to "*do equal law, and execution of right, to all the king's subjects, rich and poor, without having regard to any person;*" and that they will "*deny no man common right;*" * but they were *not* sworn to obey or execute any statutes of the king, or of the king and parliament. Indeed, they are virtually sworn *not* to obey any statutes that are against "*common right,*" or contrary to "*the common law,*" or "*law of the land;*" but to "certify the king thereof" — that is, notify him that his statutes are against the common law; — and then proceed to execute the *common law,* notwithstanding such legislation to the contrary. The words of the oath on this point are these:

"*That ye deny no man common right by (virtue of) the king's letters, nor none other man's, nor for none other cause; and in case any letters come to you contrary to the law,* (that is, the common law, as will be seen on reference to the entire oath given in the note,) *that ye do nothing by such letters, but*

---

* "*Common right*" was the *common law.* 1 *Coke's Inst.* 142 a. 2 do. 55, 6.

certify the king thereof, and proceed to execute the law, (that is, the common law,) *notwithstanding the same letters."*

When it is considered that the king was the sole legislative power, and that he exercised this power, to a great extent, by orders in council, and by writs and "letters" addressed oftentimes to some sheriff, or other person, and that his commands, when communicated to his justices, or any other person, "by letters," or writs, *under seal*, had as much legal authority as laws promulgated in any other form whatever, it will be seen that this oath of the justices *absolutely required* that they disregard any legislation that was contrary to "*common right*," or "*the common law*," and notify the king that it was contrary to common right, or the common law, and then proceed to execute the common law, notwithstanding such legislation.*

If there could be any doubt that such was the meaning of this oath, that doubt would be removed by a statute passed by the king two years afterwards, which fully explains this oath, as follows:

"Edward, by the Grace of God, &c., to the Sheriff of *Stafford*, greeting: Because that by divers complaints made to us, we have perceived that *the Law of the Land, which we by our oath are bound to maintain*, is the less well kept, and the execution of the same disturbed many times by maintenance and procurement, as well in the court as in the country; we

---

* The oath of the justices is in these words:

"Ye shall swear, that well and lawfully ye shall serve our lord the king *and his people*, in the office of justice, and that lawfully ye shall counsel the king in his business, and that ye shall not counsel nor assent to anything which may turn him in damage or disherison in any manner, way, or color. And that ye shall not know the damage or disherison of him, whereof ye shall not cause him to be warned by yourself, or by other; *and that ye shall do equal law and execution of right to all his subjects, rich and poor, without having regard to any person.* And that ye take not by yourself, or by other, privily nor apertly, gift nor reward of gold nor silver, nor of any other thing that may turn to your profit, unless it be meat or drink, and that of small value, of any man that shall have any plea or process hanging before you, as long as the same process shall be so hanging, nor after for the same cause. And that ye take no fee, as long as ye shall be justice, nor robe of any man great or small, but of the king himself. And that ye give none advice or counsel to no man great or small, in no case where the king is party. And in case that any, of what estate or condition they be, come before you in your sessions with force and arms, or otherwise against the peace, or against the form of the statute thereof made, *to disturb execution of the common law*," (mark the term, "*common law*,") "or to menace the people that they may not

greatly moved of conscience in this matter, and for this cause desiring as much for the pleasure of God, and ease and quietness of our subjects, as to save our conscience, and for to save and keep our said oath, by the assent of the great men and other wise men of our council, we have ordained these things following:

"First, we have commanded all our justices, that they shall from henceforth *do equal law and execution of right to all our subjects, rich and poor, without having regard to any person, and without omitting to do right for any letters or commandment which may come to them from us, or from any other, or by any other cause. And if that any letters, writs, or commandments come to the justices, or to other deputed to do law and right according to the usage of the realm, in disturbance of the law, or of the execution of the same, or of right to the parties, the justices and other aforesaid shall proceed and hold their courts and processes, where the pleas and matters be depending before them, as if no such letters, writs, or commandments were come to them; and they shall certify us and our council of such commandments which be contrary to the law,* (that is, " the law of the land," or common law,) *as afore is said."** And to the intent that our justices shall do even right to all people in the manner aforesaid, without more favor showing to one than to another, we have ordained and caused our said justices to be sworn, that they shall not from henceforth, as long as they shall be in the office of justice, take fee nor robe of any man, but of ourself, and that they shall take no gift nor reward by themselves, nor by other, privily nor

---

pursue the law, that ye shall cause their bodies to be arrested and put in prison; and in case they be such that ye cannot arrest them, that ye certify the king of their names, and of their misprision, hastily, so that he may thereof ordain a convenable remedy. And that ye by yourself, nor by other, privily nor apertly, maintain any plea or quarrel hanging in the king's court, or elsewhere in the country. *And that ye deny no man common right by the king's letters, nor none other man's, nor for none other cause; and in case any letters come to you contrary to the law,*" (that is, the " common law" before mentioned,) "*that ye do nothing by such letters, but certify the king thereof, and proceed to execute the law,*" (the " common law" before mentioned,) "*notwithstanding the same letters.* And that ye shall do and procure the profit of the king and of his crown, with all things where ye may reasonably do the same. And in case ye be from henceforth found in default in any of the points aforesaid, ye shall be at the king's will of body, lands, and goods, thereof to be done as shall please him, as God you help and all saints." — 18 *Edward III.*, st. 4. (1344.)

* That the terms " *Law* " and " *Right*," as used in this statute, mean the *common law*, is shown by the preamble, which declares the motive of the statute to be that " *the Law of the Land, (the common law,) which we (the king) by our oath are bound to maintain*," may be the better kept, &c.

apertly, of any man that hath to do before them by any way, except meat and drink, and that of small value; and that they shall give no counsel to great men or small, in case where we be party, or which do or may touch us in any point, upon pain to be at our will, body, lands, and goods, to do thereof as shall please us, in case they do contrary. And for this cause we have increased the fees of the same, our justices, in such manner as it ought reasonably to suffice them." — 20 *Edward III.*, ch. 1. (1346.)

Other statutes of similar tenor have been enacted, as follows:

"It is accorded and established, that it shall not be commanded by the great seal, nor the little seal, to disturb or delay *common right;* and though such commandments do come, the justices shall not therefore leave (omit) to do right in any point." — *St.* 2 *Edward III.*, ch. 8. (1328.)

"That by commandment of the great seal, or privy seal, no point of this statute shall be put in delay; nor that the justices of whatsoever place it be shall let (omit) to do the *common law,* by commandment, which shall come to them under the great seal, or the privy seal." — 14 *Edward III.*, st. 1, ch. 14. (1340.)

"It is ordained and established, that neither letters of the signet, nor of the king's privy seal, shall be from henceforth sent in damage or prejudice of the realm, nor in disturbance of the law" (the common law). — 11 *Richard II.*, ch. 10. (1387.)

It is perfectly apparent from these statutes, and from the oath administered to the justices, that it was a matter freely confessed by the king himself, that his statutes were of no validity, if contrary to the common law, or "common right."

The oath of the justices, before given, is, I presume, the same that has been administered to judges in England from the day when it was first prescribed to them, (1344,) until now. I do not find from the English statutes that the oath has ever been changed. The Essay on Grand Juries, before referred to, and supposed to have been written by *Lord Somers,* mentions this oath (page 73) as being still administered to judges, that is, in the time of Charles II., more than three hundred years after the oath was first ordained. If the oath has never been changed, it follows that judges have not only never been sworn to support any statutes whatever of the king, or of parliament, but that, for five hundred years past, they actually have been sworn to treat as invalid all statutes that were contrary to the common law.

SECTION VI.

The Coronation Oath.

That the legislation of the king was of no authority over a jury, is further proved by the oath taken by the kings at their coronation. This oath seems to have been substantially the same, from the time of the *Saxon* kings, down to the seventeenth century, as will be seen from the authorities hereafter given.

The purport of the oath is, that the king swears *to maintain the law of the land*—that is, *the common law.* In other words, he swears "*to concede and preserve to the English people the laws and customs conceded to them by the ancient, just, and pious English kings,* * * *and especially the laws, customs, and liberties conceded to the clergy and people by the illustrious king Edward;*" * * and "*the just laws and customs which the common people have chosen,* (*quas vulgus elegit*)."

These are the same laws and customs which were called by the general name of "*the law of the land,*" or "*the common law,*" and, with some slight additions, were embodied in *Magna Carta.*

This oath not only forbids the king to enact any statutes contrary to the common law, but it proves that his statutes could be of no authority over the consciences of a jury; since, as has already been sufficiently shown, it was one part of this very common law itself,—that is, of the ancient "laws, customs, and liberties," mentioned in the oath,—that juries should judge of all questions that came before them, according to their own consciences, independently of the legislation of the king.

It was impossible that this right of the jury could subsist consistently with any right, on the part of the king, to impose any authoritative legislation upon them. His oath, therefore, to maintain the law of the land, or the ancient "laws, customs, and liberties," was equivalent to an oath that he would never *assume* to impose laws upon juries, as imperative rules of decision, or take from them the right to try all cases according to their own consciences. It is also an admission that he had no constitutional power to do so, if he should ever desire it. This oath, then, is conclusive proof that his legislation was of no authority with a jury, and that they were under no obligation whatever to enforce it, unless it coincided with their own ideas of justice.

The ancient coronation oath is printed with the Statutes of the Realm, vol. i., p. 168, and is as follows:*

TRANSLATION.

"*Form of the Oath of the King of England, on his Coronation.*

(The Archbishop of Canterbury, to whom, of right and custom of the Church of Canterbury, ancient and approved, it pertains to anoint and crown the kings of England, on the day of the coronation of the king, and before the king is crowned, shall propound the underwritten questions to the king.)

The laws and customs, conceded to the English people by the ancient, just, and pious English kings, will you concede and preserve to the same people, with the confirmation of an oath? and especially the laws, customs, and liberties conceded to the clergy and people by the illustrious king Edward?

---

* The following is a copy of the original :

"*Forma Juramenti Regis Angliæ in Coronacione sua :*

(Archiepiscopus Cantuariæ, ad quo de jure et consuetudine Ecclesiæ Cantuariæ, antiqua et approbata, pertinet Reges Angliæ inungere et coronare, die coronacionis Regis, anteque Rex coronetur, faciet Regi Interrogationes subscriptas.)

Si leges et consuetudines ab antiquis justis et Deo devotis Regibus plebi Anglicano concessas, cum sacramenti confirmacione eidem plebi concedere et servare (volueris :) Et præsertim leges et consuetudines et libertates a glorioso Rege Edwardo clero populoque concessas ?

(Et respondeat Rex,) Concedo et servare volo, et sacramento confirmare.

Servabis Ecclesiæ Dei, Cleroque, et Populo, pacem ex integro et concordiam in Deo secundum vires tuas ?

(Et respondeat Rex,) Servabo.

Facies fieri in omnibus Judiciis tuis equam et rectam justiciam, et discrecionem, in misericordia et veritate, secundum vires tuas ?

(Et respondeat Rex,) Faciam.

Concedis justas, leges et consuetudines esse tenendas, et promittis per te eas esse protegendas, et ad honorem Dei corroborandas, *quas vulgus elegit,* secundum vires tuas ?

(Et respondeat Rex,) Concedo et promitto."

(And the king shall answer,) I do concede, and will preserve them, and confirm them by my oath.

Will you preserve to the church of God, the clergy, and the people, entire peace and harmony in God, according to your powers?

(And the king shall answer,) I will.

In all your judgments, will you cause equal and right justice and discretion to be done, in mercy and truth, according to your powers?

(And the king shall answer,) I will.

Do you concede that the just laws and customs, *which the common people have chosen*, shall be preserved; and do you promise that they shall be protected by you, and strengthened to the honor of God, according to your powers?

(And the king shall answer,) I concede and promise."

The language used in the last of these questions, "Do you concede that the just laws and customs, *which the common people have chosen, (quas vulgus elegit,)* shall be preserved?" &c., is worthy of especial notice, as showing that the laws, which were to be preserved, were not necessarily *all* the laws which the kings enacted, *but only such of them as the common people had selected or approved.*

And how had the common people made known their approbation or selection of these laws? Plainly, in no other way than this — *that the juries composed of the common people had voluntarily enforced them.* The common people had no other *legal* form of making known their approbation of particular laws.

The word "concede," too, is an important word. In the English statutes it is usually translated *grant* — as if with an intention to indicate that "the laws, customs, and liberties" of the English people were mere *privileges, granted* to them by the king; whereas it should be translated *concede*, to indicate simply an *acknowledgment*, on the part of the king, that such were the laws, customs, and liberties, which had been chosen and established by the people themselves, and of right belonged to them, and which he was bound to respect.

I will now give some authorities to show that the foregoing oath has, *in substance*, been the coronation oath from the times of William the Conqueror, (1066,) down to the time of James the First, and probably until 1688.

It will be noticed, in the quotation from Kelham, that he says this oath (or the oath of William the Conqueror) is "in sense and substance the very same with that which the *Saxon* kings used to take at their coronations."

Hale says:

" Yet the English were very zealous for them," (that is, for the laws of Edward the Confessor,) " no less or otherwise than they are at this time for the Great Charter; insomuch that they were never satisfied till the said laws were reënforced, and mingled, for the most part, with the coronation oath of king William I., and some of his successors." — 1 *Hale's History of Common Law*, 157.

Also, " William, on his coronation, had sworn to govern by the laws of Edward the Confessor, some of which had been reduced into writing, but the greater part consisted of the immemorial customs of the realm." — *Ditto*, p. 202, note L.

Kelham says:

" Thus stood the laws of England at the entry of William I., and it seems plain that the laws, commonly called the laws of Edward the Confessor, were at that time the standing laws of the kingdom, and considered the great rule of their rights and liberties; and that the English were so zealous for them, ' that they were never satisfied till the said laws were reënforced, and mingled, for the most part, with the coronation oath.' Accordingly, we find that this great conqueror, at his coronation on the Christmas day succeeding his victory, took an oath at the altar of St. Peter, Westminster, *in sense and substance the very same with that which the Saxon kings used to take at their coronations.* * * And at Barkhamstead, in the fourth year of his reign, in the presence of Lanfranc, Archbishop of Canterbury, for the quieting of the people, he swore that he would inviolably observe the good and approved ancient laws which had been made by the devout and pious kings of England, his ancestors, and chiefly by King Edward; and we are told that the people then departed in good humor." — *Kelham's Preliminary Discourse to the Laws of William the Conqueror.* See, also, 1 *Hale's History of the Common Law*, 186.

Crabbe says that William the Conqueror "solemnly swore that he would observe the good and approved laws of Edward the Confessor." — *Crabbe's History of the English Law*, p. 43.

The successors of William, up to the time of Magna Carta,

probably all took the same oath, according to the custom of the kingdom; although there may be no historical accounts extant of the oath of each separate king. But history tells us specially that Henry I., Stephen, and Henry II., confirmed these ancient laws and customs. It appears, also, that the barons desired of John (what he afterwards granted by Magna Carta) *"that the laws and liberties of King Edward,* with other privileges granted to the kingdom and church of England, might be confirmed, as they were contained in the charters of Henry the First; further alleging, *that at the time of his absolution, he promised by his oath to observe these very laws and liberties."* — *Echard's History of England,* p. 105–6.

It would appear, from the following authorities, that since Magna Carta the form of the coronation oath has been "*to maintain the law of the land,*" — meaning that law as embodied in Magna Carta. Or perhaps it is more probable that the ancient form has been still observed, but that, as its substance and purport were "*to maintain the law of the land,*" this latter form of expression has been used, in the instances here cited, from motives of brevity and convenience. This supposition is the more probable, from the fact that I find no statute prescribing a change in the form of the oath until 1688.

That Magna Carta was considered as embodying "the law of the land," or "common law," is shown by a statute passed by Edward I., wherein he "grants," or concedes,

" That the Charter of Liberties and the Charter of the Forest * * shall be kept in every point, without breach, * * and that our justices, sheriffs, mayors, and other ministers, which, under us, have the *laws of our land** to guide, shall allow the said charters pleaded before them in judgment, in all their points, that is, to wit, *the Great Charter as the Common Law,* and the Charter of the Forest for the wealth of the realm.

"And we will, that if any judgment be given from henceforth, contrary to the points of the charters aforesaid, by the justices, or by any other our ministers that hold plea before them against the points of the charters, it shall be undone, and holden for naught." — 25 *Edward I.,* ch. 1 and 2. (1297.)

---

* It would appear, from the text, that the Charter of Liberties and the Charter of the Forest were sometimes called "*laws* of the land."

Blackstone also says:

"It is agreed by all our historians that the Great Charter of King John was, for the most part, *compiled from the ancient customs of the realm, or the laws of Edward the Confessor; by which they usually mean the old common law which was established under our Saxon princes.*" — *Blackstone's Introduction to the Charters.* See *Blackstone's Law Tracts*, 289.

Crabbe says:

"It is admitted, on all hands, that it (Magna Carta) contains nothing but what was confirmatory of the common law, and the ancient usages of the realm, and is, properly speaking, only an enlargement of the charter of Henry I., and his successors." — *Crabbe's History of the English Law*, p. 127.

That the coronation oath of the kings subsequent to Magna Carta was, in substance, if not in form, "*to maintain this law of the land, or common law,*" is shown by a statute of Edward Third, commencing as follows:

"Edward, by the Grace of God, &c., &c., to the Sheriff of Stafford, Greeting: Because that by divers complaints made to us, we have perceived that *the law of the land, which we by oath are bound to maintain,*" &c. — *St.* 20 *Edward III.* (1346.)

The following extract from Lord Somers' tract on Grand Juries shows that the coronation oath continued the same as late as 1616, (four hundred years after Magna Carta.) He says:

"King James, in his speech to the judges, in the Star Chamber, Anno 1616, told them, 'That he had, after many years, resolved to renew his oath, made at his coronation, concerning justice, and the promise therein contained for *maintaining the law of the land.*' And, in the next page save one, says, '*I was sworn to maintain the law of the land,* and therefore had been perjured if I had broken it. God is my judge, I never intended it.'" — *Somers on Grand Juries*, p. 82.

In 1688, the coronation oath was changed by act of Parliament, and the king was made to swear:

"To govern the people of this kingdom of England, and the dominions thereto belonging, *according to the statutes in Parliament agreed on, and the laws and customs of the same.*" — *St.* 1 *William and Mary*, ch. 6. (1688.)

The effect and legality of this oath will hereafter be considered. For the present it is sufficient to show, as has been already sufficiently done, that from the Saxon times until at least as lately as 1616, the coronation oath has been, in substance, *to maintain the law of the land, or the common law*, meaning thereby the ancient Saxon customs, as embodied in the laws of Alfred, of Edward the Confessor, and finally in Magna Carta.

It may here be repeated that this oath plainly proves that the statutes of the king were of no authority over juries, if inconsistent with their ideas of right; because it was one part of the common law that juries should try all causes according to their own consciences, any legislation of the king to the contrary notwithstanding.*

---

* As the ancient coronation oath, given in the text, has come down from the *Saxon* times, the following remarks of Palgrave will be pertinent, in connection with the oath, as illustrating the fact that, in those times, no special authority attached to the laws of the king :

"The Imperial Witenagemot was not a legislative assembly, in the strict sense of the term, for the whole Anglo-Saxon empire. Promulgating his edicts amidst his peers and prelates, the king uses the language of command; but the theoretical prerogative was modified by usage, and the practice of the constitution required that the law should be accepted by the legislatures (courts) of the several kingdoms. * * The ' Basileus ' speaks in the tone of prerogative : Edgar does not merely recommend, he commands that the law shall be adopted by all the people, whether English, Danes, or Britons, in every part of his empire. Let this statute be observed, he continues, by Earl Oslac, and all the host who dwell under his government, and let it be transmitted by *writ* to the ealdormen of the other subordinate states. And yet, in defiance of this positive injunction, the laws of Edgar were not accepted in Mercia until the reign of Canute the Dane. It might be said that the course so adopted may have been an exception to the general rule; but in the scanty and imperfect annals of Anglo-Saxon legislation, we shall be able to find so many examples of similar proceedings, *that this mode of enactment must be considered as dictated by the constitution of the empire*. Edward was the supreme lord of the Northumbrians, but more than a century elapsed before they obeyed his decrees. The laws of the glorious Athelstane had no effect in Kent, (county,) the dependent appanage of his crown, until sanctioned by the *Witan* of the *shire* (county court). And the power of Canute himself, the 'King of all England,' does not seem to have compelled the Northumbrians to receive his code, until the reign of the Confessor, when such acceptance became a part of the compact upon the accession of a new earl.

Legislation constituted but a small portion of the ordinary business transacted by the Imperial Witenagemot. The wisdom of the assembly was shown in avoiding unnecessary change. *Consisting principally of traditionary usages and ancestorial customs, the law was upheld by opinion. The people considered their jurisprudence as a part of their inheritance.* Their privileges and their duties were closely conjoined; *most frequently, the statutes themselves were only affirmances of ancient customs, or declaratory enactments.* In the Anglo-Saxon commonwealth, therefore, the legislative functions of the Witenagemot were of far less importance than the other branches of its authority. * * The members of the Witenagemot were the 'Pares Curiæ' (Peers of Court) of the kingdom. How far, on these occasions, their opinion or their equity controlled the power of the crown, cannot be ascertained. But the form of inserting their names in the ' *Testing Clause* ' was retained under the Anglo-Norman reigns ; and the sovereign, who submitted his Charter to the judgment of the *Proceres*, professed to be guided by the opinion which they gave. As the '*Pares*' of the empire, the Witenagemot decided the disputes between the great vassals of the crown. * * The jurisdiction exercised in the Parliament of Edward I., when the barony of a *Lord-Marcher* became the subject of litigation, is entirely analogous to the proceedings thus adopted by the great council of Edward, the son of Alfred, the Anglo-Saxon king.

In this assembly, the king, the prelates, the dukes, the ealdormen, and the optimates passed judgment upon all great offenders. * *

The sovereign could not compel the obedience of the different nations composing the Anglo-Saxon empire. Hence, it became more necessary for him to *conciliate their opinions,* if he solicited any service from a vassal prince or a vassal state beyond the ordinary terms of the compact; still more so, when he needed the support of a free burgh or city. And we may view the assembly (the Witenagemot) as partaking of the character of a political congress, in which the liegemen of the crown, or the communities protected by the 'Basileus,' (sovereign,) were *asked or persuaded* to relieve the exigences of the state, or to consider those measures which might be required for the common weal. The sovereign was compelled to *parley* with his dependents.

It may be doubted whether any one member of the empire had power to legislate for any other member. The Regulus of Cumbria was unaffected by the vote of the Earl of East Angliæ, if he chose to stand out against it. These dignitaries constituted a congress, in which the sovereign could treat more conveniently and effectually with his vassals than by separate negotiations. * * But the determinations of the Witan bound those only who were present, or who concurred in the proposition; and a vassal denying his assent to the grant, might assert that the engagement which he had contracted with his superior did not involve any pecuniary subsidy, but only rendered him liable to perform service in the field." — 1 *Palgrave's Rise and Progress of the English Commonwealth,* 637 to 642.

10

CHAPTER IV.

THE RIGHTS AND DUTIES OF JURIES IN CIVIL SUITS.

The evidence already given in the preceding chapters proves that the rights and duties of jurors, in civil suits, were anciently the same as in criminal ones; that the laws of the king were of no obligation upon the consciences of the jurors, any further than the laws were seen by them to be just; that very few laws were enacted applicable to civil suits; that when a new law was enacted, the nature of it could have been known to the jurors only by report, and was very likely not to be known to them at all; that nearly all the law involved in civil suits was *unwritten;* that there was *usually* no one in attendance upon juries who could possibly enlighten them, unless it were sheriffs, stewards, and bailiffs, who were unquestionably too ignorant and untrustworthy to instruct them authoritatively; that the jurors must therefore necessarily have judged for themselves of the whole case; and that, *as a general rule,* they could judge of it by no law but the law of nature, or the principles of justice as they existed in their own minds.

The ancient oath of jurors in civil suits, viz., that "*they would make known the truth according to their consciences,*" implies that the jurors were above the authority of all legislation. The modern oath, in England, viz., that they "*will well and truly try the issue between the parties, and a true verdict give, according to the evidence,*" implies the same thing. If the laws of the king had been binding upon a jury, they would have been sworn to try the cases *according to law,* or according to the laws.

The ancient writs, in civil suits, as given in Glanville, (within the half century before Magna Carta,) to wit, "Summon twelve free and legal men, (or sometimes twelve knights,) to be in court, *prepared upon their oaths to declare whether A or B have the greater right to the land in question,"* indicate that the jurors judged of the whole matter on their consciences only.

The language of Magna Carta, already discussed, establishes the same point; for, although some of the words, such as "outlawed," and "exiled," would apply only to criminal cases, nearly the whole chapter applies as well to civil as to criminal suits. For example, how could the payment of a debt ever be enforced against an unwilling debtor, if he could neither be "arrested, imprisoned, nor deprived of his freehold," and if the king could neither "proceed against him, nor send any one against him, by force or arms"? Yet Magna Carta as much forbids that any of these things shall be done against a debtor, as against a criminal, *except according to, or in execution of,* "*a judgment of his peers, or the law of the land,"* — a provision which, it has been shown, gave the jury the free and absolute right to give or withhold "judgment" according to their consciences, irrespective of all legislation.

The following provisions, in the Magna Carta of John, illustrate the custom of referring the most important matters of a civil nature, even where the king was a party, to the determination of the peers, or of twelve men, acting by no rules but their own consciences. These examples at least show that there is nothing improbable or unnatural in the idea that juries should try all civil suits according to their own judgments, independently of all laws of the king.

Chap. 65. "If we have disseized or dispossessed the Welsh of any lands, liberties, or other things, without the legal judgment of their peers, they shall be immediately restored to them. And if any dispute arises upon this head, the matter shall be determined in the Marches,* *by the judgment of their peers,"* &c.

Chap. 68. "We shall treat with Alexander, king of Scots, concerning the restoring of his sisters, and hostages, and rights and liberties, in the same form and manner as we shall do to the rest of our barons of England; unless by the engagements, which his father William. late king of Scots, hath entered into with us, it ought to be otherwise; *and this shall be left to the determination of his peers in our court.*"

---

* *Marches,* the limits, or boundaries, between England and Wales.

Chap. 56. "All evil customs concerning forests, warrens, and foresters, warreners, sheriffs, and their officers, rivers and their keepers, shall forthwith be inquired into in each county, *by twelve knights of the same shire*, chosen by the most creditable persons in the same county, *and upon oath ;* and within forty days after the said inquest, be utterly abolished, so as never to be restored."

There is substantially the same reason why a jury *ought* to judge of the justice of laws, and hold all unjust laws invalid, in civil suits, as in criminal ones. That reason is the necessity of guarding against the tyranny of the government. Nearly the same oppressions can be practised in civil suits as in criminal ones. For example, individuals may be deprived of their liberty, and robbed of their property, by judgments rendered in civil suits, as well as in criminal ones. If the laws of the king were imperative upon a jury in civil suits, the king might enact laws giving one man's property to another, or confiscating it to the king himself, and authorizing civil suits to obtain possession of it. Thus a man might be robbed of his property at the arbitrary pleasure of the king. In fact, all the property of the kingdom would be placed at the arbitrary disposal of the king, through the judgments of juries in civil suits, if the laws of the king were imperative upon a jury in such suits.*

---

* That the kings would have had no scruples to enact laws for the special purpose of plundering the people, by means of the judgments of juries, if they could have got juries to acknowledge the authority of their laws, is evident from the audacity with which they plundered them, without any judgments of juries to authorize them.

It is not necessary to occupy space here to give details as to these robberies ; but only some evidence of the general fact.

Hallam says, that "For the first three reigns (of the Norman kings) * * the intolerable exactions of tribute, the rapine of purveyance, the iniquity of royal courts, are continually in the mouths of the historians. 'God sees the wretched people,' says the Saxon Chronicler, 'most unjustly oppressed ; first they are despoiled of their possessions, and then butchered.' This was a grievous year (1124). Whoever had any property, lost it by heavy taxes and unjust decrees." — 2 *Middle Ages,* 435-6.

"In the succeeding reign of John, all the rapacious exactions usual to these Norman kings were not only redoubled, but mingled with outrages of tyranny still more intolerable. * *

"In 1207 John took a seventh of the movables of lay and spiritual persons, all murmuring, but none daring to speak against it." — *Ditto,* 446.

In Hume's account of the extortions of those times, the following paragraph occurs :

"But the most barefaced acts of tyranny and oppression were practised against the

Furthermore, it would be absurd and inconsistent to make a jury paramount to legislation in *criminal* suits, and subordinate to it in *civil* suits; because an individual, by resisting the execution of a *civil* judgment, founded upon an unjust

---

Jews, who were entirely out of the protection of the law, and were abandoned to the immeasurable rapacity of the king and his ministers. Besides many other indignities, to which they were continually exposed, it appears that they were once all thrown into prison, and the sum of 66,000 marks exacted for their liberty. At another time, Isaac, the Jew, paid alone 5100 marks; Brun, 3000 marks; Jurnet, 2000; Bennet, 500. At another, Licorica, widow of David, the Jew of Oxford, was required to pay 6000 marks." — *Hume's Hist. Eng., Appendix 2.*

Further accounts of the extortions and oppressions of the kings may be found in Hume's History, Appendix 2, and in Hallam's Middle Ages, vol. 2, p. 435 to 446.

By Magna Carta John bound himself to make restitution for some of the spoliations he had committed upon individuals " *without the legal judgment of their peers.*" — *See Magna Carta of John,* ch. 60, 61, 65 and 66.

One of the great charges, on account of which the nation rose against John, was, that he plundered individuals of their property, " *without legal judgment of their peers.*" Now it was evidently very weak and short-sighted in John to expose himself to such charges, *if his laws were really obligatory upon the peers ;* because, in that case, he could have enacted any laws that were necessary for his purpose, and then, by civil suits, have brought the cases before juries for their " judgment," and thus have accomplished all his robberies in a perfectly legal manner.

There would evidently have been no sense in these complaints, that he deprived men of their property " *without legal judgment of their peers,*" if his laws had been binding upon the peers; because he could then have made the same spoliations as well with the judgment of the peers as without it. Taking the judgment of the peers in the matter, would have been only a ridiculous and useless formality, if they were to exercise no discretion or conscience of their own, independently of the laws of the king.

It may here be mentioned, in passing, that the same would be true in criminal matters, if the king's laws were obligatory upon juries.

As an illustration of what tyranny the kings would sometimes practise, Hume says :

" It appears from the Great Charter itself, that not only John, a tyrannical prince, and Richard, a violent one, but their father Henry, under whose reign the prevalence of gross abuses is the least to be suspected, were accustomed, from their sole authority, without process of law, to imprison, banish, and attaint the freemen of their kingdom." — *Hume, Appendix 2.*

The provision, also, in the 64th chapter of Magna Carta, that " all unjust and illegal fines, and all amercements, *imposed unjustly, and contrary to the Law of the Land, shall be entirely forgiven,*" &c.; and the provision, in chapter 61, that the king " will cause full justice to be administered " in regard to " all those things, of which any person has, without legal judgment of his peers, been dispossessed or deprived, either by King Henry, our father, or our brother, King Richard," indicate the tyrannical practices that prevailed.

We are told also that John himself " had dispossessed several great men without any judgment of their peers, condemned others to cruel deaths, * * insomuch that his tyrannical will stood instead of a law." — *Echard's History of England,* 106.

Now all these things were very unnecessary and foolish, if his laws were binding

law, could give rise to a *criminal* suit, in which the jury would be bound to hold the same law invalid. So that, if an unjust law were binding upon a jury in *civil* suits, a defendant, by resisting the execution of the judgment, could, *in effect*, convert the civil action into a criminal one, in which the jury would be paramount to the same legislation, to which, in the *civil* suit, they were subordinate. In other words, in the *criminal* suit, the jury would be obliged to justify the defendant in resisting a law, which, in the *civil* suit, they had said he was bound to submit to.

To make this point plain to the most common mind — suppose a law be enacted that the property of A shall be given to B. B brings a civil action to obtain possession of it. If the jury, in this *civil* suit, are bound to hold the law obligatory, they render a judgment in favor of B, that he be put in possession of the property; *thereby declaring that A is bound to submit to a law depriving him of his property.* But when the execution of that judgment comes to be attempted — that is, when the sheriff comes to take the property for the purpose of delivering it to B — A acting, as he has a *natural* right to do, in defence of his property, resists and kills the sheriff. He is thereupon indicted for murder. On this trial his plea is, that in killing the sheriff, he was simply exercising his *natural* right of defending his property against an unjust law. The jury, not being bound, in a *criminal* case, by the authority of an unjust law, judge the act on its merits, and acquit the defendant — thus declaring that he was *not* bound to submit to the same law which the jury, in the *civil* suit, had, by their judgment, declared that he *was* bound to submit to. Here is a contradiction between the two judgments. In the *civil* suit, the law is declared to be obligatory upon A; in the *criminal* suit, the same law is declared to be of no obligation.

---

upon juries; because, in that case, he could have procured the conviction of these men in a legal manner, and thus have saved the necessity of such usurpation. In short, if the laws of the king had been binding upon juries, there is no robbery, vengeance, or oppression, which he could not have accomplished through the judgments of juries. This consideration is sufficient, of itself, to prove that the laws of the king were of no authority over a jury, in either civil or criminal cases, unless the juries regarded the laws as just in themselves.

It would be a solecism and absurdity in government to allow such consequences as these. Besides, it would be practically impossible to maintain government on such principles; for no government could enforce its *civil* judgments, unless it could support them by *criminal* ones, in case of resistance. A jury must therefore be paramount to legislation in both civil and criminal cases, or in neither. If they are paramount in neither, they are no protection to liberty. If they are paramount in both, then all legislation goes only for what it may chance to be worth in the estimation of a jury.

Another reason why Magna Carta makes the discretion and consciences of juries paramount to all legislation in *civil* suits, is, that if legislation were binding upon a jury, the jurors — (by reason of their being unable to read, as jurors in those days were, and also by reason of many of the statutes being unwritten, or at least not so many copies written as that juries could be supplied with them) — would have been necessitated — at least in those courts in which the king's justices sat — to take the word of those justices as to what the laws of the king really were. In other words, they would have been necessitated *to take the law from the court,* as jurors do now.

Now there were two reasons why, as we may rationally suppose, the people did not wish juries to take their law from the king's judges. One was, that, at that day, the people probably had sense enough to see, (what we, at this day, have not sense enough to see, although we have the evidence of it every day before our eyes,) that those judges, being dependent upon the legislative power, (the king,) being appointed by it, paid by it, and removable by it at pleasure, would be mere tools of that power, and would hold all its legislation obligatory, whether it were just or unjust. This was one reason, doubtless, why Magna Carta made juries, in civil suits, paramount to all instructions of the king's judges. The reason was precisely the same as that for making them paramount to all instructions of judges in criminal suits, viz., that the people did not choose to subject their rights of property, and all other rights involved in civil suits, to the operation of such laws as the king might please to enact. It was seen that to allow the king's judges to dictate the law to the jury would be equivalent to making the legislation of the king imperative upon the jury.

Another reason why the people did not wish juries, in civil suits, to take their law from the king's judges, doubtless was, that, knowing the dependence of the judges upon the king, and knowing that the king would, of course, tolerate no judges who were not subservient to his will, they necessarily inferred that the king's judges would be as corrupt, in the administration of justice, as was the king himself, or as he wished them to be. And how corrupt that was, may be inferred from the following historical facts.

Hume says:

"It appears that the ancient kings of England put themselves entirely upon the footing of the barbarous Eastern princes, whom no man must approach without a present, who sell all their good offices, and who intrude themselves into every business that they may have a pretence for extorting money. Even justice was avowedly bought and sold; the king's court itself, though the supreme judicature of the kingdom, was open to none that brought not presents to the king; the bribes given for expedition, delay, suspension, and doubtless for the perversion of justice, were entered in the public registers of the royal revenue, and remain as monuments of the perpetual iniquity and tyranny of the times. The barons of the exchequer, for instance, the first nobility of the kingdom, were not ashamed to insert, as an article in their records, that the county of Norfolk paid a sum that they might be fairly dealt with; the borough of Yarmouth, that the king's charters, which they have for their liberties, might not be violated; Richard, son of Gilbert, for the king's helping him to recover his debt from the Jews; * * Serlo, son of Terlavaston, that he might be permitted to make his defence, in case he were accused of a certain homicide; Walter de Burton, for free law, if accused of wounding another; Robert de Essart, for having an inquest to find whether Roger, the butcher, and Wace and Humphrey, accused him of robbery and theft out of envy and ill-will, or not; William Buhurst, for having an inquest to find whether he were accused of the death of one Godwin, out of ill-will, or for just cause. I have selected these few instances from a great number of the like kind, which Madox had selected from a still greater number, preserved in the ancient rolls of the exchequer.

Sometimes a party litigant offered the king a certain portion, a half, a third, a fourth, payable out of the debts which he, as the executor of justice, should assist in recovering. Theophania de Westland agreed to pay the half of two hundred and twelve marks, that she might recover that sum against James de Fughleston; Solomon, the Jew, engaged to pay one mark out of every seven that he should recover against Hugh de la Hose; Nicholas Morrel promised to pay sixty pounds, that the Earl of Flanders might be distrained to pay him three hundred and forty-three pounds, which the earl had taken from him; and these sixty pounds were to be paid out of the first money that Nicholas should recover from the earl." — *Hume, Appendix* 2.

"In the reign of Henry II., the best and most just of these (the Norman) princes, * * Peter, of Blois, a judicious and even elegant writer, of that age, gives a pathetic description of *the venality of justice*, and the oppressions of the poor, * * and he scruples not to complain to the king himself of these abuses. We may judge what the case would be under the government of worse princes." — *Hume, Appendix* 2.

Carte says:

"The crown exercised in those days an exorbitant and inconvenient power, ordering the justices of the king's court, in suits about lands, to turn out, put, and keep in possession, which of the litigants they pleased; to send contradictory orders; and take large sums of money from each; to respite proceedings; to direct sentences; and the judges, acting by their commission, conceived themselves bound to observe such orders, to the great delay, interruption, and preventing of justice; at least, this was John's practice." — *Carte's History of England*, vol. 1, p. 832.

Hallam says:

"But of all the abuses that deformed the Anglo-Saxon government, none was so flagitious as the sale of judicial redress. The king, we are often told, is the fountain of justice; but in those ages it was one which gold alone could unseal. Men fined (paid fines) to have right done them; to sue in a certain court; to implead a certain person; to have restitution of land which they had recovered at law. From the sale of that justice which every citizen has a right to demand, it was an easy transition to withhold or deny it. Fines were received for the king's help against the adverse suitor; that is, for perversion of justice, or for delay. Sometimes they were paid by opposite parties, and, of course, for opposite ends." — 2 *Middle Ages*, 438.

In allusion to the provision of Magna Carta on this subject, Hallam says:

"A law which enacts that justice shall neither be sold, denied, nor delayed, stamps with infamy that government under which it had become necessary." — 2 *Middle Ages*, 451.

Lingard, speaking of the times of Henry II., (say 1184,) says:

"It was universally understood that money possessed greater influence than justice in the royal courts, and instances are on record, in which one party has made the king a present to accelerate, and the other by a more valuable offer has succeeded in retarding a decision. * * But besides the fines paid to the sovereigns, *the judges often exacted presents for themselves*, and loud complaints existed against their venality and injustice." — 2 *Lingard*, 231.

In the narrative of "The costs and charges which I, Richard de Anesty, bestowed in recovering the land of William, my uncle," (some fifty years before Magna Carta,) are the following items:

"To Ralph, the king's physician, I gave thirty-six marks and one half; to the king an hundred marks; and to the queen one mark of gold." The result is thus stated. "At last, thanks to our lord the king, and by judgment of his court, my uncle's land was adjudged to me." — 2 *Palgrave's Rise and Progress of the English Commonwealth*, p. 9 and 24.

Palgrave also says:

"The precious ore was cast into the scales of justice, even when held by the most conscientious of our Anglo-Saxon kings. A single case will exemplify the practices which prevailed. Alfric, the heir of 'Aylwin, the black,' seeks to set aside the death-bed bequest, by which his kinsman bestowed four rich and fertile manors upon St. Benedict. Alfric, the claimant, was supported by extensive and powerful connexions; and Abbot Alfwine, the defendant, was well aware that there would be *danger* in the discussion of the dispute in public, or before the Folkmoot, (people's meeting, or county court); or, in other words, that the Thanes of the shire would do their best to give a judgment in favor of their compeer. The plea being removed into the Royal Court, the abbot acted with that prudence which so often calls forth the praises of the monastic scribe. He gladly emptied twenty marks of gold into the sleeve of the Confessor, (Edward,) and five marks of gold presented to Edith, the Fair, encouraged her to aid the

bishop, and to exercise her gentle influence in his favor. Alfric, with equal wisdom, withdrew from prosecuting the hopeless cause, in which his opponent might possess an advocate in the royal judge, and a friend in the king's consort. Both parties, therefore, found it desirable to come to an agreement."
— 1 *Palgrave's Rise and Progress, &c.*, p. 650.

But Magna Carta has another provision for the trial of *civil* suits, that obviously had its origin in the corruption of the king's judges. The provision is, that four knights, to be chosen in every county, by the people of the county, shall sit with the king's judges, in the Common Pleas, in jury trials, (assizes,) on the trial of three certain kinds of suits, that were among the most important that were tried at all. The reason for this provision undoubtedly was, that the corruption and subserviency of the king's judges were so well known, that the people would not even trust them to sit alone in a jury trial of any considerable importance. The provision is this:

Chap. 22, (of John's Charter.) "Common Pleas shall not follow our court, but shall be holden in some certain place. Trials upon the writ of *novel disseisin,* and of *Mort d'Ancester,* and of *Darrein Presentment,* shall be taken but in their proper counties, and after this manner: We, or, if we should be out of our realm, our chief justiciary, shall send two justiciaries through every county four times a year;* *who, with four knights chosen out of every shire, by the people, shall hold the assizes* (juries) *in the county, on the day and at the place appointed.*"

It would be very unreasonable to suppose that the king's judges were allowed to *dictate* the law to the juries, when the people would not even suffer them to sit alone in jury trials, but themselves chose four men to sit with them, to keep them honest. †

---

* By the Magna Carta of Henry III. this is changed to once a year.

† From the provision of Magna Carta, cited in the text, it must be inferred that there can be no legal trial by jury, in *civil* cases, if only the king's justices preside; that, to make the trial legal, there must be other persons, chosen by the people, to sit with them; the object being to prevent the jury's being deceived by the justices. I think we must also infer that the king's justices could sit only in the three actions specially mentioned. We cannot go beyond the letter of Magna Carta, in making innovations upon the common law, which required all presiding officers in jury trials to be elected by the people.

This practice of sending the king's judges into the counties to preside at jury trials, was introduced by the Norman kings. Under the Saxons it was not so. *No officer of the king was allowed to preside at a jury trial; but only magistrates chosen by the people.**

But the following chapter of John's charter, which immediately succeeds the one just quoted, and refers to the same suits, affords very strong, not to say conclusive, proof, that juries judged of the law in civil suits — that is, *made the law*, so far as their deciding according to their own notions of justice could make the law.

Chap. 23. "And if, on the county day, the aforesaid assizes cannot be taken, *so many knights and freeholders shall remain, of those who shall have been present on said day, as that the judgments may be rendered by them,* whether the business be more or less."

---

* "The earls, sheriffs, and head-boroughs were annually elected in the full folcmote, (people's meeting)." — *Introduction to Gilbert's History of the Common Pleas,* p. 2, *note.*

"It was the especial province of the earldomen or earl to attend the shyre-meeting, (the county court,) twice a year, and there officiate as the county judge in expounding the secular laws, as appears by the fifth of Edgar's laws." — *Same,* p. 2, *note.*

"Every ward had its proper alderman, who was *chosen,* and not imposed by the prince." — *Same,* p. 4, *text.*

"As the aldermen, or earls, were always *chosen*" (by the people) "from among the greatest thanes, who in those times were generally more addicted to arms than to letters, they were but ill-qualified for the administration of justice, and performing the civil duties of their office." — 3 *Henry's History of Great Britain,* 343.

"But none of these thanes were annually elected in the full folcmote, (people's meeting,) *as the earls, sheriffs, and head-boroughs were;* nor did King Alfred (as this author suggests) deprive the people of the election of those last mentioned magistrates and nobles, much less did he appoint them himself." — *Introd. to Gilbert's Hist. Com. Pleas,* p. 2, *note.*

"The sheriff was usually not appointed by the lord, but elected by the freeholders of the district." — *Political Dictionary,* word *Sheriff.*

"Among the most remarkable of the Saxon laws we may reckon * * the election of their magistrates by the people, originally even that of their kings, till dear-bought experience evinced the convenience and necessity of establishing an hereditary succession to the crown. But that (the election) of all subordinate magistrates, their military officers or heretochs, their sheriffs, their conservators of the peace, their coroners, their portreeves, (since changed into mayors and bailiffs,) and even their tithing-men and borsholders at the last, continued, some, till the Norman conquest, others for two centuries after, and some remain to this day." — 4 *Blackstone,* 413.

"The election of sheriffs was left to the people, *according to ancient usage.*" — *St. West.* 1, c. 27. — *Crabbe's History of English Law,* 181.

The meaning of this chapter is, that so many of the *civil* suits, as could not be tried on the day when the king's justices were present, should be tried afterwards, *by the four knights before mentioned, and the freeholders, that is, the jury.* It must be admitted, of course, that the juries, in these cases, judged the matters of law, as well as fact, unless it be presumed that the *knights* dictated the law to the jury — a thing of which there is no evidence at all.

As a final proof on this point, there is a statute enacted seventy years after Magna Carta, which, although it is contrary to the common law, and therefore void, is nevertheless good evidence, inasmuch as it contains an acknowledgment, on the part of the king himself, that juries had a right to judge of the whole matter, law and fact, in civil suits. The provision is this:

"It is ordained, that the justices assigned to take the assizes, shall not compel the jurors to say precisely whether it be disseisin, or not, so that they do show the truth of the deed, and seek aid of the justices. But if they will, of their own accord, say that it is disseisin, or not, their verdict shall be admitted at their own peril." — 13 *Edward I.*, st. 1, ch. 3, sec. 2. (1285.)

The question of "disseisin, or not," was a question of law, as well as fact. This statute, therefore, admits that the law, as well as the fact, was in the hands of the jury. The statute is nevertheless void, because the king had no authority to give jurors a dispensation from the obligation imposed upon them by their oaths and the "law of the land," that they should "make known the truth according their (own) consciences." This they were bound to do, and there was no power in the king to absolve them from the duty. And the attempt of the king thus to absolve them, and authorize them to throw the case into the hands of the judges for decision, was simply an illegal and unconstitutional attempt to overturn the "law of the land," which he was sworn to maintain, and gather power into his own hands, through his judges. He had just as much constitutional power to enact that the jurors should not be compelled to declare the *facts*, but that they might leave *them* to be determined by the king's judges, as he had to enact that they should not be compelled to declare the *law*, but might leave *it* to be decided by the king's judges. It was as much the legal duty of the jury to decide the law as to decide the fact; and no law of the king could affect their obligation to do either. And this statute is only one example of the numberless contrivances and usurpations which have been resorted to, for the purpose of destroying the original and genuine trial by jury.

CHAPTER V.

OBJECTIONS ANSWERED

The following objections will be made to the doctrines and the evidence presented in the preceding chapters.

1. That it is a *maxim* of the law, that the judges respond to the question of law, and juries only to the question of fact.

The answer to this objection is, that, since Magna Carta, judges have had more than six centuries in which to invent and promulgate pretended maxims to suit themselves; and this is one of them. Instead of expressing the law, it expresses nothing but the ambitious and lawless will of the judges themselves, and of those whose instruments they are.*

2. It will be asked, Of what use are the justices, if the jurors judge both of law and fact?

The answer is, that they are of use, 1. To assist and enlighten the jurors, if they can, by their advice and information; such advice and information to be received only for what they may chance to be worth in the estimation of the jurors. 2. To do anything that may be necessary in regard to granting appeals and new trials.

3. It is said that it would be absurd that twelve ignorant men should have power to judge of the law, while justices learned in the law should be compelled to sit by and see the law decided erroneously.

One answer to this objection is, that the powers of juries

---

* Judges do not even live up to that part of their own maxim, which requires jurors to try the matter of fact. By dictating to them the laws of evidence, — that is, by dictating what evidence they may hear, and what they may not hear, and also by dictating to them rules for weighing such evidence as they permit them to hear, — they of necessity dictate the conclusion to which they shall arrive. And thus the court really tries the question of fact, as well as the question of law, in every cause. It is clearly impossible, in the nature of things, for a jury to try a question of fact, without trying every question of law on which the fact depends.

are not granted to them on the supposition that they know the law better than the justices; but on the ground that the justices are untrustworthy, that they are exposed to bribes, are themselves fond of power and authority, and are also the dependent and subservient creatures of the legislature; and that to allow them to dictate the law, would not only expose the rights of parties to be sold for money, but would be equivalent to surrendering all the property, liberty, and rights of the people, unreservedly into the hands of arbitrary power, (the legislature,) to be disposed of at its pleasure. The powers of juries, therefore, not only place a curb upon the powers of legislators and judges, but imply also an imputation upon their integrity and trustworthiness; and *these* are the reasons why legislators and judges have formerly entertained the intensest hatred of juries, and, so fast as they could do it without alarming the people for their liberties, have, by indirection, denied, undermined, and practically destroyed their power. And it is only since all the real power of juries has been destroyed, and they have become mere tools in the hands of legislators and judges, that they have become favorites with them.

Legislators and judges are necessarily exposed to all the temptations of money, fame, and power, to induce them to disregard justice between parties, and sell the rights, and violate the liberties of the people. Jurors, on the other hand, are exposed to none of these temptations. They are not liable to bribery, for they are unknown to the parties until they come into the jury-box. They can rarely gain either fame, power, or money, by giving erroneous decisions. Their offices are temporary, and they know that when they shall have executed them, they must return to the people, to hold all their own rights in life subject to the liability of such judgments, by their successors, as they themselves have given an example for. The laws of human nature do not permit the supposition that twelve men, taken by lot from the mass of the people, and acting under such circumstances, will *all* prove dishonest. It is a supposable case that they may not be sufficiently enlightened to know and do their whole duty, in all cases whatsoever; but that they should *all* prove *dishonest*, is not within the range of probability. A jury, therefore, insures to us — what no other court does — that first and indispensable requisite in a judicial tribunal, integrity.

4. It is alleged that if juries are allowed to judge of the law, *they decide the law absolutely; that their decision must necessarily stand, be it right or wrong;* and that this power of absolute decision would be dangerous in their hands, by reason of their ignorance of the law.

One answer is, that this power, which juries have of *judging* of the law, is not a power of *absolute decision in all cases.* For example, it is a power to declare imperatively that a man's property, liberty, or life, shall *not* be taken from him; but it is not a power to declare imperatively that they *shall* be taken from him.

Magna Carta does not provide that the judgments of the peers *shall be executed;* but only that *no other than their judgments* shall ever be executed, *so far as to take a party's goods, rights, or person, thereon.*

A judgment of the peers may be reviewed, and invalidated, and a new trial granted. So that practically a jury has no absolute power to take a party's goods, rights, or person. They have only an absolute veto upon their being taken by the government. The government is not bound to do everything that a jury may adjudge. It is only prohibited from doing anything — (that is, from taking a party's goods, rights, or person) — unless a jury have first adjudged it to be done.

But it will, perhaps, be said, that if an erroneous judgment of one jury should be reäffirmed by another, on a new trial, it must *then* be executed. But Magna Carta does not command even this — although it might, perhaps, have been reasonably safe for it to have done so — for if two juries unanimously affirm the same thing, after all the light and aid that judges and lawyers can afford them, that fact probably furnishes as strong a presumption in favor of the correctness of their opinion, as can ordinarily be obtained in favor of a judgment, by any measures of a practical character for the administration of justice. Still, there is nothing in Magna Carta that *compels* the execution of even a second judgment of a jury. The only injunction of Magna Carta upon the government, as to what it *shall do*, on this point, is that it shall "do justice and right," without sale, denial, or delay. But this leaves the government all power of determining what is justice and right, except that it shall not consider anything as justice and right — so far as to carry it into execution against the goods, rights, or person of a party — unless it be something which a jury have sanctioned.

If the government had no alternative but to execute all judgments of a jury indiscriminately, the power of juries would unquestionably be dangerous; for there is no doubt that they may sometimes give hasty and erroneous judgments. But when it is considered that their judgments can be reviewed, and new trials granted, this danger is, for all practical purposes, obviated.

If it be said that juries may *successively* give erroneous judgments, and that new trials cannot be granted indefinitely, the answer is, that so far as Magna Carta is concerned, there is nothing to prevent the granting of new trials indefinitely, if the judgments of juries are contrary to "justice and right." So that Magna Carta does not *require* any judgment whatever to be executed — so far as to take a party's goods, rights, or person, thereon — unless it be concurred in by both court and jury.

Nevertheless, we may, for the sake of the argument, suppose the existence of a *practical*, if not *legal*, necessity, for executing *some* judgment or other, in cases where juries persist in disagreeing with the courts. In such cases, the principle of Magna Carta unquestionably is, that the uniform judgments of *successive* juries shall prevail over the opinion of the court. And the reason of this principle is obvious, viz., that it is the will of the country, and not the will of the court, or the government, that must determine what laws shall be established and enforced; that the concurrent judgments of successive juries, given in opposition to all the reasoning which judges and lawyers can offer to the contrary, must necessarily be presumed to be a truer exposition of the will of the country, than are the opinions of the judges.

But it may be said that, unless jurors submit to the control of the court, in matters of law, they may disagree among themselves, and *never* come to any judgment; and thus justice fail to be done.

Such a case is perhaps possible; but, if possible, it can occur but rarely; because, although one jury may disagree, a succession of juries are not likely to disagree — that is, *on matters of natural law, or abstract justice.** If such a thing should occur, it would almost certainly be owing to the attempt of the court to mislead them. It is hardly possible that any other cause should be adequate to produce such an effect; because justice comes very near to being a self-evident principle. The mind perceives it almost intuitively. If, in addition to this, the court be uniformly on the side of justice, it is not a reasonable supposition that a succession of juries should disagree about it. If, therefore, a succession of juries do disagree on the law of any case, the presumption is, not that justice fails of being done, but that injustice is prevented — *that* injustice, which would be done, if the opinion of the court were suffered to control the jury.

For the sake of the argument, however, it may be admitted to be possible that justice should sometimes fail of being done through the disagreements of jurors, notwithstanding all the light which judges and lawyers can throw upon the question in issue. If it be asked what provision the trial by jury makes for such cases, the answer is, *it makes none; and justice must fail of being done, from the want of its being made sufficiently intelligible.*

Under the trial by jury, justice can never be done — that is, by a judgment that shall take a party's goods, rights, or person — until that justice can be made intelligible or perceptible to the minds of *all* the jurors; or, at least, until it obtain the voluntary assent of all — an assent, which ought not to be given until the justice itself shall have become perceptible to all.

---

* Most disagreements of juries are on matters of fact, which are admitted to be within their province. We have little or no evidence of their disagreements on matters of natural justice. The disagreements of *courts* on matters of law, afford little or no evidence that juries would also disagree on matters of law — that is, *of justice;* because the disagreements of courts are generally on matters of *legislation,* and not on those principles of abstract justice, by which juries would be governed, and in regard to which the minds of men are nearly unanimous.

The principles of the trial by jury, then, are these:

1. That, in criminal cases, the accused is presumed innocent.

2. That, in civil cases, possession is presumptive proof of property; or, in other words, every man is presumed to be the rightful proprietor of whatever he has in his possession.

3. That these presumptions shall be overcome, in a court of justice, only by evidence, the sufficiency of which, and by law, the justice of which, are satisfactory to the understanding and consciences of *all* the jurors.

These are the bases on which the trial by jury places the property, liberty, and rights of every individual.

But some one will say, if these are the principles of the trial by jury, then it is plain that justice must often fail to be done. Admitting, for the sake of the argument, that this may be true, the compensation for it is, that positive *injustice* will also often fail to be done; whereas otherwise it would be done frequently. The very precautions used to prevent *injustice* being done, may often have the effect to prevent *justice* being done. But are we, therefore, to take no precautions against injustice? By no means, all will agree. The question then arises — Does the trial by jury, *as here explained*, involve such extreme and unnecessary precautions against injustice, as to interpose unnecessary obstacles to the doing of justice? Men of different minds may very likely answer this question differently, according as they have more or less confidence in the wisdom and justice of legislators, the integrity and independence of judges, and the intelligence of jurors. This much, however, may be said in favor of these precautions, viz., that the history of the past, as well as our constant present experience, prove how much injustice may, and certainly will, be done, systematically and continually, *for the want of these precautions* — that is, while the law is authoritatively made and expounded by legislators and judges. On the other hand, we have no such evidence of how much justice may fail to be done, *by reason of these precautions* — that is, by reason of the law being left to the judgments and consciences of jurors. We can determine the former point — that is, how much positive injustice is done under the first of these two systems — because the system is in full operation; but we cannot determine how much justice would fail to be done under the latter system, because we have, in modern times, had no experience of the use of the precautions themselves. In ancient times, when these precautions were *nominally* in force, such was the tyranny of kings, and such the poverty, ignorance, and the inability of concert and resistance, on the part of the people, that the system had no full or fair operation. It, nevertheless, under all these disadvantages, impressed itself upon the understandings, and imbedded itself in the hearts, of the people, so as no other system of civil liberty has ever done.

But this view of the two systems compares only the injustice done, and the justice omitted to be done, in the individual cases adjudged, without looking beyond them. And some persons might, on first thought, argue that, if justice failed of being done under the one system, oftener than positive injustice were done under the other, the balance was in favor of the latter system. But such a weighing of the two systems against each other gives no true idea of their comparative merits or demerits; for, possibly, in this view alone, the balance would not be very great in favor of either. To compare, or rather to contrast, the two, we must consider that, under the jury system, the failures to do justice would be only rare and exceptional cases; and would be owing either to the intrinsic difficulty of the questions, or to the fact that the parties had transacted their business in a manner unintelligible to the jury, and the effects would be confined to the individual or individuals interested in the particular suits. No permanent law would be established thereby destructive of the rights of the people in other like cases. And the people at large would continue to enjoy all their natural rights as before. But under the other system, whenever an unjust law is enacted by the legislature, and the judge imposes it upon the jury as authoritative, and they give a judgment in accordance therewith, the authority of the law is thereby established, and the whole people are thus brought under the yoke of that law; because they then understand that the law will be enforced against them in future, if they presume to exercise their rights, or refuse to comply with the exactions of the law. In this manner all unjust laws are established, and made operative against the rights of the people.

The difference, then, between the two systems is this : Under the one system, a jury, at distant intervals, would (not enforce any positive injustice, but only) fail of enforcing justice, in a dark and difficult case, or in consequence of the parties not having transacted their business in a manner intelligible to a jury; and the plaintiff would thus fail of obtaining what was rightfully due him. And there the matter would end, *for evil*, though not for good; for thenceforth parties, warned of the danger of losing their rights, would be careful to transact their business in a more clear and intelligible manner. Under the other system — the system of legislative and judicial authority — positive injustice is not only done in every suit arising under unjust laws, — that is, men's property, liberty, or lives are not only unjustly taken on those particular judgments, — but the rights of the whole people are struck down by the authority of the laws thus enforced, and a wide-sweeping tyranny at once put in operation.

But there is another ample and conclusive answer to the argument that justice would often fail to be done, if jurors were allowed to be governed by their own consciences, instead of the direction of the justices, in matters of law. That answer is this:

Legitimate government can be formed only by the voluntary association of all who contribute to its support. As a voluntary association, it can have for its objects only those things in which the members of the association are *all agreed*. If, therefore, there be any *justice*, in regard to which all the parties to the government *are not agreed*, the objects of the association do not extend to it.*

---

* This is the principle of all voluntary asssociations whatsoever. No voluntary association was ever formed, and in the nature of things there never can be one formed, for the accomplishment of any objects except those in which *all* the parties to the association are agreed. Government, therefore, must be kept within these limits, or it is no longer a voluntary association of all who contribute to its support, but a mere tyranny established by a part over the rest.

All, or nearly all, voluntary associations give to a majority, or to some other portion of the members less than the whole, the right to use some *limited* discretion as to the

If any of the members wish more than this,— if they claim to have acquired a more extended knowledge of justice than is common to all, and wish to have their pretended discoveries carried into effect, in reference to themselves,— they must either form a separate association for that purpose, or be content to wait until they can make their views intelligible to the people at large. They cannot claim or expect that the whole people shall practise the folly of taking on trust their pretended superior knowledge, and of committing blindly into their hands all their own interests, liberties, and rights, to be disposed of on principles, the justness of which the people themselves cannot comprehend.

A government of the whole, therefore, must necessarily confine itself to the administration of such principles of law as *all* the people, who contribute to the support of the government, can comprehend and see the justice of. And it can be confined within those limits only by allowing the jurors, who represent all the parties to the compact, to judge of the law, and the justice of the law, in all cases whatsoever. And if any justice be left undone, under these circumstances, it is a justice for which the nature of the association does not provide, which the association does not undertake to do, and which, as an association, it is under no obligation to do.

The people at large, the unlearned and common people, have certainly an indisputable right to associate for the establishment and maintenance of such a government as *they themselves* see the justice of, and feel the need of, for the promotion of their own interests, and the safety of their own rights, without at the same time surrendering all their property, liberty, and rights into the hands of men, who, under the pretence of a superior and incomprehensible knowledge of justice, may dispose of such property, liberties, and rights, in a manner to suit their own selfish and dishonest purposes.

---

means to be used to accomplish the ends in view; but *the ends themselves to be accomplished* are always precisely defined, and are such as every member necessarily agrees to, else he would not voluntarily join the association.

Justice is the object of government, and those who support the government, must be agreed as to the justice to be executed by it, or they cannot rightfully unite in maintaining the government itself.

If a government were to be established and supported *solely* by that portion of the people who lay claim to superior knowledge, there would be some consistency in their saying that the common people should not be received as jurors, with power to judge of the justice of the laws. But so long as the whole people (or all the male adults) are presumed to be voluntary parties to the government, and voluntary contributors to its support, there is no consistency in refusing to any one of them more than to another the right to sit as juror, with full power to decide for himself whether any law that is proposed to be enforced in any particular case, be within the objects of the association.

The conclusion, therefore, is, that, in a government formed by voluntary association, or on the *theory* of voluntary association, and voluntary support, (as all the North American governments are,) no law can rightfully be enforced by the association in its corporate capacity, against the goods, rights, or person of any individual, except it be such as *all* the members of the association agree that it may enforce. To enforce any other law, to the extent of taking a man's goods, rights, or person, would be making *some* of the parties to the association accomplices in what they regard as acts of injustice. It would also be making them consent to what they regard as the destruction of their own rights. These are things which no legitimate system or theory of government can require of any of the parties to it.

The mode adopted, by the trial by jury, for ascertaining whether all the parties to the government do approve of a particular law, is to take twelve men at random from the whole people, and accept their unanimous decision as representing the opinions of the whole. Even this mode is not theoretically accurate; for theoretical accuracy would require that every man, who was a party to the government, should individually give his consent to the enforcement of every law in every separate case. But such a thing would be impossible in practice. The consent of twelve men is therefore taken instead; with the privilege of appeal, and (in case of error found by the the appeal court) a new trial, to guard against possible mistakes. This system, it is assumed, will ascertain the sense of the whole people — "the country" — with sufficient accuracy for all practical purposes, and with as much accuracy as is practicable without too great inconvenience and expense.

5. Another objection that will perhaps be made to allowing jurors to judge of the law, and the justice of the law, is, that the law would be uncertain.

If, by this objection, it be meant that the law would be uncertain to the minds of the people at large, so that they would not know what the juries would sanction and what condemn, and would not therefore know practically what their own rights and liberties were under the law, the objection is thoroughly baseless and false. No system of law that was ever devised could be so entirely intelligible and certain to the minds of the people at large as this. Compared with it, the complicated systems of law that are compounded of the law of nature, of constitutional grants, of innumerable and incessantly changing legislative enactments, and of countless and contradictory judicial decisions, with no uniform principle of reason or justice running through them, are among the blindest of all the mazes in which unsophisticated minds were ever bewildered and lost. The uncertainty of the law under these systems has become a proverb. So great is this uncertainty, that nearly all men, learned as well as unlearned, shun the law as their enemy, instead of resorting to it for protection. They usually go into courts of justice, so called, only as men go into battle — when there is no alternative left for them. And even then they go into them as men go into dark labyrinths and caverns — with no knowledge of their own, but trusting wholly to their guides. Yet, less fortunate than other adventurers, they can have little confidence even in their guides, for the reason that the guides themselves know little of the mazes they are threading. They know the mode and place of entrance; but what they will meet with on their way, and what will be the time, mode, place, or condition of their exit; whether they will emerge into a prison, or not; whether *wholly* naked and destitute, or not; whether with their reputations left to them, or not; and whether in time or eternity; experienced and honest guides rarely venture to predict. Was there ever such fatuity as that of a nation of men madly bent on building up such labyrinths as these, for no other purpose than that of exposing all their rights of reputation, property, liberty, and life, to the hazards of being lost in them, instead of being content to live in the light of the open day of their own understandings?

What honest, unsophisticated man ever found himself involved in a lawsuit, that he did not desire, of all things, that his cause might be judged of on principles of natural justice, as those principles were understood by plain men like himself? He would then feel that he could foresee the result. These plain men are the men who pay the taxes, and support the government. Why should they not have such an administration of justice as they desire, and can understand?

If the jurors were to judge of the law, and the justice of the law, there would be something like certainty in the administration of justice, and in the popular knowledge of the law, and men would govern themselves accordingly. There would be something like certainty, because every man has himself something like definite and clear opinions, and also knows something of the opinions of his neighbors, on matters of justice. And he would know that no statute, unless it were so clearly just as to command the unanimous assent of twelve men, who should be taken at random from the whole community, could be enforced so as to take from him his reputation, property, liberty, or life. What greater certainty can men require or need, as to the laws under which they are to live? If a statute were enacted by a legislature, a man, in order to know what was its true interpretation, whether it were constitutional, and whether it would be enforced, would not be under the necessity of waiting for years until some suit had arisen and been carried through all the stages of judicial proceeding, to a final decision. He would need only to use his own reason as to its meaning and its justice, and then talk with his neighbors on the same points. Unless he found them nearly unanimous in their interpretation and approbation of it, he would conclude that juries would not unite in enforcing it, and that it would consequently be a dead letter. And he would be safe in coming to this conclusion.

There would be something like certainty in the administration of justice, and in the popular knowledge of the law, for the further reason that there would be little legislation, and men's rights would be left to stand almost solely upon the law of nature, or what was *once* called in England "the *common law,*" (before so much legislation and usurpation had become incorporated into the common law,) — in other words, upon the principles of natural justice.

Of the certainty of this law of nature, or the ancient English common law, I may be excused for repeating here what I have said on another occasion.

"Natural law, so far from being uncertain, when compared with statutory and constitutional law, is the only thing that gives any certainty at all to a very large portion of our statutory and constitutional law. The reason is this. The words in which statutes and constitutions are written are susceptible of so many different meanings, — meanings widely different from, often directly opposite to, each other, in their bearing upon men's rights, — that, unless there were some rule of interpretation for determining which of these various and opposite meanings are the true ones, there could be no certainty at all as to the meaning of the statutes and constitutions themselves. Judges could make almost anything they should please out of them. Hence the necessity of a rule of interpretation. *And this rule is, that the language of statutes and constitutions shall be construed, as nearly as possible, consistently with natural law.*

The rule assumes, what is true, that natural law is a thing certain in itself; also that it is capable of being learned. It assumes, furthermore, that it actually is understood by the legislators and judges who make and interpret the written law. Of necessity, therefore, it assumes further, that they (the legislators and judges) are *incompetent* to make and interpret the *written* law, unless they previously understand the natural law applicable to the same subject. It also assumes that the *people* must understand the natural law, before they can understand the written law.

It is a principle perfectly familiar to lawyers, and one that must be perfectly obvious to every other man that will reflect a moment, that, as a general rule, *no one can know what the written law is, until he knows what it ought to be;* that men are liable to be constantly misled by the various and conflicting senses of the same words, unless they perceive the true legal sense in which the words *ought to be taken.* And this true legal sense is the sense that is most nearly consistent with natural law of any that the words can be made to bear, consistently with the laws of language, and appropriately to the subjects to which they are applied.

Though the words *contain* the law, the *words* themselves are not the law. Were the words themselves the law, each single written law would be liable to embrace many different laws, to wit, as many different laws as there were different senses, and different combinations of senses, in which each and all the words were capable of being taken.

Take, for example, the Constitution of the United States. By adopting one or another sense of the single word "*free*," the whole instrument is changed. Yet the word *free* is capable of some ten or twenty different senses. So that, by changing the sense of that single word, some ten or twenty different constitutions could be made out of the same written instrument. But there are, we will suppose, a thousand other words in the constitution, each of which is capable of from two to ten different senses. So that, by changing the sense of only a single word at a time, several thousands of different constitutions would be made. But this is not all. Variations could also be made by changing the senses of two or more words at a time, and these variations could be run through all the changes and combinations of senses that these thousand words are capable of. We see, then, that it is no more than a literal truth, that out of that single instrument, as it now stands, without altering the location of a single word, might be formed, by construction and interpretation, more different constitutions than figures can well estimate.

But each written law, in order to be a law, must be taken only in some *one* definite and distinct sense; and that definite and distinct sense must be selected from the almost infinite variety of senses which its words are capable of. How is this selection to be made? It can be only by the aid of that perception of natural law, or natural justice, which men naturally possess.

Such, then, is the comparative certainty of the natural and the written law. Nearly all the certainty there is in the latter, so far as it relates to principles, is based upon, and derived from, the still greater certainty of the former. In fact, nearly all the uncertainty of the laws under which we live, — which are a mixture of natural and written laws, — arises from the difficulty of construing, or, rather, from the facility of misconstruing, the *written* law; while natural law has nearly or quite the same certainty as mathematics On this point, Sir William Jones, one of the most learned judges that have ever lived, learned in Asiatic as well as European law, says, — and the fact should be kept forever in mind, as one of the most important of all truths: — "*It is pleasing to remark the similarity, or, rather, the identity of those conclusions which pure, unbiassed reason, in all ages and nations, seldom fails to draw, in such juridical inquiries as are not fettered and manacled by positive institutions.*" * In short, the simple fact that the written law must be interpreted by the natural, is, of itself, a sufficient confession of the superior certainty of the latter.

The written law, then, even where it can be construed consistently with the natural, introduces labor and obscurity, instead of shutting them out. And this must always be the case, because words do not create ideas, but only recall them; and the same word may recall many different ideas. For this reason, nearly all abstract principles can be seen by the single mind more clearly than they can be expressed by words to another. This is owing to the imperfection of language, and the different senses, meanings, and shades of meaning, which different individuals attach to the same words, in the same circumstances.†

Where the written law cannot be construed consistently with the natural, there is no reason why it should ever be enacted at all. It may, indeed, be sufficiently plain and certain to be easily understood; but its certainty and plainness are but a poor compensation for its injustice. Doubtless a law forbidding men to drink water, on pain of death, might be made so intelligible as to cut off all discussion as to its meaning; but would the intelligibleness of such a law be any equivalent for the right to drink water? The principle is the same in regard to all unjust laws. Few persons could

---

* Jones on Bailments, 133.

† Kent, describing the difficulty of construing the written law, says:

"Such is the imperfection of language, and the want of technical skill in the makers of the law, that statutes often give occasion to the most perplexing and distressing doubts and discussions, arising from the ambiguity that attends them. It requires great experience, as well as the command of a perspicuous diction, to frame a law in such clear and precise terms, as to secure it from ambiguous expressions, and from all doubts and criticisms upon its meaning." — *Kent*, 460.

The following extract from a speech of Lord Brougham, in the House of Lords, confesses the same difficulty:

"There was another subject, well worthy of the consideration of government during the recess, — the expediency, *or rather the absolute necessity*, of some arrangement for the preparation of bills, not merely private, but public bills, *in order that legislation might be consistent and systematic, and that the courts might not have so large a portion of their time occupied in endeavoring to construe acts of Parliament, in many cases unconstruable, and in most cases difficult to be construed.*" — *Law Reporter*, 1848, p. 525.

reasonably feel compensated for the arbitary destruction of their rights, by having the order for their destruction made known beforehand, in terms so distinct and unequivocal as to admit of neither mistake nor evasion. Yet this is all the compensation that such laws offer.

Whether, therefore, written laws correspond with, or differ from, the natural, they are to be condemned. In the first case, they are useless repetitions, introducing labor and obscurity. In the latter case, they are positive violations of men's rights.

There would be substantially the same reason in enacting mathematics by statute, that there is in enacting natural law. Whenever the natural law is sufficiently certain to all men's minds to justify its being enacted, it is sufficiently certain to need no enactment. On the other hand, until it be thus certain, there is danger of doing injustice by enacting it; it should, therefore, be left open to be discussed by anybody who may be disposed to question it, and to be judged of by the proper tribunal, the judiciary.*

It is not necessary that legislators should enact natural law in order that it may be known to the *people*, because that would be presuming that the legislators already understand it better than the people, — a fact of which I am not aware that they have ever heretofore given any very satisfactory evidence. The same sources of knowledge on the subject are open to the people that are open to the legislators, and the people must be presumed to know it as well as they.

The objections made to natural law, on the ground of obscurity, are wholly unfounded. It is true, it must be learned, like any other science; but it is equally true that it is very easily learned. Although as illimitable in its applications as the infinite relations of men to each other, it is, nevertheless, made up of simple elementary principles, of the truth and justice of which every ordinary mind has an almost intuitive perception. *It is the science of justice,* — and almost all men have the same perceptions of what constitutes justice, or of what justice requires, when they understand alike the facts from which their inferences are to be drawn. Men living in contact with each other, and having intercourse together, *cannot avoid* learning

---

* This condemnation of written laws must, of course, be understood as applying only to cases where principles and rights are involved, and not as condemning any governmental arrangements, or instrumentalities, that are consistent with natural right, and which must be agreed upon for the purpose of carrying natural law into effect. These things may be varied, as expediency may dictate, so only that they be allowed to infringe no principle of justice. And they must, of course, be written, because they do not exist as fixed principles, or laws in nature.

natural law, to a very great extent, even if they would. The dealings of men with men, their separate possessions, and their individual wants, are continually forcing upon their minds the questions, — Is this act just? or is it unjust? Is this thing mine? or is it his? And these are questions of natural law; questions, which, in regard to the great mass of cases, are answered alike by the human mind everywhere.

Children learn many principles of natural law at a very early age. For example: they learn that when one child has picked up an apple or a flower, it is his, and that his associates must not take it from him against his will. They also learn that if he voluntarily exchange his apple or flower with a playmate, for some other article of desire, he has thereby surrendered his right to it, and must not reclaim it. These are fundamental principles of natural law, which govern most of the greatest interests of individuals and society; yet children learn them earlier than they learn that three and three are six, or five and five, ten. Talk of enacting natural law by statute, that it may be known! It would hardly be extravagant to say, that, in nine cases in ten, men learn it before they have learned the language by which we describe it. Nevertheless, numerous treatises are written on it, as on other sciences. The decisions of courts, containing their opinions upon the almost endless variety of cases that have come before them, are reported; and these reports are condensed, codified, and digested, so as to give, in a small compass, the facts, and the opinions of the courts as to the law resulting from them. And these treatises, codes, and digests are open to be read of all men. And a man has the same excuse for being ignorant of arithmetic, or any other science, that he has for being ignorant of natural law. He can learn it as well, if he will, without its being enacted, as he could if it were.

If our governments would but themselves adhere to natural law, there would be little occasion to complain of the ignorance of the people in regard to it. The popular ignorance of law is attributable mainly to the innovations that have been made upon natural law by legislation; whereby our system has become an incongruous mixture of natural and statute law, with no uniform principle pervading it. To learn such a system, — if system it can be called, and if learned it can be, — is a matter of very similar difficulty to what it would be to learn a system of mathematics, which should consist of the mathematics of nature, interspersed with such other mathematics as might be created by legislation, in violation of all the natural principles of numbers and quantities.

But whether the difficulties of learning natural law be

greater or less than here represented, they exist in the nature of things, and cannot be removed. Legislation, instead of removing, only increases them. This it does by innovating upon natural truths and principles, and introducing jargon and contradiction, in the place of order, analogy, consistency, and uniformity.

Further than this; legislation does not even profess to remove the obscurity of natural law. That is no part of its object. It only professes to substitute something arbitrary in the place of natural law. Legislators generally have the sense to see that legislation will not make natural law any clearer than it is. Neither is it the object of legislation to establish the authority of natural law. Legislators have the sense to see that they can add nothing to the authority of natural law, and that it will stand on its own authority, unless they overturn it.

The whole object of legislation, excepting that legislation which merely makes regulations, and provides instrumentalities for carrying other laws into effect, is to overturn natural law, and substitute for it the arbitrary will of power. In other words, the whole object of it is to destroy men's rights. At least, such is its only effect; and its designs must be inferred from its effect. Taking all the statutes in the country, there probably is not one in a hundred, — except the auxiliary ones just mentioned, — that does not violate natural law; that does not invade some right or other.

Yet the advocates of arbitrary legislation are continually practising the fraud of pretending that unless the legislature *make* the laws, the laws will not be known. The whole object of the fraud is to secure to the government the authority of making laws that never ought to be known."

In addition to the authority already cited, of Sir William Jones, as to the certainty of natural law, and the uniformity of men's opinions in regard to it, I may add the following:

"There is that great simplicity and plainness in the Common Law, that Lord Coke has gone so far as to assert, (and Lord Bacon nearly seconds him in observing,) that 'he never knew two questions arise merely upon common law; but that they were mostly owing to statutes ill-penned and overladen with provisos.'"— 3 *Eunomus*, 157–8.

If it still be said that juries would disagree, as to what was natural justice, and that one jury would decide one way, and another jury another; the answer is, that such a thing is hardly credible, as that twelve men, taken at random from the people at large, should *unanimously* decide a question of natural justice one way, and that twelve other men, selected in the same manner, should *unanimously* decide the same question the other way, *unless they were misled by the justices*. If, however, such things should sometimes happen, from any cause whatever, the remedy is by appeal, and new trial.

CHAPTER VI.

JURIES OF THE PRESENT DAY ILLEGAL.

IT may probably be safely asserted that there are, at this day, no legal juries, either in England or America. And if there are no legal juries, there is, of course, no legal trial, nor "judgment," by jury.

In saying that there are probably no legal juries, I mean that there are probably no juries appointed in conformity with the principles of the *common law*.

The term *jury* is a technical one, derived from the common law; and when the American constitutions provide for the trial by jury, they provide for the *common law* trial by jury; and not merely for any trial by jury that the government itself may chance to invent, and call by that name. It is the *thing*, and not merely the *name*, that is guarantied. Any legislation, therefore, that infringes any *essential principle* of the *common law*, in the selection of jurors, is unconstitutional; and the juries selected in accordance with such legislation are, of course, illegal, and their judgments void.

It will also be shown, in a subsequent chapter,* that since Magna Carta, the legislative power in England (whether king or parliament) has never had any constitutional authority to infringe, by legislation, any essential principle of the common law in the selection of jurors. All such legislation is as much unconstitutional and void, as though it abolished the trial by jury altogether. In reality it does abolish it.

What, then, are the *essential principles* of the common law, controlling the selection of jurors?

They are two.

---

* On the English Constitution.

1. That *all* the freemen, or adult male members of the state, shall be eligible as jurors.*

Any legislation which requires the selection of jurors to be made from a less number of freemen than the whole, makes the jury selected an illegal one.

If a part only of the freemen, or members of the state, are eligible as jurors, the jury no longer represent " the country," but only a part of " the country."

If the selection of jurors can be restricted to any less number of freemen than the whole, it can be restricted to a very small proportion of the whole; and thus the government be taken out of the hands of " the country," or the whole people, and be thrown into the hands of a few.

That, at common law, the whole body of freemen were eligible as jurors is sufficiently proved, not only by the reason of the thing, but by the following evidence:

1. Everybody must be presumed eligible, until the contrary be shown. We have no evidence, that I am aware of, of a prior date to Magna Carta, to *disprove* that all freemen were eligible as jurors, unless it be the law of Ethelred, which requires that they be *elderly* † men. Since no specific age is given, it is probable, I think, that this statute meant nothing more than that they be more than twenty-one years old. If it meant anything more, it was probably contrary to the common law, and therefore void.

2. Since Magna Carta, we have evidence showing quite conclusively that all freemen, above the age of twenty-one years, were eligible as jurors.

The *Mirror of Justices*, (written within a century after Magna Carta,) in the section " *Of Judges* " — that is, *jurors* — says:

"All those who are not forbidden by law may be judges

---

* Although all the freemen are legally eligible as jurors, any one may nevertheless be challenged and set aside, at the trial, for any special *personal* disqualification; such as mental or physical inability to perform the duties; having been convicted, or being under charge, of crime; interest, bias, &c. But it is clear that the common law allows none of these points to be determined by the court, but only by "*triers.*"

† What was the precise meaning of the Saxon word, which I have here called *elderly*, I do not know. In the Latin translations it is rendered by *seniores*, which may perhaps mean simply those who have attained their majority.

(jurors). To women it is forbidden by law that they be judges; and thence it is, that feme coverts are exempted to do suit in inferior courts. On the other part, a villein cannot be a judge, by reason of the two estates, which are repugnants; persons attainted of false judgments cannot be judges, nor infants, nor any under the age of twenty-one years, nor infected persons, nor idiots, nor madmen, nor deaf, nor dumb, nor parties in the pleas, nor men excommunicated by the bishop, nor criminal persons. * * And those who are not of the Christian faith cannot be judges, nor those who are out of the king's allegiance." — *Mirror of Justices*, 59–60.

In the section " *Of Inferior Courts*," it is said:

"From the first assemblies came consistories, which we now call courts, and that in divers places, and in divers manners; whereof the sheriffs held one monthly, or every five weeks, according to the greatness or largeness of the shires. And these courts are called county courts, *where the judgment is by the suitors*, if there be no writ, and is by warrant of jurisdiction ordinary. The other inferior courts are the courts of every lord of the fee, to the likeness of the hundred courts. * * There are other inferior courts which the bailiffs hold in every hundred, from three weeks to three weeks, *by the suitors of the freeholders of the hundred. All the tenants within the fees are bounden to do their suit there*, and that not for the service of their persons, but for the service of their fees. But women, infants within the age of twenty-one years, deaf, dumb, idiots, those who are indicted or appealed of mortal felony, before they be acquitted, diseased persons, and excommunicated persons are exempted from doing suit." — *Mirror of Justices*, 50–51.

In the section " *Of the Sheriff's Turns*," it is said:

"The sheriffs by ancient ordinances hold several meetings twice in the year in every hundred; *where all the freeholders within the hundred* are bound to appear for the service of their fees." — *Mirror of Justices*, 50.

The following statute was passed by Edward I., seventy years after Magna Carta:

"Forasmuch also as sheriffs, hundreders, and bailiffs of liberties, have used to grieve those which be placed under them, putting in assizes and juries men diseased and decrepit, and having continual or sudden disease; and men also that dwelled not in the country at the time of the summons; and summon also an unreasonable number of jurors, for to extort money from some of them, for letting them go in peace, and so the assizes and juries pass many times by poor men, and the rich abide at home by reason of their bribes; it is ordained that from henceforth in one assize no more shall be summoned than four and twenty; and old men above three score and ten years, being continually sick, or being diseased at the time of the summons, or not dwelling in that country, shall not be put in juries of petit assizes." — *St.* 13 *Edward I.*, ch. 38. (1285.)

Although this command to the sheriffs and other officers, not to summon, as jurors, those who, from age and disease, were physically incapable of performing the duties, may not, of itself, afford any absolute or legal implication, by which we can determine precisely who were, and who were not, eligible as jurors at common law, yet the exceptions here made nevertheless carry a seeming confession with them that, at common law, all male adults were eligible as jurors.

But the main principle of the feudal system itself shows that *all* the full and free adult male members of the state — that is, all who were free born, and had not lost their civil rights by crime, or otherwise — *must*, at common law, have been eligible as jurors. What was that principle? It was, that the state rested for support upon the land, and not upon taxation levied upon the people personally. The lands of the country were considered the property of the state, and were made to support the state *in this way*. A portion of them was set apart to the king, the rents of which went to pay his personal and official expenditures, not including the maintenance of armies, or the administration of justice. War and the administration of justice were provided for in the following manner. The freemen, or the free-born adult male members of the state — who had not forfeited their political rights — were entitled to land *of right*, (until all the land was taken up,) on condition of their rendering certain military and civil services to the state. The military services consisted in serving personally as soldiers, or contributing an equivalent in horses, provisions, or other military supplies. The civil services consisted, among other things, in serving as jurors (and, it would appear, as witnesses) in the courts of justice. For these services they received no compensation other than the use of their lands. In this way the state was sustained; and the king had no power to levy additional burdens or taxes upon the people. The persons holding lands on these terms were called *freeholders* — in later times *freemen* — meaning free and full members of the state.

Now, as the principle of the system was that the freeholders held their lands of the state, on the condition of rendering these military and civil services as *rents* for their lands, the principle implies that *all* the freeholders were liable to these rents, and were therefore eligible as jurors. Indeed, I do not know that it has ever been doubted that, at common law, *all* the freeholders were eligible as jurors. If all had not been eligible, we unquestionably should have had abundant evidence of the exceptions. And if anybody, at this day, allege any exceptions, the burden will be on him to prove them. The presumption clearly is that *all* were eligible.

The first invasion, which I find made, by the English statutes, upon this common law principle, was made in 1285, seventy years after Magna Carta. It was then enacted as follows:

"Nor shall any be put in assizes or juries, though they ought to be taken in their own shire, that hold a tenement of less than the value of *twenty shillings yearly*. And if such assizes and juries be taken out of the shire, no one shall be placed in them who holds a tenement of less value than forty shillings yearly at the least, except such as be witnesses in deeds or other writings, whose presence is necessary, so that they be able to travel." — *St.* 13 *Edward I.*, ch. 38. (1285.)

The next invasion of the common law, in this particular, was made in 1414, about two hundred years after Magna Carta, when it was enacted:

"That no person shall be admitted to pass in any inquest upon trial of the death of a man, nor in any inquest betwixt party and party in plea real, nor in plea personal, whereof the debt or the damage declared amount to forty marks, if the same person have not lands or tenements of the yearly value of *forty shillings above all charges of the same.*" — 2 *Henry V.*, st. 2, ch. 3. (1414.)

Other statutes on this subject of the property qualifications of jurors, are given in the note.*

---

* In 1483 it was enacted, by a statute entitled "Of what credit and estate those jurors must be which shall be impanelled in the Sheriff's Turn."

"That no bailiff nor other officer from henceforth return or impanel any such person in any shire of England, to be taken or put in or upon any inquiry in any of the said Turns, but such as be of good name and fame, and having lands and tenements of freehold within the same shires, to the yearly value of *twenty shillings* at the least, or else lands and tenements holden by custom of manor, commonly called *copy-hold*, within the said shires, to the yearly value of twenty-six shillings eight pence over all charges at the least." — 1 *Richard III.*, ch. 4. (1483.)

In 1486 it was enacted, "That the justices of the peace of every shire of this realm for the time being may take, by their discretion, an inquest, whereof every man shall have lands and tenements to the yearly value of *forty shillings* at the least, to inquire of the concealments of others," &c., &c. — 3 *Henry VII.*, ch. 1. (1486.)

A statute passed in 1494, in regard to jurors in the city of London, enacts:

"That no person nor persons hereafter be impanelled, summoned, or sworn in any jury or inquest in courts within the same city, (of London,) except he be of lands, tenements, *or goods and chattels*, to the value of *forty marks*;* and that no person or persons hereafter be impanelled, summoned, nor sworn in any jury or inquest in any court within the said city, for lands or tenements, or action personal, wherein the debt or damage amounteth to the sum of forty marks, or above, except he be in lands, tenements, goods, or chattels, to the value of *one hundred marks*." — 11 *Henry VII.*, ch. 21. (1494.)

The statute 4 *Henry VIII.*, ch. 3, sec. 4, (1512) requires jurors in London to have "*goods* to the value of one hundred marks."

In 1494 it was enacted that "It shall be lawful to every sheriff of the counties of *Southampton, Surry, and Sussex,* to impanel and summons twenty-four lawful men of such, inhabiting within the precinct of his or their turns, as owe suit to the same turn, whereof every one hath lands or freehold to the yearly value of *ten* shillings, or copyhold lands to the yearly value of *thirteen shillings four pence*, above all charges within any of the said counties, or men of less livelihood, if there be not so many there, notwithstanding the statute of 1 *Richard III.*, ch. 4. To endure to the next parliament." — 11 *Henry VII.*, ch. 26. (1494.)

This statute was continued in force by 19 *Henry VII.*, ch. 16. (1503.)

In 1531 it was enacted, "That every person or persons, being the king's natural subject born, which either by the name of citizen, or of a freeman, or any other name, doth enjoy and use the liberties and privileges of any city, borough, or town corporate, where he dwelleth and maketh his abode, being worth in *movable goods and substance* to the clear value of *forty pounds*, be henceforth admitted in trials of murders and felonies in every sessions and gaol delivery, to be kept and holden in and for the liberty of such cities, boroughs, and towns corporate, albeit they have no freehold; any act, statute, use, custom, or ordinance to the contrary hereof notwithstanding." — 23 *Henry VIII.*, ch. 13. (1531.)

In 1585 it was enacted, "That in all cases where any jurors to be returned for trial of any issue or issues joined in any of the Queen's majesty's courts of King's Bench, Common Pleas, and the Exchequer, or before justices of assize, by the laws of this realm now in force, ought to have estate of freehold in lands, tenements, or hereditaments, of the clear yearly value of *forty shillings*, that in every such case the jurors that shall be returned from and after the end of this present session of parliament, shall every of them have estate of freehold in lands, tenements, or hereditaments, to the clear yearly value of *four pounds* at the least." — 27 *Elizabeth*, ch. 6. (1585.)

In 1664–5 it was enacted, "That all jurors (other than strangers upon trials *per medietatem linguæ*) who are to be returned for the trials of issues joined in any of (his)

---

* A mark was thirteen shillings and four pence.

From these statutes it will be seen that, since 1285, seventy years after Magna Carta, the common law right of all free British subjects to eligibility as jurors has been abolished, and the qualifications of jurors have been made a subject of arbitrary legislation. In other words, the government has usurped the authority of *selecting* the jurors that were to sit in judgment upon its own acts. This is destroying the vital principle of the trial by jury itself, which is that the legislation of the government shall be subjected to the judgment of a tribunal, taken indiscriminately from the whole people, without any choice by the government, and over which the government can exercise no control. If the government can select the jurors, it will, of course, select those whom it supposes will be favorable to its enactments. And an exclusion of *any* of the freemen from eligibility is a *selection* of those not excluded.

It will be seen, from the statutes cited, that the most absolute authority over the jury box — that is, over the right of the people to sit in juries — has been usurped by the govern-

---

majesty's courts of king's bench, common pleas, or the exchequer, or before justices of assize, or nisi prius, oyer and terminer, gaol delivery, or general or quarter sessions of the peace, from and after the twentieth day of April, which shall be in the year of our Lord one thousand six hundred and sixty-five, in any county of this realm of England, shall every of them then have, in their own name, or in trust for them, within the same county, *twenty pounds by the year*, at least, above reprises, in their own or their wives' right, of freehold lands, or of ancient demesne, or of rents in fee, fee-tail, or for life. And that in every county within the dominion of Wales every such juror shall then have, within the same, *eight pounds by the year*, at the least, above reprises, in manner aforesaid. All which persons having such estate as aforesaid are hereby enabled and made liable to be returned and serve as jurors for the trial of issues before the justices aforesaid, any law or statute to the contrary in any wise notwithstanding." — 16 *and* 17 *Charles II.*, ch. 3. (1664–5.)

By a statute passed in 1692, jurors in England are to have landed estates of the value of *ten pounds a year;* and jurors in Wales to have similar estates of the realm of *six pounds a year.* — 4 and 5 *William and Mary*, ch. 24, sec. 14. (1692.)

By the same statute, (sec. 18,) persons may be returned to serve upon the *tales* in any county of England, who shall have, within the same county, *five pounds by the year*, above reprises, in the manner aforesaid.

By St. 3 *George II.*, ch. 25, sec. 19, 20, no one is to be a juror in London, who shall not be "an householder within the said city, and have lands, tenements, or personal estate, to the value of *one hundred pounds.*"

By another statute, applicable only to the county of *Middlesex*, it is enacted,

"That all leaseholders, upon leases where the improved rents or value shall amount to *fifty pounds or upwards per annum*, over and above all ground rents or other reservations payable by virtue of the said leases, shall be liable and obliged to serve upon juries when they shall be legally summoned for that purpose." — 4 *George II.*, ch. 7, sec. 3. (1731.)

ment; that the qualifications of jurors have been repeatedly changed, and made to vary from a freehold of *ten shillings yearly,* to one of "*twenty pounds by the year at least above reprises.*" They have also been made different, in the counties of Southampton, Surrey, and Sussex, from what they were in the other counties; different in Wales from what they were in England; and different in the city of London, and in the county of Middlesex, from what they were in any other part of the kingdom.

But this is not all. The government has not only assumed arbitrarily to classify the people, on the basis of property, but it has even assumed to give to some of its judges entire and absolute personal discretion in the selection of the jurors to be impanelled *in criminal cases,* as the following statutes show.

" Be it also ordained and enacted by the same authority, that all panels hereafter to be returned, which be not at the suit of any party, that shall be made and put in afore any justice of gaol delivery or justices of peace in their open sessions *to inquire for the king, shall hereafter be reformed by additions and taking out of names of persons by discretion of the same justices before whom such panel shall be returned; and the same justices shall hereafter command the sheriff, or his ministers in his absence, to put other persons in the same panel by their discretions; and that panel so hereafter to be made, to be good and lawful.* This act to endure only to the next Parliament."
— 11 *Henry VII.,* ch. 24, sec. 6. (1495.)

This act was continued in force by 1 Henry VIII., ch. 11, (1509,) to the end of the then next Parliament.

It was reënacted, and made perpetual, by 3 Henry VIII., ch. 12. (1511.)

These acts gave unlimited authority to the king's justices to pack juries at their discretion; and abolished the last vestige of the common law right of the people to sit as jurors, and judge of their own liberties, in the courts to which the acts applied.

Yet, as matters of law, these statutes were no more clear violations of the common law, the fundamental and paramount "law of the land," than were those statutes which affixed the property qualifications before named; because, if the king, or the government, can select the jurors on the ground of property, it can select them on any other ground whatever.

13*

Any infringement or restriction of the common law right of the whole body of the freemen of the kingdom to eligibility as jurors, was legally an abolition of the trial by jury itself. The juries no longer represented "the country," but only a part of the country; that part, too, on whose favor the government chose to rely for the maintenance of its power, and which it therefore saw fit to select as being the most reliable instruments for its purposes of oppression towards the rest. And the selection was made on the same principle, on which tyrannical governments generally select their supporters, viz., that of conciliating those who would be most dangerous as enemies, and most powerful as friends — that is, the wealthy.*

These restrictions, or indeed any one of them, of the right of eligibility as jurors, was, in principle, a complete abolition of the English constitution; or, at least, of its most vital and valuable part. It was, in principle, an assertion of a right, on the part of the government, to *select* the individuals who were to determine the authority of its own laws, and the extent of its own powers. It was, therefore, *in effect*, the assertion of a right, on the part of the government itself, to determine its own powers, and the authority of its own legislation, over the people; and a denial of all right, on the part of the people, to judge of or determine their own liberties against the government. It was, therefore, in reality, a declaration of entire absolutism on the part of the government. It was an act as purely despotic, *in principle*, as would have been the express abolition of all juries whatsoever. By "the law of the land," which the kings were sworn to maintain, every free adult male British subject was eligible to the jury box, with full power to exercise his own judgment as to the authority and obligation of every statute of the king, which might come

---

* Suppose these statutes, instead of disfranchising all whose freeholds were of less than the standard value fixed by the statutes, had disfranchised all whose freeholds were of greater value than the same standard — would anybody ever have doubted that such legislation was inconsistent with the English constitution; or that it amounted to an entire abolition of the trial by jury? Certainly not. Yet it was as clearly inconsistent with the common law, or the English constitution, to disfranchise those whose freeholds fell below any arbitrary standard fixed by the government, as it would have been to disfranchise all whose freeholds rose above that standard.

before him. But the principle of these statutes (fixing the qualifications of jurors) is, that nobody is to sit in judgment upon the acts or legislation of the king, or the government, except those whom the government itself shall select for that purpose. A more complete subversion of the essential principles of the English constitution could not be devised.

The juries of England are illegal for another reason, viz., that the statutes cited require the jurors (except in London and a few other places) to be *freeholders*. All the other free British subjects are excluded; whereas, at common law, all such subjects are eligible to sit in juries, whether they be freeholders or not.

It is true, the ancient common law required the jurors to be freeholders; but the term *freeholder* no longer expresses the same idea that it did in the ancient common law; because no land is now holden in England on the same principle, or by the same tenure, as that on which all the land was held in the early times of the common law.

As has heretofore been mentioned, in the early times of the common law the land was considered the property of the state; and was all holden by the *tenants*, so called, (that is, *holders*,) on the condition of their rendering certain military and civil services to the state, (or to the king as the representative of the state,) under the name of *rents*. Those who held lands on these terms were called free *tenants*, that is, *free holders* — meaning free persons, or members of the state, holding lands — to distinguish them from villeins, or serfs, who were not members of the state, but held their lands by a more servile tenure, and also to distinguish them from persons of foreign birth, outlaws, and all other persons, who were not members of the state.

Every freeborn adult male Englishman (who had not lost his civil rights by crime or otherwise) was entitled to land *of right;* that is, by virtue of his civil freedom, or membership of the body politic. Every member of the state was therefore a freeholder; and every freeholder was a member of the state. And the members of the state were therefore called freeholders. But what is material to be observed, is, that a man's right to land was an incident to his *civil freedom ;* not his civil freedom an incident to his right to land. He was a freeholder because he was a *freeborn* member of the state ; and not a freeborn member of the state because he was a freeholder ; for this last would be an absurdity.

As the tenures of lands changed, the term *freeholder* lost its original significance, and no longer described a man who held land of the state by virtue of his civil freedom, but only one who held it in fee-simple — that is, free of any liability to military or civil services. But the government, in fixing the qualifications of jurors, has adhered to the term *freeholder* after that term has ceased to express the *thing* originally designated by it.

The principle, then, of the common law, was, that every freeman, or freeborn male Englishman, of adult age, &c., was eligible to sit in juries, by virtue of his civil freedom, or his being a member of the state, or body politic. But the principle of the present English statutes is, that a man shall have a right to sit in juries because he owns lands in fee-simple. At the common law a man was *born* to the right to sit in juries. By the present statutes he *buys* that right when he buys his land. And thus this, the greatest of all the political rights of an Englishman, has become a mere article of merchandise ; a thing that is bought and sold in the market for what it will bring.

Of course, there can be no legality in such juries as these ; but only in juries to which every free or natural born adult male Englishman is eligible.

The second essential principle of the common law, controlling the selection of jurors, is, that when the selection of the actual jurors comes to be made, (from the whole body of male adults,) that selection shall be made in some mode that excludes the possibility of choice *on the part of the government.*

Of course, this principle forbids the selection to be made *by any officer of the government.*

There seem to have been at least three modes of selecting the jurors, at the common law. 1. By lot.* 2. Two knights, or other freeholders, were appointed, (probably by the sheriff,)

---

* *Lingard* says : " These compurgators or jurors * * were sometimes * * *drawn by lot.*" — 1 *Lingard's History of England*, p. 300.

to select the jurors. 3. By the sheriff, bailiff, or other person, who held the court, or rather acted as its ministerial officer. Probably the latter mode may have been the most common, although there may be some doubt on this point.

At the common law the sheriffs, bailiffs, and other officers *were chosen by the people, instead of being appointed by the king.* (4 *Blackstone*, 413. *Introduction to Gilbert's History of the Common Pleas*, p. 2, *note*, and p. 4.) This has been shown in a former chapter.* At common law, therefore, jurors selected by these officers were legally selected, so far as the principle now under discussion is concerned; that is, they were not selected by any officer who was dependent on the government.

But in the year 1315, one hundred years after Magna Carta, the choice of sheriffs was taken from the people, and it was enacted:

"That the sheriffs shall henceforth be assigned by the chancellor, treasurer, barons of the exchequer, and by the justices. And in the absence of the chancellor, by the treasurer, barons and justices." — 9 *Edward II.*, st. 2. (1315.)

These officers, who appointed the sheriffs, were themselves appointed by the king, and held their offices during his pleasure. Their appointment of sheriffs was, therefore, equivalent to an appointment by the king himself. And the sheriffs, thus appointed, held their offices only during the pleasure of the king, and were of course mere tools of the king; and their selection of jurors was really a selection by the king himself. In this manner the king usurped the selection of the jurors who were to sit in judgment upon his own laws.

Here, then, was another usurpation, by which the common law trial by jury was destroyed, so far as related to the *county* courts, in which the sheriffs presided, and which were the most important courts of the kingdom. From this cause alone, if there were no other, there has not been a legal jury in a *county* court in England, for more than five hundred years.

In nearly or quite all the States of the United States the juries are illegal, for one or the other of the same reasons that make the juries in England illegal.

---

* Chapter 4, p. 120, note.

In order that the juries in the United States may be legal — that is, in accordance with the principles of the common law — it is necessary that every adult male member of the state should have his name in the jury box, or be eligible as a juror. Yet this is the case in hardly a single state.

In New Jersey, Maryland, North Carolina, Tennessee, and Mississippi, the jurors are required to be *freeholders*. But this requirement is illegal, for the reason that the term *freeholder*, in this country, has no meaning analogous to the meaning it had in the ancient common law.

In Arkansas, Missouri, Indiana, and Alabama, jurors are required to be "freeholders or householders." Each of these requirements is illegal.

In Florida, they are required to be "householders."

In Connecticut, Maine, Ohio, and Georgia, jurors are required to have the qualifications of "electors."

In Virginia, they are required to have a property qualification of one hundred dollars.

In Maine, Massachusetts, Vermont, Connecticut, New York, Ohio, Indiana, Michigan, and Wisconsin, certain civil authorities of the towns, cities, and counties are authorized to select, once in one, two, or three years, a certain number of the people — a small number compared with the whole — from whom jurors are to be taken when wanted; thus disfranchising all except the few thus selected.

In Maine and Vermont, the inhabitants, by vote in town meeting, have a veto upon the jurors selected by the authorities of the town.

In Massachusetts, the inhabitants, by vote in town meeting, can strike out any names inserted by the authorities, and insert others; thus making jurors elective by the people, and, of course, representatives only of a majority of the people.

In Illinois, the jurors are selected, for each term of court, by the county commissioners.

In North Carolina, "*the courts of pleas and quarter sessions* * * shall select the names of such persons only as are freeholders, and as are well qualified to act as jurors, &c.; thus giving the courts power to pack the juries." — (*Revised Statutes*, 147.)

In Arkansas, too, "It shall be the duty of the *county court* of each county * * to make out and cause to be delivered to the sheriff a list of not less than sixteen, nor more than twenty-three persons, qualified to serve as *grand* jurors;" and the sheriff is to summon such persons to serve as *grand* jurors.

In Tennessee, also, the jurors are to be selected by the *county courts*.

In Georgia, the jurors are to be selected by "the justices of the inferior courts of each county, together with the sheriff and clerk, or a majority of them."

In Alabama, "the sheriff, judge of the county court, and clerks of the circuit and county courts," or "a majority of" them, select the jurors.

In Virginia, the jurors are selected by the sheriffs; but the sheriffs are appointed by the governor of the state, and that is enough to make the juries illegal. Probably the same objection lies against the legality of the juries in some other states.

How jurors are appointed, and what are their qualifications, in New Hampshire, Rhode Island, Pennsylvania, Delaware, South Carolina, Kentucky, Iowa, Texas, and California, I know not. There is little doubt that there is some valid objection to them, of the kinds already suggested, in all these states.

In regard to jurors in the courts of the United States, it is enacted, by act of Congress:

"That jurors to serve in the courts of the United States, in each state respectively, shall have the like qualifications, and be entitled to the like exemptions, as jurors of the highest court of law of such state now have and are entitled to, and shall hereafter, from time to time, have and be entitled to. and shall be designated by ballot, lot, or otherwise, according to the mode of forming such juries now practised and hereafter to be practised therein, in so far as such mode may be practicable by the courts of the United States, or the officers thereof; and for this purpose, the said courts shall have power to make all necessary rules and regulations for conforming the designation and empanelling of jurors, in substance, to the laws and usages now in force in such state; and, further, shall have power, by rule or order, from time to time, to conform the same to any change in these respects which may be hereafter adopted by the legislatures of the respective states for the state courts." — *St.* 1840, ch. 47, *Statutes at Large*, vol. 5, p. 394.

In this corrupt and lawless manner, Congress, instead of taking care to preserve the trial by jury, so far as they might, by providing for the appointment of legal juries — incomparably the most important of all our judicial tribunals, and the only ones on which the least reliance can be placed for the preservation of liberty — have given the selection of them over entirely to the control of an indefinite number of state legislatures, and thus authorized each state legislature to adapt the juries of the United States to the maintenance of any and every system of tyranny that may prevail in such state.

Congress have as much constitutional right to give over all the functions of the United States government into the hands of the state legislatures, to be exercised within each state in such manner as the legislature of such state shall please to exercise them, as they have to thus give up to these legislatures the selection of juries for the courts of the United States.

There has, probably, never been a legal jury, nor a legal trial by jury, in a single court of the United States, since the adoption of the constitution.

These facts show how much reliance can be placed in written constitutions, to control the action of the government, and preserve the liberties of the people.

If the real trial by jury had been preserved in the courts of the United States — that is, if we had had legal juries, and the jurors had known their rights — it is hardly probable that one tenth of the past legislation of Congress would ever have been enacted, or, at least, that, if enacted, it could have been enforced.

Probably the best mode of appointing jurors would be this: Let the names of *all* the adult male members of the state, in each township, be kept in a jury box, by the officers of the township; and when a court is to be held for a county or other district, let the officers of a sufficient number of townships be required (without seeing the names) to draw out a name from their boxes respectively, to be returned to the court as a juror. This mode of appointment would guard against collusion and selection; and juries so appointed would be likely to be a fair epitome of " the country."

CHAPTER VII.

ILLEGAL JUDGES.

It is a principle of Magna Carta, and therefore of the trial by jury, (for all parts of Magna Carta must be construed together,) that no judge or other officer *appointed by the king*, shall preside in jury trials, *in criminal cases*, or "pleas of the crown."

This provision is contained in the great charters of both John and Henry, and is second in importance only to the provision guaranteeing the trial by jury, of which it is really a part. Consequently, without the observance of this prohibition, there can be no genuine or *legal* — that is, *common law* — trial by jury.

At the common law, all officers who held jury trials, whether in civil or criminal cases, were chosen by the people.*

---

* The proofs of this principle of the common law have already been given on page 120, *note*.

There is much confusion and contradiction among authors as to the manner in which sheriffs and other officers were appointed; some maintaining that they were appointed by the king, others that they were elected by the people. I imagine that both these opinions are correct, and that several of the king's officers bore the same official names as those chosen by the people; and that this is the cause of the confusion that has arisen on the subject.

It seems to be a perfectly well established fact that, at common law, several magistrates, bearing the names of aldermen, sheriffs, stewards, coroners and bailiffs, were chosen by the people; and yet it appears, from Magna Carta itself, that some of the *king's* officers (of whom he must have had many) were also called "sheriffs, constables, coroners, and bailiffs."

But Magna Carta, in various instances, speaks of sheriffs and bailiffs as "*our* sheriffs and bailiffs;" thus apparently intending to recognize the distinction between officers *of the king*, bearing those names, and other officers, bearing the same official names, but chosen by the people. Thus it says that "no sheriff or bailiff *of ours*, or any other (officer), shall take horses or carts of any freeman for carriage, unless with the consent of the freeman himself." — *John's Charter*, ch. 36.

In a kingdom subdivided into so many counties, hundreds, tithings, manors, cities

But previous to Magna Carta, the kings had adopted the practice of sending officers of their own appointment, called justices, into the counties, to hold jury trials in some cases; and Magna Carta authorizes this practice to be continued so far as it relates to *three* kinds of *civil* actions, to wit: "novel disseisin, mort de ancestor, and darrein presentment;" * but specially forbids its being extended to criminal cases, or pleas of the crown.

This prohibition is in these words:

"*Nullus vicecomes, constabularius, coronator, vel alii balivi nostri, teneant placita coronæ nostræ.*" (No sheriff, constable, coroner, *or other our bailiffs*, shall hold pleas of our crown.) — *John's Charter*, ch. 53. *Henry's ditto*, ch. 17.

Some persons seem to have supposed that this was a prohibition merely upon officers *bearing the specific names of* "*sheriffs, constables, coroners and bailiffs,*" to hold criminal trials. But such is not the meaning. If it were, the *name*

---

and boroughs, each having a judicial or police organization of its own, it is evident that many of the officers must have been chosen by the people, else the government could not have maintained its popular character. On the other hand, it is evident that the king, the executive power of the nation, must have had large numbers of officers of his own in every part of the kingdom. And it is perfectly natural that these different sets of officers should, in many instances, bear the same official names; and, consequently that the king, when speaking of his own officers, as distinguished from those chosen by the people, should call them "*our* sheriffs, bailiffs," &c., as he does in Magna Carta.

I apprehend that inattention to these considerations has been the cause of all the confusion of ideas that has arisen on this subject, — a confusion very evident in the following paragraph from Dunham, which may be given as an illustration of that which is exhibited by others on the same points.

"Subordinate to the ealdormen were the *gerefas,* the sheriffs, or reeves, *of whom there were several in every shire, or county.* There was one in every borough, as a judge. There was one at every gate, who witnessed purchases outside the walls; and there was one, higher than either, — the high sheriff, — who was probably the reeve of the shire. This last *appears* to have been appointed by the king. Their functions were to execute the decrees of the king, or ealdormen, to arrest prisoners, to require bail for their appearance at the sessions, to collect fines or penalties levied by the court of the shire, to preserve the public peace, *and to preside in a subordinate tribunal of their own.*" — *Dunham's Middle Ages*, sec. 2, B. 2, ch. 1. 57 *Lardner's Cab. Cyc.*, p. 41.

The confusion of *duties* attributed to these officers indicates clearly enough that different officers, bearing the same official names, must have had different duties, and have derived their authority from different sources, — to wit, the king, and the people.

* *Darrein presentment* was an inquest to discover who presented the last person to a church; *mort de ancestor,* whether the last possessor was seized of land in demesne of his own fee; and *novel disseisin,* whether the claimant had been unjustly disseized of his freehold.

could be changed, and the *thing* retained; and thus the prohibition be evaded. The prohibition applies (as will presently be seen) to all officers of the king whatsoever; and it sets up a distinction between officers *of the king*, ("*our* bailiffs,") and officers chosen by the people.

The prohibition upon the king's *justices* sitting in criminal trials, is included in the words "*vel alii balivi nostri*," (or other our bailiffs.) The word *bailiff* was anciently a sort of general name for *judicial officers* and persons employed in and about the administration of justice. In modern times its use, as applied to the higher grades of judicial officers, has been superseded by other words; and it therefore now, more generally, if not universally, signifies an executive or police officer, *a servant of courts*, rather than one whose functions are purely judicial.

The word is a French word, brought into England by the Normans.

Coke says, "*Baylife* is a French word, and signifies an officer concerned in the administration of justice of a certain province; and because a sheriff hath an office concerning the administration of justice within his county, or bailiwick, therefore he called his county *baliva sua*, (his bailiwick.)

"I have heard great question made what the true exposition of this word *balivus* is. In the statute of Magna Carta, cap. 28, the letter of that statute is, *nullus balivus de cætero ponat aliquem ad legem manifestam nec ad juramentum simplici loquela sua sine testibus fidelibus ad hoc inductis.*" (No bailiff from henceforth shall put any one to his open law, nor to an oath (of self-exculpation) upon his own simple accusation, or complaint, without faithful witnesses brought in for the same.) "And some have said that *balivus* in this statute signifieth *any judge;* for the law must be waged and made before the judge. And this statute (say they) extends to *the courts of common pleas, king's bench*, &c., for they must bring with them *fideles testes,* (faithful witnesses,) &c., *and so hath been the usage to this day.*" — 1 *Coke's Inst.*, 168 b.

Coke makes various references, in his margin to Bracton, Fleta, and other authorities, which I have not examined, but which, I presume, support the opinion expressed in this quotation.

Coke also, in another place, under the head of the chapter

just cited from Magna Carta, that "*no bailiff shall put any man to his open law,*" &c., gives the following commentary upon it, from the *Mirror of Justices,* from which it appears that in the time of Edward I., (1272 to 1307,) this word *balivus* was understood to include *all judicial,* as well as all other, officers of the king.

The Mirror says: "The point which forbiddeth that no *bailiff* put a freeman to his oath without suit, is to be understood in this manner, — *that no justice, no minister of the king,* nor other steward, nor bailiff, have power to make a freeman make oath, (of self-exculpation,) *without the king's command,** nor receive any plaint, without witnesses present who testify the plaint to be true." — *Mirror of Justices,* ch. 5, sec. 2, p. 257.

Coke quotes this commentary, (in the original French,) and then endorses it in these words:

"By this it appeareth, that under this word *balivus,* in this act, is comprehended *every justice, minister of the king,* steward, and bailiff." — *2 Inst.,* 44.

Coke also, in his commentary upon this very chapter of Magna Carta, that provides that "*no sheriff, constable, coroner, or other our bailiffs, shall hold pleas of our crown,*" expresses the opinion that it "*is a general law,*" (that is, applicable to all officers of the king,) "by reason of the words *vel alii balivi nostri,* (or other our bailiffs,) *under which words are comprehended all judges or justices of any courts of justice.*" And he cites a decision in the king's bench, in the 17th year of Edward I., (1289,) as authority; which decision he calls "a notable and leading judgment." — *2 Inst.,* 30—1.

And yet Coke, in flat contradiction of this decision, which he quotes with such emphasis and approbation, and in flat contradiction also of the definition he repeatedly gives of the word *balivus,* showing that it embraced *all ministers of the king whatsoever,* whether high or low, judicial or executive, fabricates an entirely gratuitous interpretation of this chapter

---

* He has no power to do it, *either with, or without, the king's command.* The prohibition is absolute, containing no such qualification as is here interpolated, viz., "*without the king's command.*" If it could be done *with* the king's command, the king would be invested with arbitrary power in the matter.

of Magna Carta, and pretends that after all it only required that *felonies* should be tried before the king's *justices, on account of their superior learning;* and that it permitted all lesser offences to be tried before inferior officers, (meaning of course the *king's* inferior officers.) — 2 *Inst.*, 30.

And thus this chapter of Magna Carta, which, according to his own definition of the word *balivus*, applies to all officers of the king; and which, according to the common and true definition of the term "pleas of the crown," applies to all criminal cases without distinction, and which, therefore, forbids any officer or minister of the king to preside in a jury trial in any criminal case whatsoever, he coolly and gratuitously interprets into a mere senseless provision for simply restricting the discretion of the king in giving *names* to his own officers who should preside at the trials of particular offences; as if the king, who made and unmade all his officers by a word, could not defeat the whole object of the prohibition, by appointing such individuals as he pleased, to try such causes as he pleased, and calling them by such names as he pleased, *if he were but permitted to appoint and name such officers at all;* and as if it were of the least importance what *name* an officer bore, whom the king might appoint to a particular duty.*

---

* The absurdity of this doctrine of Coke is made more apparent by the fact that, at that time, the "justices" and other persons appointed by the king to hold courts were not only dependent upon the king for their offices, and removable at his pleasure, *but that the usual custom was, not to appoint them with any view to permanency, but only to give them special commissions for trying a single cause, or for holding a single term of a court, or for making a single circuit;* which, being done, their commissions expired. The king, therefore, could, *and undoubtedly did, appoint any individual he pleased, to try any cause he pleased, with a special view to the verdicts he desired to obtain in the particular cases.*

This custom of commissioning particular persons to hold jury trials, in *criminal* cases, (and probably also in *civil* ones,) was of course a usurpation upon the common law, but had been practised more or less from the time of William the Conqueror. Palgrave says:

"The frequent absence of William from his insular dominions occasioned another mode of administration, *which ultimately produced still greater changes in the law.* It was the practice of appointing justiciars to represent the king's person, to hold his court, to decide his pleas, to dispense justice on his behalf, to command the military levies, and to act as conservators of the peace in the king's name.* . . The justices who were

* In this extract, Palgrave seems to assume that the king himself had a right to sit as judge, in *jury* trials, in the *county* courts, in both civil and criminal cases. I apprehend he had no such power at the *common law*, but only to sit in the trial of appeals, and in the trial of peers, and of civil suits in which peers were parties, and possibly in the courts of ancient demesne.

Coke evidently gives this interpretation solely because, as he was giving a general commentary on Magna Carta, he was bound to give some interpretation or other to every chapter of it; and for this chapter he could invent, or fabricate, (for it is

---

assigned in the name of the sovereign, and whose powers were revocable at his pleasure, derived their authority merely from their grant. . . Some of those judges were usually deputed for the purpose of relieving the king from the burden of his judicial functions. . . The number as well as the variety of names of the justices appearing in the early chirographs of 'Concords,' leave reason for doubting whether, anterior to the reign of Henry III., (1216 to 1272,) *a court, whose members were changing at almost every session, can be said to have been permanently constituted. It seems more probable that the individuals who composed the tribunal were selected as suited the pleasure of the sovereign, and the convenience of the clerks and barons;* and the history of our legal administration will be much simplified, if we consider all those courts which were afterwards denominated the Exchequer, the King's Bench, the Common Pleas, and the Chancery, *as being originally committees, selected by the king when occasion required,* out of a large body, for the despatch of peculiar branches of business, *and which committees, by degrees, assumed an independent and permanent existence.* . . Justices itinerant, who, despatched throughout the land, decided the 'Pleas of the Crown,' may be obscurely traced in the reign of the Conqueror; *not, perhaps, appointed with much regularity, but despatched upon peculiar occasions and emergencies.*" — 1 *Palgrave's Rise and Progress,* &c., p. 289 to 293.

The following statute, passed in 1354, (139 years after Magna Carta,) shows that even after this usurpation of appointing "justices" of his own, to try criminal cases, had probably become somewhat established in practice, in defiance of Magna Carta, the king was in the habit of granting special commissions to still other persons, (especially to sheriffs, — *his* sheriffs, no doubt,) to try particular cases :

"Because that the people of the realm have suffered many evils and mischiefs, for that sheriffs of divers counties, by virtue of commissions and general writs granted to them at their own suit, for their singular profit to gain of the people, have made and taken divers inquests to cause to indict the people at their will, and have taken fine and ransom of them to their own use, and have delivered them; whereas such persons indicted were not brought before the king's justices to have their deliverance, it is accorded and established, for to eschew all such evils and mischiefs, that such commissions and writs before this time made shall be utterly repealed, and that from henceforth no such commissions shall be granted." — *St.* 28 *Edward III.,* ch. 9, (1354.)

How silly to suppose that the illegality of these commissions to try criminal cases, could have been avoided by simply granting them to persons under the title of "*justices,*" instead of granting them to "*sheriffs.*" The statute was evidently a cheat, or at least designed as such, inasmuch as it virtually asserts the right of the king to appoint his tools, under the name of "justices," to try criminal cases, while it *disavows* his right to appoint them under the name of "sheriffs."

Millar says : "When the king's bench came to have its usual residence at Westminster, the sovereign was induced to *grant special commissions, for trying particular crimes,* in such parts of the country as were found most convenient; and this practice was *gradually* modelled into a regular appointment of certain commissioners, empowered, at stated seasons, to perform circuits over the kingdom, and to hold courts in particular towns, for the trial of all sorts of crimes. These judges of the circuit, however, *never obtained an ordinary jurisdiction, but continued, on every occasion, to derive their authority from two special commissions :* that of *oyer and terminer,* by which they were appointed to hear and determine all treasons, felonies and misdemeanors, within certain districts ; and that of *gaol delivery,* by which they were directed to try every prisoner confined in the gaols of the several towns falling under their inspection." — *Millar's Hist. View of Eng. Gov.,* vol. 2, ch. 7, p. 282.

The following extract from Gilbert shows to what lengths of usurpation the kings

a sheer fabrication,) no interpretation better suited to his purpose than this. It seems never to have entered his mind, (or if it did, he intended that it should never enter the mind of anybody else,) that the object of the chapter could be to deprive the king of the power of putting his creatures into criminal courts, to pack, cheat, and browbeat juries, and thus maintain his authority by procuring the conviction of those who should transgress his laws, or incur his displeasure.

This example of Coke tends to show how utterly blind, or how utterly corrupt, English judges, (dependent upon the crown and the legislature), have been in regard to everything in Magna Carta, that went to secure the liberties of the people, or limit the power of the government.

Coke's interpretation of this chapter of Magna Carta is of a piece with his absurd and gratuitous interpretation of the words "*nec super eum ibimus, nec super eum mittemus*," which was pointed out in a former article, and by which he attempted to give a *judicial* power to the king and his judges, where Magna Carta had given it only to a jury. It is also of a piece with his pretence that there was a difference between

---

would sometimes go, in their attempts to get the judicial power out of the hands of the people, and entrust it to instruments of their own choosing :

"From the time of the *Saxons*," (that is, from the commencement of the reign of William the Conqueror,) "till the reign of Edward the first, (1272 to 1307,) the several county courts and sheriffs courts did decline in their interest and authority. The methods by which they were broken were two-fold. *First, by granting commissions to the sheriffs by writ of* JUSTICIES, *whereby the sheriff had a particular jurisdiction granted him to be judge of a particular cause, independent of the suitors of the county court*," (that is, *without a jury;*) "*and these commissions were after the Norman form, by which (according to which) all power of judicature was immediately derived from the king.*"—*Gilbert on the Court of Chancery*, p. 1.

The several authorities now given show that it was the custom of the *Norman* kings, not only to appoint persons to sit as judges in jury trials, in criminal cases, but that they also commissioned individuals to sit in singular and particular cases, as occasion required ; and that they therefore readily *could*, and naturally *would*, and therefore undoubtedly *did*, commission individuals with a special view to their adaptation or capacity to procure such judgments as the kings desired.

The extract from Gilbert suggests also the usurpation of the *Norman* kings, in their assumption that *they*, (and *not the people*, as by the *common law*,) were the fountains of justice. It was only by virtue of this illegal assumption that they could claim to appoint their tools to hold courts.

All these things show how perfectly lawless and arbitrary the kings were both before and after Magna Carta, and how necessary to liberty was the principle of Magna Carta and the common law, that no person appointed by the king should hold jury trials in criminal cases.

fine and *amercement*, and that *fines* might be imposed by the king, and that juries were required only for fixing *amercements*.

These are some of the innumerable frauds by which the English people have been cheated out of the trial by jury.

Ex uno disce omnes. From one judge learn the characters of all.*

I give in the note additional and abundant authorities for

---

* The opinions and decisions of judges and courts are undeserving of the least reliance, (beyond the intrinsic merit of the arguments offered to sustain them,) and are unworthy even to be quoted as evidence of the law, *when those opinions or decisions are favorable to the power of the government, or unfavorable to the liberties of the people.* The only reasons that their opinions, *when in favor of liberty*, are entitled to any confidence, are, first, that all presumptions of law are in favor of liberty; and, second, that the admissions of all men, the innocent and the criminal alike, *when made against their own interests*, are entitled to be received as true, because it is contrary to human nature for a man to confess anything but truth against himself.

More solemn farces, or more gross impostures, were never practised upon mankind, than are all, or very nearly all, those oracular responses by which courts assume to determine that certain statutes, in restraint of individual liberty, are within the constitutional power of the government, and are therefore valid and binding upon the people.

The reason why these courts are so intensely servile and corrupt, is, that they are not only parts of, but the veriest creatures of, the very governments whose oppressions they are thus seeking to uphold. They receive their offices and salaries from, and are impeachable and removable by, the very governments upon whose acts they affect to sit in judgment. Of course, no one with his eyes open ever places himself in a position so incompatible with the liberty of declaring his honest opinion, unless he do it with the intention of becoming a mere instrument in the hands of the government for the execution of all its oppressions.

As proof of this, look at the judicial history of England for the last five hundred years, and of America from its settlement. In all that time (so far as I know, or presume) no bench of judges, (probably not even any single judge,) dependent upon the legislature that passed the statute, has ever declared a single *penal* statute invalid, on account of its being in conflict either with the common law, which the judges in England have been sworn to preserve, or with the written constitutions, (recognizing men's natural rights,) which the American judges were under oath to maintain. Every oppression, every atrocity even, that has ever been enacted in either country, by the legislative power, in the shape of a criminal law, (or, indeed, in almost any other shape,) has been as sure of a sanction from the judiciary that was dependent upon, and impeachable by, the legislature that enacted the law, as if there were a physical necessity that the legislative enactment and the judicial sanction should go together. Practically speaking, the sum of their decisions, all and singular, has been, that there are no limits to the power of the government, and that the people have no rights except what the government pleases to allow to them.

It is extreme folly for a people to allow such dependent, servile, and perjured creatures to sit either in civil or criminal trials; but to allow them to sit in criminal trials, and judge of the people's liberties, is not merely fatuity, — it is suicide.

the meaning ascribed to the word *bailiff*. The importance of the principle involved will be a sufficient excuse for such an accumulation of authorities as would otherwise be tedious and perhaps unnecessary.*

The foregoing interpretation of the chapter of Magna Carta now under discussion, is corroborated by another chapter of

---

* Coke, speaking of the word *bailiffs*, as used in the statute of 1 *Westminster*, ch. 35, (1275,) says:

"Here *bailiffs* are taken for the *judges of the court*, as manifestly appeareth hereby." — 2 *Inst.*, 229.

Coke also says, "It is a maxim in law, *aliquis non debet esse judex in propria causa*, (no one ought to be judge in his own cause;) and therefore a fine levied before the *baylifes* of *Salop* was reversed, because one of the *baylifes* was party to the fine, *quia non potest esse judex et pars*," (because one cannot be *judge* and party.) — 1 *Inst.*, 141 a.

In the statute of Gloucester, ch. 11 and 12, (1278,) "the mayor and *bailiffs* of London (undoubtedly chosen by the people, or at any rate not appointed by the king) are manifestly spoken of as *judges*, or magistrates, holding *jury* trials, as follows:

Ch. II. "It is provided, also, that if any man lease his tenement in the city of London, for a term of years, and he to whom the freehold belongeth causeth himself to be impleaded by collusion, and maketh default after default, or cometh into court and giveth it up, for to make the termor (lessee) lose his term, (lease,) and the demandant hath his suit, so that the termor may recover by writ of covenant; *the mayor and bailiffs may inquire by a good inquest,* (*jury,*) in the presence of the termor and the demandant, whether the demandant moved his plea upon good right that he had, or by collusion, or fraud, to make the termor lose his term; and if it be found by the inquest (jury) that the demandant moved his plea upon good right that he had, the judgment shall be given forthwith; and if it be found by the inquest (jury) that he impleaded him (self) by fraud, to put the termor from his term, then shall the termor enjoy his term, and the execution of judgment for the demandant shall be suspended until the term be expired." — 6 *Edward I.*, ch. 11, (1278.)

Coke, in his commentary on this chapter, calls this court of "the mayor and *bailiffs*" of London, "*the court of the hustings, the greatest and highest court in London;*" and adds, "other cities have the like court, and so called, as York, Lincoln, Winchester, &c. Here the city of London is named; but it appeareth by that which hath been said out of Fleta, that this act extends to such cities and boroughs privileged, — that is, such as have such privilege to hold plea as London hath." — 2 *Inst.*, 322.

The 12th chapter of the same statute is in the following words, which plainly recognize the fact that "the mayor and *bailiffs* of London" are *judicial* officers holding courts in London.

"It is provided, also, that if a man, impleaded for a tenement in the same city, (London,) doth vouch a foreigner to warranty, that he shall come into the chancery, and have a writ to summon his warrantor at a certain day before the justices of the bench, *and another writ to the mayor and bailiffs of London, that they shall surcease* (suspend proceedings) *in the matter that is before them by writ,* until the plea of the warrantee be determined before the justices of the bench; and when the plea at the bench shall be determined, then shall he that is vouched be commanded to go into the city," (that is, before "the mayor and *bailiffs'*" court,) "to answer unto the chief plea; and a writ shall be awarded at the suit of the demandant by the justices *unto the mayor and bailiffs, that they shall proceed in the plea,*" &c. — 6 *Edward I.*, ch. 12, (1278.)

Coke, in his commentary on this chapter, also speaks repeatedly of "the mayor and *bailiffs*" *as judges holding courts;* and also speaks of this chapter as applicable not only to "the citie of London, specially named for the cause aforesaid, but extended by equity to all other privileged places," (that is, privileged to have a court of "mayor and bail-

Magna Carta, which specially provides that the king's justices shall "go through every county" to "take the assizes" (hold jury trials) in three kinds of *civil* actions, to wit, "novel disseisin, mort de ancestor, and darrein presentment;" but makes no mention whatever of their holding jury trials in *criminal* cases, — an omission wholly unlikely to be made, if it were

---

iffs,") "where foreign voucher is made, as to Chester, Durham, Salop," &c. — 2 *Inst.*, 325-7.

BAILIE. — In Scotch law, a municipal magistrate, corresponding with the English *alderman.** — *Burrill's Law Dictionary.*

BAILIFFE. — *Baillif.* Fr. A bailiff: a ministerial officer with duties similar to those of a sheriff. . . *The judge of a court.* A municipal magistrate, &c. — *Burrill's Law Dict.*

BAILIFF. . . The word *bailiff* is of Norman origin, and was applied in England, at an early period, (after the example, it is said, of the French,) to the chief magistrates of counties, or shires, such as the alderman, the reeve, or sheriff, and also of inferior jurisdictions, such as hundreds and wapentakes. — *Spelman, voc. Balivus;* 1 *Bl. Com.*, 344. *See Bailli, Ballivus.* The Latin *ballivus* occurs, indeed, in the laws of Edward the Confessor, but Spelman thinks it was introduced by a later hand. *Balliva* (bailiwick) was the word formed from *ballivus*, to denote the extent of territory comprised within a bailiff's jurisdiction; and *bailiwick* is still retained in writs and other proceedings, as the name of a sheriff's county. — 1 *Bl. Com.*, 344. *See Balliva. The office of bailiff was at first strictly, though not exclusively, a judicial one.* In France, the word had the sense of what Spelman calls *justitia tutelaris. Ballivus* occurs frequently in the *Regiam Majestatem*, in the sense of a *judge.* — *Spelman.* In its sense of a *deputy*, it was formerly applied, in England, to those officers who, by virtue of a deputation, either from the sheriff or the lords of private jurisdictions, exercised within the hundred, or whatever might be the limits of their bailiwick, certain *judicial* and ministerial functions. With the disuse of private and local jurisdictions, the meaning of the term became commonly restricted to such persons as were deputed by the sheriff to assist him in the merely ministerial portion of his duty; such as the summoning of juries, and the execution of writs. — *Brande.* . . The word *bailiff* is also applied in England to the chief magistrates of certain towns and jurisdictions, to the keepers of castles, forests and other places, and to the stewards or agents of lords of manors. — *Burrill's Law Dict.*

"BAILIFF, (from the Lat. *ballivus*; Fr. *baillif*, i. e., *Præfectus provinciæ*,) signifies an officer appointed for the administration of justice within a certain district. The office, as well as the name, appears to have been derived from the French," &c. — *Brewster's Encyclopedia.*

Millar says, "The French monarchs, about this period, were not content with the power of receiving appeals from the several courts of their barons. An expedient was devised of sending royal *bailiffs* into different parts of the kingdom, with a commission to take cognizance of all those causes in which the sovereign was interested, and in reality for the purpose of abridging and limiting the subordinate jurisdiction of the

---

* *Alderman* was a title anciently given to various *judicial* officers, as the Alderman of all England, Alderman of the King, Alderman of the County, Alderman of the City or Borough, alderman of the Hundred or Wapentake. These were all *judicial* officers. See Law Dictionaries.

ILLEGAL JUDGES. 167

designed they should attend the trial of such causes. Besides, the chapter here spoken of (in John's charter) does not allow these justices to sit *alone* in jury trials, even in *civil* actions; but provides that four knights, chosen by the county, shall sit

---

neighboring feudal superiors. By an edict of Phillip Augustus, in the year 1190, those *bailiffs* were appointed in all the principal towns of the kingdom." — *Millar's Hist. View of the Eng. Gov.*, vol. ii., ch. 3, p. 126.

"BAILIFF-*office*. — Magistrates who formerly administered justice in the parliaments or courts of France, answering to the English sheriffs, as mentioned by Bracton." — *Bouvier's Law Dict.*

"There be several officers called *bailiffs*, whose offices and employments seem quite different from each other. . . The chief magistrate, in divers ancient corporations, are called *bailiffs*, as in Ipswich, Yarmouth, Colchester, &c. There are, likewise, officers of the forest, who are termed bailiffs." — 1 *Bacon's Abridgment*, 498-9.

"BAILIFF signifies a keeper or superintendent, and is directly derived from the French word *bailli*, which appears to come from the word *balivus*, and that from *bagalus*, a Latin word signifying generally a governor, tutor, or superintendent. . . The French word *bailli* is thus explained by Richelet, (*Dictionaire*, &c.:) *Bailli*. — *He who in a province has the superintendence of justice, who is the ordinary judge of the nobles,* who is their head for the *ban* and *arriere ban*,* and who maintains the right and property of others against those who attack them. . . All the various officers who are called by this name, though differing as to the nature of their employments, seem to have some kind of superintendence intrusted to them by their superior." — *Political Dictionary.*

"BAILIFF, *balivus*. From the French word *bayliff*, that is, *præfectus provinciæ*, and as the name, so the office itself was answerable to that of France, where there were eight parliaments, which were high courts from whence there lay no appeal, and within the precincts of the several parts of that kingdom which belonged to each parliament, *there were several provinces to which justice was administered by certain officers called bailiffs;* and in England we have several counties in which justice hath been, and still is, in small suits, administered to the inhabitants by the officer whom we now call *sheriff*, or *viscount;* (one of which names descends from the Saxons, the other from the Normans.) And, though the sheriff is not called *bailiff*, yet it was probable that was one of his names also, because the county is often called *balliva;* as in the return of a writ, where the person is not arrested, the sheriff saith, *infra-nominatus, A. B. non est inventus in balliva mea*, &c.; (the within named A. B. is not found in my bailiwick, &c.) And in the statute of Magna Carta, ch. 28, and 14 Ed. 3, ch. 9, the word *bailiff* seems to comprise as well sheriffs, as bailiffs of hundreds.

"*Bailies*, in Scotland, are magistrates of burghs, possessed of certain jurisdictions, having the same power within their territory as sheriffs in the county. . .

"As England is divided into counties, so every county is divided into hundreds; within which, in ancient times, the people had justice administered to them by the several officers of every hundred, which were the *bailiffs*. And it appears by Bracton, (*lib.* 3, *tract.* 2, ch. 34,) that *bailiffs* of hundreds might anciently hold plea of appeal and approvers; but since that time the hundred courts, except certain franchises, are swallowed in the county courts; and now the *bailiff's* name and office is grown into contempt, they being

* "*Ban* and *arriere ban*, a proclamation, whereby all that hold lands of the crown, (except some privileged officers and citizens,) are summoned to meet at a certain place in order to serve the king in his wars, either personally, or by proxy." — *Boyer.*

with them to keep them honest. When the king's justices were known to be so corrupt and servile that the people would not even trust them to sit alone, in jury trials, in *civil* actions,

---

generally officers to serve writs, &c., within their liberties; though, in other respects, the name is still in good esteem, for the chief magistrates in divers towns are called *bailiffs;* and sometimes the persons to whom the king's castles are committed are termed *bailiffs*, as the *bailiff* of Dover Castle, &c.

" Of the ordinary *bailiffs* there are several sorts, viz., *bailiffs* of liberties; sheriffs' *bailiffs; bailiffs* of lords of manors; *bailiffs* of husbandry, &c. . .

" *Bailiffs* of liberties or franchises are to be sworn to take distresses, *truly impanel jurors*, make returns by indenture between them and sheriffs, &c. . .

" *Bailiffs of courts baron* summon those courts, and execute the process thereof. . .

" Besides these, there are also *bailiffs of the forest*. . . " — *Jacob's Law Dict. Tomlin's do.*

" BAILIWICK, *balliva*, — is not only taken for the county, but signifies generally that liberty which is exempted from the sheriff of the county, over which the lord of the liberty appointeth a *bailiff*, with such powers within his precinct as an under-sheriff exerciseth under the sheriff of the county; such as the *bailiff* of Westminster." — *Jacob's Law Dict. Tomlin's do.*

"*A bailiff of a Leet, Court-baron, Manor, Balivus Letæ, Baronis, Manerii.* — He is one that is appointed by the lord, or his steward, within every manor, to do such offices as appertain thereunto, as to summon the court, warn the tenants and resiants; also, to summon the Leet and Homage, levy fines, and make distresses, &c., of which you may read at large in *Kitchen's Court-leet and Court-baron.*" — *A Law Dictionary, anonymous,* (in Suffolk Law Library.)

" BAILIFF. — In England an officer appointed by the sheriff. Bailiffs are either special, and appointed, for their adroitness, to arrest persons; or bailiffs of hundreds, who collect fines, summon juries, attend the assizes, and execute writs and processes. *The sheriff in England is the king's bailiff.* . .

" *The office of bailiff formerly was high and honorable in England, and officers under that title on the continent are still invested with important functions.*" — *Webster.*

" BAILLI, (Scotland.) — An alderman; a magistrate who is second in rank in a royal burgh." — *Worcester.*

" *Baili, or Bailiff.* — (Sorte d'officier de justice.) A bailiff; a sort of magistrate." — *Boyer's French Dict.*

" By some opinions, a *bailiff*, in Magna Carta, ch. 28, signifies *any judge.*" — *Cunningham's Law Dict.*

" BAILIFF. — In the court of the Greek emperors there was a grand *bajulos*, first tutor of the emperor's children. The superintendent of foreign merchants seems also to have been called *bajulos;* and, as he was appointed by the Venetians, this title (balio) was transferred to the Venetian ambassador. From Greece, the official *bajulos* (*ballivus, bailli,* in France; *bailiff,* in England,) was introduced into the south of Europe, and denoted a superintendent; hence the eight *ballivi* of the knights of St. John, which constitute its supreme council. In France, the royal bailiffs were commanders of the militia, administrators or stewards of the domains, *and judges of their districts.* In the course of time, only the first duty remained to the bailiff; hence he was *bailli d'épée,* and laws were administered in his name by a lawyer, as his deputy, lieutenant de robe. The seigniories, with which high courts were connected, employed bailiffs, who thus consti-

how preposterous is it to suppose that they would not only suffer them to sit, but to sit alone, in *criminal* ones.

It is entirely incredible that Magna Carta, which makes such careful provision in regard to the king's justices sitting in *civil* actions, should make no provision whatever as to their sitting in *criminal* trials, if they were to be allowed to sit in them at all. Yet Magna Carta has no provision whatever on the subject.*

---

tuted, almost everywhere, *the lowest order of judges.* From the courts of the nobility, the appellation passed to the royal courts; from thence to the parliaments. In the greater bailiwicks of cities of importance, Henry II. established a collegial constitution under the name of *presidial courts.* . . *The name of bailiff was introduced into England with William I.* The counties were also called *bailiwicks,* (*ballivæ,*) while the subdivisions were called *hundreds;* but, as the courts of the hundreds have long since ceased, the English bailiffs are only a kind of subordinate officers of justice, like the French *huissiers.* These correspond very nearly to the officers called *constables* in the United States. Every sheriff has some of them under him, for whom he is answerable. In some cities the highest municipal officer yet bears this name, as the high bailiff of Westminster. In London, the Lord Mayor is at the same time bailiff, (which title he bore before the present became usual,) *and administers, in this quality, the criminal jurisdiction of the city, in the court of old Bailey,* where there are, annually, eight sittings of the court, for the city of London and the county of Middlesex. *Usually, the recorder of London supplies his place as judge.* In some instances the term *bailiff*, in England, is applied to the chief magistrates of towns, or to the commanders of particular castles, as that of Dover. The term *baillie,* in Scotland, is applied to a judicial police-officer, having powers very similar to those of justices of peace in the United States." — *Encyclopædia Americana.*

* Perhaps it may be said (and such, it has already been seen, is the opinion of Coke and others) that the chapter of Magna Carta, that "no *bailiff* from henceforth shall put any man to his open law, (put him on trial,) nor to an oath (that is, an oath of self-exculpation) upon his (the bailiff's) own accusation or testimony, without credible witnesses brought in to prove the charge," *is itself* a " provision in regard to the king's justices sitting in criminal trials," and therefore implies that they *are to sit* in such trials.

But, although the word *bailiff* includes all *judicial,* as well as other, officers, and would therefore in this case apply to the king's justices, *if* they were to sit in criminal trials; yet this particular chapter of Magna Carta evidently does not contemplate " *bailiffs* " while acting in their *judicial* capacity, (for they were not allowed to sit in criminal trials at all,) but only in the character of *witnesses;* and that the meaning of the chapter is, that the simple testimony (simplici loquela) of "no bailiff," (of whatever kind,) unsupported by other and " credible witnesses," shall be sufficient to put any man on trial, or to his oath of self-exculpation.*

It will be noticed that the words of this chapter are *not*, " no bailiff *of ours*," — that is, *of the king*, — as in some other chapters of Magna Carta; but simply " no bailiff," &c. The prohibition, therefore, applies to all " bailiffs," — to those chosen by the peo-

* At the common law, parties, in both civil and criminal cases, were allowed to swear in their own behalf; and it will be so again, if the true trial by jury should be reëstablished.

But what would appear to make this matter absolutely certain is, that unless the prohibition that "no bailiff, &c., *of ours* shall hold pleas of our crown," apply to all officers of the king, justices as well as others, it would be wholly nugatory for any practical or useful purpose, because the prohibition could be evaded by the king, at any time, by simply changing the titles of his officers. Instead of calling them "sheriffs, coroners, constables and bailiffs," he could call them "*justices*," or anything else he pleased; and this prohibition, so important to the liberty of the people, would then be entirely defeated. The king also could make and unmake "justices" at his pleasure; and if he could appoint any officers whatever to preside over juries in criminal trials, he could appoint any tool that he might at any time find adapted to his purpose. It was as easy to make justices of Jeffreys and Scroggs, as of any other material; and to have prohibited all the king's officers, *except his justices*, from presiding in criminal trials, would therefore have been mere fool's play.

We can all perhaps form some idea, though few of us will be likely to form any adequate idea, of what a different thing

---

ple, as well as those appointed by the king. And the prohibition is obviously founded upon the idea (a very sound one in that age certainly, and probably also in this) that public officers (whether appointed by king or people) have generally, or at least frequently, too many interests and animosities against accused persons, to make it safe to convict any man on their testimony alone.

The idea of Coke and others, that the object of this chapter was simply to forbid *magistrates* to put a man on trial, when there were no witnesses against him, but only the simple accusation or testimony of the magistrates themselves, before whom he was to be tried, is preposterous; for that would be equivalent to supposing that magistrates acted in the triple character of judge, jury and witnesses, *in the same trial;* and that, therefore, *in such cases*, they needed to be prohibited from condemning a man on their own accusation or testimony alone. But such a provision would have been unnecessary and senseless, for two reasons; first, because the bailiffs or magistrates had no power to "hold pleas of the crown," still less to try or condemn a man; that power resting wholly with the juries; second, because if bailiffs or magistrates *could* try and condemn a man, without a jury, the prohibition upon their doing so upon their own accusation or testimony alone, would give no additional protection to the accused, so long as these same bailiffs or magistrates were allowed to decide what weight should be given, *both to their own testimony and that of other witnesses;* for, if they wished to convict, they would of course decide that *any* testimony, however frivolous or irrelevant, *in addition to their own*, was sufficient. Certainly a magistrate could always procure witnesses enough to testify to something or other, which *he himself* could decide to be corroborative of his own testimony. And thus the prohibition would be defeated in fact, though observed in form.

the trial by jury would have been *in practice*, and of what would have been the difference to the liberties of England, for five hundred years last past, had this prohibition of Magna Carta, upon the king's officers sitting in the trial of criminal cases, been observed.

The principle of this chapter of Magna Carta, as applicable to the governments of the United States of America, forbids that any officer appointed either by the executive or *legislative* power, or dependent upon them for their salaries, or responsible to them by impeachment, should preside over a jury in criminal trials. To have the trial a legal (that is, a *common law*) and true trial by jury, the presiding officers must be chosen by the people, and be entirely free from all dependence upon, and all accountability to, the executive and legislative branches of the government.*

---

* In this chapter I have called the justices "*presiding* officers," solely for the want of a better term. They are not "*presiding* officers," in the sense of having any authority over the jury; but are only assistants to, and teachers and servants of, the jury. The foreman of the jury is properly the "presiding officer," so far as there is such an officer at all. The sheriff has no authority except over other persons than the jury.

CHAPTER VIII.

THE FREE ADMINISTRATION OF JUSTICE.

The free administration of justice was a principle of the common law; and it must necessarily be a part of every system of government which is not designed to be an engine in the hands of the rich for the oppression of the poor.

In saying that the free administration of justice was a principle of the common law, I mean only that parties were subjected to no costs for jurors, witnesses, writs, or other necessaries for the trial, *preliminary to the trial itself.* Consequently, no one could lose the benefit of a trial, for the want of means to defray expenses. *But after the trial*, the plaintiff or defendant was liable to be amerced, (by the jury, of course,) for having troubled the court with the prosecution or defence of an unjust suit.* But it is not likely that the losing party was subjected to an amercement as a matter of course, but only in those cases where the injustice of his cause was so evident as to make him inexcusable in bringing it before the courts.

All the freeholders were required to attend the courts, that they might serve as jurors and witnesses, and do any other service that could legally be required of them; and their attendance was paid for by the state. In other words, their attendance and service at the courts were part of the rents which they paid the state for their lands.

The freeholders, who were thus required always to attend

---

* 2 *Sullivan Lectures*, 234–5. 3 *Blackstone*, 274–5, 376. Sullivan says that both plaintiffs and defendants were liable to amercement. Blackstone speaks of plaintiffs being liable, without saying whether defendants were so or not. What the rule really was I do not know. There would seem to be some reason in allowing defendants to defend themselves, *at their own charges*, without exposing themselves to amercement in case of failure.

the courts, were doubtless the only witnesses who were *usually* required in *civil* causes. This was owing to the fact that, in those days, when the people at large could neither write nor read, few contracts were put in writing. The expedient adopted for proving contracts, was that of making them in the presence of witnesses, who could afterwards testify to the transactions. Most contracts in regard to lands were made at the courts, in the presence of the freeholders there assembled.*

In the king's courts it was specially provided by Magna Carta that "justice and right" should not be "sold;" that is, that the king should take nothing from the parties for administering justice.

The oath of a party to the justice of his cause was all that was necessary to entitle him to the benefit of the courts free of all expense; (except the risk of being amerced after the trial, in case the jury should think he deserved it.†)

This principle of the free administration of justice connects itself necessarily with the trial by jury, because a jury could not rightfully give judgment against any man, in either a civil or criminal case, if they had any reason to suppose he had been unable to procure his witnesses.

The true trial by jury would also compel the free administration of justice from another necessity, viz., that of preventing private quarrels; because, unless the government enforced a man's rights and redressed his wrongs, *free of expense to him*, a jury would be bound to protect him in taking the law into his own hands. A man has a natural right to enforce his own rights and redress his own wrongs. If one man owe another a debt, and refuse to pay it, the creditor has a natural right to seize sufficient property of the debtor, wherever he

---

* When any other witnesses than freeholders were required in a civil suit, I am not aware of the manner in which their attendance was procured; but it was doubtless done at the expense either of the state or of the witnesses themselves. And it was doubtless the same in criminal cases.

† "All claims were established in the first stage by the oath of the plaintiff, except when otherwise specially directed by the law. The oath, by which any claim was supported, was called the fore-oath, or ' Præjuramentum,' and it was the foundation of his suit. One of the cases which did not require this initiatory confirmation, was when cattle could be tracked into another man's land, and then the foot-mark stood for the fore-oath." — 2 *Palgrave's Rise and Progress*, &c., 114.

can find it, to satisfy the debt. If one man commit a trespass upon the person, property or character of another, the injured party has a natural right, either to chastise the aggressor, or to take compensation for the injury out of his property. But as the government is an impartial party as between these individuals, it is more likely to do *exact* justice between them than the injured individual himself would do. The government, also, having more power at its command, is likely to right a man's wrongs more peacefully than the injured party himself could do it. If, therefore, the government will do the work of enforcing a man's rights, and redressing his wrongs, *promptly, and free of expense to him*, he is under a moral obligation to leave the work in the hands of the government; but not otherwise. When the government forbids him to enforce his own rights or redress his own wrongs, and deprives him of all means of obtaining justice, except on the condition of his employing the government to obtain it for him, *and of paying the government for doing it*, the government becomes itself the protector and accomplice of the wrong-doer. If the government will forbid a man to protect his own rights, it is bound to do it for him, *free of expense to him*. And so long as government refuses to do this, juries, if they knew their duties, would protect a man in defending his own rights.

Under the prevailing system, probably one half of the community are virtually deprived of all protection for their rights, except what the criminal law affords them. Courts of justice, for all civil suits, are as effectually shut against them, as though it were done by bolts and bars. Being forbidden to maintain their own rights by force, — as, for instance, to compel the payment of debts, — and being unable to pay the expenses of civil suits, they have no alternative but submission to many acts of injustice, against which the government is bound either to protect them, *free of expense*, or allow them to protect themselves.

There would be the same reason in compelling a party to pay the judge and jury for their services, that there is in compelling him to pay the witnesses, or any other *necessary* charges.*

---

* Among the necessary expenses of suits, should be reckoned reasonable compensation to counsel, for they are nearly or quite as important to the administration of justice,

THE FREE ADMINISTRATION OF JUSTICE. 175

This compelling parties to pay the expenses of civil suits is one of the many cases in which government is false to the fundamental principles on which free government is based. What is the object of government, but to protect men's rights? On what principle does a man pay his taxes to the government, except on that of contributing his proportion towards the necessary cost of protecting the rights of all? Yet, when his own rights are actually invaded, the government, which he contributes to support, instead of fulfilling its implied contract, becomes his enemy, and not only refuses to protect his rights, (except at his own cost,) but even forbids him to do it himself.

All free government is founded on the theory of voluntary association; and on the theory that all the parties to it *voluntarily* pay their taxes for its support, on the condition of receiving protection in return. But the idea that any *poor* man would voluntarily pay taxes to build up a government, which will neither protect his rights, (except at a cost which he cannot meet,) nor suffer himself to protect them by such means as may be in his power, is absurd.

Under the prevailing system, a large portion of the lawsuits determined in courts, are mere contests of purses rather than of rights. And a jury, sworn to decide causes "according to the evidence" produced, are quite likely, *for aught they themselves can know*, to be deciding merely the comparative length of the parties' purses, rather than the intrinsic strength of their respective rights. Jurors ought to refuse to decide a cause at all, except upon the assurance that all the evidence, necessary

---

as are judges, jurors, or witnesses; and the universal practice of employing them, both on the part of governments and of private persons, shows that their importance is generally understood. As a mere matter of economy, too, it would be wise for the government to pay them, rather than they should not be employed; because they collect and arrange the testimony and the law beforehand, so as to be able to present the whole case to the court and jury intelligibly, and in a short space of time. Whereas, if they were not employed, the court and jury would be under the necessity either of spending much more time than now in the investigation of causes, or of despatching them in haste, and with little regard to justice. They would be very likely to do the latter, thus defeating the whole object of the people in establishing courts.

To prevent the abuse of this right, it should perhaps be left discretionary with the jury in each case to determine whether the counsel should receive any pay — and, if any, how much — from the government.

to a full knowledge of the cause, is produced. This assurance they can seldom have, unless the government itself produces all the witnesses the parties desire.

In criminal cases, the atrocity of accusing a man of crime, and then condemning him unless he prove his innocence at his own charges, is so evident that a jury could rarely, if ever, be justified in convicting a man under such circumstances.

But the free administration of justice is not only indispensable to the maintenance of right between man and man; it would also promote simplicity and stability in the laws. The mania for legislation would be, in an important degree, restrained, if the government were compelled to pay the expenses of all the suits that grew out of it.

The free administration of justice would diminish and nearly extinguish another great evil, — that of malicious *civil* suits. It is an old saying, that "*multi litigant in foro, non ut aliquid lucrentur, sed ut vexant alios.*" (Many litigate in court, not that they may gain anything, but that they may harass others.) Many men, from motives of revenge and oppression, are willing to spend their own money in prosecuting a groundless suit, if they can thereby compel their victims, who are less able than themselves to bear the loss, to spend money in the defence. Under the prevailing system, in which the parties pay the expenses of their suits, nothing but money is necessary to enable any malicious man to commence and prosecute a groundless suit, to the terror, injury, and perhaps ruin, of another man. In this way, a court of justice, into which none but a conscientious *plaintiff* certainly should ever be allowed to enter, becomes an arena into which any rich and revengeful oppressor may drag any man poorer than himself, and harass, terrify, and impoverish him, to almost any extent. It is a scandal and an outrage, that government should suffer itself to be made an instrument, in this way, for the gratification of private malice. We might nearly as well have no courts of justice, as to throw them open, as we do, for such flagitious uses. Yet the evil probably admits of no remedy except a free administration of justice. Under a free system, plaintiffs could rarely be influenced by motives of this kind; because they could put their victim to little or no expense, *neither pending the suit*, (which it is the object of the oppressor to do,) nor at its termination. Besides, if the ancient common law practice should be adopted, of amercing a party for troubling the courts with groundless suits, the prosecutor himself would, in the end, be likely to be amerced by the jury, in such a manner as to make courts of justice a very unprofitable place for a man to go to seek revenge.

In estimating the evils of this kind, resulting from the present system, we are to consider that they are not, by any means, confined to the actual suits in which this kind of oppression is practised; but we are to include all those cases in which the fear of such oppression is used as a weapon to compel men into a surrender of their rights.

CHAPTER IX.

THE CRIMINAL INTENT.

It is a maxim of the common law that there can be no crime without a criminal intent. And it is a perfectly clear principle, although one which judges have in a great measure overthrown in practice, that *jurors* are to judge of the moral intent of an accused person, and hold him guiltless, whatever his act, unless they find him to have acted with a criminal intent; that is, with a design to do what he knew to be criminal.

This principle is clear, because the question for a jury to determine is, whether the accused be *guilty*, or *not guilty*. *Guilt* is a personal quality of the actor, — not *necessarily* involved in the act, but depending also upon the intent or motive with which the act was done. Consequently, the jury must find that he acted from a criminal motive, before they can declare him *guilty*.

There is no moral justice in, nor any political necessity for, punishing a man for any act whatever that he may have committed, if he have done it without any criminal intent. There can be no *moral justice* in punishing for such an act, because, there having been no *criminal motive*, there can have been no other motive which justice can take cognizance of, as demanding or justifying punishment. There can be no *political necessity* for punishing, to warn against similar acts in future, because, if one man have injured another, however unintentionally, he is liable, and justly liable, to a *civil* suit for damages; and in this suit he will be compelled to make compensation for the injury, notwithstanding his innocence of any intention to injure. He must bear the consequences of his own act, instead of throwing them upon another, however innocent he may have been of any intention to do wrong. And the damages he will have to pay will be a sufficient warning to him not to do the like act again.

If it be alleged that there are crimes against the public, (as treason, for example, or any other resistance to government,) for which private persons can recover no damages, and that there is a political necessity for punishing for such offences, even though the party acted conscientiously, the answer is, — the government must bear with all resistance that is not so clearly wrong as to give evidence of criminal intent. In other words, the government, in all its acts, must keep itself so *clearly* within the limits of justice, as that twelve men, taken at random, will all agree that it is in the right, or it must incur the risk of resistance, without any power to punish it. This is the mode in which the trial by jury operates to prevent the government from falling into the hands of a party, or a faction, and to keep it within such limits as *all*, or substantially *all*, the people are agreed that it may occupy.

This necessity for a criminal intent, to justify conviction, is proved by the issue which the jury are to try, and the verdict they are to pronounce. The "issue" they are to try is, "*guilty*," or "*not guilty.*" And those are the terms they are required to use in rendering their verdicts. But it is a plain falsehood to say that a man is "*guilty*," unless he have done an act which he knew to be criminal.

This necessity for a criminal intent — in other words, for *guilt* — as a preliminary to conviction, makes it impossible that a man can be rightfully convicted for an act that is intrinsically innocent, though forbidden by the government; because guilt is an intrinsic quality of actions and motives, and not one that can be imparted to them by arbitrary legislation. All the efforts of the government, therefore, to "*make offences by statute*," out of acts that are not criminal by nature, must necessarily be ineffectual, unless a jury will declare a man "*guilty*" for an act that is really innocent.

The corruption of judges, in their attempts to uphold the arbitrary authority of the government, by procuring the conviction of individuals for acts innocent in themselves, and forbidden only by some tyrannical statute, and the commission of which therefore indicates no criminal intent, is very apparent.

To accomplish this object, they have in modern times held it to be unnecessary that indictments should charge, as by the common law they were required to do, that an act was done "*wickedly*," "*feloniously*," "*with malice aforethought*," or in any other manner that implied a criminal intent, without which there can be no criminality; but that it is sufficient to charge simply that it was done "*contrary to the form of the statute in such case made and provided.*" This form of indictment proceeds plainly upon the assumption that the government is absolute, and that it has authority to prohibit any act it pleases, however innocent in its nature the act may be. Judges have been driven to the alternative of either sanctioning this new form of indictment, (which they never had any constitutional right to sanction,) or of seeing the authority of many of the statutes of the government fall to the ground; because the acts forbidden by the statutes were so plainly innocent in their nature, that even the government itself had not the face to allege that the commission of them implied or indicated any criminal intent.

To get rid of the necessity of showing a criminal intent, and thereby further to enslave the people, by reducing them to the necessity of a blind, unreasoning submission to the arbitrary will of the government, and of a surrender of all right, on their own part, to judge what are their constitutional and natural rights and liberties, courts have invented another idea, which they have incorporated among the pretended *maxims*, upon which they act in criminal trials, viz., that "*ignorance of the law excuses no one.*" As if it were in the nature of things possible that there could be an excuse more absolute and complete. What else than ignorance of the law is it that excuses persons under the years of discretion, and men of imbecile minds? What else than ignorance of the law is it that excuses judges themselves for all their erroneous decisions? Nothing. They are every day committing errors, which would be crimes, but for their ignorance of the law. And yet these same judges, who claim to be *learned* in the law, and who yet could not hold their offices for a day, but for the allowance which the law makes for their ignorance, are continually asserting it to be a "maxim" that "ignorance of the law excuses no one;" (by which, of course, they really mean that it excuses no one but themselves; and especially that it excuses no *unlearned* man, who comes before them charged with crime)

This preposterous doctrine, that "ignorance of the law excuses no one," is asserted by courts because it is an indispensable one to the maintenance of absolute power in the government. It is indispensable for this purpose, because, if it be once admitted that the people *have* any rights and liberties which the government cannot lawfully take from them, then the question arises in regard to every statute of the government, whether it be law, or not; that is, whether it infringe, or not, the rights and liberties of the people. Of this question every man must of course judge according to the light in his own mind. And no man can be convicted unless the jury find, not only that the statute is *law*, — that it does *not* infringe the rights and liberties of the people, — but also that it was so clearly law, so clearly consistent with the rights and liberties of the people, as that the individual himself, who transgressed it, *knew it to be so*, and therefore had no moral excuse for transgressing it. Governments see that if ignorance of the law were allowed to excuse a man for any act whatever, it must excuse him for transgressing all statutes whatsoever, which he himself thinks inconsistent with his rights and liberties. But such a doctrine would of course be inconsistent with the maintenance of arbitrary power by the government; and hence governments will not allow the plea, although they will not confess their true reasons for disallowing it.

The only reasons, (if they deserve the name of reasons), that I ever knew given for the doctrine that ignorance of the law excuses no one, are these:

1. "The reason for the maxim is that of necessity. It prevails, 'not that all men know the law, but because it is an excuse which every man will make, and no man can tell how to confute him.'— *Selden*, (as quoted in the 2d edition of *Starkie on Slander*, Prelim. Disc., p. 140, note.)" — *Law Magazine*, (*London*,) vol. 27, p. 97.

This reason impliedly admits that ignorance of the law is, *intrinsically*, an ample and sufficient excuse for a crime; and that the excuse ought to be allowed, if the fact of ignorance could but be ascertained. But it asserts that this fact is incapable of being ascertained, and that therefore there is a necessity for punishing the ignorant and the knowing — that is, the innocent and the guilty — without discrimination.

This reason is worthy of the doctrine it is used to uphold; as if a plea of ignorance, any more than any other plea, must necessarily be believed simply because it is urged; and as if it were not a common and every-day practice of courts and juries, in both civil and criminal cases, to determine the mental capacity of individuals; as, for example, to determine whether they are of sufficient mental capacity to make reasonable contracts; whether they are lunatic; whether they are *compotes mentis*, "of sound mind and memory," &c. &c. And there is obviously no more difficulty in a jury's determining whether an accused person knew the law in a criminal case, than there is in determining any of these other questions that are continually determined in regard to a man's mental capacity. For the question to be settled by the jury is not whether the accused person knew the particular *penalty* attached to his act, (for at common law no one knew what penalty a *jury* would attach to an offence,) but whether he knew that his act was *intrinsically criminal*. If it were *intrinsically criminal*, it was criminal at common law. If it was not intrinsically criminal, it was not criminal at common law. (At least, such was the general principle of the common law. There may have been exceptions in practice, owing to the fact that the opinions of men, as to what was intrinsically criminal, may not have been in all cases correct.)

A jury, then, in judging whether an accused person knew his act to be illegal, were bound first to use their own judgments, as to whether the act were *intrinsically* criminal. If their own judgments told them the act was *intrinsically* and *clearly* criminal, they would naturally and reasonably infer that the accused also understood that it was intrinsically criminal, (and consequently illegal,) unless it should appear that he was either below themselves in the scale of intellect, or had

had less opportunities of knowing what acts were criminal. In short, they would judge, from any and every means they might have of judging; and if they had any reasonable doubt that he knew his act to be criminal in itself, they would be bound to acquit him.

The second reason that has been offered for the doctrine that ignorance of the law excuses no one, is this:

"Ignorance of the municipal law of the kingdom, or of the penalty thereby inflicted on offenders, doth not excuse any that is of the age of discretion and compos mentis, from the penalty of the breach of it; because every person, of the age of discretion and compos mentis, *is bound to know the law*, and presumed to do so. *Ignorantia eorum, quæ quis scire tenetur non excusat.*" (Ignorance of those things which every one is bound to know, does not excuse.) — 1 *Hale's Pleas of the Crown*, 42. *Doctor and Student, Dialog.* 2, ch. 46. *Law Magazine*, (*London,*) vol. 27, p. 97.

The sum of this reason is, that ignorance of the law excuses no one, (who is of the age of discretion and is compos mentis,) because every such person "*is bound to know the law.*" But this is giving no reason at all for the doctrine, since saying that a man "is bound to know the law," is only saying, *in another form*, that "ignorance of the law does not excuse him." There is no difference at all in the two ideas. To say, therefore, that "ignorance of the law excuses no one, *because* every one is bound to know the law," is only equivalent to saying that "ignorance of the law excuses no one, *because* ignorance of the law excuses no one." It is merely reässerting the doctrine, without giving any reason at all.

And yet these reasons, which are really no reasons at all, are the only ones, so far as I know, that have ever been offered for this absurd and brutal doctrine.

The idea suggested, that " the age of discretion " determines the guilt of a person, — that there is a particular age, prior to which *all* persons alike should be held incapable of knowing *any* crime, and subsequent to which *all* persons alike should be held capable of knowing *all* crimes, — is another of this most ridiculous nest of ideas. All mankind acquire their knowledge of crimes, as they do of other things, *gradually*. Some they learn at an early age; others not till a later one. One individual acquires a knowledge of crimes, as he does of arithmetic, at an earlier age than others do. And to apply the same presumption to all, on the ground of age alone, is not only gross injustice, but gross folly. A universal presumption might, with nearly or quite as much reason, be founded upon weight, or height, as upon age.*

This doctrine, that "ignorance of the law excuses no one," is constantly repeated in the form that "every one is bound to know the law." The doctrine is true in *civil* matters, especially in contracts, so far as this: that no man, who has the *ordinary* capacity to make reasonable contracts, can escape the consequences of his own agreement, on the ground that he did not know the law applicable to it. When a man makes a contract, he gives the other party rights; and he must of necessity judge for himself, and take his own risk, as to what those rights are, — otherwise the contract would not be binding, and men could not make contracts that would convey rights to each other. Besides, the capacity to make reasonable con-

---

* This presumption, founded upon age alone, is as absurd in civil matters as in criminal. What can be more entirely ludicrous than the idea that all men (not manifestly imbecile) become mentally competent to make all contracts whatsoever on the day they become twenty-one years of age ? — and that, previous to that day, no man becomes competent to make any contract whatever, except for the present supply of the most obvious wants of nature ? In reason, a man's *legal* competency to make *binding* contracts, in any and every case whatever, depends wholly upon his *mental* capacity to make *reasonable* contracts in each particular case. It of course requires more capacity to make a reasonable contract in some cases than in others. It requires, for example, more capacity to make a reasonable contract in the purchase of a large estate, than in the purchase of a pair of shoes. But the mental capacity to make a reasonable contract, in any particular case, is, in reason, the only legal criterion of the legal competency to make a binding contract in that case. The age, whether more or less than twenty-one years, is of no legal consequence whatever, except that it is entitled to some consideration *as evidence of capacity.*

It may be mentioned, in this connection, that the rules that prevail, that every man is entitled to freedom from parental authority at twenty-one years of age, and no one before that age, are of the same class of absurdities with those that have been mentioned. The only ground on which a parent is ever entitled to exercise authority over his child, is that the child is incapable of taking reasonable care of himself. The child would be entitled to his freedom from his birth, if he were at that time capable of taking reasonable care of himself. Some become capable of taking care of themselves at an earlier age than others. And whenever any one becomes capable of taking reasonable care of himself, and not until then, he is entitled to his freedom, be his age more or less.

These principles would prevail under the true trial by jury, the jury being the judges of the capacity of every individual whose capacity should be called in question.

tracts, *implies and includes* a capacity to form a reasonable judgment as to the law applicable to them. But in *criminal* matters, where the question is one of punishment, or not; where no second party has acquired any right to have the crime punished, unless it were committed with criminal intent, (but only to have it compensated for by damages in a civil suit;) and when the criminal intent is the only moral justification for the punishment, the principle does not apply, and a man is bound to know the law *only as well as he reasonably may.* The criminal law requires neither impossibilities nor extraordinaries of any one. It requires only thoughtfulness and a good conscience. It requires only that a man fairly and properly use the judgment he possesses, and the means he has of learning his duty. It requires of him only the same care to know his duty in regard to the law, that he is morally bound to use in other matters of equal importance. *And this care it does require of him.* Any ignorance of the law, therefore, that is unnecessary, or that arises from indifference or disregard of one's duty, is no excuse. An accused person, therefore, may be rightfully held responsible for such a knowledge of the law as is common to men in general, having no greater natural capacities than himself, and no greater opportunities for learning the law. And he can rightfully be held to no greater knowledge of the law than this. To hold him responsible for a greater knowledge of the law than is common to mankind, when other things are equal, would be gross injustice and cruelty. The mass of mankind can give but little of their attention to acquiring a knowledge of the law. Their other duties in life forbid it. Of course, they cannot investigate abstruse or difficult questions. All that can rightfully be required of each of them, then, is that he exercise such a candid and conscientious judgment as it is common for mankind generally to exercise in such matters. If he have done this, it would be monstrous to punish him criminally for his errors; errors not of conscience, but only of judgment. It would also be contrary to the first principles of a free government (that is, a government formed by voluntary association) to punish men in such cases, because it would be absurd to suppose that any man would voluntarily assist to establish or support a government that would punish himself for acts which he himself did not know to be crimes. But a man may reasonably unite with his fellow-men to maintain a government to punish those acts which he himself considers criminal, and may reasonably acquiesce in his own liability to be punished for such acts. As those are the only grounds on which any one can be supposed to render any voluntary support to a government, it follows that a government formed by voluntary association, and of course having no powers except such as *all* the associates have consented that it may have, can have no power to punish a man for acts which he did not himself know to be criminal.

The safety of society, which is the only object of the criminal law, requires only that those acts *which are understood by mankind at large to be intrinsically criminal*, should be punished as crimes. The remaining few (if there are any) may safely be left to go unpunished. Nor does the safety of society require that any individuals, other than those who have sufficient mental capacity to understand that their acts are criminal, should be criminally punished. All others may safely be left to their liability, under the *civil* law, to compensate for their unintentional wrongs.

The only real object of this absurd and atrocious doctrine, that "ignorance of the law (that is, of crime) excuses no one," and that "every one is bound to know the *criminal* law," (that is, bound to know what is a crime,) is to maintain an entirely arbitrary authority on the part of the government, and to deny to the people all right to judge for themselves what their own rights and liberties are. In other words, the whole object of the doctrine is to deny to the people themselves all right to judge what statutes and other acts of the government are consistent or inconsistent with their own rights and liberties; and thus to reduce the people to the condition of mere slaves to a despotic power, such as the people themselves would never have voluntarily established, and the justice of whose laws the people themselves cannot understand.

Under the true trial by jury all tyranny of this kind would be abolished. A jury would not only judge what acts were really criminal, but they would judge of the mental capacity of an accused person, and of his opportunities for understanding the true character of his conduct. In short, they would judge of his moral intent from all the circumstances of the case, and acquit him, if they had any reasonable doubt that he knew that he was committing a crime.*

---

* In contrast to the doctrines of the text, it may be proper to present more distinctly the doctrines that are maintained by judges, and that prevail in courts of justice.

Of course, no judge, either of the present day, or perhaps within the last five hundred years, has admitted the right of a jury to judge of the *justice* of a law, or to hold any law invalid for its injustice. Every judge asserts the power of the government to punish for acts that are intrinsically innocent, and which therefore involve or evince no criminal intent. To accommodate the administration of law to this principle, all judges, so far as I am aware, hold it to be unnecessary that an indictment should charge, or that a jury should find, that an act was done with a criminal intent, except in those cases where the act is *malum in se*, — criminal in itself. In all other cases, so far as I am aware, they hold it sufficient that the indictment charge, and consequently that the jury find, simply that the act was done " contrary to the form of the statute in such case made and provided ;" in other words, contrary to the orders of the government.

All these doctrines prevail universally among judges, and are, I think, uniformly practised upon in courts of justice ; and they plainly involve the most absolute despotism on the part of the government.

But there is still another doctrine that extensively, and perhaps most generally, prevails in practice, although judges are not agreed in regard to its soundness. It is this : that it is not even necessary that the jury should see or know, *for themselves*, what the law *is* that is charged to have been violated; nor to see or know, *for themselves*, that the act charged was in violation of any law whatever; — but that it is sufficient that they be simply *told by the judge* that any act whatever, charged in an indictment, is in violation of law, and that they are then bound blindly to receive the declaration as true, and convict a man accordingly, if they find that he has done the act charged.

This doctrine is adopted by many among the most eminent judges, and the reasons for it are thus given by Lord Mansfield :

" They (the jury) do not know, and are not presumed to know, the law. They are not sworn to decide the law;* they are not required to do it. . . The jury ought not to assume the jurisdiction of law. They do not know, and are not presumed to know, anything of the matter. They do not understand the language in which it is conceived, or the meaning of the terms. They have no rule to go by but their passions and wishes." — 3 *Term Rep.*, 428, note.

What is this but saying that the people, who are supposed to be represented in juries, and who institute and support the government, (of course for the protection of their own rights and liberties, *as they understand them*, for plainly no other motive can be attributed to them,) are really the slaves of a despotic power, whose arbitrary commands even they are not supposed competent to understand, but for the transgression of which they are nevertheless to be punished as criminals ?

This is plainly the sum of the doctrine, because the jury are the peers (equals) of the accused, and are therefore supposed to know the law as well as he does, and as well as it is known by the people at large. If *they* (the jury) are not presumed to know the

---

* This declaration of Mansfield, that juries in England " are not sworn to decide the law " in criminal cases, is a plain falsehood. They are sworn to try the whole case at issue between the king and the prisoner, and that includes the law as well as the fact. See *juror's oath*, page 86.

law, neither the accused nor the people at large can be presumed to know it. Hence, it follows that one principle of the *true* trial by jury is, that no accused person shall be held responsible for any other or greater knowledge of the law than is common to his political equals, who will generally be men of nearly similar condition in life. But the doctrine of Mansfield is, that the body of the people, from whom jurors are taken, are responsible to a law, *which it is agreed they cannot understand.* What is this but despotism? — and not merely despotism, but insult and oppression of the intensest kind?

This doctrine of Mansfield is the doctrine of all who deny the right of juries to judge of the law, although all may not choose to express it in so blunt and unambiguous terms. But the doctrine evidently admits of no other interpretation or defence.

CHAPTER X.

MORAL CONSIDERATIONS FOR JURORS.

THE trial by jury must, if possible, be construed to be such that a man can rightfully sit in a jury, and unite with his fellows in giving judgment. But no man can rightfully do this, unless he hold in his own hand alone a veto upon any judgment or sentence whatever to be rendered by the jury against a defendant, which veto he must be permitted to use according to his own discretion and conscience, and not bound to use according to the dictation of either legislatures or judges.

The prevalent idea, that a juror may, at the mere dictation of a legislature or a judge, and without the concurrence of his own conscience or understanding, declare a man "*guilty*," and thus in effect license the government to punish him; and that the legislature or the judge, and not himself, has in that case all the moral responsibility for the correctness of the principles on which the judgment was rendered, is one of the many gross impostures by which it could hardly have been supposed that any sane man could ever have been deluded, but which governments have nevertheless succeeded in inducing the people at large to receive and act upon.

As a moral proposition, it is perfectly self-evident that, unless juries have all the legal rights that have been claimed for them in the preceding chapters, — that is, the rights of judging what the law is, whether the law be a just one, what evidence is admissible, what weight the evidence is entitled to, whether an act were done with a criminal intent, and the right also to *limit* the sentence, free of all dictation from any quarter, — they have no *moral* right to sit in the trial at all, and cannot do so without making themselves accomplices in any injustice that they may have reason to believe may result from their verdict. It is absurd to say that they have no moral responsibility for the use that may be made of their verdict by the government, when they have reason to suppose it will be used for purposes of injustice.

It is, for instance, manifestly absurd to say that jurors have no moral responsibility for the enforcement of an unjust law, when they consent to render a verdict of *guilty* for the transgression of it; which verdict they know, or have good reason to believe, will be used by the government as a justification for inflicting a penalty.

It is absurd, also, to say that jurors have no moral responsibility for a punishment inflicted upon a man *against law*, when, at the dictation of a judge as to what the law is, they have consented to render a verdict against their own opinions of the law.

It is absurd, too, to say that jurors have no moral responsibility for the conviction and punishment of an innocent man, when they consent to render a verdict against him on the strength of evidence, or laws of evidence, dictated to them by the court, if any evidence or laws of evidence have been excluded, which *they* (the jurors) think ought to have been admitted in his defence.

It is absurd to say that jurors have no moral responsibility for rendering a verdict of "*guilty*" against a man, for an act which he did not know to be a crime, and in the commission of which, therefore, he could have had no criminal intent, in obedience to the instructions of courts that "ignorance of the law (that is, of crime) excuses no one."

It is absurd, also, to say that jurors have no moral responsibility for any cruel or unreasonable *sentence* that may be inflicted even upon a *guilty* man, when they consent to render a verdict which they have reason to believe will be used by the government as a justification for the infliction of such sentence.

The consequence is, that jurors must have the whole case in their hands, and judge of law, evidence, and sentence, or they incur the moral responsibility of accomplices in any injustice which they have reason to believe will be done by the government on the authority of their verdict.

The same principles apply to civil cases as to criminal. If a jury consent, at the dictation of the court, as to either law or evidence, to render a verdict, on the strength of which they have reason to believe that a man's property will be taken from him and given to another, against their own notions of justice, they make themselves morally responsible for the wrong.

Every man, therefore, ought to refuse to sit in a jury, and to take the oath of a juror, unless the form of the oath be such as to allow him to use his own judgment, on every part of the case, free of all dictation whatsoever, and to hold in his own hand a veto upon any verdict that can be rendered against a defendant, and any sentence that can be inflicted upon him, even if he be guilty.

Of course, no man can rightfully take an oath as juror, to try a case "according to law," (if by law be meant anything other than his own ideas of justice,) nor "according to the law and the evidence, *as they shall be given him.*" Nor can he rightfully take an oath even to try a case "*according to the evidence*," because in all cases he may have good reason to believe that a party has been unable to produce all the evidence legitimately entitled to be received. The only oath which it would seem that a man can rightfully take as juror, in either a civil or criminal case, is, that he " will try the case *according to his conscience.*" Of course, the form may admit of variation, but this should be the substance. Such, we have seen, were the ancient common law oaths.

CHAPTER XI.

AUTHORITY OF MAGNA CARTA.

PROBABLY no political compact between king and people was ever entered into in a manner to settle more authoritatively the fundamental law of a nation, than was Magna Carta. Probably no people were ever more united and resolute in demanding from their king a definite and unambiguous acknowledgment of their rights and liberties, than were the English at that time. Probably no king was ever more completely stripped of all power to maintain his throne, and at the same time resist the demands of his people, than was John on the 15th day of June, 1215. Probably no king every consented, more deliberately or explicitly, to hold his throne subject to specific and enumerated limitations upon his power, than did John when he put his seal to the Great Charter of the Liberties of England. And if any political compact between king and people was ever valid to settle the liberties of the people, or to limit the power of the crown, that compact is now to be found in Magna Carta. If, therefore, the constitutional authority of Magna Carta had rested solely upon the compact of John with his people, that authority would have been entitled to stand forever as the supreme law of the land, unless revoked by the will of the people themselves.

But the authority of Magna Carta does not rest alone upon the compact with *John*. When, in the next year, (1216,) his son, Henry III., came to the throne, the charter was ratified by him, and again in 1217, and again in 1225, in substantially the same form, and especially without allowing any new powers, legislative, judicial, or executive, to the king or his judges, and without detracting in the least from the powers of the jury. And from the latter date to this, the charter has remained unchanged.

In the course of two hundred years the charter was confirmed by Henry and his successors more than thirty times. And although they were guilty of numerous and almost continual breaches of it, and were constantly seeking to evade it, yet such were the spirit, vigilance and courage of the nation, that the kings held their thrones only on the condition of their renewed and solemn promises of observance. And it was not until 1429, (as will be more fully shown hereafter,) when a truce between themselves, and a formal combination against the mass of the people, had been entered into, by the king, the nobility, and the "*forty shilling freeholders,*" (a class whom Mackintosh designates as "*a few freeholders then accounted wealthy,*"*) by the exclusion of all others than such freeholders from all voice in the election of knights to represent the counties in the House of Commons, that a repetition of these confirmations of Magna Carta ceased to be demanded and obtained.†

The terms and the formalities of some of these "confirmations" make them worthy of insertion at length.

Hume thus describes one which took place in the 38th year of Henry III. (1253):

"But as they (the barons) had experienced his (the king's) frequent breach of promise, they required that he should ratify the Great Charter in a manner still more authentic and solemn than any which he had hitherto employed. All the prelates and abbots were assembled. They held burning tapers in their hands. The Great Charter was read before them. They denounced the sentence of excommunication against every one who should thenceforth violate that fundamental law. They threw their tapers on the ground, and exclaimed, *May the soul of every one who incurs this sentence so stink and corrupt in hell!* The king bore a part in this ceremony, and subjoined, 'So help me God! I will keep all these articles inviolate, as I am a man, as I am a Christian, as I am a knight, and as I am a king crowned and anointed.' " — *Hume,* ch. 12. See also

---

* *Mackintosh's Hist. of Eng.*, ch. 3. 45 *Lardner's Cab. Cyc.*, 354.

† "*Forty shilling freeholders*" were those "people dwelling and resident in the same counties, whereof every one of them shall have free land or tenement to the value of forty shillings by the year at the least above all charges." By statute 8 *Henry* 6, ch. 7, (1429,) these freeholders only were allowed to vote for members of Parliament from the *counties.*

Blackstone's Introd. to the Charters. Black. Law Tracts,
Oxford ed., p. 332. *Mackintosh's Hist. of Eng.*, ch. 3.
Lardner's Cab. Cyc., vol. 45, p. 233-4.

The following is the form of "the sentence of excommunication" referred to by Hume:

"*The Sentence of Curse, Given by the Bishops, against the Breakers of the Charters.*

"The year of our Lord a thousand two hundred and fifty-three, the third day of May, in the great Hall of the King at Westminster, *in the presence, and by the assent, of the Lord Henry, by the Grace of God King of England*, and the Lords Richard, Earl of Cornwall, his brother, Roger (Bigot) Earl of Norfolk and Suffolk, marshal of England, Humphrey, Earl of Hereford, Henry, Earl of Oxford, John, Earl of Warwick, and other estates of the Realm of England: We, Boniface, by the mercy of God Archbishop of Canterbury, Primate of all England, F. of London, H. of Ely, S. of Worcester, E. of Lincoln, W. of Norwich, P. of Hereford, W. of Salisbury, W. of Durham, R. of Exeter, M. of Carlisle, W. of Bath, E. of Rochester, T. of Saint David's, Bishops, apparelled in Pontificals, with tapers burning, against the breakers of the Church's Liberties, and of the Liberties or free customs of the Realm of England, and especially of those which are contained in the Charter of the Common Liberties of the Realm, and the Charter of the Forest, have solemnly denounced the sentence of Excommunication in this form. By the authority of Almighty God, the Father, the Son, and the Holy Ghost, and of the glorious Mother of God, and perpetual Virgin Mary, of the blessed Apostles Peter and Paul, and of all apostles, of the blessed Thomas, Archbishop and Martyr, and of all martyrs, of blessed Edward of England, and of all Confessors and virgins, and of all the saints of heaven: We excommunicate, accurse, and from the thresholds (liminibus) of our Holy Mother the Church, We sequester, all those that hereafter willingly and maliciously deprive or spoil the Church of her right: And all those that by any craft or wiliness do violate, break, diminish, or change the Church's Liberties, or the ancient approved customs of the Realm, and especially the Liberties and free Customs contained in the Charters of the Common Liberties, and of the Forest, conceded by our Lord the King, to Archbishops, Bishops, and other Prelates of England; and likewise to the Earls, Barons, Knights, and other Freeholders of the Realm: And all that secretly, or openly, by deed, word, or counsel, *do make statutes, or observe them being made,* and that bring in Customs, or keep them when they be brought in, against the said

Liberties, or any of them, the Writers and Counsellors of said statutes, and the Executors of them, and all those that shall presume to judge according to them. All and every which persons before mentioned, that wittingly shall commit anything of the premises, let them well know that they incur the aforesaid sentence, *ipso facto*, (i. e., upon the deed being done.) And those that ignorantly do so, and be admonished, except they reform themselves within fifteen days after the time of the admonition, and make full satisfaction for that they have done, at the will of the ordinary, shall be from that time forth included in the same sentence. And with the same sentence we burden all those that presume to perturb the peace of our sovereign Lord the King, and of the Realm. To the perpetual memory of which thing, We, the aforesaid Prelates, have put our seals to these presents." — *Statutes of the Realm*, vol. 1, p. 6. *Ruffhead's Statutes*, vol. 1, p. 20.

One of the Confirmations of the Charters, by Edward I., was by statute, in the 25th year of his reign, (1297,) in the following terms. The statute is usually entitled "*Confirmatio Cartarum*," (Confirmation of the Charters.)

Ch. 1. "Edward, by the Grace of God, King of England, Lord of Ireland, and Duke of Guyan, To all those that these presents shall hear or see, Greeting. Know ye, that We, to the honor of God, and of Holy Church, and to the profit of our Realm, have granted, for us and our heirs, that the Charter of Liberties, and the Charter of the Forest, which were made by common assent of all the Realm, in the time of King Henry our Father, shall be kept in every point without breach. And we will that the same Charters shall be sent under our seal, as well to our justices of the Forest, as to others, and to all Sheriffs of shires, and to all our other officers, and to all our cities throughout the Realm, together with our writs, in the which it shall be contained, that they cause the aforesaid Charters to be published, and to declare to the people that We have confirmed them at all points; and to our Justices, Sheriffs, Mayors, and other ministers, which under us have the Laws of our Land to guide, that they allow the same Charters, in all their points, in pleas before them, and in judgment; that is, to wit, the Great Charter as the Common Law, and the Charter of the Forest for the wealth of our Realm.

Ch. 2. "And we will that if any judgment be given from henceforth contrary to the points of the charters aforesaid by the justices, or by any others our ministers that hold plea before them, against the points of the Charters, it shall be undone and holden for naught.

Ch. 3. "And we will, that the same Charters shall be sent, under our seal, to Cathedral Churches throughout our Realm, there to remain, and shall be read before the people two times in the year.

Ch. 4. "And that all Archbishops and Bishops shall pronounce the sentence of excommunication against all those that by word, deed, or counsel, do contrary to the foresaid charters, or that in any point break or undo them. And that the said Curses be twice a year denounced and published by the prelates aforesaid. And if the same prelates, or any of them, be remiss in the denunciation of the said sentences, the Archbishops of Canterbury and York, for the time being, shall compel and distrain them to make the denunciation in the form aforesaid." — *St.* 25 *Edward I.*, (1297.) *Statutes of the Realm*, vol. 1, p. 123.

It is unnecessary to repeat the terms of the various confirmations, most of which were less formal than those that have been given, though of course equally authoritative. Most of them are brief, and in the form of a simple statute, or promise, to the effect that "The Great Charter, and the Charter of the Forest, shall be firmly kept and maintained in all points." They are to be found printed with the other statutes of the realm. One of them, after having "again granted, renewed and confirmed" the charters, requires as follows:

"That the Charters be delivered to every sheriff of England under the king's seal, to be read four times in the year before the people in the full county," (that is, at the county court,) "that is, to wit, the next county (court) after the feast of Saint Michael, and the next county (court) after Christmas, and at the next county (court) after Easter, and at the next county (court) after the feast of Saint John." — 28 *Edward I.*, ch. 1, (1300.)

Lingard says, "The Charter was ratified four times by Henry III., twice by Edward I., fifteen times by Edward III., seven times by Richard II., six times by Henry IV., and once by Henry V.;" making thirty-five times in all. — 3 *Lingard*, 50, note, Philad. ed.

Coke says Magna Carta was confirmed thirty-two times. — *Preface to* 2 *Inst.*, p. 6.

Lingard calls these "thirty-five successive ratifications" of the charter, "a sufficient proof how much its provisions were abhorred by the sovereign, and how highly they were prized by the nation." — 3 *Lingard*, 50.

Mackintosh says, "For almost five centuries (that is, until 1688) it (Magna Carta) was appealed to as the decisive authority on behalf of the people, though commonly so far only as the necessities of each case demanded." — *Mackintosh's Hist. of Eng.* ch. 3. 45 *Lardner's Cab. Cyc.*, 221.

Coke, who has labored so hard to overthrow the most vital principles of Magna Carta, and who, therefore, ought to be considered good authority when he speaks in its favor,* says:

"It is called Magna Carta, not that it is great in quantity, for there be many voluminous charters commonly passed, specially in these later times, longer than this is; nor comparatively in respect that it is greater than *Charta de Foresta*, but in respect of the great importance and weightiness of the matter, as hereafter shall appear; and likewise for the same cause *Charta de Foresta;* and both of them are called *Magnæ Chartæ Libertatum Angliæ*, (The Great Charters of the Liberties of England.) . .

"And it is also called *Charta Libertatum regni*, (Charter of the Liberties of the kingdom;) and upon great reason it is so called of the effect, *quia liberos facit*, (because it makes men free.) Sometime for the same cause (it is called) *communis libertas*, (common liberty,) and *le chartre des franchises*, (the charter of franchises.) . .

"It was for the most part declaratory of the principal grounds of the fundamental laws of England, and for the residue it is additional to supply some defects of the common law. . .

"Also, by the said act of 25 Edward I., (called *Confirmatio Chartarum*,) it is adjudged in parliament that the Great Charter and the Charter of the Forest shall be taken as the common law. . .

"They (Magna Carta and Carta de Foresta) were, for the most part, but declarations of the ancient common laws of England, to the observation and keeping whereof, the king was bound and sworn.

"After the making of Magna Charta, and Charta de Foresta, divers learned men in the laws, that I may use the words of the record, kept schools of the law in the city of London, and taught such as resorted to them the laws of the realm,

---

* He probably speaks in its favor only to blind the eyes of the people to the frauds he has attempted upon its true meaning.

taking their foundation of Magna Charta and Charta de Foresta.

"And the said two charters have been confirmed, established, and commanded to be put in execution by thirty-two several acts of parliament in all.

"This appeareth partly by that which hath been said, for that it hath so often been confirmed by the wise providence of so many acts of parliament.

"And albeit judgments in the king's courts are of high regard in law, and *judicia* (judgments) are accounted as *jurisdicta*, (the speech of the law itself,) yet it is provided by act of parliament, that if any judgment be given contrary to any of the points of the Great Charter and Charta de Foresta, by the justices, or by any other of the king's ministers, &c., it shall be undone, and holden for naught.

"And that both the said charters shall be sent under the great seal to all cathedral churches throughout the realm, there to remain, and shall be read to the people twice every year.

"The highest and most binding laws are the statutes which are established by parliament; and by authority of that highest court it is enacted (only to show their tender care of Magna Carta and Carta de Foresta) that if any statute be made contrary to the Great Charter, or the Charter of the Forest, that shall be holden for none; by which words all former statutes made against either of those charters are now repealed; and the nobles and great officers were to be sworn to the observation of Magna Charta and Charta de Foresta.

"*Magna fuit quondam magnæ reverentia chartæ.*" (Great was formerly the reverence for Magna Carta.) — *Coke's Proem to* 2 *Inst.*, p. 1 to 7.

Coke also says, "All pretence of prerogative against Magna Charta is taken away." — 2 *Inst.*, 36.

He also says, "That after this parliament (52 *Henry* III., in 1267) neither Magna Carta nor Carta de Foresta was ever attempted to be impugned or questioned." — 2 *Inst.*, 102.*

---

* It will be noticed that Coke calls these confirmations of the charter "acts of parliament," instead of acts of the king alone. This needs explanation.

It was one of Coke's ridiculous pretences, that laws anciently enacted by the king, at the *request*, or with the *consent*, or by the *advice*, of his parliament, was " an act of parliament," instead of the act of the king. And in the extracts cited, he carries this idea so far as to pretend that the various confirmations of the Great Charter were "acts of parliament," instead of the acts of the kings. He might as well have pretended that the original grant of the Charter was an "act of parliament;" because it was not only granted at the request, and with the consent, and by the advice, but on the compulsion even, of those who commonly constituted his parliaments. Yet this did

AUTHORITY OF MAGNA CARTA.

To give all the evidence of the authority of Magna Carta, it would be necessary to give the constitutional history of England since the year 1215. This history would show that Magna Carta, although continually violated and evaded, was still acknowl-

---

not make the grant of the charter "an act of parliament." It was simply an act of the king.

The object of Coke, in this pretence, was to furnish some color for the palpable falsehood that the legislative authority, which parliament was trying to assume in his own day, and which it finally succeeded in obtaining, had a precedent in the ancient constitution of the kingdom.

There would be as much reason in saying that, because the ancient kings were in the habit of passing laws in special answer to the *petitions* of their subjects, therefore those *petitioners* were a part of the legislative power of the kingdom.

One great objection to this argument of Coke, for the legislative authority of the ancient parliaments, is that a very large — probably much the larger — number of legislative acts were done *without* the advice, consent, request, or even presence, of a parliament. Not only were many formal statutes passed without any mention of the consent or advice of parliament, but a simple order of the king in council, or a simple proclamation, writ, or letter under seal, issued by his command, had the same force as what Coke calls "an act of parliament." And this practice continued, to a considerable extent at least, down to Coke's own time.

The kings were always in the habit of consulting their parliaments, more or less, in regard to matters of legislation, — not because their consent was constitutionally necessary, but in order to make influence in favor of their laws, and thus induce the people to observe them, and the juries to enforce them.

The general duties of the ancient parliaments were not legislative, but judicial, as will be shown more fully hereafter. The *people* were not represented in the parliaments at the time of Magna Carta, but only the archbishops, bishops, earls, barons, and knights; so that little or nothing would have been gained for liberty by Coke's idea that parliament had a legislative power. He would only have substituted an aristocracy for a king. Even after the Commons were represented in parliament, they for some centuries appeared only as *petitioners*, except in the matter of taxation, when their *consent* was asked. And almost the only source of their influence on legislation was this: that they would sometimes refuse their consent to the taxation, unless the king would pass such laws as they petitioned for; or, as would seem to have been much more frequently the case, unless he would abolish such laws and practices as they remonstrated against.

The *influence* or power of parliament, and especially of the Commons, in the *general* legislation of the country, was a thing of slow growth, having its origin in a device of the king to get money contrary to law, (as will be seen in the next volume,) and not at all a part of the constitution of the kingdom, nor having its foundation in the consent of the people. The power, *as at present exercised*, was not fully established until 1688, (near five hundred years after Magna Carta,) when the House of Commons (falsely so called) had acquired such influence as the representative, *not of the people, but of the wealth*, of the nation, that they compelled the king to discard the oath fixed by the constitution of the kingdom; (which oath has been already given in a former chapter,* and was, in substance, to preserve and execute the Common Law, the Law of the Land,

---

* See page 101.

edged as law by the government, and was held up by the people as the great standard and proof of their rights and liber-

---

— or, in the words of the oath, "*the just laws and customs which the common people had chosen;*") and to swear that he would "govern the people of this kingdom of England, and the dominions thereto belonging, *according to the statutes in parliament agreed on*, and the laws and customs of the same."*

The passage and enforcement of this statute, and the assumption of this oath by the king, were plain violations of the English constitution, inasmuch as they abolished, so far as such an oath could abolish, the legislative power of the king, and also "those just laws and customs which the common people (through their juries) had chosen," and substituted the will of parliament in their stead.

Coke was a great advocate for the legislative power of parliament, as a means of restraining the power of the king. As he denied all power to *juries* to decide upon the obligation of laws, and as he held that the legislative power was "*so transcendent and absolute as (that) it cannot be confined, either for causes or persons, within any bounds,*" † he was perhaps honest in holding that it was safer to trust this terrific power in the hands of parliament, than in the hands of the king. His error consisted in holding that either the king or parliament had any such power, or that they had any power at all to pass laws that should be binding upon a jury.

These declarations of Coke, that the charter was confirmed by thirty-two "acts of parliament," have a mischievous bearing in another respect. They tend to weaken the authority of the charter, by conveying the impression that the charter itself might be *abolished* by "act of parliament." Coke himself admits that it could not be revoked or rescinded by the *king;* for he says, "All pretence of prerogative against Magna Carta is taken away." (2 *Inst.*, 36.)

He knew perfectly well, and the whole English nation knew, that the *king* could not lawfully infringe Magna Carta. Magna Carta, therefore, made it impossible that absolute power could ever be practically established in England, *in the hands of the king*. Hence, as Coke was an advocate for absolute power, — that is, for a legislative power "so transcendent and absolute as (that) it cannot be confined, either for causes or persons, within any bounds," — there was no alternative for him but to vest this absolute power in parliament. Had he not vested it in parliament, he would have been obliged to abjure it altogether, and to confess that the people, *through their juries*, had the right to judge of the obligation of all legislation whatsoever; in other words, that they had the right to confine the government within the limits of "those just laws and customs which the common people (acting as jurors) had chosen." True to his instincts, as a judge, and as a tyrant, he *assumed* that this absolute power was vested in the hands of parliament.

But the truth was that, as by the English constitution parliament had no authority at all for *general* legislation, it could no more confirm, than it could abolish, Magna Carta.

These thirty-two confirmations of Magna Carta, which Coke speaks of as "acts of parliament," were merely acts of the king. The parliaments, indeed, by refusing to grant him money, except on that condition, and otherwise, had contributed to oblige him to make the confirmations; just as they had helped to oblige him by arms to grant the charter in the first place. But the confirmations themselves were nevertheless constitutionally, as well as formally, the acts of the king alone.

* St. 1 *William and Mary*, ch. 6, (1688.)   † 4 *Inst.*, 36.

ties. It would show also that the judicial tribunals, *whenever it suited their purposes to do so*, were in the habit of referring to Magna Carta as authority, in the same manner, and with the same real or pretended veneration, with which American courts now refer to the constitution of the United States, or the constitutions of the states. And, what is equally to the point, it would show that these same tribunals, the mere tools of kings and parliaments, would resort to the same artifices of assumption, *precedent*, construction, and false interpretation, to evade the requirements of Magna Carta, and to emasculate it of all its power for the preservation of liberty, that are resorted to by American courts to accomplish the same work on our American constitutions.

I take it for granted, therefore, that if the authority of Magna Carta had rested simply upon its character as a *compact* between the king and the people, it would have been forever binding upon the king, (that is, upon the government, for the king was the government,) in his legislative, judicial, and executive character; and that there was no *constitutional* possibility of his escaping from its restraints, unless the people themselves should freely discharge him from them.

But the authority of Magna Carta does not rest, either wholly or mainly, upon its character as a compact. For centuries before the charter was granted, its main principles constituted "the Law of the Land," — the fundamental and constitutional law of the realm, which the kings were sworn to maintain. And the principal benefit of the charter was, that it contained a *written* description and acknowledgment, by the king himself, of what the constitutional law of the kingdom was, which his coronation oath bound him to observe. Previous to Magna Carta, this constitutional law rested mainly in precedents, customs, and the memories of the people. And if the king could but make one innovation upon this law, without arousing resistance, and being compelled to retreat from his usurpation, he would cite that innovation as a precedent for another act of the same kind; next, assert a custom; and, finally, raise a controversy as to what the Law of the Land really was. The great object of the barons and people, in demanding from the king a written description and acknowledgment of the Law of the Land, was to put an end to all disputes of this kind, and to put it out of the power of the king to plead any misunderstanding of the constitutional law of the kingdom. And the charter, no doubt, accomplished very much in this way. After Magna Carta, it required much more audacity, cunning, or strength, on the part of the king, than it had before, to invade the people's liberties with impunity. Still, Magna Carta, like all other written constitutions, proved inadequate to the full accomplishment of its purpose; for when did a parchment ever have power adequately to restrain a government, that had either cunning to evade its requirements, or strength to overcome those who attempted its defence? The work of usurpation, therefore, though seriously checked, still went on, to a great extent, after Magna Carta. Innovations upon the Law of the Land are still made by the government. One innovation was cited as a precedent; precedents made customs; and customs became laws, so far as practice was concerned; until the government, composed of the king, the high functionaries of the church, the nobility, a House of Commons representing the "forty shilling freeholders," and a dependent and servile judiciary, all acting in conspiracy against the mass of the people, became practically absolute, as it is at this day.

As proof that Magna Carta embraced little else than what was previously recognized as the common law, or Law of the Land, I repeat some authorities that have been already cited.

Crabbe says, "It is admitted on all hands that it (Magna Carta) contains nothing but what was confirmatory of the common law and the ancient usages of the realm; and is, properly speaking, only an enlargement of the charter of Henry I. and his successors." — *Crabbe's Hist. of the Eng. Law*, p. 127.

Blackstone says, "It is agreed by all our historians that the Great Charter of King John was, for the most part, compiled from the ancient customs of the realm, or the laws of Edward the Confessor; by which they mean the old common law which was established under our Saxon princes." — *Blackstone's Introd. to the Charters.* See *Blackstone's Law Tracts*, Oxford ed., p. 289.

Coke says, "The common law is the most general and ancient law of the realm. . . The common law appeareth in the statute of *Magna Carta*, and other ancient statutes, (which for the most part are affirmations of the common law,) in the original writs, in judicial records, and in our books of terms and years." — 1 *Inst.*, 115 b.

Coke also says, "It (Magna Carta) was for the most part declaratory of the principal grounds of the fundamental laws of England, and for the residue it was additional to supply some defects of the common law. . . They (Magna Carta and Carta de Foresta) were, for the most part, but declarations of the ancient common laws of England, *to the observation and keeping whereof the king was bound and sworn.*" — *Preface to* 2 *Inst.*, p. 3 and 5.

Hume says, "We may now, from the tenor of this charter, (Magna Carta,) conjecture what those laws were of King Edward, (the Confessor,) which the English nation during so many generations still desired, with such an obstinate perseverance, to have recalled and established. They were chiefly these latter articles of Magna Carta; and the barons who, at the beginning of these commotions, demanded the revival of the Saxon laws, undoubtedly thought that they had sufficiently satisfied the people, by procuring them this concession, which comprehended the principal objects to which they had so long aspired."— *Hume*, ch. 11.

Edward the First confessed that the Great Charter was substantially identical with the common law, as far as it went, when he commanded his justices to allow "the Great Charter as the Common Law," "in pleas before them, and in judgment," as has been already cited in this chapter. — 25 *Edward* I., ch. 1, (1297.)

In conclusion of this chapter, it may be safely asserted that the veneration, attachment, and pride, which the English nation, for more than six centuries, have felt towards Magna Carta, are in their nature among the most irrefragable of all proofs that it was the fundamental law of the land, and constitutionally binding upon the government; for, otherwise, it would have been, in their eyes, an unimportant and worthless thing. What those sentiments were I will use the words of others to describe, — the words, too, of men, who, like all modern authors who have written on the same topic, had utterly inadequate ideas of the true character of the instrument on which they lavished their eulogiums.

Hume, speaking of the Great Charter and the Charter of the Forest, as they were confirmed by Henry III., in 1217, says:

"Thus these famous charters were brought nearly to the shape in which they have ever since stood; and they were, during many generations, the peculiar favorites of the English nation, and esteemed the most sacred rampart to national liberty and independence. As they secured the rights of all orders of men, they were anxiously defended by all, and became the basis, in a manner, of the English monarchy, and a kind of original contract, which both limited the authority of the king and ensured the conditional allegiance of his subjects. Though often violated, they were still claimed by the nobility and people; and, as no precedents were supposed valid that infringed them, they rather acquired than lost authority, from the frequent attempts made against them in several ages, by regal and arbitrary power." — *Hume*, ch. 12.

Mackintosh says, "It was understood by the simplest of the unlettered age for whom it was intended. It was remembered by them. . . For almost five centuries it was appealed to as the decisive authority on behalf of the people. . . To have produced it, to have preserved it, to have matured it, constitute the immortal claim of England on the esteem of mankind. Her Bacons and Shakspeares, her Miltons and Newtons, with all the truth which they have revealed, and all the generous virtues which they have inspired, are of inferior value when compared with the subjection of men and their rulers to the principles of justice; if, indeed, it be not more true that these mighty spirits could not have been formed except under equal laws, nor roused to full activity without the influence of that spirit which the Great Charter breathed over their forefathers." — *Mackintosh's Hist. of Eng.*, ch. 3.*

Of the Great Charter, the trial by jury is the vital part, and the only part that places the liberties of the people in their own keeping. Of this Blackstone says:

"The trial by jury, or the country, *per patriam*, is also that trial by the peers of every Englishman, which, as the grand bulwark of his liberties, is secured to him by the Great Charter; *nullus liber homo capiatur, vel imprisonetur, aut exuletur, aut aliquo modo destruatur, nisi per legale judicium parium suorum, vel per legem terrae.* . .

The liberties of England cannot but subsist so long as this palladium remains sacred and inviolate, not only from all

---

* Under the head of "*John.*"

open attacks, which none will be so hardy as to make, but also from all secret machinations which may sap and undermine it." *

"The trial by jury ever has been, and I trust ever will be, looked upon as the glory of the English law. . . It is the most transcendent privilege which any subject can enjoy or wish for, that he cannot be affected in his property, his liberty, or his person, but by the unanimous consent of twelve of his neighbors and equals." †

Hume calls the trial by jury "An institution admirable in itself, and the best calculated for the preservation of liberty and the administration of justice, that ever was devised by the wit of man." ‡

An old book, called "English Liberties," says:

"English Parliaments have all along been most zealous for preserving this great Jewel of Liberty, trials by juries having no less than fifty-eight several times, since the Norman Conquest, been established and confirmed by the legislative power, no one privilege besides having been ever so often remembered in parliament." §

---

* 4 *Blackstone*, 349-50. † 3 *Blackstone*, 379. ‡ *Hume*, ch. 2.
§ Page 203, 5th edition, 1721.

CHAPTER XII.

LIMITATIONS IMPOSED UPON THE MAJORITY BY THE TRIAL BY JURY.

The principal objection, that will be made to the doctrine of this essay, is, that under it, a jury would paralyze the power of the majority, and veto all legislation that was not in accordance with the will of the whole, or nearly the whole, people.

The answer to this objection is, that the limitation, which would be thus imposed upon the legislative power, (whether that power be vested in the majority, or minority, of the people,) is the crowning merit of the trial by jury. It has other merits; but, though important in themselves, they are utterly insignificant and worthless in comparison with this.

It is this power of vetoing all partial and oppressive legislation, and of restricting the government to the maintenance of such laws as the *whole*, or substantially the whole, people *are agreed in*, that makes the trial by jury " the palladium of liberty." Without this power it would never have deserved that name.

The will, or the pretended will, of the majority, is the last lurking place of tyranny at the present day. The dogma, that certain individuals and families have a divine appointment to govern the rest of mankind, is fast giving place to the one that the larger number have a right to govern the smaller; a dogma, which may, or may not, be less oppressive in its practical operation, but which certainly is no less false or tyrannical in principle, than the one it is so rapidly supplanting. Obviously there is nothing in the nature of majorities, that insures justice at their hands. They have the same passions as minorities, and they have no qualities whatever that should be expected to prevent them from practising the same tyranny as minorities, if they think it will be for their interest to do so.

There is no particle of truth in the notion that the majority have a *right* to rule, or to exercise arbitrary power over, the minority, simply because the former are more numerous than the latter. Two men have no more natural right to rule one, than one has to rule two. Any single man, or any body of men, many or few, have a natural right to maintain justice for themselves, and for any others who may need their assistance, against the injustice of any and all other men, without regard to their numbers; and majorities have no right to do any more than this. The relative numbers of the opposing parties have nothing to do with the question of right. And no more tyrannical principle was ever avowed, than that the will of the majority ought to have the force of law, without regard to its justice; or, what is the same thing, that the will of the majority ought always to be presumed to be in accordance with justice. Such a doctrine is only another form of the doctrine that might makes right.

When *two* men meet *one* upon the highway, or in the wilderness, have they a right to dispose of his life, liberty, or property at their pleasure, simply because they are the more numerous party? Or is he bound to submit to lose his life, liberty, or property, if they demand it, merely because he is the less numerous party? Or, because they are more numerous than he, is he bound to presume that they are governed only by superior wisdom, and the principles of justice, and by no selfish passion that can lead them to do him a wrong? Yet this is the principle, which it is claimed should govern men in all their civil relations to each other. Mankind fall in company with each other on the highway or in the wilderness of life, and it is claimed that the more numerous party, simply by virtue of their superior numbers, have the right arbitrarily to dispose of the life, liberty, and property of the minority; and that the minority are bound, by reason of their inferior numbers, to practise abject submission, and consent to hold their natural rights,— any, all, or none, as the case may be,— at the mere will and pleasure of the majority; as if all a man's natural rights expired, or were suspended by the operation of a paramount law, the moment he came into the presence of superior numbers.

If such be the true nature of the relations men hold to each other in this world, it puts an end to all such things as crimes, unless they be perpetrated upon those who are equal or superior, in number, to the actors. All acts committed against persons *inferior* in number to the aggressors, become but the exercise of rightful authority. And consistency with their own principles requires that all governments, founded on the will of the majority, should recognize this plea as a sufficient justification for all crimes whatsoever.

If it be said that the majority should be allowed to rule, not because they are stronger than the minority, but because their superior numbers furnish a *probability* that they are in the right; one answer is, that the lives, liberties, and properties of men are too valuable to them, and the natural presumptions are too strong in their favor, to justify the destruction of them by their fellow-men on a mere balancing of probabilities, *or on any ground whatever short of certainty beyond a reasonable doubt.* This last is the moral rule universally recognized to be binding upon single individuals. And in the forum of conscience the same rule is equally binding upon governments, for governments are mere associations of individuals. This *is* the rule on which the trial by jury is based. And it is plainly the only rule that ought to induce a man to submit his rights to the adjudication of his fellow-men, or dissuade him from a forcible defence of them.

Another answer is, that if two opposing parties could be supposed to have no personal interests or passions involved, to warp their judgments, or corrupt their motives, the fact that one of the parties was more numerous than the other, (a fact that leaves the comparative intellectual competency of the two parties entirely out of consideration,) might, perhaps, furnish a slight, but at best only a very slight, probability that such party was on the side of justice. But when it is considered that the parties are liable to differ in their intellectual capacities, and that one, or the other, or both, are undoubtedly under the influence of such passions as rivalry, hatred, avarice, and ambition,— passions that are nearly certain to pervert their judgments, and very likely to corrupt their motives,— all probabilities founded upon a mere numerical majority, in one party, or the other, vanish at once; and the decision of the majority becomes, to all practical purposes, a mere decision of chance. And to dispose of men's properties, liberties, and lives, by the mere process of enumerating such parties, is not only as palpable gambling as was ever practised, but it is also the most atrocious that was ever practised, except in matters of government. And where government is instituted on this principle, (as in the United States, for example,) the nation is at once converted into one great gambling establishment; where all the rights of men are the stakes; a few bold bad men throw the dice — (dice loaded with all the hopes, fears, interests, and passions which rage in the breasts of ambitious and desperate men,) — and all the people, from the interests they have depending, become enlisted, excited, agitated, and generally corrupted, by the hazards of the game.

The trial by jury disavows the majority principle altogether; and proceeds upon the ground that every man should be presumed to be entitled to life, liberty, and such property as he has in his possession; and that the government should lay its hand upon none of them, (except for the purpose of bringing them before a tribunal for adjudication,) unless it be first ascertained, *beyond a reasonable doubt*, in every individual case, that justice requires it.

To ascertain whether there be such reasonable doubt, it takes twelve men *by lot* from the whole body of mature men. If any of these twelve are proved to be under the influence of any *special* interest or passion, that may either pervert their judgments, or corrupt their motives, they are set aside as unsuitable for the performance of a duty requiring such absolute impartiality and integrity; and others substituted in their stead. When the utmost practicable impartiality is attained on the part of the whole twelve, they are sworn to the observance of justice; and their unanimous concurrence is then held to be necessary to remove that reasonable doubt, which, unremoved, would forbid the government to lay its hand on its victim.

Such is the caution which the trial by jury both practises

and inculcates, against the violation of justice, on the part of the government, towards the humblest individual, in the smallest matter affecting his civil rights, his property, liberty, or life. And such is the contrast, which the trial by jury presents, to that gambler's and robber's rule, that the majority have a right, by virtue of their superior numbers, and without regard to justice, to dispose at pleasure of the property and persons of all bodies of men less numerous than themselves.

The difference, in short, between the two systems, is this. The trial by jury protects person and property, inviolate to their possessors, from the hand of the law, unless *justice, beyond a reasonable doubt,* require them to be taken. The majority principle takes person and property from their possessors, at the mere arbitrary will of a majority, who are liable and likely to be influenced, in taking them, by motives of oppression, avarice, and ambition.

If the relative numbers of opposing parties afforded sufficient evidence of the comparative justice of their claims, the government should carry the principle into its courts of justice; and instead of referring controversies to impartial and disinterested men,— to judges and jurors, sworn to do justice, and bound patiently to hear and weigh all the evidence and arguments that can be offered on either side,— it should simply *count* the plaintiffs and defendants in each case, (where there were more than one of either,) and then give the case to the majority; after ample opportunity had been given to the plaintiffs and defendants to reason with, flatter, cheat, threaten, and bribe each other, by way of inducing them to change sides. Such a process would be just as rational in courts of justice, as in halls of legislation; for it is of no importance to a man, who has his rights taken from him, whether it be done by a legislative enactment, or a judicial decision.

In legislation, the people are all arranged as plaintiffs and defendants in their own causes; (those who are in favor of a particular law, standing as plaintiffs, and those who are opposed to the same law, standing as defendants); and to allow these causes to be decided by majorities, is plainly as absurd as it would be to allow judicial decisions to be determined by the relative number of plaintiffs and defendants.

If this mode of decision were introduced into courts of justice, we should see a parallel, and only a parallel, to that system of legislation which we witness daily. We should see large bodies of men conspiring to bring perfectly groundless suits, against other bodies of men, for large sums of money, and to carry them by sheer force of numbers; just as we now continually see large bodies of men conspiring to carry, by mere force of numbers, some scheme of legislation that will, directly or indirectly, take money out of other men's pockets, and put it into their own. And we should also see distinct bodies of men, parties in separate suits, combining and agreeing all to appear and be counted as plaintiffs or defendants in each other's suits, for the purpose of ekeing out the necessary majority; just as we now see distinct bodies of men, interested in separate schemes of ambition or plunder, conspiring to carry through a batch of legislative enactments, that shall accomplish their several purposes.

This system of combination and conspiracy would go on, until at length whole states and a whole nation would become divided into two great litigating parties, each party composed of several smaller bodies, having their separate suits, but all confederating for the purpose of making up the necessary majority in each case. The individuals composing each of these two great parties, would at length become so accustomed to acting together, and so well acquainted with each others' schemes, and so mutually dependent upon each others' fidelity for success, that they would become organized as permanent associations; bound together by that kind of honor that prevails among thieves; and pledged by all their interests, sympathies, and animosities, to mutual fidelity, and to unceasing hostility to their opponents; and exerting all their arts and all their resources of threats, injuries, promises, and bribes, to drive or seduce from the other party enough to enable their own to retain or acquire such a majority as would be necessary to gain their own suits, and defeat the suits of their opponents. All the wealth and talent of the country would become enlisted in the service of these rival associations; and both would at length become so compact, so well organized, so powerful, and yet always so much in need of recruits, that a private person would be nearly or quite unable to obtain justice in the most paltry suit with his neighbor, except on the condition of joining one of these great litigating associations, who would agree to carry through his cause, on condition of his assisting them to carry through all the others, good and bad, which they had already undertaken. If he refused this, they would threaten to make a similar offer to his antagonist, and suffer their whole numbers to be counted against him.

Now this picture is no caricature, but a true and honest likeness. And such a system of administering justice, would be no more false, absurd, or atrocious, than that system of working by majorities, which seeks to accomplish, by legislation, the same ends which, in the case supposed, would be accomplished by judicial decisions.

Again, the doctrine that the minority ought to submit to the will of the majority, proceeds, not upon the principle that government is formed by voluntary association, and for an *agreed purpose*, on the part of all who contribute to its support, but upon the presumption that all government must be practically a state of war and plunder between opposing parties; and that, in order to save blood, and prevent mutual extermination, the parties come to an agreement that they will count their respective numbers periodically, and the one party shall then be permitted quietly to rule and plunder, (restrained only by their own discretion,) and the other submit quietly to be ruled and plundered, until the time of the next enumeration.

Such an agreement may possibly be wiser than unceasing and deadly conflict; it nevertheless partakes too much of the ludicrous to deserve to be seriously considered as an expedient for the maintenance of civil society. It would certainly seem that mankind might agree upon a cessation of hostilities, upon more rational and equitable terms than that of unconditional submission on the part of the less numerous body. Unconditional submission is usually the last act of one who confesses himself subdued and enslaved. How any one ever came to imagine that condition to be one of freedom, has never been explained. And as for the system being adapted to the maintenance of justice among men, it is a mystery that any human mind could ever have been visited with an insanity wild enough to originate the idea.

If it be said that other corporations, than governments, surrender their affairs into the hands of the majority, the answer is, that they allow majorities to determine only trifling matters, that are in their nature mere questions of discretion, and where there is no natural presumption of justice or right on one side rather than the other. They *never* surrender to the majority the power to dispose of, or, what is practically the same thing, to *determine*, the *rights* of any individual member. The *rights* of every member are determined by the written compact, to which all the members have voluntarily agreed.

For example. A banking corporation allows a majority to determine such questions of discretion as whether the note of A or of B shall be discounted; whether notes shall be discounted on one, two, or six days in the week; how many hours in a day their banking-house shall be kept open; how many clerks shall be employed; what salaries they shall receive, and such like matters, which are in their nature mere subjects of discretion, and where there are no natural presumptions of justice or right in favor of one course over the other. But no banking corporation allows a majority, or any other number of its members less than the whole, to divert the funds of the corporation to any other purpose than the one to which *every member* of the corporation has legally agreed that they may be devoted; nor to take the stock of one member and give it to another; nor to distribute the dividends among the stockholders otherwise than to each one the proportion which he has agreed to accept, and all the others have agreed that he shall receive. Nor does any banking corporation allow a majority to impose taxes upon the members for the payment of the corporate expenses, except in such proportions as *every member* has consented that they may be imposed. All these questions, involving the *rights* of the members as against each other, are fixed by the articles of the association,— that is, by the agreement to which *every member* has personally assented.

What is also specially to be noticed, and what constitutes a vital difference between the banking corporation and the political corporation, or government, is, that in case of controversy among the members of the banking corporation, as to the *rights* of any member, the question is determined, not by any number, either majority, or minority, of the corporation itself, *but by persons out of the corporation;* by twelve men acting as jurors, or by other tribunals of justice, of which no member of the corporation is allowed to be a part. But in the case of the political corporation, controversies among the parties to it, as to the rights of individual members, must of necessity be settled by members of the corporation itself, because there are no persons out of the corporation to whom the question can be referred.

Since, then, all questions as to the *rights* of the members of the political corporation, must be determined by members of the corporation itself, the trial by jury says that no man's *rights*,— neither his right to his life, his liberty, nor his property,— shall be determined by any such standard as the mere will and pleasure of majorities; but only by the unanimous verdict of a tribunal fairly representing the whole people,— that is, a tribunal of twelve men, taken at random from the whole body, and ascertained to be as impartial as the nature of the case will admit, *and sworn to the observance of justice.* Such is the difference in the two kinds of corporations; and the custom of managing by majorities the mere discretionary matters of business corporations, (the majority having no power to determine the *rights* of any member,) furnishes no analogy to the practice, adopted by political corporations, of disposing of all the *rights* of their members by the arbitrary will of majorities.

But further. The doctrine that the majority have a *right* to rule, proceeds upon the principle that minorities have no *rights* in the government; for certainly the minority cannot be said to have any *rights* in a government, so long as the majority alone determine what their rights shall be. They hold everything, or nothing, as the case may be, at the mere will of the majority.

It is indispensable to a "*free* government," (in the political sense of that term,) that the minority, the weaker party, have a veto upon the acts of the majority. Political liberty is liberty for the *weaker party* in a nation. It is only the weaker party that lose their liberties, when a government becomes oppressive. The stronger party, in all governments, are free by virtue of their superior strength. They never oppress themselves.

Legislation is the work of this stronger party; and if, in addition to the sole power of legislating, they have the sole power of determining what legislation shall be enforced, they have all power in their hands, and the weaker party are the subjects of an absolute government.

Unless the weaker party have a veto, either upon the making, or the enforcement of laws, they have no power whatever in the government, and can of course have no liberties except such as the stronger party, in their arbitrary discretion, see fit to permit them to enjoy.

In England and the United States, the trial by jury is the only institution that gives the weaker party any veto upon the power of the stronger. Consequently it is the only institution, that gives them any effective voice in the government, or any guaranty against oppression.

Suffrage, however free, is of no avail for this purpose; because the suffrage of the minority is overborne by the suffrage of the majority, and is thus rendered powerless for purposes of legislation. The responsibility of officers can be made of no avail, because they are responsible only to the majority. The minority, therefore, are wholly without rights in the government, wholly at the mercy of the majority, unless, through the trial by jury, they have a veto upon such legislation as they think unjust.

Government is established for the protection of the weak against the strong. This is the principal, if not the sole, motive for the establishment of all legitimate government. Laws, that are sufficient for the protection of the weaker party, are of course sufficient for the protection of the stronger party; because the strong can certainly need no more protection than the weak. It is, therefore, right that the weaker party should be represented in the tribunal which is finally to determine what legislation may be enforced; and that no legislation shall be enforced against their consent. They being presumed to be competent judges of what kind of legislation makes for their safety, and what for their injury, it must be presumed that any legislation, which *they* object to enforcing, tends to their oppression, and not to their security.

There is still another reason why the weaker party, or the minority, should have a veto upon all legislation which they disapprove. *That reason is, that that is the only means by which the government can be kept within the limits of the contract, compact, or constitution, by which the whole people agree to establish government.* If the majority were allowed to interpret the compact for themselves, and enforce it according to their own interpretation, they would, of course, make it authorize them to do whatever they wish to do.

The theory of free government is that it is formed by the voluntary contract of the people individually with each other. This is the theory, (although it is not, as it ought to be, the fact,) in all the governments in the United States, as also in the government of England. The theory assumes that each man, who is a party to the government, and contributes to its support, has individually and freely consented to it. Otherwise the government would have no right to tax him for its support,— for taxation without consent is robbery. This theory, then, necessarily supposes that this government, which is formed by the free consent of all, has no powers except such as *all* the parties to it have individually agreed that it shall have; and especially that it has no power to pass any *laws*, except such as *all* the parties have agreed that it may pass.

This theory supposes that there may be certain laws that will be beneficial to *all*,— so beneficial that *all* consent to be taxed for their maintenance. For the maintenance of these specific laws, in which all are interested, all associate. And they associate for the maintenance of those laws *only*, in which *all* are interested. It would be absurd to suppose that all would associate, and consent to be taxed, for purposes which were beneficial only to a part; and especially for purposes that were injurious to any. A government of the whole, therefore, can have no powers except such as *all* the parties consent that it may have. It can do nothing except what *all* have consented that it may do. And if any portion of the people,— no matter how large their number, if it be less than the whole,— desire a government for any purposes other than those that are common to all, and desired by all, they must form a separate association for those purposes. They have no right,— by perverting this government of the whole, to the accomplishment of purposes desired only by a part,— to compel any one to contribute to purposes that are either useless or injurious to himself.

Such being the principles on which the government is formed, the question arises, how shall this government, when formed, be kept within the limits of the contract by which it was established? How shall this government, instituted by the whole people, agreed to by the whole people, supported by the contributions of the whole people, be confined to the accomplishment of those purposes alone, which the whole people desire? How shall it be preserved from degenerating into a mere government for the benefit of a part only of those who established, and who support it? How shall it be prevented from even injuring a part of its own members, for the aggrandizement of the rest? Its laws must be, (or at least now are,) passed, and most of its other acts performed, by mere agents,— agents chosen by a part of the people, and not by the whole. How can these agents be restrained from seeking their own interests, and the interests of those who elected them, at the expense of the rights of the remainder of the people, by the passage and enforcement of laws that shall be partial, unequal, and unjust in their operation? That is the great question. And the trial by jury answers it. And how does the trial by jury answer it? It answers it, as has already been shown throughout this volume, by saying that these mere agents and attorneys, who are chosen by a part only of the people, and are liable to be influenced by partial and unequal purposes,-shall not have unlimited authority in the enactment and enforcement of laws; that they shall not exercise *all* the functions of government. It says that they shall never exercise that ultimate power of compelling obedience to the laws by punishing for disobedience, or of executing the laws against the person or property of any man, without first getting the consent of the people, through a tribunal that may fairly be presumed to represent the whole, or substantially the whole, people. It says that if the power to make laws, and the power also to enforce them, were committed to these agents, they would have all power,— would be absolute masters of the people, and could deprive them of their rights at pleasure. It says, therefore, that the people themselves will hold a veto upon the enforcement of any and every law, which these agents may enact, and that whenever the occasion arises for them to give or withhold their consent,— inasmuch as the whole people cannot assemble, or devote the time and attention necessary to the investigation of each case,— twelve of their number shall be taken by lot, or otherwise at random, from the whole body; that they shall not be chosen by majorities, (the same majorities that elected the agents who enacted the laws to be put in issue,) nor by any interested or suspected party; that they shall not be appointed by, or be in any way dependent upon, those who enacted the law; that their opinions, whether for or against the law that is in issue, shall not be inquired of beforehand; and that if these twelve men give their consent to the enforcement of the law, their consent shall stand for the consent of the whole.

This is the mode, which the trial by jury provides, for keeping the government within the limits designed by the whole people, who have associated for its establishment. And it is the only mode, provided either by the English or American constitutions, for the accomplishment of that object.

But it will, perhaps, be said that if the minority can defeat the will of the majority, then the minority *rule* the majority. But this is not true in any unjust sense. The minority enact no laws of their own. They simply refuse their assent to such laws of the majority as they do not approve. The minority assume no authority over the majority; they simply defend themselves. They do not interfere with the right of the majority to seek their own happiness in their own way, so long as they (the majority) do not interfere with the minority. They claim simply not to be oppressed, and not to be compelled to assist in doing anything which they do not approve. They say to the majority, "We will unite with you, if you desire it, for the accomplishment of all those purposes, in which we have a common interest with you. You can certainly expect us to do nothing more. If you do not choose to associate with us on those terms, there must be two separate associations. You must associate for the accomplishment of your purposes; we for the accomplishment of ours."

In this case, the minority assume no authority over the majority; they simply refuse to surrender their own liberties into the hands of the majority. They propose a union; but decline submission. The majority are still at liberty to refuse the connection, and to seek their own happiness in their own way, except that they cannot be gratified in their desire to become absolute masters of the minority.

But, it may be asked, how can the minority be trusted to enforce even such legislation as is equal and just? The answer is, that they are as reliable for that purpose as are the majority; they are as much presumed to have associated, and are as likely to have associated, for that object, as are the majority; and they have as much interest in such legislation as have the majority. They have even more interest in it; for, being the weaker party, they must rely on it for their security,—having no other security on which they can rely. Hence their consent to the establishment of government, and to the *taxation* required for its support, is *presumed*, (although it ought not to be presumed,) without any express consent being given. This presumption of their consent to be taxed for the maintenance of laws, would be absurd, if they could not themselves be trusted to act in good faith in enforcing those laws. And hence they cannot be presumed to have consented to be taxed for the maintenance of any laws, except such as they are themselves ready to aid in enforcing. It is therefore unjust to tax them, unless they are eligible to seats in a jury, with power to judge of the justice of the laws. Taxing them for the support of the laws, on the assumption that they are in favor of the laws, and at the same time refusing them the right, as jurors, to judge of the justice of the laws, on the assumption that they are opposed to the laws, are flat contradictions.

But, it will be asked, what motive have the majority, when

they have all power in their own hands, to submit their will to the veto of the minority?

One answer is, that they have the motive of justice. It would be *unjust* to compel the minority to contribute, by taxation, to the support of any laws which they did not approve.

Another answer is, that if the stronger party wish to use their power only for purposes of justice, they have no occasion to fear the veto of the weaker party; for the latter have as strong motives for the maintenance of *just* government, as have the former.

Another answer is, that if the stronger party use their power *unjustly*, they will hold it by an uncertain tenure, especially in a community where knowledge is diffused; for knowledge will enable the weaker party to make itself in time the stronger party. It also enables the weaker party, even while it remains the weaker party, perpetually to annoy, alarm, and injure their oppressors. Unjust power,— or rather power that is *grossly* unjust, and that is known to be so by the minority, — can be sustained only at the expense of standing armies, and all the other machinery of force; for the oppressed party are always ready to risk their lives for purposes of vengeance, and the acquisition of their rights, whenever there is any tolerable chance of success. Peace, safety, and quiet for all, can be enjoyed only under laws that obtain the consent of all. Hence tyrants frequently yield to the demands of justice from those weaker than themselves, as a means of buying peace and safety.

Still another answer is, that those who are in the majority on one law, will be in the minority on another. All, therefore, need the benefit of the veto, at some time or other, to protect themselves from injustice.

That the limits, within which legislation would, by this process, be confined, would be exceedingly narrow, in comparison with those it at present occupies, there can be no doubt. All monopolies, all special privileges, all sumptuary laws, all restraints upon any traffic, bargain, or contract, that was naturally lawful,* all restraints upon men's natural

---

* Such as restraints upon banking, upon the rates of interest, upon traffic with foreigners, &c., &c.

rights, the whole catalogue of *mala prohibita*, and all taxation to which the taxed parties had not individually, severally, and freely consented, would be at an end; because all such legislation implies a violation of the rights of a greater or less minority. This minority would disregard, trample upon, or resist, the execution of such legislation, and then throw themselves upon a jury of the whole people for justification and protection. In this way all legislation would be nullified, except the legislation of that general nature which impartially protected the rights, and subserved the interests, of all. The only legislation that could be sustained, would probably be such as tended directly to the maintenance of justice and liberty; such, for example, as should contribute to the enforcement of contracts, the protection of property, and the prevention and punishment of acts intrinsically criminal. In short, government in practice would be brought to the necessity of a strict adherence to natural law, and natural justice, instead of being, as it now is, a great battle, in which avarice and ambition are constantly fighting for and obtaining advantages over the natural rights of mankind.

APPENDIX.

TAXATION.

It was a principle of the Common Law, as it is of the law of nature, and of common sense, that no man can be taxed without his personal consent. The Common Law knew nothing of that system, which now prevails in England, of *assuming* a man's own consent to be taxed, because some pretended representative, whom he never authorized to act for him, has taken it upon himself to consent that he may be taxed. That is one of the many frauds on the Common Law, and the English constitution, which have been introduced since Magna Carta. Having finally established itself in England, it has been stupidly and servilely copied and submitted to in the United States.

If the trial by jury were reëstablished, the Common Law principle of taxation would be reëstablished with it; for it is not to be supposed that juries would enforce a tax upon an individual which he had never agreed to pay. Taxation without consent is as plainly robbery, when enforced against one man, as when enforced against millions; and it is not to be imagined that juries could be blind to so self-evident a principle. Taking a man's money without his consent, is also as much robbery, when it is done by millions of men, acting in concert, and calling themselves a government, as when it is done by a single individual, acting on his own responsibility, and calling himself a highwayman. Neither the numbers engaged in the act, nor the different characters they assume as a cover for the act, alter the nature of the act itself.

If the government can take a man's money without his consent, there is no limit to the additional tyranny it may practise upon him; for, with his money, it can hire soldiers to stand over him, keep him in subjection, plunder him at discretion, and kill him if he resists. And governments always will do this, as they everywhere and always have done it, except where the Common Law principle has been established. It is therefore a first principle, a very *sine qua non* of political freedom, that a man can be taxed only by his personal consent. And the establishment of this principle, *with trial by jury*, insures freedom of course; because: 1. No man would pay his money unless he had first contracted for such a government as he was willing to support; and, 2. Unless the government then kept itself within the terms of its contract, juries would not enforce the payment of the tax. Besides, the agreement to be taxed would probably be entered into but for a year at a time. If, in that year, the government proved itself either inefficient or tyrannical, to any serious degree, the contract would not be renewed.

APPENDIX.   223

The dissatisfied parties, if sufficiently numerous for a new organization, would form themselves into a separate association for mutual protection. If not sufficiently numerous for that purpose, those who were conscientious would forego all governmental protection, rather than contribute to the support of a government which they deemed unjust.

All legitimate government is a mutual insurance company, voluntarily agreed upon by the parties to it, for the protection of their rights against wrong-doers. In its voluntary character it is precisely similar to an association for mutual protection against fire or shipwreck. Before a man will join an association for these latter purposes, and pay the premium for being insured, he will, if he be a man of sense, look at the articles of the association; see what the company promises to do; what it is likely to do; and what are the rates of insurance. If he be satisfied on all these points, he will become a member, pay his premium for a year, and then hold the company to its contract. If the conduct of the company prove unsatisfactory, he will let his policy expire at the end of the year for which he has paid; will decline to pay any further premiums, and either seek insurance elsewhere, or take his own risk without any insurance. And as men act in the insurance of their ships and dwellings, they would act in the insurance of their properties, liberties and lives, in the political association, or government.

The political insurance company, or government, have no more right, in nature or reason, to *assume* a man's consent to be protected by them, and to be taxed for that protection, when he has given no actual consent, than a fire or marine insurance company have to assume a man's consent to be protected by them, and to pay the premium, when his actual consent has never been given. To take a man's property without his consent is robbery; and to assume his consent, where no actual consent is given, makes the taking none the less robbery. If it did, the highwayman has the same right to assume a man's consent to part with his purse, that any other man, or body of men, can have. And his assumption would afford as much moral justification for his robbery as does a like assumption, on the part of the government, for taking a man's property without his consent. The government's pretence of protecting him, as an equivalent for the taxation, affords no justification. It is for himself to decide whether he desires such protection as the government offers him. If he do not desire it, or do not bargain for it, the government has no more right than any other insurance company to impose it upon him, or make him pay for it.

Trial by the country, and no taxation without consent, were the two pillars of English liberty, (when England had any liberty,) and the first principles of the Common Law. They mutually sustain each other; and neither can stand without the other. Without both, no people have any guaranty for their freedom; with both, no people can be otherwise than free.*

---

* Trial by the country, and no taxation without consent, mutually sustain each other, and can be sustained only by each other, for these reasons: 1. Juries would refuse to enforce a tax against a man who had never agreed to pay it. They would also protect men in forcibly resisting the collection of taxes to which they had never consented. Otherwise the jurors would authorize the government to tax themselves without their consent, — a thing which no jury would be likely to do. In these two ways, then, trial by the country would sustain the principle of no taxation without consent. 2. On the other hand, the principle of no taxation without consent would sustain the trial by the country, because men in general would not consent to be taxed for the support of a

By what force, fraud, and conspiracy, on the part of kings, nobles, and "a few wealthy freeholders," these pillars have been prostrated in England, it is designed to show more fully in the next volume, if it should be necessary.

---

government under which trial by the country was not secured. Thus these two principles mutually sustain each other.

But, if either of these principles were broken down, the other would fall with it, and for these reasons: 1. If trial by the country were broken down, the principle of no taxation without consent would fall with it, because the government would then be *able* to tax the people without their consent, inasmuch as the legal tribunals would be mere tools of the government, and would enforce such taxation, and punish men for resisting such taxation, as the government ordered. 2. On the other hand, if the principle of no taxation without consent were broken down, trial by the country would fall with it, because the government, if it could tax people without their consent, would, of course, take enough of their money to enable it to employ all the force necessary for sustaining its own tribunals, (in the place of juries,) and carrying their decrees into execution.

A LETTER

TO

GROVER CLEVELAND,

ON

His False Inaugural Address, The Usurpations and Crimes of Lawmakers and Judges, and The Consequent Poverty, Ignorance, and Servitude of the People.

BY
LYSANDER SPOONER.

BOSTON:
BENJ. R. TUCKER, PUBLISHER.
1886.

The author reserves his copyright in this letter.

First pamphlet edition published in July, 1886.*

---

*Under a somewhat different title, to wit, "*A Letter to Grover Cleveland, on his False, Absurd, Self-contradictory, and Ridiculous Inaugural Address,*" this letter was first published, in instalments, in "LIBERTY" (a paper published in Boston); the instalments commencing June 20, 1885, and continuing to May 22, 1886: notice being given, in each paper, of the reservation of copyright.

A LETTER TO GROVER CLEVELAND.

Section I.

To Grover Cleveland:

Sir,—Your inaugural address is probably as honest, sensible, and consistent a one as that of any president within the last fifty years, or, perhaps, as any since the foundation of the government. If, therefore, it is false, absurd, self-contradictory, and ridiculous, it is not (as I think) because you are personally less honest, sensible, or consistent than your predecessors, but because the government itself—according to your own description of it, and according to the practical administration of it for nearly a hundred years—is an utterly and palpably false, absurd, and criminal one. Such praises as you bestow upon it are, therefore, necessarily false, absurd, and ridiculous.

Thus you describe it as "a government pledged to do equal and exact justice to all men."

Did you stop to think what that means? Evidently you did not; for nearly, or quite, all the rest of your address is in direct contradiction to it.

Let me then remind you that justice is an immutable, natural principle; and not anything that can be made, unmade, or altered by any human power.

It is also a subject of science, and is to be learned, like mathematics, or any other science. It does not derive its authority from the commands, will, pleasure, or discretion of any possible combination of men, whether calling themselves a government, or by any other name.

It is also, at all times, and in all places, the supreme law. And being everywhere and always the supreme law, it is necessarily everywhere and always the only law.

Lawmakers, as they call themselves, can add nothing to it, nor take anything from it. Therefore all their laws, as they call them,—that is, all the laws of their own making,—have no color of authority or obligation. It is a falsehood to call them laws; for there is nothing in them that either creates men's duties or rights, or enlightens them as to their duties or rights. There is consequently nothing binding or obligatory about them. And nobody is bound to take the least notice of them, unless it be to trample them under foot, as usurpations. If they command men to do justice, they add nothing to men's obligation to do it, or to any man's right to enforce it. They are therefore mere idle wind, such as would be commands to consider the day as day, and the night as night. If they command or license any man to do injustice, they are criminal on their face. If they command any man to do anything which justice does not require him to do, they are simple, naked usurpations and tyrannies. If they forbid any man to do anything, which justice would permit him to do, they are criminal invasions of his natural and rightful liberty. In whatever light, therefore, they are viewed, they are utterly destitute of everything like authority or obligation. They are all necessarily either the impudent, fraudulent, and criminal usurpations of tyrants, robbers, and murderers, or the senseless work of ignorant or thoughtless men, who do not know, or certainly do not realize, what they are doing.

This science of justice, or natural law, is the only science that tells us what are, and what are not, each man's natural, inherent, inalienable, *individual* rights, as against any and all other men. And to say that any, or all, other men may rightfully compel him to obey any or all such other laws as they may see fit to *make*, is to say that he has no rights of his own, but is their subject, their property, and their slave.

For the reasons now given, the simple maintenance of justice, or natural law, is plainly the one only purpose for which any coercive power — or anything bearing the name of government — has a right to exist.

It is intrinsically just as false, absurd, ludicrous, and ridiculous to say that lawmakers, so-called, can invent and make any laws, *of their own*, authoritatively fixing, or declaring, the rights of individuals, or that shall be in any manner authoritative or obligatory upon individuals, or that individuals may rightfully be compelled to obey, as it would be to say that they can invent and make such mathematics, chemistry, physiology, or other sciences, as they see fit, and rightfully compel individuals to conform all their actions to them, instead of conforming them to the mathematics, chemistry, physiology, or other sciences of nature.

Lawmakers, as they call themselves, might just as well claim the right to abolish, by statute, the natural law of gravitation, the natural laws of light, heat, and electricity, and all the other natural laws of matter and mind, and institute laws of their own in the place of them, and compel conformity to them, as to claim the right to set aside the natural law of justice, and compel obedience to such other laws as they may see fit to manufacture, and set up in its stead.

Let me now ask you how you imagine that your so-called lawmakers can "do equal and exact justice to all men," by any so-called laws of their own making. If their laws command anything but justice, or forbid anything but injustice, they are themselves unjust and criminal. If they simply command justice, and forbid injustice, they add nothing to the natural authority of justice, or to men's obligation to obey it. It is, therefore, a simple impertinence, and sheer impudence, on their part, to assume that *their* commands, *as such*, are of any authority whatever. It is also sheer impudence, on their part, to assume that their commands are at all necessary to teach other men what is, and what is not, justice. The science of justice is as open to be learned by all other men, as by themselves; and it is, in general, so simple and easy to be learned, that there is no need of, and no place for, any man, or body of men, to teach it, declare it, or command it, on their own authority.

For one, or another, of these reasons, therefore, each and every law, so-called, that forty-eight different congresses have presumed to make, within the last ninety-six years, have been utterly destitute of all legitimate authority. That is to say, they have either been criminal, as commanding or licensing men to do what justice forbade them to do, or as forbidding them to do what justice would have permitted them to do; or else they have been superfluous, as adding nothing to men's knowledge of justice, or to their obligation to do justice, or abstain from injustice.

What excuse, then, have you for attempting to enforce upon the people that great mass of superfluous or criminal laws (so-called) which ignorant and foolish, or impudent and criminal, men have, for so many years, been manufacturing, and promulgating, and enforcing, in violation of justice, and of all men's natural, inherent, and inalienable rights?

Section II.

Perhaps you will say that there is no such science as that of justice. If you do say this, by what right, or on what reason, do you proclaim your intention "to do equal and exact justice to all men"? If there is no science of justice, how do you know that there is any such principle as justice? Or how do you know what is, and what is not, justice? If there is no science of justice,—such as the people can learn and understand for themselves,—why do you say anything about justice *to them?* Or why do you promise *them* any such thing as "equal and exact justice," if they do not know, and are incapable of learning, what justice is? Do you use this phrase to deceive those whom you look upon as being so ignorant, so destitute of reason, as to be deceived by idle, unmeaning words? If you do not, you are plainly bound to let us all know what you do mean, by doing "equal and exact justice to all men."

I can assure you, sir, that a very large portion of the people of this country do not believe that the government is doing "equal and exact justice to all men." And some persons are earnestly promulgating the idea that the government is not attempting to do, and has no intention of doing, anything like "equal and exact justice to all men"; that, on the contrary, it is knowingly, deliberately, and wilfully doing an incalculable amount of injustice; that it has always been doing this in the past, and that it has no intention of doing anything else in the future; that it is a mere tool in the hands of a few ambitious, rapacious, and unprincipled men; that its purpose, in doing all this injustice, is to keep—so far as they can without driving the people to rebellion—all wealth, and all political power, in as few hands as possible; and that this injustice is the direct cause of all the widespread poverty, ignorance, and servitude among the great body of the people.

Now, Sir, I wish I could hope that you would do something to show that you are not a party to any such scheme as that; something to show that you are neither corrupt enough, nor blind enough, nor coward enough, to be made use of for any such purpose as that; something to show that when you profess your intention "to do equal and exact justice to all men," you attach some real and definite meaning to your words. Until you do that, is it not plain that the people have a right to consider you a tyrant, and the confederate and tool of tyrants, and to get rid of you as unceremoniously as they would of any other tyrant?

Section III.

Sir, if any government is to be a rational, consistent, and honest one, it must evidently be based on some fundamental, immutable, eternal principle; such as every man may reasonably agree to, and such as every man may rightfully be compelled to abide by, and obey. And the whole power of the government must be limited to the maintenance of that single principle. And that one principle is justice. There is no other principle that any man can rightfully enforce upon others, or ought to consent to have enforced against himself. Every man claims the protection of this principle for himself, whether he is willing to accord it to others, or not. Yet such is the inconsistency of human nature, that some men— in fact, many men— who will risk their lives for this principle, when their own liberty or property is at stake, will violate it in the most flagrant manner, if they can thereby obtain arbitrary power over the persons or property of others. We have seen this fact illustrated in this country, through its whole history—especially during the last hundred years—and in the case of many of the most conspicuous persons. And their example and influence have been employed to pervert the whole character of the government. It is against such men, that all others, who desire nothing but justice for themselves, and are willing to unite to secure it for all others, must combine, if we are ever to have justice established for any.

Section IV.

It is self-evident that no number of men, by conspiring, and calling themselves a government, can acquire any rights whatever over other men, or other men's property, which they had not before, as individuals. And whenever any number of men, calling themselves a government, do anything to another man, or to his property, which they had no right to do as individuals, they thereby declare themselves trespassers, robbers, or murderers, according to the nature of their acts.

Men, *as individuals*, may rightfully *compel* each other to obey this one law of justice. And it is the only law which any man can rightfully be compelled, *by his fellow men*, to obey. All other laws, it is optional with each man to obey, or not, as he may choose. But this one law of justice he may rightfully be compelled to obey; and all the force that is reasonably necessary to compel him, may rightfully be used against him.

But the right of every man to do anything, and everything, *which justice does not forbid him to do*, is a natural, inherent, inalienable right. It is his right, as against any and all other men, whether they be many, or few. It is a right indispensable to every man's highest happiness; and to every man's power of judging and determining for himself what will, and what will not, promote his happiness. Any restriction upon the exercise of this right is a restriction upon his rightful power of providing for, and accomplishing, his own well-being.

Sir, these natural, inherent, inalienable, *individual* rights are sacred things. *They are the only human rights.* They are the only rights by which any man can protect his own property, liberty, or life against any one who may be disposed to take it away. Consequently they are not things that any set of either blockheads or villains, calling themselves a government, can rightfully take into their own hands, and dispose of at their pleasure, as they have been accustomed to do in this, and in nearly or quite all other countries.

Section V.

Sir, I repeat that individual rights are the only human rights. *Legally speaking*, there are no such things as *"public rights,"* as distinguished from individual rights. *Legally speaking*, there is no such creature or thing as *"the public."* The term "the public" is an utterly vague and indefinite one, applied arbitrarily and at random to a greater or less number of individuals, each and every one of whom have their own separate, individual rights, *and none others*. And the protection of these separate, *individual* rights is the one only legitimate purpose, for which anything in the nature of a governing, or coercive, power has a right to exist. And these separate, individual rights all rest upon, and can be ascertained only by, the one science of justice.

Legally speaking, the term "public *rights*" is as vague and indefinite as are the terms "public *health*," "public *good*," "public *welfare*," and the like. It has no legal meaning, except when used to describe the separate, private, *individual* rights of a greater or less number of individuals.

In so far as the separate, private, natural rights of *individuals* are secured, in just so far, and no farther, are the "public rights" secured. In so far as the separate, private, natural rights of *individuals* are disregarded or violated, in just so far are "public rights" disregarded or violated. Therefore all the pretences of so-called lawmakers, that they are protecting "public rights," by violating private rights, are sheer and utter contradictions and frauds. They are just as false and absurd as it would be to say that they are protecting the public *health*, by arbitrarily poisoning and destroying the health of single individuals.

The pretence of the lawmakers, that they are promoting the "public *good*," by violating individual "*rights*," is just as false and absurd as is the pretence that they are protecting "public *rights*" by violating "private rights." Sir, the greatest "public *good*," of which any coercive power, calling itself a government, or by any other name, is capable, is the protection of each and every individual in the quiet and peaceful enjoyment and exercise of *all* his own natural, inherent, inalienable, *individual* "rights." This is a "good" that comes home to each and every individual, of whom "the public" is composed. It is also a "good," which each and every one of these individuals, composing "the public," can appreciate. It is a "good," for the loss of which governments can make no compensation whatever. *It is a universal and impartial "good*," of the highest importance to each and every human being; and not any such vague, false, and criminal thing as the lawmakers —when violating private rights—tell us they are trying to accomplish, under the name of "the public good." It is also the only "equal and exact justice," which you, or anybody else, are capable of securing, or have any occasion to secure, to any human being. Let but this "equal and exact justice" be secured "to all men," and they will then be abundantly able to take care of themselves, and secure their own highest "good." Or if any one should ever chance to need anything more than this, he may safely trust to the voluntary kindness of his fellow men to supply it.

It is one of those things not easily accounted for, that men who would scorn to do an injustice to a fellow man, in a private transaction,—who would scorn to usurp any arbitrary dominion over him, or his property,—who would be in the highest degree indignant, if charged with any private injustice,—and who, at a moment's warning, would take their lives in their hands, to defend their own rights, and redress their own wrongs,—will, the moment they become members of what they call a government, assume that they are absolved from all principles and all obligations that were imperative upon them, as individuals; will assume that they are invested with a right of arbitrary and irresponsible dominion over other men, and other men's property. Yet they are doing this continually. And all the laws they *make* are based upon the assumption that they have now become invested with rights that are more than human, and that those, on whom their laws are to operate, have lost even their human rights. They seem to be utterly blind to the fact, that the only reason there can be for their existence as a government, is that they may protect those very "rights," which they before scrupulously respected, but which they now unscrupulously trample upon.

Section VI.

But you evidently believe nothing of what I have now been saying. You evidently believe that justice is no law at all, unless in cases where the lawmakers may chance to prefer it to any law which they themselves can invent.

You evidently believe that a certain paper, called the constitution, which nobody ever signed, which few persons ever read, which the great body of the people never saw, and as to the meaning of which no two persons were ever agreed, is the supreme law of this land, anything in the law of nature—anything in the natural, inherent, inalienable, *individual* rights of fifty millions of people—to the contrary notwithstanding.

Did folly, falsehood, absurdity, assumption, or criminality ever reach a higher point than that?

You evidently believe that those great volumes of statutes, which the people at large have never read, nor even seen, and never will read, nor see, but which such men as you and your lawmakers have been manufacturing for nearly a hundred years, to restrain them of their liberty, and deprive them of their natural rights, were all made for their benefit, by men wiser than they—wiser even than justice itself—and having only their welfare at heart!

You evidently believe that the men who made those laws were duly authorized to make them; and that you yourself have been duly authorized to enforce them. But in this you are utterly mistaken. You have not so much as the honest, responsible scratch of one single pen, to justify you in the exercise of the power you have taken upon yourself to exercise. For example, you have no such evidence of your right to take any man's property for the support of your government, as would be required of you, if you were to claim pay for a single day's honest labor.

It was once said, in this country, that taxation without consent was robbery. And a seven years' war was fought to maintain that principle. But if that principle were a true one in behalf of three millions of men, it is an equally true one in behalf of three men, or of one man.

Who are ever taxed? Individuals only. Who have property that can be taxed? Individuals only. Who can give their consent to be taxed? Individuals only. Who are ever taxed without their consent? Individuals only. Who, then, are robbed, if taxed without their consent? Individuals only.

If taxation without consent is robbery, the United States government has never had, has not now, and is never likely to have, a single honest dollar in its treasury.

If taxation without consent is *not* robbery, then any band of robbers have only to declare themselves a government, and all their robberies are legalized.

If any man's money can be taken by a so-called government, without his own personal consent, all his other rights are taken with it; for with his money the government can, and will, hire soldiers to stand over him, compel him to submit to its arbitrary will, and kill him if he resists.

That your whole claim of a right to any man's money for the support of your government, without his consent, is the merest farce and fraud, is proved by the fact that you have no such evidence of your right to take it, as would be required of you, by one of your own courts, to prove a debt of five dollars, that might be honestly due you.

You and your lawmakers have no such evidence of your right of dominion over the people of this country, as would be required to prove your right to any material property, that you might have purchased.

When a man parts with any considerable amount of such material property as he has a natural right to part with,—as, for example, houses, or lands, or food, or clothing, or anything else of much value,—he usually gives, and the purchaser usually demands, some *written* acknowledgment, receipt, bill of sale, or other evidence, that will prove that he voluntarily parted with it, and that the purchaser is now the real and true owner of it. But you hold that fifty millions of people have voluntarily parted, not only with their natural right of dominion over all their material property, but also with all their natural right of dominion over their own souls and bodies; when not one of them has ever given you a scrap of writing, or even "made his mark," to that effect.

You have not so much as the honest signature of a single human being, granting to you or your lawmakers any right of dominion whatever over him or his property.

You hold your place only by a title, which, on no just principle of law or reason, is worth a straw. And all who are associated with you in the government—whether they be called senators, representatives, judges, executive officers, or what not—all hold their places, directly or indirectly, only by the same worthless title. That title is nothing more nor less than votes given in secret (by secret ballot), by not more than one-fifth of the whole population. These votes were given in secret solely because those who gave them did not dare to make themselves personally responsible, either for their own acts, or the acts of their agents, the lawmakers, judges, etc.

These voters, having given their votes in secret (by secret ballot), have put it out of your power—and out of the power of all others associated with you in the government—to designate your principals *individually*. That is to say, you have no legal knowledge as to who voted for you, or who voted against you. And being unable to designate your principals *individually*, you have no right to say that you have any principals. And having no right to say that you have any principals, you are bound, on every just principle of law or reason, to confess that you are mere usurpers, making laws, and enforcing them, upon your own authority alone.

A secret ballot makes a secret government; and a secret government is nothing else than a government by conspiracy. And a government by conspiracy is the only government we now have.

You say that "*every voter exercises a public trust.*"

Who appointed him to that trust? Nobody. He simply usurped the power; he never accepted the trust. And because he usurped the power, he dares exercise it only in secret. Not one of all the ten millions of voters, who helped to place you in power, would have dared to do so, if he had known that he was to be held personally responsible, before any just tribunal, for the acts of those for whom he voted.

Inasmuch as all the votes, given for you and your lawmakers, were given in secret, all that you and they can say, in support of your authority as rulers, is that you venture upon your acts as lawmakers, etc., not because you have any open, authentic, written, legitimate authority granted you by any human being, — for you can show nothing of the kind, — but only because, from certain reports made to you of votes given in secret, you have reason to believe that you have at your backs a secret association strong enough to sustain you by force, in case your authority should be resisted.

Is there a government on earth that rests upon a more false, absurd, or tyrannical basis than that?

Section VII.

But the falsehood and absurdity of your whole system of government do not result solely from the fact that it rests wholly upon votes given in secret, or by men who take care to avoid all personal responsibility for their own acts, or the acts of their agents. On the contrary, if every man, woman, and child in the United States had openly signed, sealed, and delivered to you and your associates, a written document, purporting to invest you with all the legislative, judicial, and executive powers that you now exercise, they would not thereby have given you the slightest legitimate authority. Such a contract, purporting to surrender into your hands all their natural rights of person and property, to be disposed of at your pleasure or discretion, would have been simply an absurd and void contract, giving you no real authority whatever.

It is a natural impossibility for any man to make a *binding* contract, by which he shall surrender to others a single one of what are commonly called his "natural, inherent, *inalienable* rights."

It is a natural impossibility for any man to make a *binding* contract, that shall invest others with any right whatever of arbitrary, irresponsible dominion over him.

The right of arbitrary, irresponsible dominion is the right of property; and the right of property is the right of arbitrary, irresponsible dominion. The two are identical. There is no difference between them. Neither can exist without the other. If, therefore, our so-called lawmakers really have that right of arbitrary, irresponsible dominion over us, which they claim to have, and which they habitually exercise, it must be because they own us as property. If they own us as property, it must be because nature made us their property; for, as no man can sell himself as a slave, we could never make a binding contract that should make us their property — or, what is the same thing, give them any right of arbitrary, irresponsible dominion over us.

As a lawyer, you certainly ought to know that all this is true.

Section VIII.

Sir, consider, for a moment, what an utterly false, absurd, ridiculous, and criminal government we now have.

It all rests upon the false, ridiculous, and utterly groundless assumption, that fifty millions of people not only could voluntarily surrender, but actually have voluntarily surrendered, all their natural rights, as human beings, into the custody of some four hundred men, called lawmakers, judges, etc., who are to be held utterly irresponsible for the disposal they may make of them.*

The only right, which any individual is supposed to retain, or possess, under the government, *is a purely fictitious one, — one that nature never gave him,* — to wit, his right (so-called), as one of some ten millions of male adults, to give away, by his vote, not only all his own natural, inherent, inalienable, human rights, but also all the natural, inherent, inalienable, human rights of forty millions of other human beings — that is, women and children.

To suppose that any one of all these ten millions of male adults would voluntarily surrender a single one of all his natural, inherent, inalienable, human rights into the hands of irresponsible men, is an absurdity; because, first, he has no

---

*The irresponsibility of the senators and representatives is guaranteed to them in this wise:

For any speech or debate [or vote] in either house, they [the senators and representatives] shall not be questioned [held to any legal responsibility] in any other place.—*Constitution, Art.* 1, *Sec.* 6.

The judicial and executive officers are all equally guaranteed against all responsibility *to the people.* They are made responsible only to the senators and representatives, whose laws they are to administer and execute. So long as they sanction and execute all these laws, to the satisfaction of the lawmakers, they are safe against all responsibility. *In no case can the people, whose rights they are continually denying and trampling upon, hold them to any accountability whatever.*

Thus it will be seen that all departments of the government, legislative, judicial, and executive, are placed entirely beyond any responsibility *to the people,* whose agents they profess to be, and whose rights they assume to dispose of at pleasure.

Was a more absolute, irresponsible government than that ever invented?

power to do so, any contract he may make for that purpose being absurd, and necessarily void; and, secondly, because he can have no rational motive for doing so. To suppose him to do so, is to suppose him to be an idiot, incapable of making any rational and obligatory contract. It is to suppose he would voluntarily give away everything in life that was of value to himself, and get nothing in return. To suppose that he would attempt to give away all the natural rights *of other persons*—that is, the women and children—as well as his own, is to suppose him to attempt to do something that he has no right, or power, to do. It is to suppose him to be both a villain and a fool.

And yet this government now rests wholly upon the assumption that some ten millions of male adults—men supposed to be *compos mentis*—have not only attempted to do, but have actually succeeded in doing, these absurd and impossible things.

It cannot be said that men put all their rights into the hands of the government, in order to have them protected; because there can be no such thing as a man's being protected in his rights, *any longer than he is allowed to retain them in his own possession.* The only possible way, in which any man can be protected in his rights, *is to protect him in his own actual possession and exercise of them.* And yet our government is absurd enough to assume that a man can be protected in his rights, after he has surrendered them altogether into other hands than his own.

This is just as absurd as it would be to assume that a man had given himself away as a slave, in order to be protected in the enjoyment of his liberty.

A man wants his rights protected, solely that he himself may possess and use them, and have the full benefit of them. But if he is compelled to give them up to somebody else,—to a government, so-called, or to any body else,—he ceases to have any rights of his own to be protected.

To say, as the advocates of our government do, that a man must give up *some* of his natural rights, to a government, in order to have the rest of them protected—the government being all the while the sole and irresponsible judge as to what rights he does give up, and what he retains, and what are to be protected—is to say that he gives up all the rights that the government chooses, *at any time,* to assume that he has given up; and that he retains none, and is to be protected in none, except such as the government shall, *at all times,* see fit to protect, and to permit him to retain. This is to suppose that he has retained no rights at all, that he can, *at any time,* claim as his own, *as against the government.* It is to say that he has really given up every right, and reserved none.

For a still further reason, it is absurd to say that a man must give up *some* of his rights to a government, in order that government may protect him in the rest. That reason is, that every right he gives up diminishes his own power of self-protection, and makes it so much more difficult for the government to protect him. And yet our government says a man must give up *all* his rights, in order that it may protect him. It might just as well be said that a man must consent to be bound hand and foot, in order to enable a government, or his friends, to protect him against an enemy. Leave him in full possession of his limbs, and of all his powers, and he will do more for his own protection than he otherwise could, and will have less need of protection from a government, or any other source.

Finally, if a man, who is *compos mentis*, wants any outside protection for his rights, he is perfectly competent to make his own bargain for such as he desires; and other persons have no occasion to thrust their protection upon him, against his will; or to insist, as they now do, that he shall give up all, or any, of his rights to them, in consideration of such protection, and only such protection, as they may afterwards *choose* to give him.

It is especially noticeable that those persons, who are so impatient to protect other men in their rights that they cannot wait until they are requested to do so, have a somewhat inveterate habit of killing all who do not voluntarily accept their protection; or do not consent to give up to them all their rights in exchange for it.

If A were to go to B, a merchant, and say to him, "Sir, I am a night-watchman, and I insist upon your employing me as such in protecting your property against burglars; and to enable me to do so more effectually, I insist upon your letting me tie your own hands and feet, so that you cannot interfere with me; and also upon your delivering up to me all your keys to your store, your safe, and to all your valuables; and that you authorize me to act solely and fully according to my own will, pleasure, and discretion in the matter; and I demand still further, that you shall give me an absolute guaranty that you will not hold me to any accountability whatever for anything I may do, or for anything that may happen to your goods while they are under my protection; and unless you comply with this proposal, I will now kill you on the spot,"—if A were to say all this to B, B would naturally conclude that A himself was the most impudent and dangerous burglar that he (B) had to fear; and that if he (B) wished to secure his property against burglars, his best way would be to kill A in the first place, and then take his chances against all such other burglars as might come afterwards.

Our government constantly acts the part that is here supposed to be acted by A. And it is just as impudent a scoundrel as A is here supposed to be. It insists that every man shall give up all his rights unreservedly into its custody, and then hold it wholly irresponsible for any disposal it may make of them. And it gives him no alternative but death.

If by putting a bayonet to a man's breast, and giving him his choice, to die, or be "protected in his rights," it secures his consent to the latter alternative, it then proclaims itself a free government,—a government resting on consent!

You yourself describe such a government as "the best government ever vouchsafed to man."

Can you tell me of one that is worse in principle?

But perhaps you will say that ours is not so bad, in principle, as the others, for the reason that here, once in two, four, or six years, each male adult is permitted to have one vote in ten millions, in choosing the public protectors. Well, if you think that that materially alters the case, I wish you joy of your remarkable discernment.

Section IX.

Sir, if a government is to "do equal and exact justice to all men," *it must do simply that, and nothing more.* If it does more than that to any, — that is, if it gives monopolies, privileges, exemptions, bounties, or favors to any, — it can do so only by doing injustice to more or less others. *It can give to one only what it takes from others; for it has nothing of its own to give to any one.* The best that it can do for all, and the only honest thing it can do for any, is simply to secure to each and every one his own rights, — the rights that nature gave him, — his rights of person, and his rights of property; leaving him, then, to pursue his own interests, and secure his own welfare, by the free and full exercise of his own powers of body and mind; so long as he trespasses upon the equal rights of no other person.

If he desires any favors from any body, he must, I repeat, depend upon the voluntary kindness of such of his fellow men as may be willing to grant them. No government can have any right to grant them; because no government can have a right to take from one man any thing that is his, and give it to another.

If this be the only true idea of an honest government, it is plain that it can have nothing to do with men's "interests," "welfare," or "prosperity," *as distinguished from their "rights."* Being secured in their rights, each and all must take the sole charge of, and have the sole responsibility for, their own "interests," "welfare," and "prosperity."

By simply protecting every man in his rights, a government necessarily keeps open to every one the widest possible field, that he honestly can have, for such industry as he may choose to follow. It also insures him the widest possible field for obtaining such capital as he needs for his industry, and the widest possible markets for the products of his labor. With the possession of these rights, he must be content.

No honest government can go into business with any individuals, be they many, or few. It cannot furnish capital to any, nor prohibit the loaning of capital to any. It can give to no one any special aid to competition; nor protect any one from competition. It must adhere inflexibly to the principle of entire freedom for all honest industry, and all honest traffic. It can do to no one any favor, nor render to any one any assistance, which it withholds from another. It must hold the scales impartially between them; taking no cognizance of any man's "interests," "welfare," or "prosperity," otherwise than by simply protecting him in his "*rights.*"

In opposition to this view, lawmakers profess to have weighty duties laid upon them, to promote men's "interests," "welfare," and "prosperity," *as distinguished from their "rights."* They seldom have any thing to say about men's *"rights."* On the contrary, they take it for granted that they are charged with the duty of promoting, superintending, directing, and controlling the "business" of the country. In the performance of this supposed duty, all ideas of individual *"rights"* are cast aside. Not knowing any way — because there is no way — in which they can impartially promote all men's "interests," "welfare," and "prosperity," *otherwise than by protecting impartially all men's rights,* they boldly proclaim that *"individual rights must not be permitted to stand in the way of the public good, the public welfare, and the business interests of the country."*

Substantially all their lawmaking proceeds upon this theory; for there is no other theory, on which they can find any justification whatever for any lawmaking at all. So they proceed to give monopolies, privileges, bounties, grants, loans, etc., etc., to particular persons, or classes of persons; justifying themselves by saying that these privileged persons will "give employment" to the unprivileged; and that this employment, given by the privileged to the unprivileged, will compensate the latter for the loss of their *"rights."* And they carry on their lawmaking of this kind to the greatest extent they think is possible, without causing rebellion and revolution, on the part of the injured classes.

Sir, I am sorry to see that you adopt this lawmaking theory to its fullest extent; that although, for once only, and in a dozen words only, — and then merely incidentally, — you describe the government as "a government pledged to do equal and exact justice to all men," you show, throughout the rest of your address, that you have no thought of abiding by that principle; that you are either utterly ignorant, or utterly regardless, of what that principle requires of you; that the government, so far as your influence goes, is to be given up to the business of lawmaking, — that is, to the business of abolishing justice, and establishing injustice in its place; that you hold it to be the proper duty and function of the government to be constantly looking after men's "interests," "welfare," "prosperity," etc., etc., *as distinguished from their rights;* that it must consider men's "rights" as no guide to the promotion of their "interests"; that it must give favors to some, and withhold the same favors from others; that in order to give these favors to some, it must take from others their *rights;* that, in reality, it must traffic in both men's interests and their rights; that it must keep open shop, and sell men's interests and rights to the highest bidders; and that this is your only plan for promoting "the general welfare," "the common interest," etc., etc.

That such is your idea of the constitutional duties and functions of the government, is shown by different parts of your address: but more fully, perhaps, by this:

The large variety of diverse and *competing interests* subject to *federal control, persistently seeking recognition of their claims,* need give us no fear that the greatest good of the greatest number will fail to be accomplished, if, *in the halls of national legislation*, that spirit of amity and mutual concession shall prevail, in which the constitution had its birth. If this involves the *surrender* or *postponement* of *private interests*, and the *abandonment* of *local advantages*, compensation will be found in the assurance that thus the *common interest* is subserved, and *the general welfare* advanced.

What is all this but saying that the government is not at all an institution for "doing equal and exact justice to all men," or for the impartial protection of all men's *rights;* but that it is its proper business to take sides, for and against, a "large variety of diverse and *competing interests*"; that it has this "large variety of diverse and *competing interests*" under its arbitrary "*control*"; that it can, at its pleasure, make such laws as will give success to some of them, and insure the defeat of others; that these "various, diverse, and *competing interests*" will be "*persistently seeking recognition of their claims* . . . . *in the halls of national legislation*," — that is, will be "persistently" clamoring for laws to be made in their favor; that, in fact, "the halls of national legislation" are to be mere arenas, into which the government actually invites the advocates and representatives of all the selfish schemes of avarice and ambition that unprincipled men can devise; that these schemes will there be free to "*compete*" with each other in their corrupt offers for government favor and support; and that it is to be the proper and ordinary business of the lawmakers to listen to all these schemes; to adopt some of them, and sustain them with all the money and power of the government; and to "postpone," "abandon," oppose, and defeat all others; it being well known, all the while, that the lawmakers will, *individually*, favor, or oppose, these various schemes, according to their own irresponsible will, pleasure, and discretion, — that is, according as they can better serve their own personal interests and ambitions by doing the one or the other.

Was a more thorough scheme of national villainy ever invented?

Sir, do you not know that in this conflict, between these "various, diverse, and *competing interests*," all ideas of individual "*rights*" — all ideas of "equal and exact justice to all men" — will be cast to the winds; that the boldest, the strongest, the most fraudulent, the most rapacious, and the most corrupt, men will have control of the government, and make it a mere instrument for plundering the great body of the people?

Your idea of the real character of the government is plainly this: The lawmakers are to assume absolute and irresponsible "*control*" of all the financial resources, all the legislative, judicial, and executive powers, of the government, and employ them all for the promotion of such schemes of plunder and ambition as they may select from all those that may be submitted to them for their approval; that they are to keep "the halls of national legislation" wide open for the admission of all persons having such schemes to offer; and that they are to grant monopolies, privileges, loans, and bounties to all such of these schemes as they can make subserve their own individual interests and ambitions, and reject or "postpone" all others. And that there is to be no limit to their operations of this kind, except their fear of exciting rebellion and resistance on the part of the plundered classes.

And you are just fool enough to tell us that such a government as this may be relied on to "accomplish the greatest good to the greatest number," "to subserve the common interest," and "advance the general welfare," "if," only, "in the halls of national legislation, that spirit of amity and mutual concession shall prevail, in which the constitution had its birth."

You here assume that "the general welfare" is to depend, not upon the free and untrammelled enterprise and industry of the whole people, acting individually, and each enjoying and exercising all his natural rights; but wholly or principally upon the success of such particular schemes as the government may take under its special "control." And this means that "the general welfare" is to depend, wholly or principally, upon such privileges, monopolies, loans, and bounties as the government may grant to more or less of that "large variety of diverse and competing *interests*"—that is, schemes—that may be "persistently" pressed upon its attention.

But as you impliedly acknowledge that the government cannot take all these "interests" (schemes) under its "control," and bestow its favors upon all alike, you concede that some of them must be "surrendered," "postponed," or "abandoned"; and that, consequently, the government cannot get on at all, unless, "in the halls of national legislation, that spirit of amity and mutual concession shall prevail, in which the constitution had its birth."

This "spirit of amity and mutual concession in the halls of legislation," you explain to mean this: a disposition, on the part of the lawmakers respectively—whose various schemes of plunder cannot all be accomplished, by reason of their being beyond the financial resources of the government, or the endurance of the people—to "surrender" some of them, "postpone" others, and "abandon" others, in order that the general business of robbery may go on to the greatest extent possible, and that each one of the lawmakers may succeed with as many of the schemes he is specially intrusted with, as he can carry through by means of such bargains, for mutual help, as he may be able to make with his fellow lawmakers.

Such is the plan of government, to which you say that you "consecrate" yourself, and "engage your every faculty and effort."

Was a more shameless avowal ever made?

You cannot claim to be ignorant of what crimes such a government will commit. You have had abundant opportunity to know—and if you have kept your eyes open, you do know—what these schemes of robbery have been in the past; and from these you can judge what they will be in the future.

You know that under such a system, every senator and representative—probably without an exception—will come to the congress as the champion of the dominant scoundrelisms of his own State or district; that he will be elected solely to serve those "interests," as you call them; that in offering himself as a candidate, he will announce the robbery, or robberies, to which all his efforts will be directed; that he will call these robberies his "policy"; or if he be lost to all decency, he will call them his "principles"; that they will always be such as he thinks will best subserve his own interests, or ambitions; that he will go to "the halls of national legislation" with his head full of plans for making bargains with other lawmakers — as corrupt as himself — for mutual help in carrying their respective schemes.

Such has been the character of our congresses nearly, or quite, from the beginning. It can scarcely be said that there has ever been an honest man in one of them. A man has sometimes gained a reputation for honesty, in his own State or district, by opposing some one or more of the robberies that were proposed by members from other portions of the country. But such a man has seldom, or never, deserved his reputation; for he has, generally, if not always, been the advocate of some one or more schemes of robbery, by which more or less of his own constituents were to profit, and which he knew it would be indispensable that he should advocate, in order to give him votes at home.

If there have ever been any members, who were consistently honest throughout, — who were really in favor of "doing equal and exact justice to all men," — and, of course, nothing more than that to any, — their numbers have been few; so few as to have left no mark upon the general legislation. They have but constituted the exceptions that proved the rule. If you were now required to name such a lawmaker, I think you would search our history in vain to find him.

That this is no exaggerated description of our national lawmaking, the following facts will prove.

For the first seventy years of the government, one portion of the lawmakers would be satisfied with nothing less than permission to rob one-sixth, or one-seventh, of the whole population, not only of their labor, but even of their right to their own persons. In 1860, this class of lawmakers comprised all the senators and representatives from fifteen, of the then thirty-three, States.*

This body of lawmakers, standing always firmly together, and capable of turning the scale for, or against, any scheme of robbery, in which northern men were interested, but on which northern men were divided, — such as navigation acts, tariffs, bounties, grants, war, peace, etc., — could purchase immunity for their own crime, by supporting such, and so many, northern crimes — second only to their own in atrocity — as could be mutually agreed on.

---

*In the Senate they stood thirty to thirty-six, in the house ninety to one hundred and forty-seven, in the two branches united one hundred and twenty to one hundred and eighty-three, relatively to the non-slaveholding members.

From the foundation of the government — without a single interval, I think — the lawmakers from the slaveholding States had been, *relatively*, as strong, or stronger, than in 1860.

In this way the slaveholders bargained for, and secured, protection for slavery and the slave trade, by consenting to such navigation acts as some of the northern States desired, and to such tariffs on imports — such as iron, coal, wool, woollen goods, etc., — as should enable the home producers of similar articles to make fortunes by robbing everybody else in the prices of their goods.

Another class of lawmakers have been satisfied with nothing less than such a monopoly of money, as should enable the holders of it to suppress, as far as possible, all industry and traffic, except such as they themselves should control; such a monopoly of money as would put it wholly out of the power of the great body of wealth-producers to hire the capital needed for their industries; and thus compel them — especially the mechanical portions of them — by the alternative of starvation — to sell their labor to the monopolists of money, for just such prices as these latter should choose to pay. This monopoly of money has also given, to the holders of it, a control, so nearly absolute, of all industry — agricultural as well as mechanical — and all traffic, as has enabled them to plunder all the producing classes in the prices of their labor, or the products of their labor.

Have you been blind, all these years, to the existence, or the effects, of this monopoly of money?

Still another class of lawmakers have demanded unequal taxation on the various kinds of home property, that are subject to taxation; such unequal taxation as would throw heavy burdens upon some kinds of property, and very light burdens, or no burdens at all, upon other kinds.

And yet another class of lawmakers have demanded great appropriations, or loans, of money, or grants of lands, to enterprises intended to give great wealth to a few, at the expense of everybody else.

These are some of the schemes of downright and outright robbery, which you mildly describe as "the large variety of diverse and competing interests, *subject to federal control*, persistently seeking recognition of their claims . . . . . in the halls of national legislation"; and each having its champions and representatives among the lawmakers.

You know that all, or very nearly all, the legislation of congress is devoted to these various schemes of robbery; and that little, or no, legislation goes through, except by means of such bargains as these lawmakers may enter into with each other, for mutual support of their respective robberies. And yet you have the mendacity, or the stupidity, to tell us that so much of this legislation as does go through, may be relied on to "accomplish the greatest good to the greatest number," to "subserve the common interest," and "advance the general welfare."

And when these schemes of robbery become so numerous, atrocious, and unendurable that they can no longer be reconciled "in the halls of national legislation," by "surrendering" some of them, "postponing" others, and "abandoning" others, you assume — for such has been the prevailing opinion, and you say nothing to the contrary—that it is the right of the strongest party, or parties, to murder a half million of men, if that be necessary,—and as we once did,—not to secure liberty or justice to any body,—but to compel the weaker of these would-be robbers to submit to all such robberies as the stronger ones may choose to practise upon them.

SECTION X.

Sir, your idea of the true character of our government is plainly this: you assume that all the natural, inherent, inalienable, individual, *human* rights of fifty millions of people—all their individual rights to preserve their own lives, and promote their own happiness—have been thrown into one common heap,—into hotchpotch, as the lawyers say: and that this hotchpotch has been given into the hands of some four hundred champion robbers, each of whom has pledged himself to carry off as large a portion of it as possible, to be divided among those men—well known to himself, but who—to save themselves from all responsibility for his acts—have secretly (by secret ballot) appointed him to be their champion.

Sir, if you had assumed that all the people of this country had thrown all their wealth, all their rights, all their means of living, into hotchpotch; and that this hotchpotch had been given over to four hundred ferocious hounds; and that each of these hounds had been selected and trained to bring to his masters so much of this common plunder as he, in the general fight, or scramble, could get off with, you would scarcely have drawn a more vivid picture of the true character of the government of the United States, than you have done in your inaugural address.

No wonder that you are obliged to confess that such a government can be carried on only "amid the din of party strife"; that it will be influenced—you should have said *directed*—by "purely partisan zeal"; and that it will be attended by "the animosities of political strife, the bitterness of partisan defeat, and the exultation of partisan triumph."

What gang of robbers, quarrelling over the division of their plunder, could exhibit a more shameful picture than you thus acknowledge to be shown by the government of the United States?

Sir, nothing of all this "din," and "strife," and "animosity," and "bitterness," is caused by any attempt, on the part of the government, to simply "do equal and exact justice to all men,"—to simply protect every man impartially in all his natural rights to life, liberty, and property. It is all caused simply and solely by the government's violation of some men's "*rights*," to promote other men's "*interests.*" If you do not know this, you are mentally an object of pity.

Sir, men's "*rights*" are always harmonious. That is to say, each man's "rights" are always consistent and harmonious with each and every other man's "rights." But their "*interests*," as you estimate them, constantly clash; especially such "interests" as depend on government grants of monopolies, privileges, loans, and bounties. And these "interests," like the interests of other gamblers, clash with a fury proportioned to the amounts at stake. It is these clashing "*interests*," and not any clashing "*rights*," that give rise to all the strife you have here depicted, and to all this necessity for "that spirit of amity and mutual concession," which you hold to be indispensable to the accomplishment of such legislation as you say is necessary to the welfare of the country.

Each and every man's "*rights*" being consistent and harmonious with each and every other man's "*rights*"; and all men's rights being immutably fixed, and easily ascertained, by a science that is open to be learned and known by all; a government that does nothing but "equal and exact justice to all men"—that simply gives to every man his own, and nothing more to any—has no cause and no occasion for any "political *parties*." What are these "political parties" but standing armies of robbers, each trying to rob the other, and to prevent being itself robbed by the other? A government that seeks only to "do equal and exact justice to all men," has no cause and no occasion to enlist all the fighting men in the nation in two hostile ranks; to keep them always in battle array, and burning with hatred towards each other. It has no cause and no occasion for any "political *warfare*," any "political *hostility*," any "political *campaigns*," any "political *contests*," any "political *fights*," any "political *defeats*," or any "political *triumphs*." It has no cause and no occasion for any of those "political *leaders*," so called, whose whole business is to invent new schemes of robbery, and organize the people into opposing bands of robbers; all for their own aggrandizement alone. It has no cause and no occasion for the toleration, or the existence, of that vile horde of political bullies, and swindlers, and blackguards, who enlist on one side or the other, and fight for pay; who, year in and year out, employ their lungs and their ink in spreading lies among ignorant people, to excite their hopes of gain, or their fears of loss, and thus obtain their votes. In short, it has no cause and no occasion for all this "din of party strife," for all this "purely partisan zeal," for all "the bitterness of partisan defeat," for all "the exultation of partisan triumph," nor, worst of all, for any of "that spirit of amity and mutual concession [by which you evidently mean that readiness, "in the halls of national legislation," to sacrifice some men's "rights" to promote other men's "interests"] in which [you say] the constitution had its birth."

If the constitution does really, or naturally, give rise to all this "strife," and require all this "spirit of amity and mutual concession,"—and I do not care now to deny that it does,—so much the worse for the constitution. And so much the worse for all those men who, like yourself, swear to "preserve, protect, and defend it."

And yet you have the face to make no end of professions, or pretences, that the impelling power, the real motive, in all this robbery and strife, is nothing else than "the service of the people," "their interests," "the promotion of their welfare," "good government," "government by the people," "the popular will," "the general weal," "the achievements of our national destiny," "the benefits which our happy form of government can bestow," "the lasting welfare of the country," "the priceless benefits of the constitution," "the greatest good to the greatest number," "the common interest," "the general welfare," "the people's will," "the mission of the American people," "our civil policy," "the genius of our institutions," "the needs of our people in their home life," "the settlement and development of the resources of our vast territory," "the prosperity of our republic," "the interests and prosperity of all the people," "the safety and confidence of business interests," "making the wage of labor sure and steady," "a due regard to the interests of capital invested and workingmen employed in American industries," "reform in the administration of the government," "the application of business principles to public affairs," "the constant and ever varying wants of an active and enterprising population," "a firm determination to secure to all the people of the land the full benefits of the best form of government ever vouchsafed to man," "the blessings of our national life," etc., etc.

Sir, what is the use of such a deluge of unmeaning words, unless it be to gloss over, and, if possible, hide, the true character of the acts of the government?

Such "generalities" as these do not even "glitter." They are only the stale phrases of the demagogue, who wishes to appear to promise everything, but commits himself to nothing. Or else they are the senseless talk of a mere political parrot, who repeats words he has been taught to utter, without knowing their meaning. At best, they are the mere gibberish of a man destitute of all political ideas, but who imagines that "good government," "the general welfare," "the common interest," "the best form of government ever vouchsafed to man," etc., etc., must be very good things, if anybody can ever find out what they are. There is nothing definite, nothing real, nothing tangible, nothing honest, about them. Yet they constitute your entire stock in trade. In resorting to them—in holding them up to public gaze as comprising your political creed—you assume that they have a meaning; that they are matters of overruling importance; that they require the action of an omnipotent, irresponsible, lawmaking government; that all these "interests" must be represented, and can be secured, only "in the halls of national legislation"; and by such political hounds as have been selected and trained, and sent there, solely that they may bring off, to their respective masters, as much as possible of the public plunder they hold in their hands; that is, as much as possible of the earnings of all the honest wealth-producers of the country.

And when these masters count up the spoils that their hounds have thus brought home to them, they set up a corresponding shout that "the public prosperity," "the common interest," and "the general welfare" have been "advanced." And the scoundrels by whom the work has been accomplished, "in the halls of national legislation," are trumpeted to the world as "great statesmen." And you are just stupid enough to be deceived into the belief, or just knave enough to pretend to be deceived into the belief, that all this is really the truth.

One would infer from your address that you think the people of this country incapable of doing anything for themselves, *individually;* that they would all perish, but for the employment given them by that "large variety of diverse and competing interests"—that is, such purely selfish schemes—as may be "persistently seeking recognition of their claims . . . . . in the halls of national legislation," and secure for themselves such monopolies and advantages as congress may see fit to grant them.

Instead of your recognizing the right of each and every individual to judge of, and provide for, his own well-being, according to the dictates of his own judgment, and by the free exercise of his own powers of body and mind,—so long as he infringes the equal rights of no other person,—you assume that fifty millions of people, who never saw you, and never will see you, who know almost nothing about you, and care very little about you, are all so weak, ignorant, and degraded as to be humbly and beseechingly looking to you—and to a few more lawmakers (so called) whom they never saw, and never will see, and of whom they know almost nothing—to enlighten, direct, and *"control"* them in their daily labors to supply their own wants, and promote their own happiness!

You thus assume that these fifty millions of people are so debased, mentally and morally, that they look upon you and your associate lawmakers as their earthly gods, holding their destinies in your hands, and anxiously studying their welfare; instead of looking upon you—as most of you certainly ought to be looked upon—as a mere cabal of ignorant, selfish, ambitious, rapacious, and unprincipled men, who know very little, and care to know very little, except how you can get fame, and power, and money, by trampling upon other men's rights, and robbing them of the fruits of their labor.

Assuming yourself to be the greatest of these gods, charged with the "welfare" of fifty millions of people, you enter upon the mighty task with all the mock solemnity, and ridiculous grandiloquence, of a man ignorant enough to imagine that he is really performing a solemn duty, and doing an immense public service, instead of simply making a fool of himself. Thus you say:

Fellow citizens: In the presence of this vast assemblage of my countrymen, I am about to supplement and seal, by the oath which I shall take, the manifestation of the will of a great and free people. In the exercise of their power and right of self-government, they have committed to one of their fellow citizens a supreme and sacred trust, and he here consecrates himself to their service. This impressive ceremony adds little to the solemn sense of responsibility with which I contemplate the duty I owe to all the people of the land. Nothing can relieve me from anxiety lest by any act of mine their *interests* [not their *rights*] may suffer, and nothing is needed to strengthen my resolution to engage every faculty and effort in the promotion of their *welfare*. [Not in "doing equal and exact justice to all men." After having once described the government as one "pledged to do equal and exact justice to all men," you drop that subject entirely, and wander off into "interests," and "welfare," and an astonishing number of other equally unmeaning things.]

Sir, you would have no occasion to take all this tremendous labor and responsibility upon yourself, if you and your lawmakers would but keep your hands off the "*rights*" of your "countrymen." Your "countrymen" would be perfectly competent to take care of their own "*interests*," and provide for their own "*welfare*," if their hands were not tied, and their powers crippled, by such fetters as men like you and your lawmakers have fastened upon them.

Do you know so little of your "countrymen," that you need to be told that their own strength and skill must be their sole reliance for their own well-being? Or that they are abundantly able, and willing, and anxious above all other things, to supply their own "needs in their home life," and secure their own "welfare"? Or that they would do it, not only without jar or friction, but as their highest duty and pleasure, if their powers were not manacled by the absurd and villainous laws you propose to execute upon them? Are you so stupid as to imagine that putting chains on men's hands, and fetters on their feet, and insurmountable obstacles in their paths, is the way to supply their "needs," and promote their "welfare"? Do you think your "countrymen" need to be told, either by yourself, or by any such gang of ignorant or unprincipled men as all lawmakers are, what to do, and what not to do, to supply their own "needs in their home life"? Do they not know how to grow their own food, make their own clothing, build their own houses, print their own books, acquire all the knowledge, and create all the wealth, they desire, without being domineered over, and thwarted in all their efforts, by any set of either fools or villains, who may call themselves their lawmakers? And do you think they will never get their eyes open to see what blockheads, or impostors, you and your lawmakers are? Do they not now — at least so far as you will permit them to do it — grow their own food, build their own houses, make their own clothing, print their own books? Do they not make all the scientific discoveries and mechanical inventions, by which all wealth is created? *Or are all these things done by "the government"?* Are you an idiot, that you can talk as you do, about what you and your lawmakers are doing to provide for the real wants, and promote the real "welfare," of fifty millions of people?

Section XI.

But perhaps the most brilliant idea in your whole address, is this:

Every citizen owes the country a vigilant watch and close scrutiny of its public servants, and a fair and reasonable estimate of their fidelity and usefulness. Thus is the people's will impressed upon the whole framework of our civil policy, municipal, State, and federal; *and this is the price of our liberty*, and the inspiration of our faith in the republic.

The essential parts of this declaration are these:

"*Every citizen owes the country a vigilant watch and close scrutiny of its public servants, ... and this is the price of our liberty.*"

Who are these "public servants," that need all this watching? Evidently they are the lawmakers, and the lawmakers only. They are not only the *chief* "public servants," but they are absolute masters of all the other "public servants." These other "public servants," judicial and executive,—the courts, the army, the navy, the collectors of taxes, etc., etc.,—have no function whatever, except that of simple obedience to the lawmakers. They are appointed, paid, and have their duties prescribed to them, by the lawmakers; and are made responsible only to the lawmakers. They are mere puppets in the hands of the lawmakers. Clearly, then, the lawmakers are the only ones we have any occasion to watch.

Your declaration, therefore, amounts, practically, to this, and this only:

Every citizen owes the country a vigilant watch and close scrutiny of ITS LAWMAKERS, ... and this is the price of our liberty.

Sir, your declaration is so far true, as that all the danger to "our liberty" *comes solely from the lawmakers.*

And why are the lawmakers dangerous to "our liberty"? Because it is a natural impossibility that they can *make* any law—that is, any law of their own invention—that does *not* violate "our liberty."

The law of justice is the one only law that does not violate "our liberty." And that is not a law that was made by the lawmakers. It existed before they were born, and will exist after they are dead. It derives not one particle of its authority from any commands of theirs. It is, therefore, in no sense, one of *their* laws. Only laws of their own invention are *their* laws. And as it is naturally impossible that they can invent any law of their own, that shall not conflict with the law of justice, it is naturally impossible that they can *make* a law—that is, a law of their own invention—that shall *not* violate "our liberty."

The law of justice is the precise measure, and the only precise measure, of the rightful "liberty" of each and every human being. Any law—made by lawmakers—that should give to any man more liberty than is given him by the law of justice, would be a license to commit an injustice upon one or more other persons. On the other hand, any law —made by lawmakers—that should take from any human being any "liberty" that is given him by the law of justice, would be taking from him a part of his own rightful "liberty."

Inasmuch, then, as every possible law, that can be made by lawmakers, must either give to some one or more persons more "liberty" than the law of nature—or the law of justice—gives them, and more "liberty" than is consistent with the natural and equal "liberty" of all other persons; or else must take from some one or more persons some portion of that "liberty" which the law of nature — or the law of justice — gives to every human being, it is inevitable that every law, that can be made by lawmakers, must be a violation of the natural and rightful "liberty" of some one or more persons.

Therefore the very idea of a *lawmaking* government — a government that is to make laws of its own invention — is necessarily in direct and inevitable conflict with "our liberty." In fact, the whole, sole, and only real purpose of any *lawmaking* government whatever is to take from some one or more persons their "liberty." Consequently the only way in which all men can preserve their "liberty," is not to have any *lawmaking* government at all.

We have been told, time out of mind, that "*Eternal vigilance is the price of liberty.*" But this admonition, by reason of its indefiniteness, has heretofore fallen dead upon the popular mind. It, in reality, tells us nothing that we need to know, to enable us to preserve "our liberty." It does not even tell us what "our liberty" is, or how, or when, or through whom, it is endangered, or destroyed.

1. It does not tell us that *individual* liberty is the only *human* liberty. It does not tell us that "national liberty," "political liberty," "republican liberty," "democratic liberty," "constitutional liberty," "liberty under law," and all the other kinds of liberty that men have ever invented, and with which tyrants, as well as demagogues, have amused and cheated the ignorant, are not liberty at all, unless in so far as they may, under certain circumstances, have chanced to contribute something to, or given some impulse toward, *individual* liberty.

2. It does not tell us that *individual* liberty means freedom from all compulsion to do anything whatever, except what justice requires us to do, and freedom to do everything whatever that justice permits us to do. It does not tell us that individual liberty means freedom from all human restraint or coercion whatsoever, so long as we "live honestly, hurt nobody, and give to every one his due."

3. It does not tell us that there is any *science of liberty;* any science, which every man may learn, and by which every man may know, what is, and what is not, his own, and every other man's, rightful "liberty."

4. It does not tell us that this right of individual liberty rests upon an immutable, natural principle, which no human power can make, unmake, or alter; nor that all human authority, that claims to set it aside, or modify it, is nothing but falsehood, absurdity, usurpation, tyranny, and crime.

5. It does not tell us that this right of individual liberty is a *natural, inherent, inalienable right; that therefore no man can part with it, or delegate it to another, if he would;* and that, consequently, all the claims that have ever been made, by governments, priests, or any other powers, that individuals have voluntarily surrendered, or "delegated," their liberty to others, are all impostures and frauds.

6. It does not tell us that all human laws, so called, and all human lawmaking, — all commands, either by one man, or any number of men, calling themselves a

government, or by any other name—requiring any individual to do this, or forbidding him to do that—so long as he "lives honestly, hurts no one, and gives to every one his due"—are all false and tyrannical assumptions of a right of authority and dominion over him; are all violations of his natural, inherent, inalienable, rightful, individual liberty; and, as such, are to be resented and resisted to the utmost, by every one who does not choose to be a slave.

7. And, finally, it does not tell us that all *lawmaking* governments whatsoever— whether called monarchies, aristocracies, republics, democracies, or by any other name—are all alike violations of men's natural and rightful liberty.

We can now see why lawmakers are the only enemies, from whom "our liberty" has anything to fear, or whom we have any occasion to watch. They are to be watched, because they claim the right to abolish justice, and establish injustice in its stead; because they claim the right to command us to do things which justice does not require us to do, and to forbid us to do things which justice permits us to do; because they deny our right to be, *individually, and absolutely,* our own masters and owners, so long as we obey the one law of justice towards all other persons; because they claim to be our masters, and that *their* commands, *as such*, are authoritative and binding upon us as law; and that they may rightfully compel us to obey them.

"Our liberty" is in danger only from the lawmakers, because it is only through the agency of lawmakers, that anybody pretends to be able to take away "our liberty." It is only the lawmakers that claim to be above all responsibility for taking away "our liberty." Lawmakers are the only ones who are impudent enough to assert for themselves the right to take away "our liberty." They are the only ones who are impudent enough to tell us that we have voluntarily surrendered "our liberty" into their hands. They are the only ones who have the insolent condescension to tell us that, in consideration of our having surrendered into their hands "our liberty," and all our natural, inherent, inalienable rights as human beings, they are disposed to give us, in return, "good government," "the best form of government ever vouchsafed to man"; to "protect" us, to provide for our "welfare," to promote our "interests," etc., etc.

And yet you are just blockhead enough to tell us that if "Every citizen"—fifty millions and more of them—will but keep "a vigilant watch and close scrutiny" upon these lawmakers, "our liberty" may be preserved!

Don't you think, sir, that you are really the wisest man that ever told "a great and free people" how they could preserve "their liberty"?

To be entirely candid, don't you think, sir, that a surer way of preserving "our liberty" would be to have no lawmakers at all?

Section XII.

But, in spite of all I have said, or, perhaps, can say, you will probably persist in your idea that the world needs a great deal of lawmaking; that mankind in general are not entitled to have any will, choice, judgment, or conscience of their own; that, if not very wicked, they are at least very ignorant and stupid; that they know very little of what is for their own good, or how to promote their own "interests," "welfare," or "prosperity"; that it is therefore necessary that they should be put under guardianship to lawmakers; that these lawmakers, being a very superior race of beings,—wise beyond the rest of their species,—and entirely free from all those selfish passions which tempt common mortals to do wrong,—must be intrusted with absolute and irresponsible dominion over the less favored of their kind; must prescribe to the latter, authoritatively, what they may, and may not, do; and, in general, manage the affairs of this world according to their discretion, free of all accountability to any human tribunals.

And you seem to be perfectly confident that, under this absolute and irresponsible dominion of the lawmakers, the affairs of this world will be rightly managed; that the "interests," "welfare," and "prosperity" of "a great and free people" will be properly attended to; that "the greatest good of the greatest number" will be accomplished, etc., etc.

And yet you hold that all this lawmaking, and all this subjection of the great body of the people to the arbitrary, irresponsible dominion of the lawmakers, will not interfere at all with "our liberty," if only "every citizen" will but keep "a vigilant watch and close scrutiny" of the lawmakers.

Well, perhaps this is all so; although this subjection to the arbitrary will of any man, or body of men, whatever, and under any pretence whatever, seems, on the face of it, to be much more like slavery, than it does like "liberty."

If, therefore, you really intend to continue this system of lawmaking, it seems indispensable that you should explain to us what you mean by the term "our liberty."

So far as your address gives us any light on the subject, you evidently mean, by the term "our liberty," just such, and only such, "liberty," as the lawmakers may see fit to allow us to have.

You seem to have no conception of any other "liberty" whatever.

You give us no idea of any other "liberty" that we can secure to ourselves, even though "every citizen"—fifty millions and more of them—shall all keep "a vigilant watch and close scrutiny" upon the lawmakers.

Now, inasmuch as the human race always have had all the "liberty" their lawmakers have seen fit to permit them to have; and inasmuch as, under your system of lawmaking, they always will have as much "liberty" as their lawmakers shall see fit to give them; and inasmuch as you apparently concede the right, which the lawmakers have always claimed, of killing all those who are not content with so much "liberty" as their lawmakers have seen fit to allow them,—it seems very plain that you have not added anything to our stock of knowledge on the subject of "our liberty."

Leaving us thus, as you do, in as great darkness as we ever were, on this all-important subject of "our liberty," I think you ought to submit patiently to a little questioning on the part of those of us, who feel that all this lawmaking— each and every separate particle of it—is a violation of "our liberty."

Will you, therefore, please tell us whether any, and, if any, how much, of that *natural* liberty—of that natural, inherent, inalienable, *individual* right to liberty— with which it has generally been supposed that God, or Nature, has endowed every human being, will be left to us, if the lawmakers are to continue, as you would have them do, the exercise of their arbitrary, irresponsible dominion over us?

Are you prepared to answer that question?

No. You appear to have never given a thought to any such question as that.

I will therefore answer it for you.

And my answer is, that from the moment it is conceded that any man, or body of men, whatever, under any pretence whatever, have the right to *make laws of their own invention*, and compel other men to obey them, every vestige of man's *natural* and rightful liberty is denied him.

That this is so is proved by the fact that *all* a man's *natural* rights stand upon one and the same basis, *viz.*, that they are the gift of God, or Nature, to him, *as an individual*, for his own uses, and for his own happiness. If any one of these natural rights may be arbitrarily taken from him by other men, *all* of them may be taken from him on the same reason. No one of these rights is any more sacred or inviolable in its nature, than are all the others. The denial of any one of these rights is therefore equivalent to a denial of all the others. The violation of any one of these rights, by lawmakers, is equivalent to the assertion of a right to violate all of them.

Plainly, unless *all* a man's natural rights are inviolable by lawmakers, *none* of them are. It is an absurdity to say that a man has any rights *of his own*, if other men, whether calling themselves a government, or by any other name, have the right to take them from him, without his consent. Therefore the very idea of a lawmaking government necessarily implies a denial of all such things as individual liberty, or individual rights.

From this statement it does not follow that every lawmaking government will, in practice, take from every man *all* his natural rights. It will do as it pleases about it. It will take some, leaving him to enjoy others, just as its own pleasure or discretion shall dictate at the time. It would defeat its own ends, if it were wantonly to take away *all* his natural rights,—as, for example, his right to live, and to breathe,—for then he would be dead, and the government could then get nothing more out of him. The most tyrannical government will, therefore, if it have any sense, leave its victims enough liberty to enable them to provide for their own subsistence, to pay their taxes, and to render such military or other service as the government may have need of. *But it will do this for its own good, and not for theirs.* In allowing them this liberty, it does not at all recognize their right to it, but only consults its own interests.

Now, sir, this is the real character of the government of the United States, as it is of all other *lawmaking* governments. There is not a single human right, which the government of the United States recognizes as inviolable. It tramples upon any and every individual right, whenever its own will, pleasure, or discretion shall so dictate. It takes men's property, liberty, and lives whenever it can serve its own purposes by doing so.

All these things prove that the government does not exist at all for the protection of men's *rights;* but that it absolutely denies to the people any rights, or any liberty, whatever, except such as it shall see fit to permit them to have for the time being. It virtually declares that it does not itself exist at all for the good of the people, but that the people exist solely for the use of the government.

All these things prove that the government is not one voluntarily established and sustained by the people, for the protection of their natural, inherent, individual rights, but that it is merely a government of usurpers, robbers, and tyrants, who claim to own the people as their slaves, and claim the right to dispose of them, and their property, at their (the usurpers') pleasure or discretion.

Now, sir, since you may be disposed to deny that such is the real character of the government, I propose to prove it, by evidences so numerous and conclusive that you cannot dispute them.

My proposition, then, is, that there is not a single *natural*, human right, that the government of the United States recognizes as inviolable; that there is not a single *natural*, human right, that it hesitates to trample under foot, whenever it thinks it can promote its own interests by doing so.

The proofs of this proposition are so numerous, that only a few of the most important can here be enumerated.

1. The government does not even recognize a man's natural right to his own life. If it have need of him, for the maintenance of its power, it takes him, against his will (conscripts him), and puts him before the cannon's mouth, to be blown in pieces, as if he were a mere senseless thing, having no more *rights* than if he were a shell, a canister, or a torpedo. It considers him simply as so much senseless war material, to be consumed, expended, and destroyed for the maintenance of its power. It no more recognizes his right to have anything to say in the matter, than if he were but so much weight of powder or ball. It does not recognize him at all as a human being, having any rights whatever of his own, but only as an instrument, a weapon, or a machine, to be used in killing other men.

2. The government not only denies a man's right, as a moral human being, to have any will, any judgment, or any conscience of his own, as to whether he himself will be killed in battle, but it equally denies his right to have any will, any judgment, or any conscience of his own, as a moral human being, as to whether he shall be used as a mere weapon for killing other men. If he refuses to kill any, or all, other men, whom it commands him to kill, it takes his own life, as unceremoniously as if he were but a dog.

Is it possible to conceive of a more complete denial of all a man's *natural, human* rights, than is the denial of his right to have any will, judgment, or conscience of his own, either as to his being killed himself, or as to his being used as a mere weapon for killing other men?

3. But in still another way, than by its conscriptions, the government denies a man's right to any will, choice, judgment, or conscience of his own, in regard either to being killed himself, or used as a weapon in its hands for killing other people.

If, in private life, a man enters into a perfectly voluntary agreement to work for another, at some innocent and useful labor, for a day, a week, a month, or a year, he cannot lawfully be compelled to fulfil that contract; because such compulsion would be an acknowledgment of his right to sell his own liberty. And this is what no one can do.

This right of personal liberty is inalienable. No man can sell it, or transfer it to another; or give to another any right of arbitrary dominion over him. All contracts for such a purpose are absurd and void contracts, that no man can rightfully be compelled to fulfil.

But when a deluded or ignorant young man has once been enticed into a contract to kill others, and to take his chances of being killed himself, in the service of the government, for any given number of years, the government holds that such a contract to sell his liberty, his judgment, his conscience, and his life, is a valid and binding contract; and that if he fails to fulfil it, he may rightfully be shot.

All these things prove that the government recognizes no right of the individual, to his own life, or liberty, or to the exercise of his own will, judgment, or conscience, in regard to his killing his fellow-men, or to being killed himself, if the government sees fit to use him as mere war material, in maintaining its arbitrary dominion over other human beings.

4. The government recognizes no such thing as any *natural* right of property, on the part of individuals.

This is proved by the fact that it takes, for its own uses, any and every man's property—when it pleases, and as much of it as it pleases—without obtaining, or even asking, his consent.

This taking of a man's property, without his consent, is a denial of his right of property; for the right of property is the right of supreme, absolute, and irresponsible dominion over anything that is naturally a subject of property,—that is, of ownership. *It is a right against all the world.* And this right of property — this right of supreme, absolute, and irresponsible dominion over anything that is naturally a subject of ownership — is subject only to this qualification, *viz.*, that each man must so use his own, as not to injure another.

If A uses his own property so as to injure the person or property of B, his own property may rightfully be taken to any extent that is necessary to make reparation for the wrong he has done.

This is the only qualification to which the *natural* right of property is subject.

When, therefore, a government takes a man's property, for its own support, or for its own uses, without his consent, it practically denies his right of property altogether; for it practically asserts that *its* right of dominion is superior to his.

No man can be said to have any right of property at all, in any thing — that is, any right of supreme, absolute, and irresponsible dominion over any thing — of which any other men may rightfully deprive him at their pleasure.

Now, the government of the United States, in asserting its right to take at pleasure the property of individuals, without their consent, virtually denies their right of property altogether, because it asserts that *its* right of dominion over it, is superior to theirs.

5. The government denies the *natural* right of human beings to live on this planet. This it does by denying their *natural* right to those things that are indispensable to the maintenance of life. It says that, for every thing necessary to the maintenance of life, they must have a special permit from the government; and that the government cannot be required to grant them any other means of living than it chooses to grant them.

All this is shown as follows, *viz.*:

The government denies the *natural* right of individuals to take possession of wilderness land, and hold and cultivate it for their own subsistence.

It asserts that wilderness land is the property of the government; and that individuals have no right to take possession of, or cultivate, it, unless by special grant of the government. And if an individual attempts to exercise this natural right, the government punishes him as a trespasser and a criminal.

The government has no more right to claim the ownership of wilderness lands, than it has to claim the ownership of the sunshine, the water, or the atmosphere. And it has no more right to punish a man for taking possession of wilderness land, and cultivating it, without the consent of the government, than it has to punish him for breathing the air, drinking the water, or enjoying the sunshine, without a special grant from the government.

In thus asserting the government's right of property in wilderness land, and in denying men's right to take possession of and cultivate it, except on first obtaining a grant from the government, — which grant the government may withhold if it pleases, — the government plainly denies the *natural* right of men to live on this planet, by denying their *natural* right to the means that are indispensable to their procuring the food that is necessary for supporting life.

In asserting its right of arbitrary dominion over that natural wealth that is indispensable to the support of human life, it asserts its right to withhold that wealth from those whose lives are dependent upon it. In this way it denies the *natural* right of human beings to live on the planet. It asserts that government owns the planet, and that men have no right to live on it, except by first getting a permit from the government.

This denial of men's *natural* right to take possession of and cultivate wilderness land is not altered at all by the fact that the government consents to sell as much land as it thinks it expedient or profitable to sell; nor by the fact that, in certain cases, it gives outright certain lands to certain persons. Notwithstanding these sales and gifts, the fact remains that the government claims the original ownership of the lands; and thus denies the *natural* right of individuals to take possession of and cultivate them. In denying this *natural* right of individuals, it denies their *natural* right to live on the earth; and asserts that they have no other right to life than the government, by its own mere will, pleasure, and discretion, may see fit to grant them.

In thus denying man's *natural* right to life, it of course denies every other *natural* right of human beings; and asserts that they have no *natural* right to anything; but that, for all other things, as well as for life itself, they must depend wholly upon the good pleasure and discretion of the government.

Section XIII.

In still another way, the government denies men's *natural* right to life. And that is by denying their *natural* right to make any of those contracts with each other, for buying and selling, borrowing and lending, giving and receiving, property, which are necessary, if men are to exist in any considerable numbers on the earth.

Even the few savages, who contrive to live, mostly or wholly, by hunting, fishing, and gathering wild fruits, without cultivating the earth, and almost wholly without the use of tools or machinery, are yet, *at times*, necessitated to buy and sell, borrow and lend, give and receive, articles of food, if no others, as their only means of preserving their lives. But, in civilized life, where but a small portion of men's labor is necessary for the production of food, and they employ themselves in an almost infinite variety of industries, and in the production of an almost infinite variety of commodities, it would be impossible for them to live, if they were wholly prohibited from buying and selling, borrowing and lending, giving and receiving, the products of each other's labor.

Yet the government of the United States—either acting separately, or jointly with the State governments—has heretofore constantly denied, and still constantly denies, the *natural* right of the people, *as individuals*, to make their own contracts, for such buying and selling, borrowing and lending, and giving and receiving, such commodities as they produce for each other's uses.

I repeat that both the national and State governments have constantly denied the *natural* right of individuals to make their own contracts. They have done this, sometimes by arbitrarily forbidding them to make particular contracts, and sometimes by arbitrarily qualifying the obligations of particular contracts, when the contracts themselves were naturally and intrinsically as just and lawful as any others that men ever enter into; and were, consequently, such as men have as perfect a *natural* right to make, as they have to make any of those contracts which they are permitted to make.

The laws arbitrarily prohibiting, or arbitrarily qualifying, certain contracts, that are naturally and intrinsically just and lawful, are so numerous, and so well known, that they need not all be enumerated here. But any and all such prohibitions, or qualifications, are a denial of men's *natural* right to make their own contracts. They are a denial of men's right to make any contracts whatever, except such as the governments shall see fit to permit them to make.

It is the *natural* right of any and all human beings, who are mentally competent to make reasonable contracts, to make any and every possible contract, that is naturally and intrinsically just and honest, for buying and selling, borrowing and lending, giving and receiving, any and all possible commodities, that are naturally vendible, loanable, and transferable, and that any two or more individuals may, at any time, without force or fraud, choose to buy and sell, borrow and lend, give and receive, of and to each other.

And it is plainly only by the untrammelled exercise of this *natural* right, that all the loanable capital, that is required by men's industries, can be lent and borrowed, or that all the money can be supplied for the purchase and sale of that almost infinite diversity and amount of commodities, that men are capable of producing, and that are to be transferred from the hands of the producers to those of the consumers.

But the government of the United States—and also the governments of the States—utterly deny the *natural* right of any individuals whatever to make any contracts whatever, for buying and selling, borrowing and lending, giving and receiving, any and all such commodities, as are naturally vendible, loanable, and transferable, and as the producers and consumers of such commodities may wish to buy and sell, borrow and lend, give and receive, of and to each other.

These governments (State and national) deny this *natural* right of buying and selling, etc., by arbitrarily prohibiting, or qualifying, all such, and so many, of these contracts, as they choose to prohibit, or qualify.

The prohibition, or qualification, of *any one* of these contracts—that are intrinsically just and lawful — is a denial of all individual *natural* right to make any of them. For the right to make any and all of them stands on the same grounds of *natural* law, natural justice, and men's natural rights. If a government has the right to prohibit, or qualify, any one of these contracts, it has the same right to prohibit, or qualify, all of them. Therefore the assertion, by the government, of a right to prohibit, or qualify, any one of them, is equivalent to a denial of all *natural* right, on the part of individuals, to make any of them.

The power that has been thus usurped by governments, to arbitrarily prohibit or qualify all contracts that are naturally and intrinsically just and lawful, has been the great, perhaps the greatest, of all the instrumentalities, by which, in this, as in other countries, nearly all the wealth, accumulated by the labor of the many, has been, and is now, transferred into the pockets of the few.

It is by this arbitrary power over contracts, that the monopoly of money is sustained. Few people have any real perception of the power, which this monopoly gives to the holders of it, over the industry and traffic of all other persons. And the one only purpose of the monopoly is to enable the holders of it to rob everybody else in the prices of their labor, and the products of their labor.

The theory, on which the advocates of this monopoly attempt to justify it, is simply this: *That it is not at all necessary that money should be a bona fide equivalent of the labor or property that is to be bought with it;* that if the government will but specially license a small amount of money, and prohibit all other money, the holders of the licensed money will then be able to buy with it the labor and property of all other persons for a half, a tenth, a hundredth, a thousandth, or a millionth, of what such labor and property are really and truly worth.

David A. Wells, one of the most prominent — perhaps at this time, the most prominent — advocate of the monopoly, in this country, states the theory thus:

> A three-cent piece, if it could be divided into a sufficient number of pieces, with each piece capable of being handled, would undoubtedly suffice for doing all the business of the country in the way of facilitating exchanges, if no other better instrumentality was available. — *New York Herald, February* 13, 1875.

He means here to say, that "a three-cent piece" contains *as much real, true, and natural market value,* as it would be necessary that all the money of the country should have, *if the government would but prohibit all other money;* that is, if the government, by its arbitrary legislative power, would but make all other and better money unavailable.

And this is the theory, on which John Locke, David Hume, Adam Smith, David Ricardo, J. R. McCulloch, and John Stuart Mill, in England, and Amasa Walker, Charles H. Carroll, Hugh McCulloch, in this country, and all the other conspicuous advocates of the monopoly, both in this country and in England, have attempted to justify it. They have all held that it was not necessary that money should be a *bona fide* equivalent of the labor or property to be bought with it; but that, by the prohibition of all other money, the holders of a comparatively worthless amount of licensed money would be enabled to buy, at their own prices, the labor and property of all other men.

And this is the theory on which the governments of England and the United States have always, with immaterial exceptions, acted, in prohibiting all but such small amounts of money as they (the governments) should specially license. *And it is the theory upon which they act now.* And it is so manifestly a theory of pure robbery, that scarce a word can be necessary to make it more evidently so than it now is.

But inasmuch as your mind seems to be filled with the wildest visions of the excellency of this government, and to be strangely ignorant of its wrongs; and inasmuch as this monopoly of money is, in its practical operation, one of the greatest — possibly the greatest — of all these wrongs, and the one that is most relied upon for robbing the great body of the people, and keeping them in poverty and servitude, it is plainly important that you should have your eyes opened on the subject. I therefore submit, for your consideration, the following self-evident propositions:

1. That to make all traffic just and equal, it is indispensable that, in each separate purchase and sale, the money paid should be a *bona fide* equivalent of the labor or property bought with it.

Dare you, or any other man, of common sense and common honesty, dispute the truth of that proposition? If not, let us consider that principle established. It will then serve as one of the necessary and infallible guides to the true settlement of all the other questions that remain to be settled.

2. That so long as no force or fraud is practised by either party, the parties themselves, to each separate contract, have the sole, absolute, and unqualified right to decide for themselves, *what money, and how much of it,* shall be considered a *bona fide* equivalent of the labor or property that is to be exchanged for it. All this is necessarily implied in the *natural* right of men to make their own contracts, for buying and selling their respective commodities.

Will you dispute the truth of that proposition?

3. That any one man, who has an honest dollar, of any kind whatsoever, has as perfect a right, as any other man can have, to offer it in the market, in competition with any and all other dollars, in exchange for such labor or property as may be in the market for sale.

Will you dispute the truth of that proposition?

4. That where no fraud is practised, every person, who is mentally competent to make reasonable contracts, must be presumed to be as competent to judge of the value of the money that is offered in the market, as he is to judge of the value of all the other commodities that are bought and sold for money.

Will you dispute the truth of that proposition?

5. That the free and open market, in which all honest money and all honest commodities are free to be given and received in exchange for each other, is the true, final, absolute, and only test of the true and natural market value of all money, as of all the other commodities that are bought and sold for money.

Will you dispute the truth of that proposition?

6. That any prohibition, by a government, of any such kind or amount of money—provided it be honest in itself—as the parties to contracts may voluntarily agree to give and receive in exchange for labor or property, is a palpable violation of their natural right to make their own contracts, and to buy and sell their labor and property on such terms as they may find to be necessary for the supply of their wants, or may think most beneficial to their interests.

Will you dispute the truth of that proposition?

7. That any government, that licenses a small amount of an article of such universal necessity as money, and that gives the control of it into a few hands, selected by itself, and then prohibits any and all other money—that is intrinsically honest and valuable—palpably violates all other men's natural right to make their own contracts, and infallibly proves its purpose to be to enable the few holders of the licensed money to rob all other persons in the prices of their labor and property.

Will you dispute the truth of that proposition?

Are not all these propositions so self-evident, or so easily demonstrated, that they cannot, with any reason, be disputed?

If you feel competent to show the falsehood of any one of them, I hope you will attempt the task.

Section XIV.

If, now, you wish to form some rational opinion of the extent of the robbery practised in this country, by the holders of this monopoly of money, you have only to look at the following facts.

There are, in this country, I think, at least twenty-five millions of persons, male and female, sixteen years old, and upwards, mentally and physically capable of running machinery, producing wealth, and supplying their own needs for an independent and comfortable subsistence.

To make their industry most effective, and to enable them, *individually*, to put into their own pockets as large a portion as possible of their own earnings, they need, *on an average*, one thousand dollars each of *money capital*. Some need one, two, three, or five hundred dollars, others one, two, three, or five thousand. These persons, then, need, *in the aggregate*, twenty-five thousand millions of dollars ($25,000,000,000), of money capital.

They need all this *money capital* to enable them to buy the raw materials upon which to bestow their labor, the implements and machinery with which to labor, and their means of subsistence while producing their goods for the market.

Unless they can get this capital, they must all either work at a disadvantage, or not work at all. A very large portion of them, to save themselves from starvation, have no alternative but to sell their labor to others, at just such prices as these others choose to pay. And these others choose to pay only such prices as are far below what the laborers could produce, if they themselves had the necessary capital to work with.

But this needed capital your lawmakers arbitrarily forbid them to have; and for no other reason than to reduce them to the condition of servants; and subject them to all such extortions as their employers — the holders of the privileged money — may choose to practise upon them.

If, now, you ask me where these twenty-five thousand millions of dollars of money capital, which these laborers need, are to come from, I answer:

Theoretically there are, in this country, fifty thousand millions of dollars of money capital ($50,000,000,000) — or twice as much as I have supposed these laborers to need — NOW LYING IDLE! *And it is lying idle, solely because the circulation of it, as money, is prohibited by the lawmakers.*

If you ask how this can be, I will tell you.

Theoretically, every dollar's worth of material property, that is capable of being taken by law, and applied to the payment of the owner's debts, is capable of being represented by a promissory note, that shall circulate as money.

But taking all this material property at *only half* its actual value, it is still capable of supplying the twenty-five thousand millions of dollars — or one thousand dollars each — which these laborers need.

Now, we know — because experience has taught us — that *solvent* promissory notes, made payable in coin on demand, are the best money that mankind have ever had; (although probably not the best they ever will have).

To make a note solvent, and suitable for circulation as money, it is only necessary that it should be made payable in coin on demand, and be issued by a person, or persons, who are known to have in their hands abundant material property, that can be taken by law, and applied to the payment of the note, with all costs and damages for non-payment on demand.

Theoretically, I repeat, all the material property in the country, that can be taken by law, and applied to the payment of debts, can be used as banking capital; and be represented by promissory notes, made payable in coin on demand. And, *practically*, so much of it can be used as banking capital as may be required for supplying all the notes that can be kept in circulation as money.

Although these notes are made legally payable in coin on demand, it is seldom that such payment is demanded, *if only it be publicly known that the notes are solvent:*

that is, if it be publicly known that they are issued by persons who have so much material property, that can be taken by law, and sold, as may be necessary to bring the coin that is needed to pay the notes. In such cases, the notes are preferred to the coin, because they are so much more safe and convenient for handling, counting, and transportation, than is the coin; and also because we can have so many times more of them.

These notes are also a legal tender, to the banks that issue them, in payment of the notes discounted; that is, in payment of the notes given by the borrowers to the banks. And, in the ordinary course of things, *all* the notes, issued by the banks for circulation, are wanted, and come back to the banks, in payment of the notes discounted; thus saving all necessity for redeeming them with coin, except in rare cases. For meeting these rare cases, the banks find it necessary to keep on hand small amounts of coin; probably not more than one per cent. of the amount of notes in circulation.

As the notes discounted have usually but a short time to run, — say three months on an average, — the bank notes issued for circulation will *all* come back, *on an average*, once in three months, and be redeemed by the bankers, by being accepted in payment of the notes discounted.

Then the bank notes will be re-issued, by discounting new notes, and will go into circulation again; to be again brought back, at the end of another three months, and redeemed, by being accepted in payment of the new notes discounted.

In this way the bank notes will be continually re-issued, and redeemed, in the greatest amounts that can be kept in circulation long enough to earn such an amount of interest as will make it an object for the bankers to issue them.

Each of these notes, issued for circulation, if known to be solvent, will always have the same value in the market, as the same nominal amount of coin. And this value is a just one, because the notes are in the nature of a lien, or mortgage, upon so much property of the bankers as is necessary to pay the notes, and as can be taken by law, and sold, and the proceeds applied to their payment.

There is no danger that any more of these notes will be issued than will be wanted for buying and selling property at its true and natural market value, relatively to coin; for as the notes are all made legally payable in coin on demand, if they should ever fall below the value of coin in the market, the holders of them will at once return them to the banks, and demand coin for them; *and thus take them out of circulation.*

The bankers, therefore, have no motive for issuing more of them than will remain long enough in circulation, to earn so much interest as will make it an object to issue them; the only motive for issuing them being to draw interest on them while they are in circulation.

The bankers readily find how many are wanted for circulation, by the time those issued remain in circulation, before coming back for redemption. If they come back immediately, or very quickly, after being issued, the bankers know that they have over-issued, and that they must therefore pay in coin — to their inconvenience, and perhaps loss — notes that would otherwise have remained in circulation long enough to earn so much interest as would have paid for issuing them; and would then have come back to them in payment of notes discounted, instead of coming back on a demand for redemption in coin.

Now, the best of all possible banking capital is real estate. It is the best, because it is visible, immovable, and indestructible. It cannot, like coin, be removed, concealed, or carried out of the country. And its aggregate value, in all civilized countries, is probably a hundred times greater than the amount of coin in circulation. It is therefore capable of furnishing a hundred times as much money as we can have in coin.

The owners of this real estate have the greatest inducements to use it as banking capital, because all the banking profit, over and above expenses, is a clear profit; inasmuch as the use of the real estate as banking capital does not interfere at all with its use for other purposes.

Farmers have a double, and much more than a double, inducement to use their lands as banking capital; because they not only get a direct profit from the loan of their notes, but, by loaning them, they furnish the necessary capital for the greatest variety of manufacturing purposes. They thus induce a much larger portion of the people, than otherwise would, to leave agriculture, and engage in mechanical employments; and thus become purchasers, instead of producers, of agricultural commodities. They thus get much higher prices for their agricultural products, and also a much greater variety and amount of manufactured commodities in exchange.

The amount of money, capable of being furnished by this system, is so great that every man, woman, and child, who is worthy of credit, could get it, and do business for himself, or herself — either singly, or in partnerships — and be under no necessity to act as a servant, or sell his or her labor to others. All the great establishments, of every kind, now in the hands of a few proprietors, but employing a great number of wage laborers, would be broken up; for few, or no persons, who could hire capital, and do business for themselves, would consent to labor for wages for another.

The credit furnished by this system would always be stable; for the system is probably capable of furnishing, *at all times*, all the credit, and all the money, that can be needed. It would also introduce a substantially universal system of cash payments. Everybody, who could get credit at all, would be able to get it at bank, *in money*. With the money, he would buy everything he needed for cash. He would also sell everything for cash; for when everybody buys for cash, everybody sells for cash; since buying for cash, and selling for cash, are necessarily one and the same thing.

We should, therefore, never have another crisis, panic, revulsion of credit, stagnation of industry, or fall of prices; for these are all caused by the lack of money, and the consequent necessity of buying and selling on credit; whereby the amount of indebtedness becomes so great, so enormous, in fact, in proportion to the amount of money extant, with which to meet it, that the whole system of credit breaks down; to the ruin of everybody, except the few holders of the monopoly of money, who reap a harvest in the fall of prices, and the consequent bankruptcy of everybody who is dependent on credit for his means of doing business.

It would be inadmissible for me, in this letter, to occupy the space that would be necessary, to expose all the false, absurd, and ridiculous pretences, by which the advocates of the monopoly of money have attempted to justify it. The only real argument they ever employed has been that, by means of the monopoly, the few holders of it were enabled to rob everybody else in the prices of their labor and property.

And our governments, State and national, have hitherto acted together in maintaining this monopoly, in flagrant violation of men's natural right to make their own contracts, and in flagrant violation of the self-evident truth, that, to make all traffic just and equal, it is indispensable that the money paid should be, in all cases, a *bona fide* equivalent of the labor or property that is bought with it.

The holders of this monopoly now rule and rob this nation; and the government, in all its branches, is simply their tool. And being their tool for this gigantic robbery, it is equally their tool for all the lesser robberies, to which it is supposed that the people at large can be made to submit.

Section XV.

But although the monopoly of money is one of the most glaring violations of men's natural right to make their own contracts, and one of the most effective — perhaps *the* most effective — for enabling a few men to rob everybody else, and for keeping the great body of the people in poverty and servitude, it is not the only one that our government practises, nor the only one that has the same robbery in view.

The so-called taxes or duties, which the government levies upon imports, are a practical violation both of men's natural right of property, and of their natural right to make their own contracts.

A man has the same *natural* right to traffic with another, who lives on the opposite side of the globe, as he has to traffic with his next-door neighbor. And any obstruction, price, or penalty, interposed by the government, to the exercise of that right, is a practical violation of the right itself.

The ten, twenty, or fifty per cent. of a man's property, which is taken from him, for the reason that he purchased it in a foreign country, must be considered either as the price he is required to pay for the *privilege* of buying property in that country, or else as a penalty for having exercised his *natural right* of buying it in that country. Whether it be considered as a price paid for a privilege, or a penalty for having exercised a natural right, it is a violation both of his natural right of property, and of his natural right to make a contract in that country.

In short, it is nothing but downright robbery.

And when a man seeks to avoid this robbery, by evading the government robbers who are lying in wait for him, — that is, the so-called revenue officers, — whom he has as perfect a right to evade, as he has to evade any other robbers, who may be lying in wait for him, — the seizure of his whole property, — instead of the ten, twenty, or fifty per cent. that would otherwise have been taken from him, — is not merely adding so much to the robbery itself, but is adding insult to the robbery. It is punishing a man as a criminal, for simply trying to save his property from robbers.

But it will be said that these taxes or duties are laid to raise revenue for the support of the government.

Be it so, for the sake of the argument. All taxes, levied upon a man's property for the support of government, without his consent, are mere robbery; a violation of his natural right of property. And when a government takes ten, twenty, or fifty per cent. of a man's property, for the reason that he bought it in a foreign country, such taking is as much a violation of his natural right of property, or of his natural right to purchase property, as is the taking of property which he has himself produced, or which he has bought in his own village.

A man's natural right of property, in a commodity he has bought in a foreign country, is intrinsically as sacred and inviolable as it is in a commodity produced at home. The foreign commodity is bought with the commodity produced at home; and therefore it stands on the same footing as the commodity produced at home. And it is a plain violation of one's right, for a government to make any distinction between them.

Government assumes to exist for the impartial protection of all rights of property. If it really exists for that purpose, it is plainly bound to make each kind of property pay its proper proportion, and only its proper proportion, of the cost of protecting all kinds. To levy upon a few kinds the cost of protecting all, is a naked robbery of the holders of those few kinds, for the benefit of the holders of all other kinds.

But the pretence that heavy taxes are levied upon imports, solely, or mainly, for the support of government, while light taxes, or no taxes at all, are levied upon property at home, is an utterly false pretence. They are levied upon the imported commodity, mainly, if not solely, for the purpose of enabling the producers of competing home commodities to extort from consumers a higher price than the home commodities would bring in free and open market. And this additional price is sheer robbery, and is known to be so. And the amount of this robbery — which goes into the pockets of the home producers — is five, ten, twenty, or fifty times greater than the amount that goes into the treasury, for the support of the government, according as the amount of the home commodities is five, ten, twenty, or fifty times greater than the amount of the imported competing commodities.

Thus the amounts that go to the support of the government, and also the amounts that go into the pockets of the home producers, in the higher prices they get for their goods, are all sheer robberies; and nothing else.

But it will be said that the heavy taxes are levied upon the foreign commodity, not to put great wealth into a few pockets, but *"to protect the home laborer against the competition of the pauper labor of other countries."*

This is the great argument that is relied on to justify the robbery.

This argument must have originated with the employers of home labor, and not with the home laborers themselves.

The home laborers themselves could never have originated it, because they must have seen that, so far as they were concerned, the object of the "protection," so-called, was, *at best*, only to benefit them, by robbing others who were as poor as themselves, and who had as good a right as themselves to live by their labor. That is, they must have seen that the object of the "protection" was to rob the foreign laborers, in whole, or in part, of the pittances on which they were already necessitated to live; and, secondly, to rob consumers at home, — in the increased prices of the protected commodities, — when many or most of these home consumers were also laborers as poor as themselves.

Even if any class of laborers would have been so selfish and dishonest as to wish to thus benefit themselves by injuring others, as poor as themselves, they could have had no hope of carrying through such a scheme, if they alone were to profit by it; because they could have had no such influence with governments, as would be necessary to enable them to carry it through, in opposition to the rights and interests of consumers, both rich and poor, and much more numerous than themselves.

For these reasons it is plain that the argument originated with the employers of home labor, and not with the home laborers themselves.

And why do the employers of home labor advocate this robbery? Certainly not because they have such an intense compassion for their own laborers, that they are willing to rob everybody else, rich and poor, for their benefit. Nobody will suspect them of being influenced by any such compassion as that. But they advocate it solely because they put into their own pockets a very large portion certainly — probably three-fourths, I should judge — of the increased prices their commodities are thus made to bring in the market. The home laborers themselves probably get not more than one-fourth of these increased prices.

Thus the argument for "protection" is really an argument for robbing foreign laborers — as poor as our own — of their equal and rightful chances in our markets; and also for robbing all the home consumers of the protected article — the poor as well as the rich — in the prices they are made to pay for it. And all this is done at the instigation, and principally for the benefit, of the employers of home labor, and not for the benefit of the home laborers themselves.

Having now seen that this argument — of "protecting our home laborers against the competition of the pauper labor of other countries" — is, of itself, an utterly dishonest argument; that it is dishonest towards foreign laborers and home consumers; that it must have originated with the employers of home labor, and not with the home laborers themselves; and that the employers of home labor, and not the home laborers themselves, are to receive the principal profits of the robbery, let us now see how utterly false is the argument itself.

1. The pauper laborers (if there are any such) of other countries have just as good a right to live by their labor, and have an equal chance in our own markets, and in all the markets of the world, as have the pauper laborers, or any other laborers, of our own country.

Every human being has the same natural right to buy and sell, of and to, any and all other people in the world, as he has to buy and sell, of and to, the people of his own country. And none but tyrants and robbers deny that right. And they deny it for their own benefit solely, and not for the benefit of their laborers.

And if a man, in our own country — either from motives of profit to himself, or from motives of pity towards the pauper laborers of other countries — *chooses* to buy the products of the foreign pauper labor, rather than the products of the laborers of his own country, he has a perfect legal right to do so. And for any government to forbid him to do so, or to obstruct his doing so, or to punish him for doing so, is a violation of his natural right of purchasing property of whom he pleases, and from such motives as he pleases.

2. To forbid our own people to buy in the best markets, is equivalent to forbidding them to sell the products of their own labor in the best markets; for they can buy the products of foreign labor, only by giving the products of their own labor in exchange. Therefore to deny our right to buy in foreign markets, is to forbid us to sell in foreign markets. And this is a plain violation of men's natural rights.

If, when a producer of cotton, tobacco, grain, beef, pork, butter, cheese, or any other commodity, in our own country, has carried it abroad, and exchanged it for iron or woolen goods, and has brought these latter home, the government seizes one-half of them, because they were manufactured abroad, the robbery committed upon the owner is the same as if the government had seized one-half of his cotton, tobacco, or other commodity, before he exported it; because the iron or woolen goods, which he purchased abroad with the products of his own home labor, are as much his own property, as was the commodity with which he purchased them.

Therefore the tax laid upon foreign commodities, that have been bought with the products of our home labor, is as much a robbery of the home laborer, as the same tax would have been, if laid directly upon the products of our home labor. It is, at best, only a robbery of one home laborer — the producer of cotton, tobacco, grain, beef, pork, butter, or cheese — for the benefit of another home laborer — the producer of iron or woolen goods.

3. But this whole argument is a false one, for the further reason that our home laborers do not have to compete with *"the pauper labor"* of any country on earth; since the *actual paupers* of no country on earth are engaged in producing commodities for export to any other country. They produce few, or no, other commodities than those they themselves consume; and ordinarily not even those.

There are a great many millions of *actual paupers* in the world. In some of the large provinces of British India, for example, it is said that nearly half the population are paupers. But I think that the commodities they are producing for export to other countries than their own, have never been heard of.

The term, "pauper labor," is therefore a false one. And when these robbers — the employers of home labor — talk of protecting their laborers against the competition of *"the pauper labor"* of other countries, they do not mean that they are protecting them against the competition of *actual paupers;* but only against the competition of that immense body of laborers, in all parts of the world, *who are kept constantly on the verge of pauperism, or starvation;* who have little, or no, means of subsistence, except such as their employers see fit to give them, — which means are usually barely enough to keep them in a condition to labor.

These are the only "pauper laborers," from whose competition our own laborers are sought to be protected. They are quite as badly off as our own laborers; and are in equal need of "protection."

What, then, is to be done? This policy of excluding foreign commodities from our markets, is a game that all other governments can play at, as well as our own. And if it is the duty of our government to "protect" our laborers against the competition of "the pauper labor," so-called, of all other countries, it is equally the duty of every other government to "protect" its laborers against the competition of the so-called "pauper labor" of all other countries. So that, according to this theory, each nation must either shut out entirely from its markets the products of all other countries; or, at least, lay such heavy duties upon them, as will, *in some measure,* "protect" its own laborers from the competition of the "pauper labor" of all other countries.

This theory, then, is that, instead of permitting all mankind to supply each other's wants, by freely exchanging their respective products with each other, the government of each nation should rob the people of every other, by imposing heavy duties upon all commodities imported from them.

The natural effect of this scheme is to pit the so-called "pauper labor" of each country against the so-called "pauper labor" of every other country; and all for the benefit of their employers. And as it holds that so-called "pauper labor" is cheaper than free labor, it gives the employers in each country a constant motive for reducing their own laborers to the lowest condition of poverty, consistent with their ability to labor at all. In other words, the theory is, that the smaller the portion of the products of labor, that is given to the laborers, the larger will be the portion that will go into the pockets of the employers.

Now, it is not a very honorable proceeding for any government to pit its own so-called "pauper laborers"—or laborers that are on the verge of pauperism—against similar laborers in all other countries: and all for the sake of putting the principal proceeds of their labor into the pockets of a few employers.

To set two bodies of "pauper laborers"—or of laborers on the verge of pauperism—to robbing each other, for the profit of their employers, is the next thing, in point of atrocity, to setting them to killing each other, as governments have heretofore been in the habit of doing, for the benefit of their rulers.

The laborers, who are paupers, or on the verge of pauperism—who are destitute, or on the verge of destitution—comprise (with their families) doubtless nine-tenths, probably nineteen-twentieths, of all the people on the globe. They are not all wage laborers. Some of them are savages, living only as savages do. Others are barbarians, living only as barbarians do. But an immense number are mere wage laborers. Much the larger portion of these have been reduced to the condition of wage laborers, by the monopoly of land, which mere bands of robbers have succeeded in securing for themselves by military power. This is the condition of nearly all the Asiatics, and of probably one-half the Europeans. But in those portions of Europe and the United States, where manufactures have been most extensively introduced, and where, by science and machinery, great wealth has been created, the laborers have been kept in the condition of wage laborers, principally, if not wholly, by the monopoly of money. This monopoly, established in all these manufacturing countries, has made it impossible for the manufacturing laborers to hire the money capital that was necessary to enable them to do business for themselves; and has consequently compelled them to sell their labor to the monopolists of money, for just such prices as these latter should choose to give.

It is, then, by the monopoly of land, and the monopoly of money, that more than a thousand millions of the earth's inhabitants—as savages, barbarians, and wage laborers—are kept in a state of destitution, or on the verge of destitution. Hundreds of millions of them are receiving, for their labor, not more than three, five, or, at most, ten cents a day.

In western Europe, and in the United States, where, within the last hundred and fifty years, machinery has been introduced, and where alone any considerable wealth is now created, the wage laborers, although they get so small a portion of the wealth they create, are nevertheless in a vastly better condition than are the laboring classes in other parts of the world.

If, now, the employers of wage labor, in this country,—who are also the monopolists of money,—and who are ostensibly so distressed lest their own wage laborers should suffer from the competition of the pauper labor of other countries,—have really any of that humanity, of which they make such profession, they have before them a much wider field for the display of it, than they seem to desire. That is to say, they have it in their power, not only to elevate immensely the condition of the laboring classes in this country, but also to set an example that will be very rapidly followed in all other countries; and the result will be the elevation of all oppressed laborers throughout the world. This they can do, by simply abolishing the monopoly of money. The real producers of wealth, with few or no exceptions, will then be able to hire all the capital they need for their industries, and will do business for themselves. They will also be able to hire their capital at very low rates of interest; and will then put into their own pockets all the proceeds of their labor, except what they pay as interest on their capital. And this amount will be too small to obstruct materially their rise to independence and wealth.

Section XVI.

But will the monopolists of money give up their monopoly? Certainly not voluntarily. They will do it only upon compulsion. They will hold on to it as long as they own and control governments as they do now. And why will they do so? Because to give up their monopoly would be to give up their control of those great armies of servants—the wage laborers—from whom all their wealth is derived, and whom they can now coerce by the alternative of starvation, to labor for them at just such prices as they (the monopolists of money) shall choose to pay.

Now these monopolists of money have no plans whatever for making their "capital," as they call it—that is, their money capital—*their privileged money capital*—profitable to themselves, *otherwise than by using it to employ other men's labor*. And they can keep control of other men's labor only by depriving the laborers themselves of all other means of subsistence. And they can deprive them of all other means of subsistence only by putting it out of their power to hire the money that is necessary to enable them to do business for themselves. And they can put it out of their power to hire money, only by forbidding all other men to lend them their credit, in the shape of promissory notes, to be circulated as money.

If the twenty-five or fifty thousand millions of loanable capital—promissory notes—which, *in this country*, are now lying idle, were permitted to be loaned, these wage laborers would hire it, and do business for themselves, instead of laboring as servants for others; and would of course retain in their own hands all the wealth they should create, except what they should pay as interest for their capital.

And what is true of this country, is true of every other where civilization exists; for wherever civilization exists, land has value, and can be used as banking capital, and be made to furnish all the money that is necessary to enable the producers of wealth to hire the capital necessary for their industries, and thus relieve them from their present servitude to the few holders of privileged money.

Thus it is that the monopoly of money is the one great obstacle to the liberation of the laboring classes all over the world, and to their indefinite progress in wealth.

But we are now to show, more definitely, what relation this monopoly of money is made to bear to the freedom of international trade; and why it is that the holders of this monopoly, *in this country*, demand heavy tariffs on imports, on the lying pretence of protecting our home labor against the competition of the so-called pauper labor of other countries.

The explanation of the whole matter is as follows.

1. The holders of the monopoly of money, in each country,—more especially in the manufacturing countries like England, the United States, and some others,—assume that the present condition of poverty, for the great mass of mankind, all over the world, is to be perpetuated forever; or at least for an indefinite period. From this assumption they infer that, if free trade between all countries is to be allowed, the so-called pauper labor of each country is to be forever pitted against the so-called pauper labor of every other country. Hence they infer that it is the duty of each government—or certainly of our government—to protect the so-called pauper labor of our own country—that is, the class of laborers who are constantly on the verge of pauperism—against the competition of the so-called pauper labor of all other countries, by such duties on imports as will secure to our own laborers a monopoly of our own home market.

This is, on the face of it, the most plausible argument—and almost, if not really, the only argument—by which they now attempt to sustain their restrictions upon international trade.

If this argument is a false one, their whole case falls to the ground. That it is a false one, will be shown hereafter.

2. These monopolists of money assume that pauper labor, so-called, is the cheapest labor in the world; and that therefore each nation, in order to compete with the pauper labor of all other nations, must itself have "cheap labor." In fact, "cheap labor" is, with them, the great *sine qua non* of all national industry. To compete with "cheap labor," say they, we must have "cheap labor." This is, with them, a self-evident proposition. And this demand for "cheap labor" means, of course, that the laboring classes, in this country, must be kept, as nearly as possible, on a level with the so-called pauper labor of all other countries.

Thus their whole scheme of national industry is made to depend upon "cheap labor." And to secure "cheap labor," they hold it to be indispensable that the laborers shall be kept constantly either in actual pauperism, or on the verge of pauperism. And, in this country, they know of no way of keeping the laborers on the verge of pauperism, but by retaining in their (the monopolists') own hands such a monopoly of money as will put it out of the power of the laborers to hire money, and do business for themselves; and thus compel them, by the alternative of starvation, to sell their labor to the monopolists of money at such prices as will enable them (the monopolists) to manufacture goods in competition with the so-called pauper laborers of all other countries.

Let it be repeated — as a vital proposition — that the whole industrial programme of these monopolists rests upon, and implies, such a degree of poverty, on the part of the laboring classes, as will put their labor in direct competition with the so-called pauper labor of all other countries. So long as they (the monopolists) can perpetuate this extreme poverty of the laboring classes, in this country, they feel safe against all foreign competition; for, in all other things than "cheap labor," we have advantages equal to those of any other nation.

Furthermore, this extreme poverty, in which the laborers are to be kept, necessarily implies that they are to receive no larger share of the proceeds of their own labor, than is necessary to keep them in a condition to labor. It implies that their industry — which is really the national industry — is not to be carried on at all for their own benefit, but only for the benefit of their employers, the monopolists of money. It implies that the laborers are to be mere tools and machines in the hands of their employers; that they are to be kept simply in running order, like other machinery; but that, beyond this, they are to have no more rights, and no more interests, in the products of their labor, than have the wheels, spindles, and other machinery, with which the work is done.

In short, this whole programme implies that the laborers — the real producers of wealth — are not to be considered at all as human beings, having rights and interests of their own; but only as tools and machines, to be owned, used, and consumed in producing such wealth as their employers — the monopolists of money — may desire for their own subsistence and pleasure.

What, then, is the remedy? Plainly it is to abolish the monopoly of money. Liberate all this loanable capital — promissory notes — that is now lying idle, and we liberate all labor, and furnish to all laborers all the capital they need for their industries. We shall then have no longer, all over the earth, the competition of pauper labor with pauper labor, but only the competition of free labor with free labor. And from this competition of free labor with free labor, no people on earth have anything to fear, but all peoples have everything to hope.

And why have all peoples everything to hope from the competition of free labor with free labor? Because when every human being, who labors at all, has, as nearly as possible, all the fruits of his labor, and all the capital that is necessary to make his labor most effective, he has all needed inducements to the best use of both his brains and his muscles, his head and his hands. He applies both his head and his hands to his work. He not only acquires, as far as possible, for his own use, all the scientific discoveries and mechanical inventions, that are made by others, but he himself makes scientific discoveries and mechanical inventions. He thus multiplies indefinitely his powers of production. And the more each one produces of his own particular commodity, the more he can buy of every other man's products, and the more he can pay for them.

With freedom in money, the scientific discoveries and mechanical inventions, made in each country, will not only be used to the utmost in that country, but will be carried into all other countries. And these discoveries and inventions, given by each country to every other, and received by each country from every other, will be of infinitely more value than all the material commodities that will be exchanged between these countries.

In this way each country contributes to the wealth of every other, and the whole human race are enriched by the increased power and stimulus given to each man's labor of body and mind.

But it is to be kept constantly in mind, that there can be no such thing as free labor, unless there be freedom in money; that is, unless everybody, who can furnish money, shall be at liberty to do so. Plainly labor cannot be free, unless the laborers are free to hire all the money capital that is necessary for their industries. And they cannot be free to hire all this money capital, unless all who can lend it to them, shall be at liberty to do so.

In short, labor cannot be free, unless each laborer is free to hire all the capital —money capital, as well as all other capital—that he honestly can hire; free to buy, wherever he can buy, all the raw material he needs for his labor; and free to sell, wherever he can sell, all the products of his labor. Therefore labor cannot be free, unless we have freedom in money, and free trade with all mankind.

We can now understand the situation. In the most civilized nations—such as Western Europe and the United States—labor is utterly crippled, robbed, and enslaved by the monopoly of money; and also, in some of these countries, by the monopoly of land. In nearly or quite all the other countries of the world, labor is not only robbed and enslaved, but to a great extent paralyzed, by the monopoly of land, and by what may properly be called the utter absence of money. There is, consequently, in these latter countries, almost literally, no diversity of industry, no science, no skill, no invention, no machinery, no manufactures, no production, and no wealth; but everywhere miserable poverty, ignorance, servitude, and wretchedness.

In this country, and in Western Europe, where the uses of money are known, there is no excuse to be offered for the monopoly of money. It is maintained, in each of these countries, by a small knot of tyrants and robbers, who have got control of the governments, and use their power principally to maintain this monopoly; understanding, as they do, that this one monopoly of money gives them a substantially absolute control of all other men's property and labor.

But not satisfied with this substantially absolute control of all other men's property and labor, the monopolists of money, *in this country*, — feigning great pity for their laborers, but really seeking only to make their monopoly more profitable to themselves, — cry out for protection against the competition of the pauper labor of all other countries; when they alone, *and such as they*, are the direct cause of all the pauper labor in the world. But for them, and others like them, there would be neither poverty, ignorance, nor servitude on the face of the earth.

But to all that has now been said, the advocates of the monopoly of money will say that, if all the material property of the country were permitted to be represented by promissory notes, and these promissory notes were permitted to be lent, bought, and sold as money, the laborers would not be able to hire them, for the reason that they could not give the necessary security for repayment.

But let those who would say this, tell us why it is that, in order to prevent men from loaning their promissory notes, for circulation as money, it has always been necessary for governments to prohibit it, either by penal enactments, or prohibitory taxation. These penal enactments and prohibitory taxation are acknowledgments that, but for them, the notes would be loaned to any extent that would be profitable to the lenders. What this extent would be, nothing but experience of freedom can determine. But freedom would doubtless give us ten, twenty, most likely fifty, times as much money as we have now, if so much could be kept in circulation. And laborers would at least have ten, twenty, or fifty times better chances for hiring capital, than they have now. And, furthermore, all labor and property would have ten, twenty, or fifty times better chances of bringing their full value in the market, than they have now.

But in the space that is allowable in this letter, it is impossible to say all, or nearly all, of what might be said, to show the justice, the utility, or the necessity, for perfect freedom in the matters of money and international trade. To pursue these topics further would exclude other matters of great importance, as showing how the government acts the part of robber and tyrant in all its legislation on contracts; and that the whole purpose of all its acts is that the earnings of the many may be put into the pockets of the few.

Section XVII.

Although, as has already been said, the constitution is a paper that nobody ever signed, that few persons have ever read, and that the great body of the people never saw; and that has, consequently, no more claim to be the supreme law of the land, or to have any authority whatever, than has any other paper, that nobody ever signed, that few persons ever read, and that the great body of the people never saw; and although it purports to authorize a government, in which the lawmakers, judges, and executive officers are all to be secured against any responsibility whatever *to the people*, whose liberty and rights are at stake; and although this government is kept in operation only by votes given in secret (by secret ballot), and in a way to save the voters from all personal responsibility for the acts of their agents,—the lawmakers, judges, etc.; and although the whole affair is so audacious a fraud and usurpation, that no people could be expected to agree to it, or ought to submit to it, for a moment; yet, inasmuch as the constitution declares itself to have been ordained and established by the people of the United States, for the maintenance of liberty and justice for themselves and their posterity; and inasmuch as all its supporters—that is, the voters, lawmakers, judges, etc.—profess to derive all their authority from it; and inasmuch as all lawmakers, and all judicial and executive officers, both national and State, swear to support it; and inasmuch as they claim the right to kill, and are evidently determined to kill, and esteem it the highest glory to kill, all who do not submit to its authority; we might reasonably expect that, from motives of common decency, if from no other, those who profess to administer it, would pay some deference to its commands, *at least in those particular cases where it explicitly forbids any violation of the natural rights of the people.*

Especially might we expect that the judiciary—whose courts claim to be courts of justice—and who profess to be authorized and sworn to expose and condemn all such violations of individual rights as the constitution itself expressly forbids —would, in spite of all their official dependence on, and responsibility to, the lawmakers, have sufficient respect for their personal characters, and the opinions of the world, to induce them to pay some regard to all those parts of the constitution that expressly require any rights of the people to be held inviolable.

If the judicial tribunals cannot be expected to do justice, even in those cases where the constitution expressly commands them to do it, and where they have solemnly sworn to do it, it is plain that they have sunk to the lowest depths of servility and corruption, and can be expected to do nothing but serve the purposes of robbers and tyrants.

But how futile have been all expectations of justice from the judiciary, may be seen in the conduct of the courts—and especially in that of the so-called Supreme Court of the United States—in regard to men's natural right to make their own contracts.

Although the State lawmakers have, more frequently than the national lawmakers, made laws in violation of men's natural right to make their own contracts, yet all laws, State and national, having for their object the destruction of that right, have always, without a single exception, I think, received the sanction of the Supreme Court of the United States. And having been sanctioned by that court, they have been, as a matter of course, sanctioned by all the other courts, State and national. And this work has gone on, until, if these courts are to be believed, nothing at all is left of men's natural right to make their own contracts.

That such is the truth, I now propose to prove.

And, first, as to the State governments.

The constitution of the United States (*Art.* 1, *Sec.* 10) declares that:

No State shall pass any law impairing the obligation of contracts.

This provision does not designate what contracts have, and what have not, an "obligation." But it clearly presupposes, implies, assumes, and asserts that there *are* contracts that *have* an "obligation." Any State law, therefore, which declares that such contracts shall have *no obligation*, is plainly in conflict with this provision of the constitution of the United States.

This provision, also, by implying that there *are* contracts, that *have* an "obligation," *necessarily implies that men have a right to enter into them;* for if men had no right to enter into the contracts, the contracts themselves could have no "obligation."

This provision, then, of the constitution of the United States, not only implies that there are contracts that *have* an obligation, *but it also implies that the people have the right to enter into all such contracts, and have the benefit of them.* And "*any*" State "*law*," conflicting with either of these implications, is necessarily unconstitutional and void.

Furthermore, the language of this provision of the constitution, to wit, "the obligation [singular] of contracts" [plural], implies *that there is one and the same* "*obligation*" *to all* "*contracts*" *whatsoever, that have any legal obligation at all.* And there obviously must be some one principle, that gives validity to all contracts alike, that have any validity.

The law, then, of this whole country, as established by the constitution of the United States, is, that all contracts whatsoever, in which this one principle of validity, or "obligation," is found, shall be held valid; and that the States shall impose no restraint whatever upon the people's entering into all such contracts.

All, therefore, that courts have to do, in order to determine whether any particular contract, or class of contracts, are valid, *and whether the people have a right to enter into them,* is simply to determine whether the contracts themselves have, or have not, this one principle of validity, or "obligation," which the constitution of the United States declares shall not be impaired.

State legislation can obviously have nothing to do with the solution of this question. It can neither create, nor destroy, that "obligation of contracts," which the constitution forbids it to impair. It can neither give, nor take away, the right to enter into any contract whatever, that has that "obligation."

On the supposition, then, that the constitution of the United States is, what it declares itself to be, *viz.*, "the supreme law of the land, ... anything in the constitutions or laws of the States to the contrary notwithstanding," this provision against "*any*" State "law impairing the obligation of contracts," is so explicit, and so authoritative, that the legislatures and courts of the States have no color of authority for violating it. And the Supreme Court of the United States has had no color of authority or justification for suffering it to be violated.

This provision is certainly one of the most important — perhaps *the* most important — of all the provisions of the constitution of the United States, *as protective of the natural rights of the people to make their own contracts, or provide for their own welfare.*

Yet it has been constantly trampled under foot, by the State legislatures, by all manner of laws, declaring who may, and who may not, make certain contracts; and what shall, and what shall not, be "the obligation" of particular contracts; thus setting at defiance all ideas of justice, of natural rights, and equal rights; conferring monopolies and privileges upon particular individuals, and imposing the most arbitrary and destructive restraints and penalties upon others; all with a view of putting, as far as possible, all wealth into the hands of the few, and imposing poverty and servitude upon the great body of the people.

And yet all these enormities have gone on for nearly a hundred years, and have been sanctioned, not only by all the State courts, but also by the Supreme Court of the United States.

And what color of excuse have any of these courts offered for thus upholding all these violations of justice, of men's natural rights, and even of that constitution which they had all sworn to support?

They have offered only this: *They have all said they did not know what "the obligation of contracts" was!*

Well, suppose, for the sake of the argument, that they have not known what "the obligation of contracts" was, what, then, was their duty? Plainly this, to neither enforce, nor annul, any contract whatever, until they should have discovered what "the obligation of contracts" was.

Clearly they could have no right to either enforce, or annul, any contract whatever, until they should have ascertained whether it had any "obligation," and, if any, what that "obligation" was.

If these courts really do not know — as perhaps they do not — what "the obligation of contracts" is, they deserve nothing but contempt for their ignorance. If they *do* know what "the obligation of contracts" is, and yet sanction the almost literally innumerable laws that violate it, they deserve nothing but detestation for their villainy.

And until they shall suspend all their judgments for either enforcing, or annulling, contracts, or, on the other hand, shall ascertain what "the obligation of contracts" is, and sweep away all State laws that impair it, they will deserve both contempt for their ignorance, and detestation for their crimes.

Individual Justices of the Supreme Court of the United States have, at least in one instance, in 1827 (*Ogden vs. Saunders*, 12 Wheaton 213), attempted to give a definition of "the obligation of contracts." But there was great disagreement among them; and no one definition secured the assent of the whole court, *or even of a majority.* Since then, so far as I know, that court has never attempted to give a definition. And, so far as the opinion of that court is concerned, the question is as unsettled now, as it was sixty years ago. And the opinions of the Supreme Courts of the States are equally unsettled with those of the Supreme Court of the United States. The consequence is, that "the obligation of contracts"—the principle on which the real validity, or invalidity, of all contracts whatsoever depends—is practically unknown, or at least unrecognized, by a single court, either of the States, or of the United States. And, as a result, every species of absurd, corrupt, and robber legislation goes on unrestrained, as it always has done.

What, now, is the reason why not one of these courts has ever so far given its attention to the subject as to have discovered what "the obligation of contracts" is? What that principle is, I repeat, which they have all sworn to sustain, and on which the real validity, or invalidity, of every contract on which they ever adjudicate, depends? Why is it that they have all gone on sanctioning and enforcing all the nakedly iniquitous laws, by which men's natural right to make their own contracts has been trampled under foot?

Surely it is not because they do not know that all men have a natural right to make their own contracts; for they know *that*, as well as they know that all men have a natural right to live, to breathe, to move, to speak, to hear, to see, or to do anything whatever for the support of their lives, or the promotion of their happiness.

Why, then, is it, that they strike down this right, without ceremony, and without compunction, whenever they are commanded to do so by the lawmakers? It is because, and solely because, they are so servile, slavish, degraded, and corrupt, as to act habitually on the principle, that justice and men's natural rights are matters of no importance, in comparison with the commands of the impudent and tyrannical lawmakers, on whom they are dependent for their offices and their salaries. It is because, and solely because, they, like the judges under all other irresponsible and tyrannical governments, are part and parcel of a conspiracy for robbing and enslaving the great body of the people, to gratify the luxury and pride of a few. It is because, and solely because, they do not recognize our governments, State or national, as institutions designed simply to maintain justice, or to protect all men in the enjoyment of all their natural rights; but only as institutions designed to accomplish such objects as irresponsible cabals of lawmakers may agree upon.

In proof of all this, I give the following.

Previous to 1824, two cases had come up from the State courts, to the Supreme Court of the United States, involving the question whether a State law, *invalidating some particular contract*, came within the constitutional prohibition of "any law impairing the obligation of contracts."

One of these cases was that of *Fletcher vs. Peck*, (6 *Cranch* 87), in the year 1810. In this case the court held simply that a grant of land, once made by the legislature of Georgia, could not be rescinded by a subsequent legislature.

But no general definition of "the obligation of contracts" was given.

Again, in the year 1819, in the case of *Dartmouth College vs. Woodward* (4 *Wheaton* 518), the court held that a charter, granted to Dartmouth College, by the king of England, before the Revolution, was a contract; and that a law of New Hampshire, annulling, or materially altering, the charter, without the consent of the trustees, was a "law impairing the obligation" of *that* contract.

But, in this case, as in that of *Fletcher vs. Peck*, the court gave no general definition of "the obligation of contracts."

But in the year 1824, and again in 1827, in the case of *Ogden vs. Saunders* (12 *Wheaton* 213) the question was, whether an insolvent law of the State of New York, which discharged a debtor from a debt, *contracted after the passage of the law*, or, as the courts would say, "*contracted under the law*" — on his giving up his property to be distributed among his creditors — was a "law impairing the obligation of contracts?"

To the correct decision of this case, it seemed indispensable that the court should give a comprehensive, precise, and *universal* definition of "the obligation of contracts"; one by which it might forever after be known what was, and what was not, that "obligation of contracts," which the State governments were forbidden to "impair" by "*any law*" whatever.

The cause was heard at two terms, that of 1824, and that of 1827.

It was argued by Webster, Wheaton, Wirt, Clay, Livingston, Ogden, Jones, Sampson, and Haines; nine in all. Their arguments were so voluminous that they could not be reported at length. Only summaries of them are given. But these summaries occupy thirty-eight pages in the reports.

The judges, at that time, were seven, *viz.*, Marshall, Washington, Johnson, Duvall, Story, Thompson, and Trimble.

The judges gave five different opinions; occupying one hundred pages of the reports.

But no one definition of "the obligation of contracts" could be agreed on; *not even by a majority.*

Here, then, sixteen lawyers and judges — many of them among the most eminent the country has ever had — were called upon to give their opinions upon a question of the highest importance to all men's natural rights, to all the interests of civilized society, and to the very existence of civilization itself; a question, upon the answer to which depended the real validity, or invalidity, of every contract that ever was made, or ever will be made, between man and man. And yet, by their disagreements, they all virtually acknowledged that they did not know what "the obligation of contracts" was!

But this was not all. Although they could not agree as to what "the obligation of contracts" was, they did all agree that it could be nothing which the State lawmakers could not prohibit and abolish, *by laws passed before the contracts were made.* That is to say, they all agreed that the State lawmakers had absolute power to prohibit all contracts whatsoever, for buying and selling, borrowing and lending, giving and receiving, property; and that, whenever they did prohibit any particular contract, or class of contracts, *all such contracts, thereafter made, could have no "obligation"!*

They said this, be it noted, not of contracts that were naturally and intrinsically criminal and void, but of contracts that were naturally and intrinsically as just, and lawful, and useful, and necessary, as any that men ever enter into; and that had as perfect a natural, intrinsic, inherent "obligation," as any of those contracts, by which the traffic of society is carried on, or by which men ever buy and sell, borrow and lend, give and receive, property, of and to each other.

Not one of these sixteen lawyers and judges took the ground that the constitution, in forbidding any State to "pass any law impairing the obligation of contracts," intended to protect, against the arbitrary legislation of the States, the only true, real, and natural "obligation of contracts," or the right of the people to enter into all really just, and naturally obligatory contracts.

Is it possible to conceive of a more shameful exhibition, or confession, of the servility, the baseness, or the utter degradation, of both bar and bench, than their refusal to say one word in favor of justice, liberty, men's natural rights, or the natural, and only real, "obligation" of their contracts?

And yet, from that day to this — a period of sixty years, save one — neither bar nor bench, so far as I know, have ever uttered one syllable in vindication of men's natural right to make their own contracts, or to have the only true, real, natural, inherent, intrinsic "obligation" of their contracts respected by lawmakers or courts.

Can any further proof be needed that all ideas of justice and men's natural rights are absolutely banished from the minds of lawmakers, and from so-called courts of justice? or that absolute and irresponsible lawmaking has usurped their place?

Or can any further proof be needed, of the utter worthlessness of all the constitutions, which these lawmakers and judges swear to support, and profess to be governed by?

Section XVIII.

If, now, it be asked, what is this constitutional "obligation of contracts," which the States are forbidden to impair, the answer is, that it is, and necessarily must be, the *natural* obligation; or that obligation, which contracts have, on principles of natural law, and natural justice, as distinguished from any arbitrary or unjust obligation, which lawmakers may assume to create, and attach to contracts.

This natural obligation is the only *one* "obligation," which *all* obligatory contracts can be said to have. It is the only *inherent* "obligation," that any contract can be said to have. It is recognized all over the world — at least as far as it is known — as the one only *true* obligation, that any, or all, contracts can have. And, so far as it is known — it is held valid all over the world, except in those exceptional cases, where arbitrary and tyrannical governments have assumed to annul it, or substitute some other in its stead.

The constitution assumes that this *one* "obligation of contracts," which it designs to protect, is the natural one, because it assumes that it existed, *and was known*, at the time the constitution itself was established; and certainly no one "obligation," *other than the natural one*, can be said to have been known, as applicable to *all* obligatory contracts, at the time the constitution was established. Unless, therefore, the constitution be presumed to have intended the natural "obligation," it cannot be said to have intended any *one* "obligation" whatever; or, consequently, to have forbidden the violation of any *one* "obligation" whatever.

It cannot be said that "the obligation," which the constitution designed to protect, was any arbitrary "obligation," that was unknown at the time the constitution was established, but that was to be created, and made known afterward; for then this provision of the constitution could have had no effect, until such arbitrary "obligation" should have been created, and made known. And as it gives us no information as to how, or by whom, this arbitrary "obligation" was to be created, or what the obligation itself was to be, or how it could ever be known to be the one that was intended to be protected, the provision itself becomes a mere nullity, having no effect to protect any "obligation" at all.

It would be a manifest and utter absurdity to say that the constitution intended to protect any "obligation" whatever, unless it be presumed to have intended some particular "obligation," *that was known at the time;* for that would be equivalent to saying that the constitution intended to establish a law, of which no man could know the meaning.

But this is not all.

The right of property is a natural right. The only real right of property, that is known to mankind, is the natural right. Men have also a natural right to convey their natural rights of property from one person to another. And there is no means known to mankind, by which this *natural* right of property can be transferred, or conveyed, by one man to another, except by such contracts as are *naturally* obligatory; that is, naturally capable of conveying and binding the right of property.

All contracts whatsoever, that are naturally capable, competent, and sufficient to convey, transfer, and bind the natural right of property, are naturally obligatory;

and really and truly do convey, transfer, and bind such rights of property as they purport to convey, transfer, and bind.

All the other modes, by which one man has ever attempted to acquire the property of another, have been thefts, robberies, and frauds. But these, of course, have never conveyed any real rights of property.

To make any contract binding, obligatory, and effectual for conveying and transferring rights of property, these three conditions only are essential, *viz.*, 1, That it be entered into by parties, who are mentally competent to make reasonable contracts. 2. That the contract be a purely voluntary one: that is, that it be entered into without either force or fraud on either side. 3. That the right of property, which the contract purports to convey, be such an one as is naturally capable of being conveyed, or transferred, by one man to another.

Subject to these conditions, all contracts whatsoever, for conveying rights of property — that is, for buying and selling, borrowing and lending, giving and receiving property — are naturally obligatory, and bind such rights of property as they purport to convey.

Subject to these conditions, all contracts, for the conveyance of rights of property, are recognized as valid, all over the world, by both civilized and savage man, except in those particular cases where governments arbitrarily and tyrannically prohibit, alter, or invalidate them.

This *natural* "obligation of contracts" must necessarily be presumed to be the one, and the only one, which the constitution forbids to be impaired, by any State law whatever, if we are to presume that the constitution was intended for the maintenance of justice, or men's natural rights.

On the other hand, if the constitution be presumed not to protect this *natural* "obligation of contracts," we know not *what* other "obligation" it did intend to protect. It mentions no other, describes no other, gives us no hint of any other; and nobody can give us the least information as to what other "obligation of contracts" was intended.

It could not have been any "obligation" which the *State* lawmakers might arbitrarily create, and annex to *all* contracts; for this is what no lawmakers have ever attempted to do. And it would be the height of absurdity to suppose they ever will invent any *one* "obligation," and attach it to *all* contracts. They have only attempted either to annul, or impair, the natural "obligation" of *particular* contracts; or, *in particular cases*, to substitute other "obligations" of their own invention. And this is the most they will ever attempt to do.

Section XIX.

Assuming it now to be proved that the "obligation of contracts," which the States are forbidden to "impair," is the *natural* "obligation"; and that, *constitutionally speaking*, this provision secures, to all the people of the United States, the right to enter into, and have the benefit of, all contracts whatsoever, that have that *one natural* "obligation," let us look at some of the more important of those State laws that have either impaired that obligation, or prohibited the exercise of that right.

1. That law, in all the States, by which any, or all, the contracts of persons, under twenty-one years of age, are either invalidated, or forbidden to be entered into.

The mental capacity of a person to make reasonable contracts, is the only criterion, by which to determine his legal capacity to make obligatory contracts. And his mental capacity to make reasonable contracts is certainly not to be determined by the fact that he is, or is not, twenty-one years of age. There would be just as much sense in saying that it was to be determined by his height, or his weight, as there is in saying that it should be determined by his age.

Nearly all persons, male and female, are mentally competent to make reasonable contracts, long before they are twenty-one years of age. And as soon as they are mentally competent to make reasonable contracts, they have the same natural right to make them, that they ever can have. And their contracts have the same natural "obligation" that they ever can have.

If a person's mental capacity to make reasonable contracts be drawn in question, that is a question of fact, to be ascertained by the same tribunal that is to ascertain all the other facts involved in the case. It certainly is not to be determined by any arbitrary legislation, that shall deprive any one of his natural right to make contracts.

2. All the State laws, that do now forbid, or that have heretofore forbidden, married women to make any or all contracts, that they are, or were, mentally competent to make reasonably, are violations of their natural right to make their own contracts.

A married woman has the same natural right to acquire and hold property, and to make all contracts that she is mentally competent to make reasonably, as has a married man, or any other man. And any law invalidating her contracts, or forbidding her to enter into contracts, on the ground of her being married, are not only absurd and outrageous in themselves, but are also as plainly violations of that provision of the constitution, which forbids any State to pass any law impairing the natural obligation of contracts, as would be laws invalidating or prohibiting similar contracts by married men.

3. All those State laws, commonly called acts of incorporation, by which a certain number of persons are licensed to contract debts, without having their individual properties held liable to pay them, are laws impairing the natural obligation of their contracts.

On natural principles of law and reason, these persons are simply partners; and their private properties, like those of any other partners, should be held liable for their partnership debts. Like any other partners, they take the profits of their business, if there be any profits. And they are naturally bound to take all the risks of their business, as in the case of any other business. For a law to say that, if they make any profits, they may put them all into their own pockets, but that, if they make a loss, they may throw it upon their creditors, is an absurdity and an outrage. Such a law is plainly a law impairing the natural obligation of their contracts.

4. All State insolvent laws, so-called, that distribute a debtor's property equally among his creditors, are laws impairing the natural obligation of his contracts.

If the natural obligation of contracts were known, and recognized as law, we should have no need of insolvent or bankrupt laws.

The only force, function, or effect of a *legal* contract is to convey and bind rights of property. A contract that conveys and binds no right of property, has no *legal* force, effect, or obligation whatever.*

Consequently, the natural obligation of a contract of debt binds the debtor's property, and nothing more. That is, it gives the creditor a mortgage upon the debtor's property, and nothing more.

A first debt is a first mortgage; a second debt is a second mortgage; a third debt is a third mortgage; and so on indefinitely.

The first mortgage must be paid in full, before anything is paid on the second. The second must be paid in full, before anything is paid on the third; and so on indefinitely.

When the mortgaged property is exhausted, the debt is cancelled; there is no other property that the contract binds.

If, therefore, a debtor, at the time his debt becomes due, pays to the extent of his ability, and has been guilty of no fraud, fault, or neglect, during the time his debt had to run, he is thenceforth discharged from all legal obligation.

If this principle were acknowledged, we should have no occasion, and no use, for insolvent or bankrupt laws.

Of course, persons who have never asked themselves what the *natural* "obligation of contracts" is, will raise numerous objections to the principle, that a legal contract binds nothing else than rights of property. But their objections are all shallow and fallacious.

I have not space here to go into all the arguments that may be necessary to prove that contracts can have no *legal* effect, except to bind rights of property; or to show the truth of that principle in its application to all contracts whatsoever. To do this would require a somewhat elaborate treatise. Such a treatise I hope sometime to publish. For the present, I only assert the principle; and assert that the ignorance of this truth is at least one of the reasons why courts and lawyers have never been able to agree as to what "the obligation of contracts" was.

---

* It may have very weighty moral obligation; but it can have no legal obligation.

In all the cases that have now been mentioned, — that is, of minors (so-called), married women, corporations, insolvents, and in all other like cases — the tricks, or pretences, by which the courts attempt to uphold the validity of all laws that forbid persons to exercise their natural right to make their own contracts, or that annul, or impair, the *natural* "obligation" of their contracts, are these:

1. They say that, if a law forbids any particular contract to be made, such contract, being then an illegal one, can have no "obligation." Consequently, say they, the law cannot be said to impair it; because the law cannot impair an "obligation," that has never had an existence.

They say this of all contracts, that are arbitrarily forbidden; although, naturally and intrinsically, they have as valid an obligation as any others that men ever enter into, or as any that courts enforce.

By such a naked trick as this, these courts not only strike down men's natural right to make their own contracts, but even seek to evade that provision of the constitution, which they are all sworn to support, and which commands them to hold valid the *natural* "obligation" of all men's contracts; "anything in the constitutions or laws of the States to the contrary notwithstanding."

They might as well have said that, if the constitution had declared that "no State shall pass any law impairing any man's natural right to life, liberty, or property" — (that is, his *natural* right to live, and do what he will with himself and his property, so long as he infringes the right of no other person) — this prohibition could be evaded by a State law declaring that, from and after such a date, no person should have any natural right to life, liberty, or property; and that, therefore, a law arbitrarily taking from a man his life, liberty, and property, could not be said to impair his right to them, because no law could impair a right that did not exist.

The answer to such an argument as this, would be, that it is a natural truth that every man, who ever has been, or ever will be, born into the world, *necessarily has been, and necessarily will be, born with an inherent right to life, liberty, and property;* and that, in forbidding this right to be impaired, *the constitution presupposes, implies, assumes, and asserts that every man has, and will have, such a right;* and that this *natural* right is the very right, which the constitution forbids any State law to impair.

Or the courts might as well have said that, if the constitution had declared that "no State shall pass any law impairing the obligation of contracts made for the purchase of food," that provision could have been evaded by a State law forbidding any contract to be made for the purchase of food; and then saying that such contract, being illegal, could have no "obligation," that could be impaired.

The answer to this argument would be that, by forbidding any State law impairing the obligation of contracts made for the purchase of food, the constitution presupposes, implies, assumes, and asserts that such contracts have, and always will have, a *natural* "obligation"; and that this *natural* "obligation" is the very "obligation," which the constitution forbids any State law to impair.

So in regard to all other contracts. The constitution presupposes, implies, assumes, and asserts the natural truth, that certain contracts have, *and always necessarily will have*, a *natural* "obligation." And this *natural* "obligation"—which is the only real obligation that any contract can have—is the very one that the constitution forbids any State law to impair, in the case of any contract whatever that has such obligation.

And yet all the courts hold the direct opposite of this. They hold that, if a State law forbids any contract to be made, such a contract can then have no obligation; and that, consequently, no State law can impair an obligation that never existed.

But if, by forbidding a contract to be made, a State law can prevent the contract's having any obligation, State laws, by forbidding any contracts at all to be made, can prevent all contracts, thereafter made, from having any obligation; and thus utterly destroy all men's natural rights to make any obligatory contracts at all.

2. A second pretence, by which the courts attempt to evade that provision of the constitution, which forbids any State to "pass any law impairing the obligation of contracts," is this: They say that the State law, that requires, or obliges, a man to fulfil his contracts, *is itself* "*the obligation*," which the constitution forbids to be impaired; and that therefore the constitution only prohibits the impairing of any law for enforcing such contracts as shall be made under it.

But this pretence, it will be seen, utterly discards the idea that contracts have any *natural* obligation. It implies that contracts have no obligation, except the laws that are made for enforcing them. But if contracts have no *natural* obligation, they have no obligation at all, *that ought to be enforced;* and the State is a mere usurper, tyrant, and robber, in passing any law to enforce them.

Plainly a State cannot rightfully enforce any contracts at all, unless they have a *natural* obligation.

3. A third pretence, by which the courts attempt to evade this provision of the constitution, is this: They say that "the law is a part of the contract" itself; and therefore cannot impair its obligation.

By this they mean that, if a law is standing upon the statute book, prescribing what obligation certain contracts shall, or shall not, have, it must then be presumed that, whenever such a contract is made, the parties intended to make it according to that law; and really to make the law a part of their contract; *although they themselves say nothing of the kind.*

This pretence, that the law is a part of the contract, is a mere trick to cheat people out of their natural right to make their own contracts; and to compel them to make only such contracts as the lawmakers choose to permit them to make.

To say that it must be presumed that the parties intended to make their contracts according to such laws as may be prescribed to them — or, what is the same thing, to make the laws a part of their contracts — is equivalent to saying that the parties must be presumed to have given up all their natural right to make their own contracts; to have acknowledged themselves imbeciles, incompetent to make reasonable contracts, and to have authorized the lawmakers to make their contracts for them; for if the lawmakers can make any part of a man's contract, and presume his consent to it, they can make a whole one, and presume his consent to it.

If the lawmakers can make any part of men's contracts, they can make the whole of them; and can, therefore, buy and sell, borrow and lend, give and receive men's property of all kinds, according to their (the lawmakers') own will, pleasure, or discretion; without the consent of the real owners of the property, and even without their knowledge, until it is too late. In short, they may take any man's property, and give it, or sell it, to whom they please, and on such conditions, and at such prices, as they please; without any regard to the rights of the owner. They may, in fact, at their pleasure, strip any, or every, man of his property, and bestow it upon whom they will; and then justify the act upon the presumption that the owner consented to have his property thus taken from him and given to others.

This absurd, contemptible, and detestable trick has had a long lease of life, and has been used as a cover for some of the greatest of crimes. By means of it, the marriage contract has been perverted into a contract, on the part of the woman, to make herself a legal non-entity, or *non compos mentis;* to give up, to her husband, all her personal property, and the control of all her real estate; and to part with her natural, inherent, inalienable right, as a human being, to direct her own labor, control her own earnings, make her own contracts, and provide for the subsistence of herself and her children.

There would be just as much reason in saying that the lawmakers have a right to make the entire marriage contract; to marry any man and woman against their will; dispose of all their personal and property rights; declare them imbeciles, incapable of making a reasonable marriage contract; then presume the consent of both the parties; and finally treat them as criminals, and their children as outcasts, if they presume to make any contract of their own.

This same trick, of holding that the law is a part of the contract, has been made to protect the private property of stockholders from liability for the debts of the corporations, of which they were members; and to protect the private property of special partners, so-called, or limited partners, from liability for partnership debts.

This same trick has been employed to justify insolvent and bankrupt laws, so-called, whereby a first creditor's right to a first mortgage on the property of his debtor, has been taken from him, and he has been compelled to take his chances with as many subsequent creditors as the debtor may succeed in becoming indebted to

All these absurdities and atrocities have been practiced by the lawmakers of the States, and sustained by the courts, under the pretence that they (the courts) did not know what the natural "obligation of contracts" was; or that, if they did know what it was, the constitution of the United States imposed no restraint upon its unlimited violation by the State lawmakers.

Section XX.

But, not content with having always sanctioned the unlimited power of the *State* lawmakers to abolish all men's natural right to make their own contracts, the Supreme Court of the United States has, within the last twenty years, taken pains to assert that congress also has the arbitrary power to abolish the same right.

1. It has asserted the arbitrary power of congress to abolish all men's right to make their own contracts, by asserting its power *to alter the meaning of all contracts, after they are made,* so as to make them widely, or wholly, different from what the parties had made them.

Thus the court has said that, after a man has made a contract to pay a certain number of dollars, at a future time, — *meaning such dollars as were current at the time the contract was made,* — congress has power to coin a dollar of less value than the one agreed on, and authorize the debtor to pay his debt with a dollar of less value than the one he had promised.

To cover up this infamous crime, the court asserts, over and over again, — what no one denies, — that congress has power (constitutionally speaking) to alter, at pleasure, the value of its coins. But it then asserts that congress has this additional, and wholly different, power, to wit, the power to declare that this alteration in the value of the coins *shall work a corresponding change in all existing contracts for the payment of money.*

In reality they say that a contract to pay money is not a contract to pay any particular amount, or value, of such money as was known and understood by the parties at the time the contract was made, *but only such, and so much, as congress shall afterwards choose to call by that name, when the debt shall become due.*

They assert that, by simply retaining the name, while altering the thing, — *or by simply giving an old name to a new thing,* — congress has power to utterly abolish the contract which the parties themselves entered into, and substitute for it any such new and different one, as they (congress) may choose to substitute.

Here are their own words:

> *The contract obligation . . . . was not a duty to pay gold or silver, or the kind of money recognized by law at the time when the contract was made, nor was it a duty to pay money of equal intrinsic value in the market. . . . . But the obligation of a contract to pay money is to pay that which the law shall recognize as money when the payment is to be made.* — Legal Tender Cases, 12 Wallace 548.

This is saying that the obligation of a contract to pay money is not an obligation to pay what both the law and the parties recognize as money, *at the time when the contract is made*, but only such substitute as congress shall afterwards prescribe, "*when the payment is to be made.*"

This opinion was given by a majority of the court in the year 1870.

In another opinion the court says:

Under the power to coin money, and to regulate its value, congress may issue coins of the same denomination [that is, bearing the same name] as those already current by law, but of less intrinsic value than those, by reason of containing a less weight of the precious metals, *and thereby enable debtors to discharge their debts by the payment of coins of the less real value.* A contract to pay a certain sum of money, without any stipulation as to the kind of money in which it shall be made, may always be satisfied by payment of that sum [that is, that *nominal* amount] *in any currency which is lawful money at the place and time at which payment is to be made.* — *Juilliard vs. Greenman*, 110 *U. S. Reports,* 449.

This opinion was given by the entire court — save one, Field — at the October term of 1883.

Both these opinions are distinct declarations of the power of congress to alter men's contracts, *after they are made*, by simply retaining the name, while altering the thing, that is agreed to be paid.

In both these cases, the court means distinctly to say that, *after the parties to a contract have agreed upon the number of dollars to be paid*, congress has power to reduce the value of the dollar, and authorize all debtors to pay the less valuable dollar, instead of the one agreed on.

In other words, the court means to say that, after a contract has been made for the payment of a certain number of dollars, *congress has power to alter the meaning of the word dollar*, and thus authorize the debtor to pay in something different from, and less valuable than, the thing he agreed to pay.

Well, if congress has power to alter men's contracts, *after they are made*, by altering the meaning of the word dollar, and thus reducing the value of the debt, it has a precisely equal power to *increase* the value of the dollar, and thus compel the debtor to pay *more* than he agreed to pay.

Congress has evidently just as much right to *increase* the value of the dollar, after a contract has been made, as it has to *reduce* its value. It has, therefore, just as much right to cheat debtors, by compelling them to pay *more* than they agreed to pay, as it has to cheat creditors, by compelling them to accept *less* than they agreed to accept.

All this talk of the court is equivalent to asserting that congress has the right to alter men's contracts at pleasure, *after they are made*, and make them over into something, or anything, wholly different from what the parties themselves had made them.

And this is equivalent to denying all men's right to make their own contracts, or to acquire any contract rights, which congress may not *afterward*, at pleasure, alter, or abolish.

It is equivalent to saying that the words of contracts are not to be taken in the sense in which they are used, by the parties themselves, at the time when the contracts are entered into, but only in such different senses as congress may choose to put upon them at any future time.

If this is not asserting the right of congress to abolish altogether men's natural right to make their own contracts, what is it?

Incredible as such audacious villainy may seem to those unsophisticated persons, who imagine that a court of law should be a court of justice, it is nevertheless true, that this court intended to declare the unlimited power of congress to alter, at pleasure, the contracts of parties, *after they have been made*, by altering the kind and amount of money by which the contracts may be fulfilled. That they intended all this, is proved, not only by the extracts already given from their opinions, but also by the whole tenor of their arguments—too long to be repeated here—and more explicitly by these quotations, *viz.*:

There is no well-founded distinction to be made between the constitutional validity of an act of congress declaring treasury notes a legal tender for the payment of debts contracted after its passage, and that of an act making them a legal tender for the discharge of *all* debts, *as well those incurred before, as those made after, its enactment.*—*Legal Tender Cases*, 12 *Wallace* 530 (1870).

Every contract for the payment of money, simply, is necessarily subject to the constitutional power of the government over the currency, whatever that power may be, *and the obligation of the parties is, therefore, assumed with reference to that power.*—12 *Wallace* 549.

Contracts for the payment of money are subject to the authority of congress, *at least so far as relates to the means of payment.*—12 *Wallace* 549.

The court means here to say that "every contract for the payment of money, simply," is necessarily made, by the parties, *subject to the power of congress to alter it afterward*—by altering the kind and value of the money with which it may be paid—*into anything, into which* they (congress) *may choose to alter it.*

And this is equivalent to saying that all such contracts are made, by the parties, *with the implied understanding that the contracts, as written and signed by themselves, do not bind either of the parties to anything;* but that they simply suggest, or initiate, some non-descript or other, which congress may afterward convert into a binding contract, *of such a sort, and only such a sort, as* they (congress) *may see fit to convert it into.*

Every one of these judges knew that no two men, having common honesty and common sense,—unless first deprived of all power to make their own contracts,—would ever enter into a contract to pay money, with any understanding that the government had any such arbitrary power as the court here ascribes to it, to alter their contract after it should be made. Such an absurd contract would, in reality, be no *legal* contract at all. It would be a mere gambling agreement, having, naturally and really, no *legal* "obligation" at all.

But further. A *solvent* contract to pay money is in reality—in law, and in equity—*a bona fide mortgage upon the debtor's property*. And this mortgage right is as veritable a right of property, as is any right of property, that is conveyed by a warranty deed. And congress has no more right to invalidate this mortgage, by a single iota, than it has to invalidate a warranty deed of land. And these judges will sometime find out that such is "the obligation of contracts," if they ever find out what "the obligation of contracts" is.

The justices of that court have had this question—what is "the obligation of contracts"?—before them for seventy years, and more. But they have never agreed among themselves—even by so many as a majority—as to what it is. And this disagreement is very good evidence that *none* of them have known what it is; for if any one of them had known what it is, he would doubtless have been able, long ago, to enlighten the rest.

Considering the vital importance of men's contracts, it would evidently be more to the credit of these judges, if they would give their attention to this question of "the obligation of contracts," until they shall have solved it, than it is to be telling fifty millions of people that they have no right to make any contracts at all, except such as congress has power to invalidate after they shall have been made. Such assertions as this, coming from a court that cannot even tell us what "the obligation of contracts" is, are not entitled to any serious consideration. On the contrary, they show us what farces and impostures these judicial opinions—or decisions, as they call them—are. They show that these judicial oracles, as men call them, are no better than some of the other so-called oracles, by whom mankind have been duped.

But these judges certainly never will find out what "the obligation of contracts" is, until they find out that men have the natural right to make their own contracts, and unalterably fix their "obligation"; and that governments can have no power whatever to make, unmake, alter, or invalidate that "obligation."

Still further. Congress has the same power over weights and measures that it has over coins. And the court has no more right or reason to say that congress has power to alter existing contracts, by altering the value of the coins, than it has to say that, after any or all men have, for value received, entered into contracts to deliver so many bushels of wheat or other grain, so many pounds of beef, pork, butter, cheese, cotton, wool, or iron, so many yards of cloth, or so many feet of lumber, congress has power, by altering these weights and measures, to alter all these existing contracts, so as to convert them into contracts to deliver only half as many, or to deliver twice as many, bushels, pounds, yards, or feet, as the parties agreed upon.

To add to the farce, as well as to the iniquity, of these judicial opinions, it must be kept in mind, that the court says that, after A has sold valuable property to B, and has taken in payment an honest and sufficient mortgage on B's property, congress has the power to compel him (A) to give up this mortgage, and to accept, in place of it, not anything of any real value whatever, but only the promissory note of a so-called government; and that government one which — if taxation without consent is robbery — never had an honest dollar in its treasury, with which to pay any of its debts, and is never likely to have one; but relies wholly on its future robberies for its means to pay them; and can give no guaranty, but its own interest at the time, that it will even make the payment out of its future robberies.

If a company of bandits were to seize a man's property for their own uses, and give him their note, promising to pay him out of their future robberies, the transaction would not be considered a very legitimate one. But it would be intrinsically just as legitimate as is the one which the Supreme Court sanctions on the part of congress.

Banditti have not usually kept supreme courts of their own, to legalize either their robberies, or their promises to pay for past robberies, out of the proceeds of their future ones. Perhaps they may now take a lesson from our Supreme Court, and establish courts of their own, that will hereafter legalize all their contracts of this kind.

Section XXI.

To justify its declaration, that congress has power to alter men's contracts after they are made, the court dwells upon the fact that, at the times when the legal-tender acts were passed, the government was in peril of its life; and asserts that it had therefore a right to do almost anything for its self-preservation, without much regard to its honesty, or dishonesty, towards private persons. Thus it says:

A civil war was then raging, which seriously threatened the overthrow of the government, and the destruction of the constitution itself. It demanded the equipment and support of large armies and navies, and the employment of money to an extent beyond the capacity of all ordinary sources of supply. Meanwhile the public treasury was nearly empty, and the credit of the government, if not stretched to its utmost tension, had become nearly exhausted. Moneyed institutions had advanced largely of their means, and more could not be expected of them. They had been compelled to suspend specie payments. Taxation was inadequate to pay even the interest on the debt already incurred, and it was impossible to await the income of additional taxes. The necessity was immediate and pressing. The army was unpaid. There was then due to the soldiers in the field nearly a score of millions of dollars. The requisitions from the War and Navy departments for supplies, exceeded fifty millions, and the current expenditure was over one million per day. . . . . Foreign credit we had none. We say nothing of the overhanging paralysis of trade, and business generally, which threatened loss of confidence in the ability of the government to maintain its continued existence, and therewith the complete destruction of all remaining national credit.

It was at such a time, and in such circumstances, that congress was called upon to devise means for maintaining the army and navy, for securing the large supplies of money needed, and indeed for the preservation of the government created by the constitution. It was at such a time, and in such an emergency, that the legal-tender acts were passed.—12 *Wallace* 540–1.

In the same case Bradley said:

Can the poor man's cattle, and horses, and corn be thus taken by the government, when the public exigency requires it, and cannot the rich man's bonds and notes be in like manner taken to reach the same end?—*p.* 561.

He also said:

It is absolutely essential to independent national existence that government should have a firm hold on the two great instrumentalities of the *sword* and the *purse, and the right to wield them without restriction, on occasions of national peril.* In certain emergencies government must have at its command, *not only the personal services—the bodies and lives—of its citizens,* but the lesser, though not less essential, power of absolute control over the resources of the country. Its armies must be filled, and its navies manned, by the citizens in person.—*p.* 563.

Also he said:

The conscription may deprive me of liberty, and destroy my life. .... *All these are fundamental political conditions on which life, property, and money are respectively held and enjoyed under our system of government, nay, under any system of government.* There are times when the exigencies of the State rightly absorb all subordinate considerations of private interest, convenience, and feeling.—*p.* 565.

Such an attempt as this, to justify one crime, by taking for granted the justice of other and greater crimes, is a rather desperate mode of reasoning, for a court of law; to say nothing of a court of justice. The answer to it is, that no government, however good in other respects—any more than any other good institution—has any right to live otherwise than on purely voluntary support. It can have no right to take either "the poor man's cattle, and horses, and corn," or "the rich man's bonds and notes," or poor men's "bodies and lives," without their consent. And when a government resorts to such measures to save its life, we need no further proof that its time to die has come. A good government, no more than a bad one, has any right to live by robbery, murder, or any other crime.

But so think not the Justices of the Supreme Court of the United States. On the contrary, they hold that, in comparison with the preservation of the government, all the rights of the people to property, liberty, and life are worthless things, not to be regarded. So they hold that in such an exigency as they describe, congress had the right to commit any crime against private persons, by which the government could be saved. And among these lawful crimes, the court holds that congress had the right to issue money that should serve as a license to all holders of it, to cheat — or rather openly rob — their creditors.

The court might, with just as much reason, have said that, to preserve the life of the government, congress had the right to issue such money as would authorize all creditors to demand twice the amount of their honest dues from all debtors.

The court might, with just as much reason, have said that, to preserve the life of the government, congress had the right to sell indulgences for all manner of crimes; for theft, robbery, rape, murder, and all other crimes, for which indulgences would bring a price in the market.

Can any one imagine it possible that, if the government had always done nothing but that "equal and exact justice to all men" — which you say it is pledged to do, — but which you must know it has never done, — it could ever have been brought into any such peril of its life, as these judges describe? Could it ever have been necessitated to take either "the poor man's cattle, and horses, and corn," or "the rich man's bonds and notes," or poor men's "bodies and lives," without their consent? Could it ever have been necessitated to "conscript" the poor man — too poor to pay a ransom of three hundred dollars — made thus poor by the tyranny of the government itself — "deprive him of his liberty, and destroy his life"? Could it ever have been necessitated to sell indulgences for crime to either debtors, or creditors, or anybody else? To preserve "the constitution" — a constitution, I repeat, that authorized nothing but "equal and exact justice to all men" — could it ever have been necessitated to send into the field millions of ignorant young men, to cut the throats of other young men as ignorant as themselves — few of whom, on either side, had ever read the constitution, or had any real knowledge of its legal meaning; and not one of whom had ever signed it, or promised to support it, or was under the least obligation to support it?

It is, I think, perfectly safe to say, that not one in a thousand, probably not one in ten thousand, of these young men, who were sent out to butcher others, and be butchered themselves, had any real knowledge of the constitution they were professedly sent out to support; or any reasonable knowledge of the real character and motives of the congresses and courts that profess to administer the constitution. If they had possessed this knowledge, how many of them would have ever gone to the field?

But further. Is it really true that the right of the government to commit all these atrocities:

Are the fundamental political conditions on which life, property, and money are respectively held and enjoyed under our system of government?

If such is the real character of the constitution, can any further proof be required of the necessity that it be buried out of sight at once and forever?

The truth was that the government was in peril, *solely because it was not fit to ex-*

ist. It, and the State governments—all but parts of one and the same system—were rotten with tyranny and crime. And being bound together by no honest tie, and existing for no honest purpose, destruction was the only honest doom to which any of them were entitled. And if we had spent the same money and blood to destroy them, that we did to preserve them, it would have been ten thousand times more creditable to our intelligence and character as a people.

Clearly the court has not strengthened its case at all by this picture of the peril in which the government was placed. It has only shown to what desperate straits a government, founded on usurpation and fraud, and devoted to robbery and oppression, may be brought, by the quarrels that are liable to arise between the different factions—that is, the different bands of robbers—of which it is composed. When such quarrels arise, it is not to be expected that either faction—having never had any regard to human rights, when acting in concert with the other—will hesitate at any new crimes that may be necessary to prolong its existence.

Here was a government that had never had any legitimate existence. It professedly rested all its authority on a certain paper called a constitution; a paper, I repeat, that nobody had ever signed, that few persons had ever read, that the great body of the people had never seen. This government had been imposed, by a few property holders, upon a people too poor, too scattered, and many of them too ignorant, to resist. It had been carried on, for some seventy years, by a mere cabal of irresponsible men, called lawmakers. In this cabal, the several local bands of robbers—the slaveholders of the South, the iron monopolists, the woollen monopolists, and the money monopolists, of the North—were represented. The whole purpose of its laws was to rob and enslave the many—both North and South—for the benefit of a few. But these robbers and tyrants quarreled—as lesser bands of robbers have done—over the division of their spoils. And hence the war. No such principle as justice to anybody—black or white—was the ruling motive on either side.

In this war, each faction—already steeped in crime—plunged into new, if not greater, crimes. In its desperation, it resolved to destroy men and money, without limit, and without mercy, for the preservation of its existence. The northern faction, having more men, money, and credit than the southern, survived the Kilkenny fight. Neither faction cared anything for human rights then, and neither of them has shown any regard for human rights since. "As a war measure," the northern faction found it necessary to put an end to the one great crime, from which the southern faction had drawn its wealth. But all other government crimes have been more rampant since the war, than they were before. Neither the conquerors, nor the conquered, have yet learned that no government can have any right to exist for any other purpose than the simple maintenance of justice between man and man.

And now, years after the fiendish butchery is over, and after men would seem to have had time to come to their senses, the Supreme Court of the United States, representing the victorious faction, comes forward with the declaration that one of the crimes — the violation of men's private contracts — resorted to by its faction, in the heat of conflict, as a means of preserving its power over the other, was not only justifiable and proper at the time, *but that it is also a legitimate and constitutional power, to be exercised forever hereafter in time of peace!*

Mark the knavery of these men. They first say that, because the government was in peril of its life, it had a right to license great crimes against private persons, if by so doing it could raise money for its own preservation. Next they say that, *although the government is no longer in peril of its life*, it may still go on forever licensing the same crimes as it was before necessitated to license!

They thus virtually say that the government may commit the same crimes in time of peace, that it is necessitated to do in time of war; and, that, consequently, it has the same right to "take the poor man's cattle, and horses, and corn," and "the rich man's bonds and notes," and poor men's "bodies and lives," in time of peace, *when no necessity whatever can be alleged*, as in time of war, when the government is in peril of its life.

In short, they virtually say, that this government exists for itself alone; and that all the natural rights of the people, to property, liberty, and life, are mere baubles, to be disposed of, at its pleasure, whether in time of peace, or in war.

Section XXII.

As if to place beyond controversy the fact, that the court may forever hereafter be relied on to sanction every usurpation and crime that congress will ever dare to put into the form of a statute, without the slightest color of authority from the constitution, necessity, utility, justice, or reason, it has, on three separate occasions, announced its sanction of the monopoly of money, as finally established by congress in 1866, and continued in force ever since.

This monopoly is established by a prohibitory tax — a tax of ten per cent. — on all notes issued for circulation as money, other than the notes of the United States and the national banks.

This ten per cent. is called a "tax," but is really a penalty, and is intended as such, and as nothing else. Its whole purpose is — *not to raise revenue* — but solely to establish a monopoly of money, by prohibiting the issue of all notes intended for circulation as money, except those issued, or specially licensed, by the government itself.

This prohibition upon the issue of all notes, except those issued, or specially licensed, by the government, is a prohibition upon all freedom of industry and traffic. It is a prohibition upon the exercise of men's natural right to lend and hire such money capital as all men need to enable them to create and distribute wealth, and supply their own wants, and provide for their own happiness. Its whole purpose is to reduce, as far as possible, the great body of the people to the condition of servants to a few — a condition but a single grade above that of chattel slavery — in which their labor, and the products of their labor, may be extorted from them at such prices only as the holders of the monopoly may choose to give.

This prohibitory tax — so-called — is therefore really a penalty imposed upon the exercise of men's natural right to create and distribute wealth, and provide for their own and each other's wants. And it is imposed solely for the purpose of establishing a practically omnipotent monopoly in the hands of a few.

Calling this penalty a "tax" is one of the dirty tricks, or rather downright lies — that of calling things by false names — to which congress and the courts resort, to hide their usurpations and crimes from the common eye.

Everybody — who believes in the government — says, of course, that congress has power to levy taxes; that it must do so to raise revenue for the support of the government. Therefore this lying congress call this penalty a "tax," instead of calling it by its true name, a penalty.

It certainly is no tax, because no revenue is raised, or intended to be raised, by it. It is not levied upon property, or persons, as such, but only upon a certain act, or upon persons for doing a certain act; an act that is not only perfectly innocent and lawful in itself, but that is naturally and intrinsically useful, and even indispensable for the prosperity and welfare of the whole people. Its whole object is simply to deter everybody — except those specially licensed — from performing this innocent, useful, and necessary act. And this it has succeeded in doing for the last twenty years; to the destruction of the rights, and the impoverishment and immeasurable injury of all the people, except the few holders of the monopoly.

If congress had passed an act, in this form, to wit:

No person, nor any association of persons, incorporated or unincorporated — *unless specially licensed by congress* — shall issue their promissory notes for circulation as money; and a *penalty* of ten per cent. upon the amount of all such notes shall be imposed upon the persons issuing them,

the act would have been the same, in effect and intention, as is this act, that imposes what it calls a "tax." The penalty would have been understood by everybody as a punishment for issuing the notes; and would have been applied to, and enforced against, those only who should have issued them. And it is the same with this so-called tax. It will never be collected, except for the same cause, and under the same circumstances, as the penalty would have been. It has no more to do with raising a revenue, than the penalty would have had. And all these lying lawmakers and courts know it.

But if congress had put this prohibition distinctly in the form of a *penalty*, the usurpation would have been so barefaced — so destitute of all color of constitutional authority—that congress dared not risk the consequences. And possibly the court might not have dared to sanction it; if, indeed, there be any crime or usurpation which the court dare not sanction. So these knavish lawmakers called this penalty a "tax"; and the court says that such a "tax" is clearly constitutional. And the monopoly has now been established for twenty years. And substantially all the industrial and financial troubles of that period have been the natural consequences of the monopoly.

If congress had laid a prohibitory tax upon all food—that is, had imposed a penalty upon the production and sale of all food—except such as it should have itself produced, or specially licensed; and should have reduced the amount of food, thus produced or licensed, to one tenth, twentieth, or fiftieth of what was really needed; the motive and the crime would have been the same, in character, if not in degree, as they are in this case, *viz.*, to enable the few holders of the licensed food to extort, from everybody else, by the fear of starvation, all their (the latter's) earnings and property, in exchange for this small quantity of privileged food.

Such a monopoly of food would have been no clearer violation of men's natural rights, than is the present monopoly of money. And yet this colossal crime—like every other crime that congress chooses to commit—is sanctioned by its servile, rotten, and stinking court.

On what *constitutional* grounds—that is, on what provisions found in the constitution itself—does the court profess to give its sanction to such a crime?

On these three only:

1. On the power of congress to lay and collect taxes, etc.
2. On the power of congress to coin money.
3. On the power of congress to borrow money.

Out of these simple, and apparently harmless provisions, the court manufactures an authority to grant, to a few persons, a monopoly that is practically omnipotent over all the industry and traffic of the country; that is fatal to all other men's natural right to lend and hire capital for any or all their legitimate industries; and fatal absolutely to all their natural right to buy, sell, and exchange any, or all, the products of their labor at their true, just, and natural prices.

Let us look at these constitutional provisions, and see how much authority congress can really draw from them.

1. The constitution says:

The congress shall have power to lay and collect taxes, duties, imposts, and excises, *to pay the debts, and provide for the common defence and general welfare of the United States.*

This provision plainly authorizes no taxation whatever, except for the raising of revenue to pay the debts and legitimate expenses of the government. It no more authorizes taxation for the purpose of establishing monopolies of any kind whatever, than it does for taking openly and boldly all the property of the many, and giving it outright to a few. And none but a congress of usurpers, robbers, and swindlers would ever think of using it for that purpose.

The court says, *in effect*, that this provision gives congress power to establish the present monopoly of money; that the power to tax all other money, is a power to prohibit all other money; and a power to prohibit all other money is a power to give the present money a monopoly.

How much is such an argument worth? Let us show by a parallel case, as follows.

Congress has the same power to tax all other property, that it has to tax money. And if the power to tax money is a power to prohibit money, then it follows that the power of congress to tax all other property than money, is a power to prohibit all other property than money; and a power to prohibit all other property than money, is a power to give monopolies to all such other property as congress may not choose to prohibit; or may choose to specially license.

On such reasoning as this, it would follow that the power of congress to tax money, and all other property, is a power to prohibit all money, and all other property; and thus to establish monopolies in favor of all such money, and all such other property, as it chooses not to prohibit; or chooses to specially license.

Thus, this reasoning would give congress power to establish all the monopolies, it may choose to establish, not only in money, but in agriculture, manufactures, and commerce; and protect these monopolies against infringement, by imposing prohibitory taxes upon all money and other property, except such as it should choose not to prohibit; or should choose to specially license.

Because the constitution says that "congress shall have power to lay and collect taxes," etc., to raise the revenue necessary for paying the current expenses of the government, the court say that congress have power to levy prohibitory taxes — taxes that shall yield no revenue at all — but shall operate only as a penalty upon all industries and traffic, and upon the use of all the means of industry and traffic, that shall compete with such monopolies as congress shall choose to grant.

This is no more than an unvarnished statement of the argument, by which the court attempts to justify a prohibitory "tax" upon money; for the same reasoning would justify the levying of a prohibitory tax — that is, penalty — upon the use of any and all other means of industry and traffic, by which any other monopolies, granted by congress, might be infringed.

There is plainly no more connection between the "power to lay and collect taxes," etc., for the necessary expenses of the government, and the power to establish this monopoly of money, than there is between such a power of taxation, and a power to punish, as a crime, any or all industry and traffic whatsoever, except such as the government may specially license.

This whole cheat lies in the use of the word "tax," to describe what is really a penalty, upon the exercise of any or all men's natural rights of providing for their subsistence and well-being. And none but corrupt and rotten congresses and courts would ever think of practising such a cheat.

2. The second provision of the constitution, relied on by the court to justify the monopoly of money, is this:

The congress shall have power to coin money, regulate the value thereof, and of foreign coins.

The only important part of this provision is that which says that "the congress shall have power to coin money, [and] regulate the value thereof."

That part about regulating the value of foreign coins — if any one can tell how congress can regulate it — is of no appreciable importance to anybody; for the coins will circulate, or not, as men may, or may not, choose to buy and sell them as money, and at such value as they will bear in free and open market, — that is, in competition with all other coins, and all other money. This is their only true and natural market value; and there is no occasion for congress to do anything in regard to them.

The only thing, therefore, that we need to look at, is simply the power of congress "to coin money."

So far as congress itself is authorized to coin money, this is simply a power to weigh and assay metals, — gold, silver, or any other, — stamp upon them marks indicating their weight and fineness, and then sell them to whomsoever may choose to buy them; and let them go in the market for whatever they may chance to bring, in competition with all other money that may chance to be offered there.

It is no power to impose any restrictions whatever upon any or all other honest money, that may be offered in the market, and bought and sold in competition with the coins weighed and assayed by the government.

The power itself is a frivolous one, of little or no utility; for the weighing and assaying of metals is a thing so easily done, and can be done by so many different persons, that there is certainly no *necessity* for its being done at all by a government. And it would undoubtedly have been far better if all coins — whether coined by governments or individuals — had all been made into pieces bearing simply the names of pounds, ounces, pennyweights, etc., and containing just the amounts of pure metal described by those weights. The coins would then have been regarded as only so much metal; and as having only the same value as the same amount of metal in any other form. Men would then have known exactly how much of certain metals they were buying, selling, and promising to pay. And all the jugglery, cheating, and robbery that governments have practised, and licensed individuals to practise — by coining pieces bearing the same names, but having different amounts of metal — would have been avoided.

And all excuses for establishing monopolies of money, by prohibiting all other money than the coins, would also have been avoided.

As it is, the constitution imposes no prohibition upon the coining of money by individuals, but only by State governments. Individuals are left perfectly free to coin it, except that they must not "*counterfeit* the securities and current coin of the United States."

For quite a number of years after the discovery of gold in California — that is, until the establishment of a government mint there — a large part of the gold that was taken out of the earth, was coined by private persons and companies; and this coinage was perfectly legal. And I do not remember to have ever heard any complaint, or accusation, that it was not honest and reliable.

The true and only value, which the coins have as money, is that value which they have as metals, for uses in the arts, — that is, for plate, watches, jewelry, and the like. This value they will retain, whether they circulate as money, or not. At this value, they are so utterly inadequate to serve as *bona fide* equivalents for such other property as is to be bought and sold for money; and, after being minted, are so quickly taken out of circulation, and worked up into articles of use — plate, watches, jewelry, etc. — that they are practically of almost no importance at all as money.

But they can be so easily and cheaply carried from one part of the world to another, that they have substantially the same market value all over the world. They are also, in but a small degree, liable to great or sudden changes in value. For these reasons, they serve well as standards — are perhaps the best standards we can have — by which to measure the value of all other money, as well as other property. But to give them any monopoly as money, is to deny the natural right of all men to make their own contracts, and buy and sell, borrow and lend, give and receive, all such money as the parties to bargains may mutually agree upon; and also to license the few holders of the coins to rob all other men in the prices of the latter's labor and property.

3. The third provision of the constitution, on which the court relies to justify the monopoly of money, is this:

The congress shall have power to borrow money.

Can any one see any connection between the power of congress "to borrow money," and its power to establish a monopoly of money?

Certainly no such connection is visible to the legal eye. But it is distinctly visible to the political and financial eye; that is, to that class of men, for whom governments exist, and who own congresses and courts, and set in motion armies and navies, whenever they can promote their own interests by doing so.

To a government, whose usurpations and crimes have brought it to the verge of destruction, these men say:

Make bonds bearing six per cent. interest; sell them to us at half their face value; then give us a monopoly of money based upon these bonds — such a monopoly as will subject the great body of the people to a dependence upon us for the necessaries of life, and compel them to sell their labor and property to us at our own prices; then, under pretence of raising revenue to pay the interest and principal of the bonds, impose such a tariff upon imported commodities as will enable us to get fifty per cent. more for our own goods than they are worth; in short, pledge to us all the power of the government to extort for us, in the future, everything that can be extorted from the producers of wealth, and we will lend you all the money you need to maintain your power.

And the government has no alternative but to comply with this infamous proposal, or give up its infamous life.

This is the only real connection there is between the power of congress "to borrow money," and its power to establish a monopoly of money. It was only by an outright sale of the rights of the whole people, for a long series of years, that the government could raise the money necessary to continue its villainous existence.

Congress had just as much constitutional power "to borrow money," by the sale of any and all the other natural rights of the people at large, as it had "to borrow money" by the sale of the people's natural rights to lend and hire money.

When the Supreme Court of the United States — assuming to be an oracle, empowered to define authoritatively the legal rights of every human being in the country — declares that congress has a constitutional power to prohibit the use of all that immense mass of money capital, in the shape of promissory notes, which the real property of the country is capable of supplying and sustaining, and which is sufficient to give to every laboring person, man or woman, the means of independence and wealth — when that court says that congress has power to prohibit the use of all this money capital, and grant to a few men a monopoly of money that shall condemn the great body of wealth-producers to hopeless poverty, dependence, and servitude — and when the court has the audacity to make these declarations on such nakedly false and senseless grounds as those that have now been stated, it is clearly time for the people of this country to inquire what constitutions and governments are good for, and whether they (the people) have any natural right, as human beings, to live for themselves, or only for a few conspirators, swindlers, usurpers, robbers, and tyrants, who employ lawmakers, judges, etc., to do their villainous work upon their fellow-men.

The court gave their sanction to the monopoly of money in these three separate cases, *viz.: Veazie Bank vs. Fenno,* 8 *Wallace,* 549 (1869). *National Bank vs. United States,* 101 *U. S. Reports,* 5 *and* 6 (1879). *Juilliard vs. Greenman,* 110 *U. S. Reports* 445–6 (1884).

Section XXIII.

If anything could add to the disgust and detestation which the monstrous falsifications of the constitution, already described, should excite towards the court that resorts to them, it would be the fact that the court, not content with falsifying to the utmost the constitution itself, *goes outside of the constitution, to the tyran-*

nical practices of what it calls the "*sovereign*" governments of "*other civilized nations,*" to justify the same practices by our own.

It asserts, over and over again, the idea that our government is a "*sovereign*" government; that it has the same rights of "*sovereignty,*" as the governments of "other civilized nations"; especially those in Europe.

What, then, is a "sovereign" government? It is a government that is "sovereign" over all the natural rights of the people. This is the only "sovereignty" that any government can be said to have. Under it, the people have no *rights*. They are simply "subjects,"—that is, slaves. They have but one law, and one duty, *viz.*, obedience, submission. They are not recognized as having any *rights*. They can claim nothing as their own. They can only accept what the government chooses to give them. The government owns them and their property; and disposes of them and their property, at its pleasure, or discretion; without regard to any consent, or dissent, on their part.

Such was the "sovereignty" claimed and exercised by the governments of those, so-called, "civilized nations of Europe," that were in power in 1787, 1788, and 1789, when our constitution was framed and adopted, and the government put in operation under it. And the court now says, virtually, that the constitution intended to give to our government the same "sovereignty" over the natural rights of the people, that those governments had then.

But how did the "civilized governments of Europe" become possessed of such "sovereignty"? Had the people ever granted it to them? Not at all. The governments spurned the idea that they were dependent on the will or consent of their people for their political power. On the contrary, they claimed to have derived it from the only source, from which such "sovereignty" could have been derived; that is, from God Himself.

In 1787, 1788, and 1789, all the great governments of Europe, except England, claimed to exist by what was called "Divine Right." That is, they claimed to have received authority from God Himself, to rule over their people. And they taught, and a servile and corrupt priesthood taught, that it was a religious duty of the people to obey them. And they kept great standing armies, and hordes of pimps, spies, and ruffians, to keep the people in subjection.

And when, soon afterwards, the revolutionists of France dethroned the king then existing—the Legitimist king, so-called—and asserted the right of the people to choose their own government, these other governments carried on a twenty years' war against her, to reëstablish the principle of "sovereignty" by "Divine Right." And in this war, the government of England, although not itself claiming to exist by Divine Right,—but really existing by brute force,—furnished men and money without limit, to reëstablish that principle in France, and to maintain it wherever else, in Europe, it was endangered by the idea of popular rights.

The principle, then, of "Sovereignty by Divine Right"—sustained by brute force—was the principle on which the governments of Europe then rested; and most of them rest on that principle today. And now the Supreme Court of the United States virtually says that our constitution intended to give to our government the same "sovereignty"—the same absolutism—the same supremacy over all the natural rights of the people—as was claimed and exercised by those "Divine Right" governments of Europe, a hundred years ago!

That I may not be suspected of misrepresenting these men, I give some of their own words as follows:

It is not doubted that the power to establish a standard of value, by which all other values may be measured, or, in other words, to determine what shall be lawful money and a legal tender, is in its nature, and of necessity, a governmental power. *It is in all countries exercised by the government.*—*Hepburn vs. Griswold,* 8 *Wallace* 615.

The court call a power,

To make treasury notes a legal tender for the payment of *all* debts [private as well as public] *a power confessedly possessed by every independent sovereignty other than the United States.*—*Legal Tender Cases,* 12 *Wallace,* p. 529.

Also, in the same case, it speaks of:

That general power over the currency, *which has always been an acknowledged attribute of sovereignty in every other civilized nation than our own.*—p. 545.

In this same case, by way of asserting the power of congress to do any dishonest thing that any so-called "sovereign government" ever did, the court say:

Has any one, in good faith, avowed his belief that even a law debasing the current coin, by increasing the alloy [and then making these debased coins a legal tender in payment of debts previously contracted], would be taking private property? It might be impolitic, and unjust, but could its constitutionality be doubted?—*p.* 552.

In the same case, Bradley said:

As a government, it [the government of the United States] was invested with *all the attributes of sovereignty.*—p. 555.

Also he said:

Such being the character of the General Government, it seems to be a self-evident proposition *that it is invested with all those inherent and implied powers, which, at the time of adopting the constitution, were generally considered to belong to every government, as such, and as being essential to the exercise of its functions.*—p. 556.

Also he said:

Another proposition equally clear is, *that at the time the constitution was adopted, it was,* and for a long time had been, the practice of most, if not all, civilized governments, to employ the public credit as a means of anticipating the national revenues for the purpose of enabling them to exercise their governmental functions. —*p.* 556.

Also he said:

It is our duty to construe the instrument [the constitution] by its words, *in the light of history, of the general nature of government, and the incidents of sovereignty.* —*p.* 55.

Also he said:

The government simply demands that its credit shall be accepted and received by public and private creditors during the pending exigency. *Every government has a right to demand this, when its existence is at stake.* —*p.* 560.

Also he said:

These views are exhibited . . . . for the purpose of showing that it [the power to make its notes a legal tender in payment of private debts] *is one of those vital and essential powers inhering in every national sovereignty,* and necessary to its self-preservation. —*p.* 564.

In still another legal tender case, the court said:

The people of the United States, by the constitution, established a national government, *with sovereign powers, legislative, executive,* and judicial. —*Juilliard vs. Greenman,* 110 *U. S. Reports, p.* 438.

Also it calls the constitution:

A constitution, establishing a form of government, declaring fundamental principles, *and creating a national sovereignty,* intended to endure for ages. —*p.* 439.

Also the court speaks of the government of the United States:

As a sovereign government. —*p.* 446.

Also it said:

It appears to us to follow, as a logical and necessary consequence, that congress has the power to issue the obligations of the United States in such form, and to impress upon them such qualities as currency, for the purchase of merchandise and the payment of debts, *as accord with the usage of other sovereign governments.* The power, as incident to the power of borrowing money, and issuing bills or notes of the government for money borrowed, of impressing upon those bills or notes the quality of being a legal tender for the payment of private debts, *was a power universally understood to belong to sovereignty, in Europe and America, at the time of the framing and adoption of the constitution of the United States.* The governments of Europe, acting through the monarch, or the legislature, according to the distribution of powers *under their respective constitutions,* had, and have, as *sovereign* a power of issuing paper money as of stamping coin. This power has been distinctly recognized in an important modern case, ably argued and fully considered, in which the Emperor of Austria, as King of Hungary, obtained from the English Court of Chancery an injunction against the issue, in England, without his license, of notes purporting to be public paper money of Hungary.—*p.* 447.

Also it speaks of:

Congress, as the legislature of a *sovereign* nation.—*p.* 449.

Also it said:

The power to make the notes of the government a legal tender in payment of private debts, *being one of the powers belonging to sovereignty in other civilized nations*, . . . we are irresistibly impelled to the conclusion that the impressing upon the treasury notes of the United States the quality of being a legal tender in payment of private debts, is an appropriate means, conducive and plainly adapted to the execution of the undoubted powers of congress, consistent with the letter and spirit of the constitution, etc.—*p.* 450.

On reading these astonishing ideas about "sovereignty"—"sovereignty" over all the natural rights of mankind—"sovereignty," as it prevailed in Europe "at the time of the framing and adoption of the constitution of the United States"—we are compelled to see that these judges obtained their constitutional law, not from the constitution itself, but from the example of the "Divine Right" governments existing in Europe a hundred years ago. These judges seem never to have heard of the American Revolution, or the French Revolution, or even of the English Revolutions of the seventeenth century—revolutions fought and accomplished to overthrow these very ideas of "sovereignty," which these judges now proclaim, as the supreme law of this country. They seem never to have heard of the Declaration of Independence, nor of any other declaration of the natural rights of human beings. To their minds, "the sovereignty of governments" is everything; human rights nothing. They apparently cannot conceive of such a thing as a people's establishing a government as a means of preserving their personal liberty and rights. They can only see what fearful calamities "sovereign governments" would be liable to, if they could not compel their "subjects"—the people—to support them against their will, and at every cost of their property, liberty, and lives. They are utterly blind to the fact, that it is this very assumption of "sovereignty" over all the natural rights of men, that brings governments into all their difficulties, and all their perils. They do not see that it is this very assumption of "sovereignty" over all men's natural rights, that makes it necessary for the "Divine Right" governments of Europe to maintain not only great standing armies, but also a vile purchased priesthood, that shall impose upon, and help to crush, the ignorant and superstitious people.

These judges talk of "the *constitutions*" of these "sovereign governments" of Europe, as they existed "at the time of the framing and adoption of the constitution of the United States." They apparently do not know that those governments had no constitutions at all, except the Will of God, their standing armies, and the judges, lawyers, priests, pimps, spies, and ruffians they kept in their service.

If these judges had lived in Russia, a hundred years ago, and had chanced to be visited with a momentary spasm of manhood — a fact hardly to be supposed of such creatures — and had been sentenced therefor to the knout, a dungeon, or Siberia, would we ever afterward have seen them, as judges of our Supreme Court, declaring that government to be the model after which ours was formed?

These judges will probably be surprised when I tell them that the constitution of the United States contains no such word as "sovereign," or "sovereignty"; that it contains no such word as "subjects"; nor any word that implies that the government is "sovereign," or that the people are "subjects." At most, it contains only the mistaken idea that a power of making laws — by lawmakers chosen by the people — was consistent with, and necessary to, the maintenance of liberty and justice for the people themselves. This mistaken idea was, in some measure, excusable in that day, when reason and experience had not demonstrated, to their minds, the utter incompatibility of all lawmaking whatsoever with men's natural rights.

The only other provision of the constitution, that can be interpreted as a declaration of "sovereignty" in the government, is this:

This constitution, and the laws of the United States *which shall be made in pursuance thereof*, and all treaties made, or which shall be made, under the authority of the United States, *shall be the supreme law of the land*, and the judges in every State shall be bound thereby, *anything in the constitution or laws of any State to the contrary notwithstanding.* — *Art.* VI.

This provision I interpret to mean simply that the constitution, laws, and treaties of the United States, shall be "the supreme law of the land" — *not anything in the natural rights of the people to liberty and justice, to the contrary notwithstanding* — but only that they shall be "the supreme law of the land," "*anything in the constitution or laws of any State to the contrary notwithstanding*," — that is, whenever the two may chance to conflict with each other.

If this is its true interpretation, the provision contains no declaration of "sovereignty" over the natural rights of the people.

Justice is "the supreme law" of this, and all other lands; anything in the constitutions or laws of any nation to the contrary notwithstanding. And if the constitution of the United States intended to assert the contrary, it was simply an audacious lie — a lie as foolish as it was audacious — that should have covered with infamy every man who helped to frame the constitution, or afterward sanctioned it, or that should ever attempt to administer it.

Inasmuch as the constitution declares itself to have been "ordained and established" by

We, the people of the United States, in order to form a more perfect union, establish justice, insure domestic tranquillity, provide for the common defence, promote the general welfare, and secure the blessings of liberty to ourselves and our posterity, everybody who attempts to administer it, is bound to give it such an interpretation, and only such an interpretation, as is consistent with, and promotive of, those objects, if its language will admit of such an interpretation.

To suppose that "the people of the United States" intended to declare that the constitution and laws of the United States should be "the supreme law of the land," *anything in their own natural rights, or in the natural rights of the rest of mankind, to the contrary notwithstanding*, would be to suppose that they intended, not only to authorize every injustice, and arouse universal violence, among themselves, but that they intended also to avow themselves the open enemies of the rights of all the rest of mankind. Certainly no such folly, madness, or criminality as this can be attributed to them by any rational man—always excepting the justices of the Supreme Court of the United States, the lawmakers, and the believers in the "Divine Right" of the cunning and the strong, to establish governments that shall deceive, plunder, enslave, and murder the ignorant and the weak.

Many men, still living, can well remember how, some fifty years ago, those famous champions of "sovereignty," of arbitrary power, Webster and Calhoun, debated the question, whether, in this country, "sovereignty" resided in the general or State governments. But they never settled the question, for the very good reason that no such thing as "sovereignty" resided in either.

And the question was never settled, until it was settled at the cost of a million of lives, and some ten thousand millions of money. And then it was settled only as the same question had so often been settled before, to wit, that "the heaviest battalions" are "sovereign" over the lighter.

The only real "sovereignty," or right of "sovereignty," in this or any other country, is that right of sovereignty which each and every human being has over his or her own person and property, so long as he or she obeys the one law of justice towards the person and property of every other human being. This is the only *natural* right of sovereignty, that was ever known among men. All other so-called rights of sovereignty are simply the usurpations of impostors, conspirators, robbers, tyrants, and murderers.

It is not strange that we are in such high favor with the tyrants of Europe, when our Supreme Court tells them that our government, although a little different in form, stands on the same essential basis as theirs of a hundred years ago; that it is as absolute and irresponsible as theirs were then; that it will spend more money, and shed more blood, to maintain its power, than they have ever been able to do; that the people have no more rights here than there; and that the government is doing all it can to keep the producing classes as poor here as they are there.

Section XXIV.

John Marshall has the reputation of having been the greatest jurist the country has ever had. And he unquestionably would have been a great jurist, if the two fundamental propositions, on which all his legal, political, and constitutional ideas were based, had been true.

These propositions were, first, that government has all power; and, secondly, that the people have no rights.

These two propositions were, with him, cardinal principles, from which, I think, he never departed.

For these reasons he was the oracle of all the rapacious classes, in whose interest the government was administered. And from them he got all his fame.

I think his record does not furnish a single instance, in which he ever vindicated men's natural rights, in opposition to the arbitrary legislation of congress.

He was chief justice thirty-four years: from 1801 to 1835. In all that time, so far as I have known, he never declared a single act of congress unconstitutional; and probably never would have done so, if he had lived to this time.

And, so far as I know, he never declared a single State law unconstitutional, on account of its injustice, or its violation of men's natural rights; but only on account of its conflict with the constitution, laws, or treaties of the United States.

He was considered very profound on questions of "sovereignty." In fact, he never said much in regard to anything else. He held that, in this country, "sovereignty" was divided: that the national government was "sovereign" over certain things; and that the State governments were "sovereign" over all other things. He had apparently never heard of any natural, individual, human rights, that had never been delegated to either the general or State governments.

As a practical matter, he seemed to hold that the general government had "sovereignty" enough to destroy as many of the natural rights of the people as it should please to destroy; and that the State governments had "sovereignty" enough to destroy what should be left, if there should be any such. He evidently considered that, to the national government, had been delegated the part of the lion, with the right to devour as much of his prey as his appetite should crave; and that the State governments were jackals, with power to devour what the lion should leave.

In his efforts to establish the absolutism of our governments, he made himself an adept in the use of all those false definitions, and false assumptions, to which courts are driven, who hold that constitutions and statute books are supreme over all natural principles of justice, and over all the natural rights of mankind.

Here is his definition of law. He professes to have borrowed it from some one, —he does not say whom,—but he accepts it as his own.

Law has been defined by a writer, whose definitions especially have been the theme of *almost* universal panegyric, " *To be a rule of civil conduct prescribed by the supreme power in a State."* In our system, the legislature of a State is the supreme power, in all cases where its action is not restrained by the constitution of the United States.— *Ogden vs. Saunders,* 12 *Wheaton* 347.

This definition is an utterly false one. It denies all the natural rights of the people; and is resorted to only by usurpers and tyrants, to justify their crimes.

The true definition of law is, that it is a fixed, immutable, natural principle; and not anything that man ever made, or can make, unmake, or alter. Thus we speak of the laws of matter, and the laws of mind; of the law of gravitation, the laws of light, heat, and electricity, the laws of chemistry, geology, botany; of physiological laws, of astronomical and atmospherical laws, etc., etc.

All these are natural laws, that man never made, nor can ever unmake, or alter.

The law of justice is just as supreme and universal in the moral world, as these others are in the mental or physical world; and is as unalterable as are these by any human power. And it is just as false and absurd to talk of anybody's having the power to abolish the law of justice, and set up their own will in its stead, as it would be to talk of their having the power to abolish the law of gravitation, or any of the other natural laws of the universe, and set up their own will in the place of them.

Yet Marshall holds that this natural law of justice is no law at all, in comparison with some "rule of civil conduct prescribed by [what he calls] the supreme power in a State."

And he gives this miserable definition, which he picked up somewhere—out of the legal filth in which he wallowed—as his sufficient authority for striking down all the natural obligation of men's contracts, and all men's natural rights to make their own contracts; and for upholding the State governments in prohibiting all such contracts as they, in their avarice and tyranny, may choose to prohibit. He does it too, directly in the face of that very constitution, which he professes to uphold, and which declares that "No State shall pass any law impairing the [natural] obligation of contracts."

By the same rule, or on the same definition of law, he would strike down any and all the other natural rights of mankind.

That such a definition of law should suit the purposes of men like Marshall, who believe that governments should have all power, and men no rights, accounts for the fact that, in this country, men have had no *"rights"*—but only such permits as lawmakers have seen fit to allow them—since the State and United States governments were established,—or at least for the last eighty years.

Marshall also said:

The right [of government] to regulate contracts, to prescribe the rules by which they may be evidenced, *to prohibit such as may be deemed mischievous, is unquestionable,* and has been universally exercised.— *Ogden vs. Saunders,* 12 *Wheaton* 347.

He here asserts that "the supreme power in a State"—that is, the legislature of a State—has "the *right*" to "*deem* it *mischievous*" to allow men to exercise their natural right to make their own contracts! Contracts that have a natural obligation! And that, if a State legislature thinks it "mischievous" to allow men to make contracts that are naturally obligatory, "*its right to prohibit them is unquestionable.*"

Is not this equivalent to saying that governments have all power, and the people no rights?

On the same principle, and under the same definition of law, the lawmakers of a State may, of course, hold it "mischievous" to allow men to exercise any of their other natural rights, as well as their right to make their own contracts; and may therefore prohibit the exercise of any, or all, of them.

And this is equivalent to saying that governments have all power, and the people no rights.

If a government can forbid the free exercise of a single one of man's natural rights, it may, for the same reason, forbid the exercise of any and all of them; and thus establish, practically and absolutely, Marshall's principle, that the government has all power, and the people no rights.

In the same case, of *Ogden vs. Saunders, Marshall's principle was agreed to by all the other justices, and all the lawyers!*

Thus Thompson, one of the justices, said:

Would it not be within the legitimate powers of a State legislature to declare *prospectively* that no one should be made responsible, upon contracts entered into before arriving at the age of *twenty-five* years? This, I presume, cannot be doubted.—*p.* 300.

On the same principle, he might say that a State legislature may declare that no person, under fifty, or seventy, or a hundred, years of age, shall exercise his natural right of making any contract that is naturally obligatory.

In the same case, Trimble, another of the justices, said:

If the positive law [that is, the statute law] of the State declares the contract shall have no obligation, *it can have no obligation, whatever may be the principles of natural law in regard to such a contract. This doctrine has been held and maintained by all States and nations. The power of controlling, modifying, and even taking away, all obligation from such contracts as, independently of positive enactions to the contrary, would have been obligatory, has been exercised by all independent sovereigns.*—*p.* 320.

Yes; and why has this power been exercised by "all States and nations," and "all independent sovereigns"? Solely because these governments have all—or at least so many of them as Trimble had in his mind—been despotic and tyrannical; and have claimed for themselves all power, and denied to the people all rights.

Thus it seems that Trimble, like all the rest of them, got his constitutional law, not from any natural principles of justice, not from men's natural rights, not from the constitution of the United States, nor even from any constitution affirming men's natural rights, but from "the doctrine [that] has been held and maintained by all [those] States and nations," and "all [those] independent sovereigns," who have usurped all power, and denied all the natural rights of mankind.

Marshall gives another of his false definitions, when, speaking for the whole court, in regard to the power of congress "to regulate commerce with foreign nations, and among the several States," he asserts the right of congress to an arbitrary, absolute dominion over all men's natural rights to carry on such commerce. Thus he says:

> What is this power? It is the power to regulate: *that is, to prescribe the rule by which commerce is to be governed. This power, like all others vested in congress, is complete in itself, may be exercised to its utmost extent, and acknowledges no limitations, other than are prescribed by the constitution.* These are expressed in plain terms, and do not affect the questions which arise in this case, or which have been discussed at the bar. If, as has always been understood, the sovereignty of congress, though limited to specific objects, is plenary as to those objects, the power over commerce with foreign nations, and among the several States, is vested in congress as absolutely as it would be in a single government, having in its constitution the same restrictions on the exercise of the power as are found in the constitution of the United States. *The wisdom and the discretion of congress, their identity with the people, and the influence which their constituents possess at elections, are, in this, as in many other instances, as that, for example, of declaring war, the sole restraints on which they* [the people] *have relied, to secure them from its abuse. They are the restraints on which the people must often rely* SOLELY, *in all representative governments.* — *Gibbons vs. Ogden,* 9 *Wheaton* 196.

This is a general declaration of absolutism over all "commerce with foreign nations and among the several States," with certain exceptions mentioned in the constitution; such as that "all duties, imposts, and excises shall be uniform throughout the United States," and "no tax or duty shall be laid on articles exported from any State," and "no preference shall be given, by any regulation of commerce or revenue, to the ports of one State over those of another; nor shall vessels bound to, or from, one State, be obliged to enter, clear, or pay duties in another."

According to this opinion of the court, congress has — subject to the exceptions referred to — absolute, irresponsible dominion over "all commerce with foreign nations, and among the several States"; and all men's natural rights to trade with each other, among the several States, and all over the world, are prostrate under the feet of a contemptible, detestable, and irresponsible cabal of lawmakers; and the people have no protection or redress for any tyranny or robbery that may be practised upon them, except "*the wisdom and the discretion of congress, their identity with the people, and the influence which their constituents possess at elections*"!

It will be noticed that the court say that "*all the other powers, vested in congress, are complete in themselves, and may be exercised to their utmost extent, and acknowledge no limitations, other than those prescribed by the constitution.*"

They say that among "all the other [practically unlimited] powers, vested in congress," is the power "of declaring war"; and, of course, of carrying on war; that congress has power to carry on war, for any reason, to any extent, and against any people, it pleases.

Thus they say, virtually, that *the natural rights of mankind* impose no *constitutional* restraints whatever upon congress, in the exercise of their lawmaking powers.

Is not this asserting that governments have all power, and the people no rights?

But what is to be particularly noticed, is the fact that Marshall gives to congress all this practically unlimited power over all "commerce with foreign nations, and among the several States," *solely on the strength of a false definition of the verb "to regulate."* He says that "the power to regulate commerce" is the power "*to prescribe the rule by which commerce is to be governed.*"

This definition is an utterly false, absurd, and atrocious one. It would give congress power arbitrarily to control, obstruct, impede, derange, prohibit, and destroy commerce.

The verb "to regulate" does not, as Marshall asserts, imply the exercise of any arbitrary control whatever over the thing regulated; nor any power "to prescribe [arbitrarily] the rule, by which" the thing regulated "is to be governed." On the contrary, it comes from the Latin word, *regula,* a rule; *and implies the pre-existence of a rule, to which the thing regulated is made to conform.*

To regulate one's diet, for example, is not, on the one hand, to starve one's self to emaciation, nor, on the other, to gorge one's self with all sorts of indigestible and hurtful substances, in disregard of the natural laws of health. But it supposes the pre-existence of the *natural laws of health,* to which the diet is made to conform.

A clock is not "regulated," when it is made to go, to stop, to go forwards, to go backwards, to go fast, to go slow, at the mere will or caprice of the person who may have it in hand. It is "regulated" only when it is made to conform to, to mark truly, the diurnal revolutions of the earth. These revolutions of the earth constitute the pre-existing rule, by which alone a clock can be regulated.

A mariner's compass is not "regulated," when the needle is made to move this way and that, at the will of an operator, without reference to the north pole. But it is regulated when it is freed from all disturbing influences, and suffered to point constantly to the north, as it is its nature to do.

A locomotive is not "regulated," when it is made to go, to stop, to go forwards, to go backwards, to go fast, to go slow, at the mere will and caprice of the engineer, and without regard to economy, utility, or safety. But it is regulated, when its motions are made to conform to a pre-existing rule, that is made up of economy, utility, and safety combined. What this rule is, in the case of a locomotive, may not be known with such scientific precision, as is the rule in the case of a clock, or a mariner's compass; but it may be approximated with sufficient accuracy for practical purposes.

The pre-existing rule, by which alone commerce can be "regulated," is a matter of science; and is already known, so far as the natural principle of justice, in relation to contracts, is known. The natural right of all men to make all contracts whatsoever, that are naturally and intrinsically just and lawful, furnishes the pre-existing rule, by which *alone* commerce can be regulated. And it is the only rule, to which congress have any constitutional power to make commerce conform.

When all commerce, that is intrinsically just and lawful, is secured and protected, and all commerce that is intrinsically unjust and unlawful, is prohibited, then commerce is regulated, and not before.*

This false definition of the verb *"to regulate"* has been used, time out of mind, by knavish lawmakers and their courts, to hide their violations of men's natural right to do their own businesses in all such ways — that are naturally and intrinsically just and lawful — as they may choose to do them in. These lawmakers and courts dare not always deny, utterly and plainly, men's right to do their own businesses in their own ways; but they will assume *"to regulate"* them; and in pretending simply *"to regulate"* them, they contrive *"to regulate"* men out of all their natural rights to do their own businesses in their own ways.

How much have we all heard (we who are old enough), within the last fifty years, of the power of congress, or of the States, *"to regulate the currency."* And *"to regulate the currency"* has always meant to fix the kind, *and limit the amount*, of currency, that men may be permitted to buy and sell, lend and borrow, give and receive, in their dealings with each other. It has also meant to say *who shall have the control of the licensed money;* instead of making it mean the suppression only of false and dishonest money, and then leaving all men free to exercise their natural right of buying and selling, borrowing and lending, giving and receiving, all such, and so much, honest and true money, or currency, as the parties to any or all contracts may mutually agree upon.

Marshall's false *assumptions* are numerous and tyrannical. They all have the same end in view as his false definitions; that is, to establish the principle that governments have all power, and the people no rights. They are so numerous that it would be tedious, if not impossible, to describe them all separately. Many, or most, of them are embraced in the following, *viz.*:

1. The assumption that, by a certain paper, called the constitution of the United States — a paper (I repeat and reiterate) which nobody ever signed, which but few persons ever read, and which the great body of the people never saw — and also by some forty subsidiary papers, called State constitutions, which also nobody ever signed, which but few persons ever read, and which the great body of the people never saw — all making a perfect system of the merest nothingness — the assumption, I say, that, by these papers, the people have all consented to the abolition of justice itself, the highest moral law of the Universe; and that all their own natural, inherent, inalienable rights to the benefits of that law, shall be annulled; and that they themselves, and everything that is theirs, shall be given over into the irresponsible custody of some forty little cabals of blockheads and villains called lawmakers — blockheads, who imagine themselves wiser than justice itself, and villains, who care nothing for either wisdom or justice, but only for the

---

*The above extracts are from a pamphlet published by me in 1864, entitled *" Considerations for Bankers,"* etc., pp. 55, 56, 57.

gratification of their own avarice and ambitions; and that these cabals shall be invested with the right to dispose of the property, liberty, and lives of all the rest of the people, at their pleasure or discretion; or, as Marshall says, "their wisdom and discretion!"

If such an assumption as that does not embrace nearly, or quite, all the other false assumptions that usurpers and tyrants can ever need, to justify themselves in robbing, enslaving, and murdering all the rest of mankind, it is less comprehensive than it appears to me to be.

2. In the following paragraph may be found another batch of Marshall's false assumptions.

> The right to contract is the attribute of a free agent, and he may rightfully coerce performance from another free agent, who violates his faith. Contracts have consequently an intrinsic obligation. [*But*] *When men come into society, they can no longer exercise this original natural right of coercion. It would be incompatible with general peace, and is therefore surrendered.* Society prohibits the use of private individual coercion, *and gives in its place a more safe and more certain remedy.* But the right to contract is not surrendered with the right to coerce performance.— *Ogden vs. Saunders,* 12 *Wheaton* 350.

In this extract, taken in connection with the rest of his opinion in the same case, Marshall convicts himself of the grossest falsehood. He acknowledges that men have a natural right to make their own contracts; that their contracts have an "intrinsic obligation"; and that they have an "original and natural right" to coerce performance of them. And yet he assumes, and virtually asserts, that men *voluntarily* "*come into society,*" and "*surrender*" to "society" their natural right to coerce the fulfilment of their contracts. He assumes, and virtually asserts, that they do this, *upon the ground, and for the reason, that* "*society gives in its place a more safe and more certain remedy*"; that is, "a more safe and more certain" enforcement of all men's contracts that have "an intrinsic obligation."

In thus saying that "men come into society," and "surrender" to society, their "original and natural right" of coercing the fulfilment of contracts, and that "*society gives in its place a more safe and certain remedy,*" he virtually says, and means to say, that, *in consideration of such* "*surrender*" *of their* "*original and natural right of coercion,*" "*society*" pledges itself to them that it will give them this "*more safe and more certain remedy*"; that is, that it will more safely and more certainly enforce their contracts than they can do it themselves.

And yet, in the same opinion — only two and three pages preceding this extract — he declares emphatically that "the right" of government — or of what he calls "society" — "*to prohibit such contracts as may be deemed mischievous,* is *unquestionable.*"—*p.* 347.

And as an illustration of the exercise of this right of "society" to prohibit such contracts "as may be deemed mischievous," he cites the usury laws, thus:

> The acts against usury declare the contract to be void in the beginning. They deny that

the instrument ever became a contract. They deny it all original obligation; and cannot impair that which never came into existence.—*p.* 348.

All this is as much as to say that, when a man has voluntarily "come into society," and has "surrendered" to society "his original and natural right of coercing" the fulfilment of his contracts, and when he has done this in the confidence that society will fulfil its pledge to "give him a more safe and more certain coercion" than he was capable of himself, "society" may then turn around to him, and say:

We acknowledge that you have a natural right to make your own contracts. We acknowledge that your contracts have "an intrinsic obligation." We acknowledge that you had "an original and natural right" to coerce the fulfilment of them. We acknowledge that it was solely in consideration of our pledge to you, that we would give you a more safe and more certain coercion than you were capable of yourself, that you "surrendered" to us your right to coerce a fulfilment of them. And we acknowledge that, *according to our pledge*, you have now a right to require of us that we coerce a fulfilment of them. But after you had "surrendered" to us your own right of coercion, we took a different view of the pledge we had given you; and concluded that it would be "mischievous" to allow you to make such contracts. We therefore "prohibited" your making them. And having prohibited the making of them, we cannot now admit that they have any "obligation." We must therefore decline to enforce the fulfilment of them. And we warn you that, if you attempt to enforce them, by virtue of your own "original and natural right of coercion," we shall be obliged to consider your act a breach of "the general peace," and punish you accordingly. We are sorry that you have lost your property, but "society" must judge as to what contracts are, and what are not, "mischievous." We can therefore give you no redress. Nor can we suffer you to enforce your own rights, or redress your own wrongs.

Such is Marshall's theory of the way in which "society" got possession of all men's "original and natural right" to make their own contracts, and enforce the fulfilment of them; and of the way in which "society" now justifies itself in prohibiting all contracts, though "intrinsically obligatory," which it may choose to consider "mischievous." And he asserts that, in this way, "society" has acquired "*an unquestionable right*" to cheat men out of all their "original and natural right" to make their own contracts, and enforce the fulfilment of them.

A man's "original and natural right" to make all contracts that are "intrinsically obligatory," and to coerce the fulfilment of them, is one of the most valuable and indispensable of all human possessions. But Marshall assumes that a man may "surrender" this right to "society," under a pledge from "society," that it will secure to him "a more safe and certain" fulfilment of his contracts, than he is capable of himself; and that "society," having thus obtained from him this "surrender," may then turn around to him, and not only refuse to fulfil its pledge to him, but may also prohibit his own exercise of his own "original and natural right," which he has "surrendered" to "society!"

This is as much as to say that, if A can but induce B to intrust his (B's) property with him (A), for safekeeping, under a pledge that he (A) will keep it more safely and certainly than B can do it himself, *A thereby acquires an "unquestionable right" to keep the property forever, and let B whistle for it!*

This is the kind of assumption on which Marshall based all his ideas of the constitutional law of this country; that *constitutional* law, which he was so famous for expounding. It is the kind of assumption, by which he expounded the people out of all their "original and natural rights."

He had just as much right to assume, and practically did assume, that the people had voluntarily "come into society," and had voluntarily "surrendered" to their governments *all their other natural rights*, as well as their "original and natural right" to make and enforce their own contracts.

He virtually said to all the people of this country:

You have voluntarily "come into society," and have voluntarily "surrendered" to your governments all your natural rights, of every name and nature whatsoever, *for safe keeping;* and now that these governments have, *by your own consent*, got possession of all your natural rights, they have an *"unquestionable right"* to withhold them from you forever.

If it were not melancholy to see mankind thus cheated, robbed, enslaved, and murdered, on the authority of such naked impostures as these, it would be, to the last degree, ludicrous, to see a man like Marshall—reputed to be one of the first intellects the country has ever had—solemnly expounding the "constitutional powers," as he called them, by which the general and State governments were authorized to rob the people of all their natural rights as human beings.

And yet this same Marshall has done more than any other one man—certainly more than any other man within the last eighty-five years—to make our governments, State and national, what they are. He has, for more than sixty years, been esteemed an oracle, not only by his associates and successors on the bench of the Supreme Court of the United States, but by all the other judges, State and national, by all the ignorant, as well as knavish, lawmakers in the country, and by all the sixty to a hundred thousand lawyers, upon whom the people have been, and are, obliged to depend for the security of their rights.

This system of false definitions, false assumptions, and fraud and usurpation generally, runs through all the operations of our governments, State and national. There is nothing genuine, nothing real, nothing true, nothing honest, to be found in any of them. They all proceed upon the principle, that governments have all power, and the people no rights.

Section XXV.

But perhaps the most absolute proof that our national lawmakers and judges are as regardless of all constitutional, as they are of all natural, law, and that their statutes and decisions are as destitute of all constitutional, as they are of all natural, authority, is to be found in the fact that these lawmakers and judges have trampled upon, and utterly ignored, certain amendments to the constitution, which had been adopted, and (constitutionally speaking) become authoritative, as early as 1791; only two years after the government went into operation.

If these amendments had been obeyed, they would have compelled all congresses and courts to understand that, if the government had any constitutional powers at all, they were simply powers to protect men's natural rights, and not to destroy any of them.

These amendments have actually forbidden any lawmaking whatever in violation of men's natural rights. And this is equivalent to a prohibition of any lawmaking at all. And if lawmakers and courts had been as desirous of preserving men's natural rights, as they have been of violating them, they would long ago have found out that, since these amendments, the constitution authorized no lawmaking at all.

These amendments were ten in number. They were recommended by the first congress, at its first session, in 1789; two-thirds of both houses concurring. And in 1791, they had been ratified by all the States: and from that time they imposed the restrictions mentioned upon all the powers of congress.

These amendments were proposed, by the first congress, for the reason that, although the constitution, as originally framed, had been adopted, its adoption had been procured only with great difficulty, and in spite of great objections. *These objections were that, as originally framed and adopted, the constitution contained no adequate security for the private rights of the people.*

These objections were admitted, by very many, if not all, the friends of the constitution themselves, to be very weighty; and such as ought to be immediately removed by amendments. And it was only because these friends of the constitution pledged themselves to use their influence to secure these amendments, that the adoption of the constitution itself was secured. And it was in fulfilment of these pledges, and to remove these objections, that the amendments were proposed and adopted.

The first eight amendments specified particularly various prohibitions upon the power of congress; such, for example, as those securing to the people the free exercise of religion, the freedom of speech and the press, the right to keep and bear arms, etc., etc. Then followed the ninth amendment, in these words:

The enumeration in the constitution, of certain rights, [retained by the people] shall not be construed to deny or disparage others retained by the people.

Here is an authoritative declaration, that "the people" have "*other rights*" than those specially "enumerated in the constitution"; and that these "*other rights*" were "*retained by the people*"; that is, *that congress should have no power to infringe them.*

What, then, were these "other rights," that had not been "enumerated"; but which were nevertheless "retained by the people"?

Plainly they were men's natural "rights"; for these are the only "rights" that "the people" ever had, or, consequently, that they could "retain."

And as no attempt is made to enumerate *all* these "other rights," or any considerable number of them, and as it would be obviously impossible to enumerate all, or any considerable number, of them; and as no exceptions are made of any of them, the necessary, the legal, the inevitable inference is, that they were *all* "retained"; and that congress should have no power to violate any of them.

Now, if congress and the courts had attempted to obey this amendment, as they were constitutionally bound to do, they would soon have found that they had really no lawmaking power whatever left to them; because they would have found that they could make no law at all, *of their own invention*, that would *not* violate men's natural rights.

All men's natural rights are co-extensive with natural law, the law of justice; or justice as a science. This law is the exact measure, and the only measure, of any and every man's natural rights. No one of these natural rights can be taken from any man, without doing him an injustice; and no more than these rights can be given to any one, unless by taking from the natural rights of one or more others.

In short, every man's natural rights are, first, the right to do, with himself and his property, everything that he pleases to do, and that justice towards others does not forbid him to do; and, secondly, to be free from all compulsion, by others, to do anything whatever, except what justice to others requires him to do.

Such, then, has been the constitutional law of this country since 1791; admitting, for the sake of the argument—what I do not really admit to be a fact—that the constitution, so called, has ever been a law at all.

This amendment, from the remarkable circumstances under which it was proposed and adopted, must have made an impression upon the minds of all the public men of the time; although they may not have fully comprehended, and doubtless did not fully comprehend, its sweeping effects upon all the supposed powers of the government.

But whatever impression it may have made upon the public men of that time, its authority and power were wholly lost upon their successors; and probably, for at least eighty years, it has never been heard of, either in congress or the courts.

John Marshall was perfectly familiar with all the circumstances, under which this, and the other nine amendments, were proposed and adopted. He was thirty-two years old (lacking seven days) when the constitution, as originally framed, was published (September 17, 1787); and he was a member of the Virginia convention that ratified it. He knew perfectly the objections that were raised to it, in that convention, on the ground of its inadequate guaranty of men's natural rights. He knew with what force these objections were urged by some of the ablest members of the convention. And he knew that, to obviate these objections, the convention, as a body, without a dissenting voice, so far as appears, recommended that very stringent amendments, for securing men's natural rights, be made to the constitution. And he knew further, that, but for these amendments being recommended, the constitution would not have been adopted by the convention.*

The amendments proposed were too numerous to be repeated here, although they would be very instructive, as showing how jealous the people were, lest their natural rights should be invaded by laws made by congress. And that the convention might do everything in its power to secure the adoption of these amendments, it resolved as follows:

And the convention do, in the name and behalf of the people of this commonwealth, enjoin it upon their representatives in congress to exert all their influence, and use all reasonable and legal methods, to obtain a ratification of the foregoing alterations and provisions, in the manner provided by the 5th article of the said Constitution; and, in all congressional laws to be passed in the meantime, to conform to the spirit of these amendments, as far as the said Constitution will admit. — *Elliot's Debates, Vol. 3, p.* 661.

In seven other State conventions, to wit, in those of Massachusetts, New Hampshire, Rhode Island, New York, Maryland, North Carolina, and South Carolina, the inadequate security for men's natural rights, and the necessity for amendments, were admitted, and insisted upon, in very similar terms to those in Virginia.

In Massachusetts, the convention proposed nine amendments to the constitution; and resolved as follows:

And the convention do, in the name and in the behalf of the people of this commonwealth, enjoin it upon their representatives in Congress, at all times, until the alterations and provisions aforesaid have been considered, agreeably to the 5th article of the said Constitution, to exert all their influence, and use all reasonable and legal methods, to obtain a ratification of the said alterations and provisions, in such manner as is provided in the said article. — *Elliot's Debates, Vol. 2, p.* 178.

The New Hampshire convention, that ratified the constitution, proposed twelve amendments, and added:

And the Convention do, in the name and behalf of the people of this State, enjoin it upon their representatives in congress, at all times, until the alterations and provisions aforesaid have been considered agreeably to the fifth article of the said Constitution, to exert all their influence, and use all reasonable and legal methods, to obtain a ratification of the said alterations and provisions, in such manner as is provided in the article. — *Elliot's Debates, Vol.* 1, *p.* 326.

---

*For the amendments recommended by the Virginia convention, see "Elliot's Debates," Vol. 3, pp. 657 to 663. For the debates upon these amendments, see pages 444 to 452, and 460 to 462, and 466 to 471, and 579 to 652.

The Rhode Island convention, in ratifying the constitution, put forth a declaration of rights, in eighteen articles, and also proposed twenty-one amendments to the constitution; and prescribed as follows:

And the Convention do, in the name and behalf of the people of the State of Rhode Island and Providence Plantations, enjoin it upon their senators and representative or representatives, which may be elected to represent this State in congress, to exert all their influence, and use all reasonable means, to obtain a ratification of the following amendments to the said Constitution, in the manner prescribed therein; and in all laws to be passed by the congress in the mean time, to conform to the spirit of the said amendments, as far as the Constitution will admit. — *Elliot's Debates, Vol. 1, p. 335.*

The New York convention, that ratified the constitution, proposed a great many amendments, and added:

And the Convention do, in the name and behalf of the people of the State of New York, enjoin it upon their representatives in congress, to exert all their influence, and use all reasonable means, to obtain a ratification of the following amendments to the said Constitution, in the manner prescribed therein; and in all laws to be passed by the congress, in the mean time, to conform to the spirit of the said amendments as far as the Constitution will admit. — *Elliot's Debates, Vol. 1, p. 329.*

The New York convention also addressed a "CIRCULAR LETTER" to the governors of all the other States, the first two paragraphs of which are as follows:

THE CIRCULAR LETTER,

From the Convention of the State of New York to the Governors of the several States in the Union.

POUGHKEEPSIE, JULY 28, 1788.

Sir, We, the members of the Convention of this State, have deliberately and maturely considered the Constitution proposed for the United States. Several articles in it appear so exceptionable to a majority of us, that nothing but the fullest confidence of obtaining a revision of them by a general convention, and an invincible reluctance to separating from our sister States, could have prevailed upon a sufficient number to ratify it, without stipulating for previous amendments. We all unite in opinion, that such a revision will be necessary to recommend it to the approbation and support of a numerous body of our constituents.

We observe that amendments have been proposed, and are anxiously desired, by several of the States, as well as by this; and we think it of great importance that effectual measures be immediately taken for calling a convention, to meet at a period not far remote; for we are convinced that the apprehensions and discontents, which those articles occasion, cannot be removed or allayed, unless an act to provide for it be among the first that shall be passed by the new congress. — *Elliot's Debates, Vol. 2, p. 413.*

In the Maryland convention, numerous amendments were proposed, and thirteen were agreed to; "most of them by a unanimous vote, and all by a great majority." Fifteen others were proposed, but there was so much disagreement in regard to them, that none at all were formally recommended to congress. But, says Elliot:

All the members, who voted for the ratification [of the constitution], declared that they would engage themselves, under every tie of honor, to support the amendments they had agreed to, both in their public and private characters, until they should become a part of the general government. — *Elliot's Debates, Vol.* 2, *pp.* 550, 552–3.

The first North Carolina convention refused to ratify the constitution, and

Resolved, That a declaration of rights, asserting and securing from encroachments the great principles of civil and religious liberty, and the inalienable rights of the people, together with amendments to the most ambiguous and exceptionable parts of the said constitution of government, ought to be laid before congress, and the convention of States that shall or may be called for the purpose of amending the said Constitution, for their consideration, previous to the ratification of the Constitution aforesaid, on the part of the State of North Carolina. — *Elliot's Debates, Vol.* 1, *p.* 332.

The South Carolina convention, that ratified the constitution, proposed certain amendments, and

Resolved, That it be a standing instruction to all such delegates as may hereafter be elected to represent this State in the General Government, to exert their utmost abilities and influence to effect an alteration of the Constitution, conformably to the foregoing resolutions. — *Elliot's Debates, Vol.* 1. *p.* 325.

In the Pennsylvania convention, numerous objections were made to the constitution, but it does not appear that the convention, as a convention, recommended any specific amendments. But a strong movement, outside of the convention, was afterwards made in favor of such amendments. ("Elliot's Debates," Vol. 2, p. 542.)

Of the debates in the Connecticut convention, Elliot gives only what he calls "*A Fragment.*"

Of the debates in the conventions of New Jersey, Delaware, and Georgia, Elliot gives no accounts at all.

I therefore cannot state the grounds, on which the adoption of the constitution was opposed. They were doubtless very similar to those in the other States. This is rendered morally certain by the fact, that the amendments, soon afterwards proposed by congress, were immediately ratified by all the States. Also by the further fact, that these States, by reason of the smallness of their representation in the popular branch of congress, would naturally be even more jealous of their rights, than the people of the larger States.

It is especially worthy of notice that, in some, if not in all, the conventions that ratified the constitution, although the ratification was accompanied by such urgent recommendations of amendments, and by an almost absolute assurance that they would be made, it was nevertheless secured only by very small majorities.

Thus in Virginia, the vote was only 89 ayes to 79 nays. (Elliot, Vol. 3, p. 654.)

In Massachusetts, the ratification was secured only by a vote of 187 yeas to 168 nays. (Elliot, Vol. 2, p. 181.)

In New York, the vote was only 30 yeas to 27 nays. (Elliot, Vol. 2, p. 413.)
In New Hampshire and Rhode Island, neither the yeas nor nays are given. (Elliot, Vol. 1, pp. 327–335.)
In Connecticut, the yeas were 128; *nays not given.* (Elliot, Vol. 1, p. 321–2.)
In New Jersey, the yeas were 38; *nays not given.* (Elliot, Vol. 1, p. 321.)
In Pennsylvania, the yeas were 46; *the nays not given.* (Elliot, Vol. 1, p. 320.)
In Delaware, the yeas were 30; *nays not given.* (Elliot, Vol. 1, p. 319.)
In Maryland, the vote was 57 yeas; *nays not given.* (Elliot, Vol. 1, p. 325.)
In North Carolina, neither the yeas nor nays are given. (Elliot, Vol. 1, p. 333.)
In South Carolina, neither the yeas nor nays are given. (Elliot, Vol. 1, p. 325.)
In Georgia, the yeas were 26; *nays not given.* (Elliot, Vol. 1, p. 324.)

We can thus see by what meagre votes the constitution was adopted. We can also see that, but for the prospect that important amendments would be made, specially for securing the natural rights of the people, the constitution would have been spurned with contempt, as it deserved to be.

And yet now, owing to the usurpations of lawmakers and courts, the original constitution — with the worst possible construction put upon it — has been carried into effect; and the amendments have been simply cast into the waste baskets.

Marshall was thirty-six years old, when these amendments became a part of the constitution in 1791. Ten years after, in 1801, he became Chief Justice. It then became his sworn constitutional duty to scrutinize severely every act of congress, and to condemn, as unconstitutional, all that should violate any of these natural rights. Yet he appears never to have thought of the matter afterwards. Or, rather, this ninth amendment, the most important of all, seems to have been so utterly antagonistic to all his ideas of government, that he chose to ignore it altogether, and, as far as he could, to bury it out of sight.

Instead of recognizing it as an absolute guaranty of all the natural rights of the people, he chose to assume — for it was all a mere assumption, a mere making a constitution out of his own head, to suit himself — that the people had all voluntarily "come into society," and had voluntarily "surrendered" to "society" all their natural rights, of every name and nature — trusting that they would be secured; and that now, "society," having thus got possession of all these natural rights of the people, had the "unquestionable right" to dispose of them, at the pleasure — or, as he would say, according to the "wisdom and discretion" — of a few contemptible, detestable, and irresponsible lawmakers, whom the constitution (thus amended) had forbidden to dispose of any one of them.

If, now, Marshall did not see, in this amendment, any legal force or authority, what becomes of his reputation as a constitutional lawyer? If he did see this force and authority, but chose to trample them under his feet, he was a perjured tyrant and traitor.

What, also, are we to think of all the judges, — forty in all, — his associates and successors, who, for eighty years, have been telling the people that the government has all power, and the people no rights? Have they all been mere blockheads, who never read this amendment, or knew nothing of its meaning? Or have they, too, been perjured tyrants and traitors?

What, too, becomes of those great constitutional lawyers, as we have called them, who have been supposed to have won such immortal honors, as "expounders of the constitution," but who seem never to have discovered in it any security for men's natural rights? Is their apparent ignorance, on this point, to be accounted for by the fact, that that portion of the people, who, by authority of the government, are systematically robbed of all their earnings, beyond a bare subsistence, are not able to pay such fees as are the robbers who are authorized to plunder them?

If any one will now look back to the records of congress and the courts, for the last eighty years, I do not think he will find a single mention of this amendment. And why has this been so? Solely because the amendment—if its authority had been recognized—would have stood as an insuperable barrier against all the ambition and rapacity—all the arbitrary power, all the plunder, and all the tyranny—which the ambitious and rapacious classes have determined to accomplish through the agency of the government.

The fact that these classes have been so successful in perverting the constitution (thus amended) from an instrument avowedly securing all men's natural rights, into an authority for utterly destroying them, is a sufficient proof that no lawmaking power can be safely intrusted to any body, for any purpose whatever.

And that this perversion of the constitution should have been sanctioned by all the judicial tribunals of the country, is also a proof, not only of the servility, audacity, and villainy of the judges, but also of the utter rottenness of our judicial system. It is a sufficient proof that judges, who are dependent upon lawmakers for their offices and salaries, and are responsible to them by impeachment, cannot be relied on to put the least restraint upon the acts of their masters, the lawmakers.

Such, then, would have been the effect of the ninth amendment, if it had been permitted to have its legitimate authority.

Section XXVI.

The tenth amendment is in these words:

The powers not delegated to the United States by the constitution, nor prohibited by it to the States, are reserved to the States respectively, *or to the people.*

This amendment, equally with the ninth, secures to "the people" all their natural rights. And why?

Because, in truth, no powers at all, neither legislative, judicial, nor executive, had been "delegated to the United States by the constitution."

But it will be said that the amendment itself implies that certain lawmaking "powers" had been "delegated to the United States by the constitution."

No. It only implies that those who adopted the amendment *believed* that such lawmaking "powers" had been "delegated to the United States by the constitution."

But in this belief, they were entirely mistaken. And why?

1. Because it is a natural impossibility that any lawmaking "powers" whatever can be delegated by any one man, or any number of men, to any other man, or any number of other men.

Men's natural rights are all inherent and inalienable; and therefore cannot be parted with, or delegated, by one person to another. And all contracts whatsoever, for such a purpose, are necessarily absurd and void contracts.

For example. I cannot delegate to another man any right to *make* laws — that is, laws of his own invention — and compel me to obey them.

Such a contract, on my part, would be a contract to part with my natural liberty; to give myself, or sell myself, to him as a slave. Such a contract would be an absurd and void contract, utterly destitute of all legal or moral obligation.

2. I cannot delegate to another any right to make laws — that is, laws of his own invention — and compel a third person to obey them.

For example. I cannot delegate to A any right to make laws — that is, laws of his own invention — and compel Z to obey them.

I cannot delegate any such right to A, because I have no such right myself; and I cannot delegate to another what I do not myself possess.

For these reasons no lawmaking powers ever could be — and therefore no lawmaking powers ever were — "delegated to the United States by the constitution"; no matter what the people of that day — any or all of them — may have attempted to do, or may have believed they had power to do, in the way of delegating such powers.

But not only were no lawmaking powers "delegated to the United States by the constitution," but neither were any *judicial* powers so delegated. And why? Because it is a natural impossibility that one man can delegate his judicial powers to another.

Every man has, by nature, certain judicial powers, or rights. That is to say, he has, by nature, the right to judge of, and enforce his own rights, and judge of, and redress his own wrongs. But, in so doing, he must act only in accordance with his own judgment and conscience, *and subject to his own personal responsibility, if, through either ignorance or design, he commits any error injurious to another.*

Now, inasmuch as no man can delegate, or impart, his own judgment or conscience to another, it is naturally impossible that he can delegate to another his judicial rights or powers.

So, too, every man has, by nature, a right to judge of, and enforce, the rights, and judge of, and redress the wrongs, of any and all other men. This right is included in his natural right to maintain justice between man and man, and to protect the injured party against the wrongdoer. But, in doing this, he must act only in accordance with his own judgment and conscience, and subject to his own personal responsibility for any error he may commit, either through ignorance or design.

But, inasmuch as, in this case, as in the preceding one, he can neither delegate nor impart his own judgment or conscience to another, he cannot delegate his judicial power or right to another.

But not only were no lawmaking or judicial powers "delegated to the United States by the constitution," neither were any executive powers so delegated. And why? Because, in a case of justice or injustice, it is naturally impossible that any one man can delegate his executive right or power to another.

Every man has, by nature, the right to maintain justice for himself, and for all other persons, by the use of so much force as may be reasonably necessary for that purpose. But he can use the force only in accordance with his own judgment and conscience, and on his own personal responsibility, if, through ignorance or design, he commits any wrong to another.

But inasmuch as he cannot delegate, or impart, his own judgment or conscience to another, he cannot delegate his executive power or right to another.

The result is, that, in all judicial and executive proceedings, for the maintenance of justice, every man must act only in accordance with his own judgment and conscience, and on his own personal responsibility for any wrong he may commit; whether such wrong be committed through either ignorance or design.

The effect of this principle of personal responsibility, in all judicial and executive proceedings, would be—or at least ought to be—that no one would give any judicial opinions, or do any executive acts, except such as his own judgment and conscience should approve, *and such as he would be willing to be held personally responsible for.*

No one could justify, or excuse, his wrong act, by saying that a power, or authority, to do it had been delegated to him, by any other men, however numerous.

For the reasons that have now been given, neither any legislative, judicial, nor executive powers ever were, or ever could have been, "delegated to the United States by the constitution"; no matter how honestly or innocently the people of that day may have believed, or attempted, the contrary.

And what is true, in this matter, in regard to the national government, is, for the same reasons, equally true in regard to all the State governments.

But this principle of personal responsibility, each for his own judicial or executive acts, does not stand in the way of men's associating, at pleasure, for the maintenance of justice; and selecting such persons as they think most suitable, for judicial and executive duties; and *requesting* them to perform those duties; and then paying them for their labor. But the persons, thus selected, must still perform their duties according to their own judgments and consciences alone, and subject to their own personal responsibility for any errors of either ignorance or design.

To make it safe and proper for persons to perform judicial duties, subject to their personal responsibility for any errors of either ignorance or design, two things would seem to be important, if not indispensable, viz.:

1. That, as far as is reasonably practicable, all judicial proceedings should be in writing; that is, that all testimony, and all judicial opinions, even to quite minute details, should be in writing, and be preserved; so that judges may always have it in their power to show fully what their acts, and their reasons for their acts, have been; and also that anybody, and everybody, interested, may forever after have the means of knowing fully the reasons on which everything has been done; and that any errors, ever afterwards discovered, may be corrected.

2. That all judicial tribunals should consist of so many judges — within any reasonable number — as either party may desire; or as may be necessary to prevent any wrong doing, by any one or more of the judges, either through ignorance or design.

Such tribunals, consisting of judges, numerous enough, and perfectly competent to settle justly probably ninety-nine one-hundredths of all the controversies that arise among men, could be obtained in every village. They could give their immediate attention to every case; and thus avoid most of the delay, and most of the expense, now attendant on judicial proceedings.

To make these tribunals satisfactory to all reasonable and honest persons, it is important, and probably indispensable, that all judicial proceedings should be had, *in the first instance*, at the expense of the association, or associations, to which the parties to the suit belong.

An association for the maintenance of justice should be a purely voluntary one; and should be formed upon the same principle as a mutual fire or marine insurance company; that is, each member should pay his just proportion of the expense necessary for protecting all.

A single individual could not reasonably be expected to delay, or forego, the exercise of his natural right to enforce his own rights, and redress his own wrongs, except upon the condition that there is an association that will do it promptly, and without expense to him. But having paid his proper proportion of the expense necessary for the protection of all, he has then a right to demand prompt and complete protection for himself.

Inasmuch as it cannot be known which party is in the wrong, until the trial has been had, the expense of both parties must, *in the first instance*, be paid by the association, or associations, to which they belong. But after the trial has been had, and it has been ascertained which party was in the wrong, and (if such should be the case) so clearly in the wrong as to have had no justification for putting the association to the expense of a trial, he then may properly be compelled to pay the cost of all the proceedings.

If the parties to a suit should belong to different associations, it would be right that the judges should be taken from both associations; or from a third association, with which neither party was connected.

If, with all these safeguards against injustice and expense, a party, accused of a wrong, should refuse to appear for trial, he might rightfully be proceeded against, in his absence, if the evidence produced against him should be sufficient to justify it.

It is probably not necessary to go into any further details here, to show how easy and natural a thing it would be, to form as many voluntary and mutually protective judicial associations, as might be either necessary or convenient, in order to bring justice home to every man's door; and to give to every honest and dishonest man, all reasonable assurance that he should have justice, and nothing else, done for him, or to him.

Section XXVII.

Of course we can have no courts of justice, under such systems of lawmaking, and supreme court decisions, as now prevail.

We have a population of fifty to sixty millions; *and not a single court of justice, State or national!*

But we have everywhere courts of injustice—open and avowed injustice—claiming sole jurisdiction of all cases affecting men's rights of both person and property; and having at their beck brute force enough to compel absolute submission to their decrees, whether just or unjust.

Can a more decisive or infallible condemnation of our governments be conceived of, than the absence of all courts of justice, and the absolute power of their courts of injustice?

Yes, they lie under still another condemnation, to wit, that their courts are not only courts of injustice, but they are also secret tribunals; adjudicating all causes according to the secret instructions of their masters, the lawmakers, and their authorized interpreters, their supreme courts.

I say *secret tribunals*, and *secret instructions*, because, to the great body of the people, whose rights are at stake, they are secret to all practical intents and purposes. They are secret, because their reasons for their decrees are to be found only in great volumes of statutes and supreme court reports, which the mass of the people have neither money to buy, nor time to read; and would not understand, if they were to read them.

These statutes and reports are so far out of reach of the people at large, that the only knowledge a man can ordinarily get of them, when he is summoned before one of the tribunals appointed to execute them, is to be obtained by employing an expert — or so-called lawyer — to enlighten him.

This expert in injustice is one who buys these great volumes of statutes and reports, and spends his life in studying them, and trying to keep himself informed of their contents. But even he can give a client very little information in regard to them; for the statutes and decisions are so voluminous, and are so constantly being made and unmade, and are so destitute of all conformity to those natural principles of justice which men readily and intuitively comprehend; and are moreover capable of so many different interpretations, that he is usually in as great doubt — perhaps in even greater doubt — than his client, as to what will be the result of a suit.

The most he can usually say to his client, is this:

> Every civil suit must finally be given to one of two persons, the plaintiff or defendant. Whether, therefore, your cause is a just, or an unjust, one, you have at least one chance in two, of gaining it. But no matter how just your cause may be, you need have no hope that the tribunal that tries it, will be governed by any such consideration, if the statute book, or the past decisions of the supreme court, are against you. So, also, no matter how unjust your cause may be, you may nevertheless expect to gain it, if the statutes and past decisions are in your favor. If, therefore, you have money to spend in such a lottery as this, I will do my best to gain your cause for you, whether it be a just, or an unjust, one.

If the charge is a criminal one, this expert says to his client:

> You must either be found guilty, or acquitted. Whether, therefore, you are really innocent or guilty, you have at least one chance in two, of an acquittal. But no matter how innocent you may be of any real crime, you need have no hope of an acquittal, if the statute book, or the past decisions of the supreme court, are against you. If, on the other hand, you have committed a real wrong to another, there may be many laws on the statute book, many precedents, and technicalities, and whimsicalities, through which you may hope to escape. But your reputation, your liberty, or perhaps your life, is at stake. To save these you can afford to risk your money, even though the result is so uncertain. Therefore you had best give me your money, and I will do my best to save you, whether you are innocent or guilty.

But for the great body of the people, — those who have no money that they can afford to risk in a lawsuit, — no matter what may be their rights in either a civil or criminal suit, — their cases are hopeless. They may have been taxed, directly and indirectly, to their last dollars, for the support of the government; they may even have been compelled to risk their lives, and to lose their limbs, in its defence; yet when they want its protection, — that protection for which their taxes and military services were professedly extorted from them, — they are coolly told that the government offers no justice, nor even any chance or semblance of justice, except to those who have more money than they.

But the point now to be specially noticed is, that in the case of either the civil or criminal suit, the client, whether rich or poor, is nearly or quite as much in the dark as to his fate, and as to the grounds on which his fate will be determined, as though he were to be tried by an English Star Chamber court, or one of the secret tribunals of Russia, or even the Spanish Inquisition.

Thus in the supreme exigencies of a man's life, whether in civil or criminal cases, where his property, his reputation, his liberty, or his life is at stake, he is really to be tried by what is, *to him*, at least, *a secret tribunal;* a tribunal that is governed by what are, *to him, the secret instructions* of lawmakers, and supreme courts; neither of whom care anything for his rights of property in a civil suit, or for his guilt or innocence in a criminal one; but only for their own authority as lawmakers and judges.

The bystanders, at these trials, look on amazed, but powerless to defend the right, or prevent the wrong. Human nature has no rights, in the presence of these infernal tribunals.

Is it any wonder that all men live in constant terror of such a government as that? Is it any wonder that so many give up all attempts to preserve their natural rights of person and property, in opposition to tribunals, to whom justice and injustice are indifferent, and whose ways are, to common minds, hidden mysteries, and impenetrable secrets.

But even this is not all. The mode of trial, if not as infamous as the trial itself, is at least so utterly false and absurd, as to add a new element of uncertainty to the result of all judicial proceedings.

A trial in one of these courts of injustice is a trial by battle, almost, if not quite, as really as was a trial by battle, five hundred or a thousand years ago.

Now, as then, the adverse parties choose their champions, to fight their battles for them.

These champions, trained to such contests, and armed, not only with all the weapons their own skill, cunning, and power can supply, but also with all the iniquitous laws, precedents, and technicalities that lawmakers and supreme courts can give them, for defeating justice, and accomplishing injustice, can — if not always, yet none but themselves know how often — offer their clients such chances of victory — independently of the justice of their causes — as to induce the dishonest to go into court to evade justice, or accomplish injustice, not less often perhaps than the honest go there in the hope to get justice, or avoid injustice.

We have now, I think, some sixty thousand of these champions, who make it the business of their lives to equip themselves for these conflicts, and sell their services for a price.

Is there any one of these men, who studies justice as a science, and regards that alone in all his professional exertions? If there are any such, why do we so seldom, or never, hear of them? Why have they not told us, hundreds of years ago, what are men's natural rights of person and property? And why have they not told us how false, absurd, and tyrannical are all these lawmaking governments? Why have they not told us what impostors and tyrants all these so-called lawmakers, judges, etc., etc., are? Why are so many of them so ambitious to become lawmakers and judges themselves?

Is it too much to hope for mankind, that they may sometime have courts of justice, instead of such courts of injustice as these?

If we ever should have courts of justice, it is easy to see what will become of statute books, supreme courts, trial by battle, and all the other machinery of fraud and tyranny, by which the world is now ruled.

If the people of this country knew what crimes are constantly committed by these courts of injustice, they would squelch them, without mercy, as unceremoniously as they would squelch so many gangs of bandits or pirates. In fact, bandits and pirates are highly respectable and honorable villains, compared with the judges of these courts of injustice. Bandits and pirates do not—like these judges—attempt to cheat us out of our common sense, in order to cheat us out of our property, liberty, or life. They do not profess to be anything but such villains as they really are. They do not claim to have received any "Divine" authority for robbing, enslaving, or murdering us at their pleasure. They do not claim immunity for their crimes, upon the ground that they are duly authorized agents of any such invisible, intangible, irresponsible, unimaginable thing as "society," or "the State." They do not insult us by telling us that they are only exercising that authority to rob, enslave, and murder us, which we ourselves have delegated to them. They do not claim that they are robbing, enslaving, and murdering us, solely to secure our happiness and prosperity, and not from any selfish motives of their own. They do not claim a wisdom so superior to that of the producers of wealth, as to know, better than they, how their wealth should be disposed of. They do not tell us that we are the freest and happiest people on earth, inasmuch as each of our male adults is allowed one voice in ten millions in the choice of the men, who are to rob, enslave, and murder us. They do not tell us that all liberty and order would be destroyed, that society itself would go to pieces, and man go back to barbarism, if it were not for the care, and supervision, and protection, they lavish upon us. They do not tell us of the almshouses, hospitals, schools, churches, etc., which, out of the purest charity and benevolence, they maintain for our benefit, out of the money they take from us. They do not carry their heads high, above all other men, and demand our reverence and admiration, as statesmen, patriots, and benefactors. They do not claim that we have voluntarily "come into their society," and "surrendered" to them all our natural rights of person and property; nor all our "original and natural right" of defending our own rights, and redressing our own wrongs. They do not tell us that they have established infallible supreme courts, to whom they refer all questions as to the legality of their acts, and that they do nothing that is not sanctioned by these courts. They do not attempt to deceive us, or mislead us, or reconcile us to their doings, by any such pretences, impostures, or insults as these. *There is not a single John Marshall among them.* On the contrary, they acknowledge themselves robbers, murderers, and villains, pure and simple. When they have once taken our money, they have the decency to get out of our sight as soon as possible; they do not persist in following us, and robbing us, again and again, so long as we produce anything that they can take from us. In short, they acknowledge themselves *hostes humani generis: enemies of the human race.* They acknowledge it to be our unquestioned right and duty to kill them, if we can; that they expect nothing else, than that we will kill them, if we can; and that we are only fools and cowards, if we do not kill them, by any and every means in our power. They neither ask, nor expect, any mercy, if they should ever fall into the hands of honest men.

For all these reasons, they are not only modest and sensible, but really frank, honest, and honorable villains, contrasted with these courts of injustice, and the lawmakers by whom these courts are established.

Such, Mr. Cleveland, is the real character of the government, of which you are the nominal head. Such are, and have been, its lawmakers. Such are, and have been, its judges. Such have been its executives. Such is its present executive. Have you anything to say for any of them?

      Yours frankly,   LYSANDER SPOONER.

BOSTON, MAY 15, 1886.

THE END.

NO TREASON...

Lysander Spooner

Lysander Spooner (1808-1887) was a Massachusetts lawyer noted for his vigorous and brilliant opposition to the encroachment of the State upon the liberty of the individual. His writings on the unconstitutionality of slavery influenced pre-Civil War thought. His challenge to the postal monopoly (he set up a thriving private post) resulted in an Act of Congress sharply reducing postage rates.

An analysis of Spooner's views appears in Dr. James J. Martin's *Men Against the State* (New York: Libertarian Book Club, Inc., 1957 and 1963), and in his introductions to *No Treason: The Constitution of No Authority* and *A Letter to Thomas F. Bayard*.

NO TREASON

The Constitution of No Authority

and

A LETTER TO
THOMAS F. BAYARD

"Challenging his right—and that of all the other so-called senators and representatives in Congress—to exercise any legislative power whatever over the people of the United States."

by

LYSANDER SPOONER

With Introductions by James J. Martin

The following two articles were published by the author in Boston. *No Treason: The Constitution of No Authority* was published in 1870 and *A Letter to Thomas F. Bayard* was published in 1882.

In keeping with the special interest created by these reprints, Pine Tree Press reproduces the actual title pages of the two articles.

Preface

James J. Martin is chairman of the Department of History, Rampart College Graduate School, Larkspur, Colorado. A revisionist, Dr. Martin has won a broad reputation for scholarship in his work as instructor at Deep Springs College, San Francisco State College, Northern Illinois University, and the University of Michigan, and for his published works which include *American Liberalism and World Politics, 1931-1941* (New York: The Devin-Adair Company, 1964); *Men Against the State* (first published in 1953 and republished in 1957); and *Meditations on the Early Wisdom of John Foster Dulles* (1958). He is the editor of Paul Eltzbacher's *Anarchism* (1960) and Max Stirner's *The Ego and His Own* (1963). He has contributed to the *Dictionary of American Biography* (1958) and the *Encyclopaedia Britannica* (1962).

Dr. Martin was born in St. Leonard, New Brunswick on September 18, 1916. He received his bachelor of arts degree in history at the University of New Hampshire in 1942, his master of arts degree (1945), and doctor of philosophy (1949) in history, at the University of Michigan at Ann Arbor, and has won many honors in the course of his career.

It is entirely due to the efforts of Dr. Martin that this publication, containing two of Lysander Spooner's most significant works, is appearing at this time. Spooner, after nearly a hundred years, remains a controversial figure. His crisp and incisive verbiage, his utter ruthlessness in pursuit of an important though possibly obscure point, have made him something of a paladin in libertarian circles. If lawyers, judges, and the host of government employees would examine what Lysander Spooner has to say about their positions in ascendancy over ordinary people, something of a long-needed humility might evolve.

In any case, Dr. Martin's untiring labor in bringing to light an almost forgotten argument in support of pure liberty has resulted in this slim volume, which includes his own valued biography of Lysander Spooner and something of the background from which Mr. Spooner wrote.

Robert LeFevre
Dean, Rampart College

Table of Contents

Preface *by Robert LeFevre* v

Introduction *by James J. Martin* 1

No Treason: The Constitution of No Authority 9

Introduction *by James J. Martin* 56

A Letter to Thomas F. Bayard 65

American Letter Mail Co. 70

Illustrations

Lysander Spooner ii
Original Title Page: No Treason 7
Original Title Page: A Letter 61
American Letter Mail Co. Cover 71

INTRODUCTION
by James J. Martin

Since late Neolithic times, men in their political capacity have lived almost exclusively by myths. And these political myths have continued to evolve, proliferate, and grow more complex and intricate, even though there has been a steady replacement of one by another, over the centuries. A series of entirely theoretical constructs, sometimes mystical, usually deductive and speculative, they seek to explain the status and relationships in the community since it became discernibly organized, politically. But in essence these constructs are all alike in that with varying degrees of persuasiveness they attempt to examine the origins of the State with little or no attention to its historic record, and then try to justify and fortify it in the face of criticism or objection.

In the long millennia during which theological authorizations of one kind or another were principally employed to sanctify the State and to promote its safety and continuity, we know very little of the critics and their products. Threats of divine retaliation by the gods upon any so sinful as to question the validity of the State may have been sufficient to inhibit the crime of deviationism. On the other hand, perhaps many ages may have had a formidable roster of adversaries of the State, but theirs must apparently have been largely an oral tradition, and has been lost to posterity with hardly a trace. A scrap or two have come down to us from the Orient, but ancient literary survivals are essentially a Statist apologia.

Undoubtedly the largest part of such criticisms may have subjectively denounced the more obvious vulnerabilities of the institution, particularly its capacity for promoting institutionalized robbery, murder, injustice, and tyranny. Traces of such protest are discernible in the traditions of many peoples.

But the unvarying, wearisome replacement of one State by another for thousands of years reveals the depth of the fixation humankind has had concerning it, in part testifying, as Ludwig Gumplowicz and Franz Oppenheimer and others have observed, to the long-standing drive to make a living without working, a stage which has been tied to the evolution of productive processes to a point where a surplus existed beyond the needs of the producer. (The steady increase in the numbers who batten upon the substance of the productive community in the name of the State testifies in turn not to a mellowing expansiveness, a generous enlargement of the preying nomad band, as Oppenheimer would have it, but to the prodigious increase in production totals beyond subsistence or survival demands of the former.)

Oppenheimer described the United States of America a half-century ago (in *The State* [Indianapolis: Bobbs-Merrill, 1914], p. 17) as "among the most powerful State-formations in all history." Its prodigious growth since that time would surely have prompted him to elevate it to first place, and perhaps decades ago, had he lived to make such observations.

There is no apparent logic or law regulating the age-old conflict between the individual and the collectivity, between the State and the idea or the reality of the voluntary social system. However, in America, the site of the evolution of the mightiest State of all time, there has been an inverse ratio between its growth and the production of native anti-Statism. Vasilii Klyuchevski, the giant of historical scholarship in the last century of Czarist Russia, put it best: "The State swells up; the people diminish." Part of the reason for this has been the much more opaque and intangible nature of the adversary. No stylized, symbolic vested agents, such as perhaps a traditional oligarchical priesthood of antiquity or a divine-right monarch, have existed here to provide a convenient target for word or deed. The tying of political tenure to astronomy instead of to dynasty has removed the possibility of a long-enduring personal symbol from the scene. And a massive obstacle has been created as a result of the homogenization growing out of mass voting, mass taxpaying, mass gun-bearing, and mass dispersal of the tidbits bestowed by the State; a vast, gray, shapeless enterprise has come into being, with which it has been difficult to come to grips, as in the manner of classical conflicts with the State.

One of the important consequences of all this has been a difference in the structure and strategy of Statist apologetics in America. There has been a marked diminution over the years in the invocation of the Deity as responsible for its installation and overall direction and protection. Divine-right and related theories have never enjoyed a vogue at all. The American genius has been concentrated in perfecting vague and generalized secular verbiage; elusive, imprecise terminology which often sets the line for seemingly interminable battlegrounds of conflicting interpretation. Expressions such as "general welfare," "public good," "social contract," "general will," and many others, come to mind.

Of course, the crowning achievement in the American experience was the production of the Constitution, the ultimate verbal bastion on which is perched the American State. Constitution-worship is our most extended public political ritual, frequently supervised as often by mountebanks as by the sincere. This is an unusual enterprise in world history, in view of the casual attitude toward such developments in most places and at most times. In point of service, it is easily the oldest such political document in history, which adds much to the awe and veneration in which it is held. For though we have had over a century of native critics and opponents of our State, from Warren, Thoreau, and Tucker down to Albert Jay Nock and Frank Chodorov, the Constitution has largely been exempted or neglected in the unfolding of this critical tradition.

In America, we see, therefore, a different basis for the defense of the State. Lacking dynastic families, entrenched aristocracies, nobilities, royalties, and other ostensible residuaries of State power and beneficiaries of State emoluments, both the attack and the defense have moved to the abstract sector. For sure, in the final analysis, the State must be viewed as *certain people*. But Marx's definition of the State as the executive committee of the ruling class means little in an American context. If one can say that such an entity has ever existed here, its composition has been so mixed and so varying, and its tenure so transitory, that for specific purposes such a description is almost useless. No sustained, unbroken line of material profiteers from our State can be established. The bewildering turnover of elected personnel and the multiplicity of their fortunes virtually eliminate such temporary wielders of power from qualifying as reliable custodians of the State. This has been dramatized many times by the dispossessed from office complaining bitterly and vehemently over their unhappy treatment by the State, in their turn. (One need not mention the electrifying phenomenon of the last fifty years, namely, the growth of administrative government, with increasingly larger amounts of power and discretion in the hands of persons who have not even been elected to anything, and who often stand at the elbow of the familiar "responsible" public figures and who are more often than not the real authors of the policies and programs for which the latter are credited or blamed, as political fortunes would have it.)

Consequently, in view of the evanescent nature of power tenure in this country, the frequent unhorsing of the holders and exercisers of State power is looked upon with equanimity and not considered a threat in any way to the State. It is the assault upon the abstract and verbal underpinnings of this institution which draws blood, so to speak. If one can consider all the participants in the struggle to control and use the State as those engaged in a game (the book by Morgenstern and Neumann on the theory of games, in which war politics are examined in this context, deserves more study),[1] then those who seek to destroy the abstract-verbal justification for such "play" are endangering the future course of *all* the players by riddling the rule books, which describe how such play is to be conducted while giving it a *raison d'être* besides. Those who attack the rationale of the game, and not the players, are its most formidable adversaries.

It is in the light of this that those who have the temerity to collide head-on with the Constitution and challenge its validity *in toto* stand out in such sharp outline and radiate a quality of uniqueness in the American anti-State library. And at the head of this category stands Lysander Spooner (1808-1887), whose major work in this offensive, *No Treason: The Constitution of No Authority,* is reproduced below from the original edition, written in 1869 and published in Boston in 1870. It is the last of a series bearing the identical main title which were to have been six in number, although this one, numbered the sixth, was actually only the third. (*No Treason* Nos. 3, 4, and 5 never appeared, for reasons never explained.) But in view of the scope of this work, it does not seem that anything pertinent was left unsaid, making necessary any further elaboration.

Spooner strips away the support from any and all who conjure up one or another persuasive explanation of the Constitution as a contract, or as an agent facilitating a contract theory of government. A practicing jurist all his adult life, Spooner puts the Constitution

---

[1] John Von Neumann and Oskar Morgenstern, *The Theory of Games and Economic Behavior* (2nd ed.; Princeton: Princeton University Press, 1947).

to the test of contracts "on general principles of law and reason," such as prevailed in public affairs and in the market place where he worked with people from day to day, and concludes that it does not meet any of the basic criteria for contracts at all, and was not valid or binding on anyone. The sort of mystical osmosis, akin to telepathy, perhaps, by which Americans were supposed to have contracted with one or another to function under the document at the launching of the post-Revolutionary War American State, evaporates in Spooner's path as he assembles his argument, line by line, in nineteen carefully reasoned sections.

Spooner does not find that the Constitution "says" anything, because it cannot talk. But he does see it as a device through which judges talk, explaining what it "said" to those who live under it. Since not even its creators signed it, the Constitution was not even binding on them, Spooner argued. (The appearance of printings of the Constitution in modern times which bear signatures of the drafters of the document does not affect Spooner's point, which remains unaltered; the intent of this latter-day device is not discernible, but can be interpreted to be little more than an annotation and not an attempt to assert that there is a contractual connotation here, as in the case of the signatures gracing the Declaration of Independence.) And as for later times, there was no evidence that it had any binding quality upon their posterity, while all who acted under it were anonymous agents of concealed persons, who were engaged in inflicting the will of these persons upon others in an invasive manner. He went on with ingenious demolition of the arguments that voting or tax-paying were evidence of voluntary submission to those who ruled in the name of the Constitution, and challenged any office-holder or wielder of power who might claim accurately and precisely to identify those in whose name he functioned, and with whose assent he acted to make their will prevail, to do so.

There is much internal evidence that Spooner believed the Constitution had been put to the supreme test by Secession and the ensuing Civil War, barely four years ended when he wrote *No Treason*, and that the document was a proven failure if it purported to be a voluntary compact entered into by all for the object of promoting various mutual benefits and comforts. The mere fact that so many lives lost and so much violence and blood had been necessary, for those who wanted the Constitution, to make it prevail over those who did not want it, was sufficient evidence to him that there was no difference between the American State experiment and that of all those before it which streamed away into the past. The party with the most men and guns had prevailed, and it angered and incensed him to hear political thimbleriggers bray of having "saved the country" and "preserved our glorious Union," while "maintaining the national honor."

Spooner was not trying to sympathize with the Southern cause, though he neglected to point out that the defeated Confederacy was no less State-minded than the Northern "Union," that it had preceded the period of hostilities with Constitution-making on its own account, ending up with one which included several sections even more objectionable than the one he was attacking. His effort instead was devoted to revealing how far removed from a "government by consent" or a "voluntary union of free men" the actual situation really was. Spooner disparaged the theory that the center of the contest concerned the institution of slavery, and advanced an economic interpretation of the war in harmony with others which have appeared since, propounded by critics of the State and others not so disposed, alike. Says Spooner in conclusion, speaking of the Constitution, "This much is certain—that it has either authorized such a government as we have had, or has been powerless to prevent it. In either case, it is unfit to exist."

For sheer audacity and breath-taking boldness, *No Treason* remains unmatched. One cannot call to mind anything to compare with it. In order to justify the continuance of the Constitution as the foundation-stone of the American State, one must seek other entrenched positions from which to make the defense than from that of any school of theoretical contractualism, after encountering Spooner.

No Treason presumes a bit more than minimum acquaintance with political and legal theory and practice, and the semantics of Statism, on the part of its readers. But one is unlikely to encounter another exercise in thinking which exceeds it in providing a more brilliant insight into the mystical speculative presumptions of the apologists for constitutionally-based Statism whose ideological roots are lodged in eighteenth century beliefs.

NO TREASON.

No. VI.

The Constitution of no Authority.

BY LYSANDER SPOONER.

BOSTON:
PUBLISHED BY THE AUTHOR.
1870.

No Treason
The Constitution of No Authority

I.

The Constitution has no inherent authority or obligation. It has no authority or obligation at all, unless as a contract between man and man. And it does not so much as even purport to be a contract between persons now existing. It purports, at most, to be only a contract between persons living eighty years ago.[1] And it can be supposed to have been a contract then only between persons who had already come to years of discretion, so as to be competent to make reasonable and obligatory contracts. Furthermore, we know, historically, that only a small portion even of the people then existing were consulted on the subject, or asked, or permitted to express either their consent or dissent in any formal manner. Those persons, if any, who did give their consent formally, are all dead now. Most of them have been dead forty, fifty, sixty, or seventy years. *And the Constitution, so far as it was their contract, died with them.* They had no natural power or right to make it obligatory upon their children. It is not only plainly impossible, in the nature of things, that they *could* bind their posterity, but they did not even attempt to bind them. That is to say, the instrument does not purport to be an agreement between any body but "the people" *then* existing; nor does it, either expressly or impliedly, assert any right, power, or disposition, on their part, to bind anybody but themselves. Let us see. Its language is:

> We, the people of the United States (that is, the people *then existing* in the United States), in order to form a more perfect union, insure domestic tranquility, provide for the common defense, promote the general welfare, and secure the blessings of liberty to ourselves *and our posterity,* do ordain and establish this Constitution for the United States of America.

---
[1][This essay was written in 1869.]

It is plain, in the first place, that this language, *as an agreement*, purports to be only what it at most really was, viz., a contract between the people then existing; and, of necessity, binding, as a contract, only upon those then existing. In the second place, the language neither expresses nor implies that they had any intention or desire, nor that they imagined they had any right or power, to bind their "posterity" to live under it. It does not say that their "posterity" will, shall, or must live under it. It only says, in effect, that their hopes and motives in adopting it were that it might prove useful to their posterity, as well as to themselves, by promoting their union, safety, tranquility, liberty, etc.

Suppose an agreement were entered into, in this form:

We, the people of Boston, agree to maintain a fort on Governor's Island, to protect ourselves and our posterity against invasion.

This agreement, as an agreement, would clearly bind nobody but the people then existing. Secondly, it would assert no right, power, or disposition, on their part, to compel their "posterity" to maintain such a fort. It would only indicate that the supposed welfare of their posterity was one of the motives that induced the original parties to enter into the agreement.

When a man says he is building a house for himself and his posterity, he does not mean to be understood as saying that he has any thought of binding them, nor is it to be inferred that he is so foolish as to imagine that he has any right or power to bind them, to live in it. So far as they are concerned, he only means to be understood as saying that his hopes and motives, in building it, are that they, or at least some of them, may find it for their happiness to live in it.

So when a man says he is planting a tree for himself and his posterity, he does not mean to be understood as saying that he has any thought of compelling them, nor is it to be inferred that he is such a simpleton as to imagine that he has any right or power to compel them, to eat the fruit. So far as they are concerned, he only means to say that his hopes and motives, in planting the tree, are that its fruit may be agreeable to them.

So it was with those who originally adopted the Constitution. Whatever may have been their personal intentions, the legal meaning of their language, so far as their "posterity" was concerned, simply was, that their hopes and motives, in entering into the agreement, were that it might prove useful and acceptable to their posterity; that it might promote their union, safety, tranquility, and welfare; and that it might tend "to secure to them the blessings of liberty." The language does not assert nor at all imply, any right, power, or disposition, on the part of the original parties to the agreement, to compel their "posterity" to live under it. If they had intended to bind their posterity to live under it, they should have said that their object was, not "to secure to them the blessings of liberty," but to make slaves of them; for if their "posterity" are bound to live under it, they are nothing less than the slaves of their foolish, tyrannical, and dead grandfathers.

It cannot be said that the Constitution formed "the people of the United States," for all time, into a corporation. It does not speak of "the people" as a corporation, but as individuals. A corporation does not describe itself as "we," nor as "people," nor as "ourselves." Nor does a corporation, in legal language, have any "posterity." It supposes itself to have, and speaks of itself as having, perpetual existence, as a single individuality.

Moreover, no body of men, existing at any one time, have the power to create a perpetual corporation. A corporation can become practically perpetual only by the voluntary accession of new members, as the old ones die off. But for this voluntary accession of new members, the corporation necessarily dies with the death of those who originally composed it.

Legally speaking, therefore, there is, in the Constitution, nothing that professes or attempts to bind the "posterity" of those who established it.

If, then, those who established the Constitution, had no power to bind, and did not attempt to bind, their posterity, the question arises, whether their posterity have bound themselves. If they have done so, they can have done so in only one or both of these two ways, viz., by voting, and paying taxes.

II.

Let us consider these two matters, voting and tax paying, separately. And first of voting.

All the voting that has ever taken place under the Constitution, has been of such a kind that it not only did not pledge the whole people to support the Constitution, but it did not even pledge any one of them to do so, as the following considerations show.

1. In the very nature of things, the act of voting could bind no-

body but the actual voters. But owing to the property qualifications required, it is probable that, during the first twenty or thirty years under the Constitution, not more than one-tenth, fifteenth, or perhaps twentieth of the whole population (black and white, men, women, and minors) were permitted to vote. Consequently, so far as voting was concerned, not more than one-tenth, fifteenth, or twentieth of those then existing, could have incurred any obligation to support the Constitution.[2]

At the present time,[3] it is probable that not more than one-sixth of the whole population are permitted to vote. Consequently, so far as voting is concerned, the other five-sixths can have given no pledge that they will support the Constitution.

2. Of the one-sixth that are permitted to vote, probably not more than two-thirds (about one-ninth of the whole population) have usually voted. Many never vote at all. Many vote only once in two, three, five, or ten years, in periods of great excitement.

No one, by voting, can be said to pledge himself for any longer period than that for which he votes. If, for example, I vote for an officer who is to hold his office for only a year, I cannot be said to have thereby pledged myself to support the government beyond that term. Therefore, on the ground of actual voting, it probably cannot be said that more than one-ninth or one-eighth, of the whole population are usually under any pledge to support the Constitution.[4]

3. It cannot be said that, by voting, a man pledges himself to support the Constitution, unless the act of voting be a perfectly voluntary one on his part. Yet the act of voting cannot properly

---

[2][In the presidential election of 1824, the first in American history for which there are reliable tabulations of popular votes, barely 350,000 votes were cast at a time when the population was approximately 11,000,000 (the figure for the decennial census of 1820 was 9,638,453; that of 1830 was 12,866,020).]

[3][In the 1868 election, which occurred just before Spooner was writing, a total of about 5,700,000 votes were cast for the candidates, Gen. Ulysses S. Grant and Horatio Seymour; the population figure for the 1870 census was nearly 40,000,000.]

[4][Relative percentages of those voting out of the total population have steadily increased since this was written but, in the main, Spooner's conjecture was borne out down until the adoption of the 19th Amendment, which ended sexual discrimination in national elections in 1920. The voters in the elections between 1870 and 1920 varied from one fifth to one eighth of the whole population. In recent years, since 1940, the figure has usually fluctuated between one-third and two-fifths.]

be called a voluntary one on the part of any very large number of those who do vote. It is rather a measure of necessity imposed upon them by others, than one of their own choice. On this point I repeat what was said in a former number,[a] viz.:

"In truth, in the case of individuals, their actual voting is not to be taken as proof of consent, *even for the time being*. On the contrary, it *is* to be considered that, without his consent having even been asked a man finds himself environed by a government that he cannot resist; a government that forces him to pay money, render service, and forego the exercise of many of his natural rights, under peril of weighty punishments. He sees, too, that other men practice this tyranny over him by the use of the ballot. He sees further, that, if he will but use the ballot himself, he has some chance of relieving himself from this tyranny of others, by subjecting them to his own. In short, he finds himself, without his consent, so situated that, if he use the ballot, he may become a master; if he does not use it, he must become a slave. And he has no other alternative than these two. In self-defence, he attempts the former. His case is analogous to that of a man who has been forced into battle, where he must either kill others, or be killed himself. Because, to save his own life in battle, a man attempts to take the lives of his opponents, it is not to be inferred that the battle is one of his own choosing. Neither in contests with the ballot —which is a mere substitute for a bullet—because, as his only chance of self-preservation, a man uses a ballot, is it to be inferred that the contest is one into which he voluntarily entered; that he voluntarily set up all his own natural rights, as a stake against those of others, to be lost or won by the mere power of numbers. On the contrary, it is to be considered that, in an exigency into which he had been forced by others, and in which no other means of self-defence offered, he, as a matter of necessity, used the only one that was left to him.

"Doubtless the most miserable of men, under the most oppressive government in the world, if allowed the ballot, would use it, if they could see any chance of thereby meliorating their condition. But it would not, therefore, be a legitimate inference that the government itself, that crushes them, was one which they had voluntarily set up, or even consented to.

"Therefore, a man's voting under the Constitution of the United States, is not to be taken as evidence that he ever freely assented to the Constitution, *even for the time being*. Consequently we have no proof that any very large portion, even of the actual voters of the United States, ever really and voluntarily consented to the Constitution, *even for the time being*. Nor can we ever have such proof, until every man is left perfectly free to consent, or not, without

---
[a] See *No Treason*, No. 2, pages 5 and 6.

thereby subjecting himself or his property to be disturbed or injured by others."

As we can have no legal knowledge as to who votes from choice, and who from the necessity thus forced upon him, we can have no legal knowledge, as to any particular individual, that he voted from choice; or, consequently, that by voting, he consented, or pledged himself, to support the government. Legally speaking, therefore, the act of voting utterly fails to pledge *any one* to support the government. It utterly fails to prove that the government rests upon the voluntary support of anybody. On general principles of law and reason, it cannot be said that the government has any voluntary supporters at all, until it can be distinctly shown who its voluntary supporters are.

4. As taxation is made compulsory on all, whether they vote or not, a large proportion of those who vote, no doubt do so to prevent their own money being used against themselves; when, in fact, they would have gladly abstained from voting, if they could thereby have saved themselves from taxation alone, to say nothing of being saved from all the other usurpations and tyrannies of the government. To take a man's property without his consent, and then to infer his consent because he attempts, by voting, to prevent that property from being used to his injury, is a very insufficient proof of his consent to support the Constitution. It is, in fact, no proof at all. And as we can have no legal knowledge as to who the particular individuals are, if there are any, who are willing to be taxed for the sake of voting, we can have no legal knowledge that any particular individual consents to be taxed for the sake of voting; or, consequently, consents to support the Constitution.

5. At nearly all elections, votes are given for various candidates for the same office. Those who vote for the unsuccessful candidates cannot properly be said to have voted to sustain the Constitution. They may, with more reason, be supposed to have voted, not to support the Constitution, but specially to prevent the tyranny which they anticipate the successful candidate intends to practice upon them under color of the Constitution; and therefore may reasonably be supposed to have voted against the Constitution itself. This supposition is the more reasonable, inasmuch as such voting is the only mode allowed to them of expressing their dissent to the Constitution.

6. Many votes are usually given for candidates who have no prospect of success. Those who give such votes may reasonably

be supposed to have voted as they did, with a special intention, not to support, but to obstruct the execution of, the Constitution; and, therefore, against the Constitution itself.

7. As all the different votes are given secretly (by secret ballot), there is no legal means of knowing, from the votes themselves, who votes for, and who against, the Constitution. Therefore, voting affords no legal evidence that any particular individual supports the Constitution. And where there can be no legal evidence that any particular individual supports the Constitution, it cannot legally be said that anybody supports it. It is clearly impossible to have any legal proof of the intentions of large numbers of men, where there can be no legal proof of the intentions of any particular one of them.

8. There being no legal proof of any man's intentions, in voting, we can only conjecture them. As a conjecture, it is probable, that a very large proportion of those who vote, do so on this principle, viz., that if, by voting, they could but get the government into their own hands (or that of their friends), and use its powers against their opponents, they would then willingly support the Constitution; but if their opponents are to have the power, and use it against them, then they would *not* willingly support the Constitution.

In short, men's voluntary support of the Constitution is doubtless, in most cases, wholly contingent upon the question whether, by means of the Constitution, they can make themselves masters, or are to be made slaves.

Such contingent consent as that is, in law and reason, no consent at all.

9. As everybody who supports the Constitution by voting (if there are any such) does so secretly (by secret ballot), and in a way to avoid all personal responsibility for the act of his agents or representatives, it cannot legally or reasonably be said that anybody at all supports the Constitution by voting. No man can reasonably or legally be said to do such a thing as to assent to, or support, the Constitution, *unless he does it openly, and in a way to make himself personally responsible for the acts of his agents, so long as they act within the limits of the power he delegates to them.*

10. As all voting is secret (by secret ballot), and as all secret governments are necessarily only secret bands of robbers, tyrants,

and murderers, the general fact that our government is practically carried on by means of such voting, only proves that there is among us a secret band of robbers, tyrants and murderers, whose purpose is to rob, enslave, and, so far as necessary to accomplish their purposes, murder, the rest of the people. The simple fact of the existence of such a band does nothing towards proving that "the people of the United States," or any one of them, voluntarily supports the Constitution.

For all the reasons that have now been given, voting furnishes no legal evidence as to who the particular individuals are (if there are any), who voluntarily support the Constitution. It therefore furnishes no legal evidence that anybody supports it voluntarily.

So far, therefore, as voting is concerned, the Constitution, legally speaking, has no supporters at all.

And, as matter of fact, there is not the slightest probability that the Constitution has a single bona fide supporter in the country. That is to say, there is not the slightest probability that there is a single man in the country, who both understands what the Constitution really is, *and sincerely supports it for what it really is.*

The ostensible supporters of the Constitution, like the ostensible supporters of most other governments, are made up of three classes, viz.: 1. Knaves, a numerous and active class, who see in the government an instrument which they can use for their own aggrandizement or wealth. 2. Dupes — a large class, no doubt — each of whom, because he is allowed one voice out of millions in deciding what he may do with his own person and his own property, and because he is permitted to have the same voice in robbing, enslaving, and murdering others, that others have in robbing, enslaving, and murdering himself, is stupid enough to imagine that he is a "free man," a "sovereign"; that this is "a free government"; "a government of equal rights," "the best government on earth,"[b] and such like absurdities. 3. A class who have some appreciation of the evils of government, but either do not see how to get rid of them, or do not choose to so far sacrifice their private interests as to give themselves seriously and earnestly to the work of making a change.

III.

The payment of taxes, being compulsory, of course furnishes no

---

[b]Suppose it be "the best government on earth," does that prove its own goodness, or only the badness of all other governments?

evidence that any one voluntarily supports the Constitution.

1. It is true that the *theory* of our Constitution is, that all taxes are paid voluntarily; that our government is a mutual insurance company, voluntarily entered into by the people with each other; that each man makes a free and purely voluntary contract with all others who are parties to the Constitution, to pay so much money for so much protection, the same as he does with any other insurance company; and that he is just as free not to be protected, and not to pay tax, as he is to pay a tax, and be protected.

But this theory of our government is wholly different from the practical fact. The fact is that the government, like a highwayman, says to a man: "Your money, or your life." And many, if not most, taxes are paid under the compulsion of that threat.

The government does not, indeed, waylay a man in a lonely place, spring upon him from the roadside, and, holding a pistol to his head, proceed to rifle his pockets. But the robbery is none the less a robbery on that account; and it is far more dastardly and shameful.

The highwayman takes solely upon himself the responsibility, danger, and crime of his own act. He does not pretend that he has any rightful claim to your money, or that he intends to use it for your own benefit. He does not pretend to be anything but a robber. He has not acquired impudence enough to profess to be merely a "protector," and that he takes men's money against their will, merely to enable him to "protect" those infatuated travellers, who feel perfectly able to protect themselves, or do not appreciate his peculiar system of protection. He is too sensible a man to make such professions as these. Furthermore, having taken your money, he leaves you, as you wish him to do. He does not persist in following you on the road, against your will; assuming to be your rightful "sovereign," on account of the "protection" he affords you. He does not keep "protecting" you, by commanding you to bow down and serve him; by requiring you to do this, and forbidding you to do that; by robbing you of more money as often as he finds it for his interest or pleasure to do so; and by branding you as a rebel, a traitor, and an enemy to your country, and shooting you down without mercy, if you dispute his authority, or resist his demands. He is too much of a gentleman to be guilty of such impostures, and insults, and villainies as these. In short, he does not, in addition to robbing you, attempt to make you either his dupe or his slave.

The proceedings of those robbers and murderers, who call themselves "the government," are directly the opposite of these of the single highwayman.

In the first place, they do not, like him, make themselves individually known; or, consequently, take upon themselves personally the responsibility of their acts. On the contrary, they secretly (by secret ballot) designate some one of their number to commit the robbery in their behalf, while they keep themselves practically concealed. They say to the person thus designated:

Go to A................ B.................., and say to him that "the government" has need of money to meet the expenses of protecting him and his property. If he presumes to say that he has never contracted with us to protect him, and that he wants none of our protection, say to him that that is our business, and not his; that we *choose* to protect him, whether he desires us to do so or not; and that we demand pay, too, for protecting him. If he dares to inquire who the individuals are, who have thus taken upon themselves the title of "the government," and who assume to protect him, and demand payment of him, without his having ever made any contract with them, say to him that that, too, is our business, and not his; that we do not *choose* to make ourselves *individually* known to him; that we have secretly (by secret ballot) appointed you our agent to give him notice of our demands, and, if he complies with them, to give him, in our name, a receipt that will protect him against any similar demand for the present year. If he refuses to comply, seize and sell enough of his property to pay not only our demands, but all your own expenses and trouble beside. If he resists the seizure of his property, call upon the bystanders to help you (doubtless some of them will prove to be members of our band). If, in defending his property, he should kill any of our band who are assisting you, capture him at all hazards; charge him (in one of our courts) with murder; convict him, and hang him. If he should call upon his neighbors, or any others who, like him, may be disposed to resist our demands, and they should come in large numbers to his assistance, cry out that they are all rebels and traitors; that "our country" is in danger; call upon the commander of our hired murderers; tell him to quell the rebellion and "save the country," cost what it may. Tell him to kill all who resist, though they should be hundreds of thousands; and thus strike terror into all others similarly disposed. See that the work of murder is thoroughly done; that we may have no further trouble of this kind hereafter. When these traitors shall have thus been taught our strength and our determination, they will be good loyal citizens for many years, and pay their taxes without a why or a wherefore.

It is under such compulsion as this that taxes, so called, are paid. And how much proof the payment of taxes affords, that the people consent to support "the government," it needs no further argument to show.

2. Still another reason why the payment of taxes implies no consent, or pledge, to support the government, is that the taxpayer does not know, and has no means of knowing, who the particular individuals are who compose "the government." To him "the government" is a myth, an abstraction, an incorporeality, with which he can make no contract, and to which he can give no consent, and make no pledge. He knows it only through its pretended agents. "The government" itself he never sees. He knows indeed, by common report, that certain persons, of a certain age, are permitted to vote; and thus to make themselves parts of, or (if they choose) opponents of, the government, for the time being. But who of them do thus vote, and especially how each one votes (whether so as to aid or oppose the government), he does not know; the voting being all done secretly (by secret ballot). Who, therefore, practically compose "the government," for the time being, he has no means of knowing. Of course he can make no contract with them, give them no consent, and make them no pledge. Of necessity, therefore, his paying taxes to them implies, on his part, no contract, consent, or pledge to support them—that is, to support "the government," or the Constitution.

3. Not knowing who the particular individuals are, who call themselves "the government," the taxpayer does not know whom he pays his taxes to. All he knows is that a man comes to him, representing himself to be the agent of "the government"—that is, the agent of a secret band of robbers and murderers, who have taken to themselves the title of "the government," and have determined to kill everybody who refuses to give them whatever money they demand. To save his life, he gives up his money to this agent. But as this agent does not make his principals individually known to the taxpayer, the latter, after he has given up his money, knows no more who are "the government"—that is, who were the robbers—than he did before. To say, therefore, that by giving up his money to their agent, he entered into a voluntary contract with them, that

he pledges himself to obey them, to support them, and to give them whatever money they should demand of him in the future, is simply ridiculous.

4. All political power, as it is called, rests practically upon this matter of money. Any number of scoundrels, having money enough to start with, can establish themselves as a "government"; because, with money, they can hire soldiers, and with soldiers extort more money; and also compel general obedience to their will. It is with government, as Caesar said it was in war, that money and soldiers mutually supported each other; that with money he could hire soldiers, and with soldiers extort money. So these villains, who call themselves governments, well understand that their power rests primarily upon money. With money they can hire soldiers, and with soldiers extort money. And, when their authority is denied, the first use they always make of money, is to hire soldiers to kill or subdue all who refuse them more money.

For this reason, whoever desires liberty, should understand these vital facts, viz.: 1. That every man who puts money into the hands of a "government" (so called), puts into its hands a sword which will be used against himself, to extort more money from him, and also to keep him in subjection to its arbitrary will. 2. That those who will take his money, without his consent, in the first place, will use it for his further robbery and enslavement, if he presumes to resist their demands in the future. 3. That it is a perfect absurdity to suppose that any body of men would ever take a man's money without his consent, for any such object as they profess to take it for, viz., that of protecting him; for why should they wish to protect him, if he does not wish them to do so? To suppose that they would do so, is just as absurd as it would be to suppose that they would take his money without his consent, for the purpose of buying food or clothing for him, when he did not want it. 4. If a man wants "protection," he is competent to make his own bargains for it; and nobody has any occasion to rob him, in order to "protect" him against his will. 5. That the only security men can have for their political liberty, consists in their keeping their money in their own pockets, until they have assurances, perfectly satisfactory to themselves, that it will be used as they wish it to be used, for their benefit, and not for their injury. 6. That no government, so called, can reasonably be trusted for a moment, or reasonably be supposed to have honest purposes in view, any longer than it depends wholly upon voluntary support.

These facts are all so vital and so self-evident, that it cannot reasonably be supposed that any one will voluntarily pay money to a "government," for the purpose of securing its protection, unless he first makes an explicit and purely voluntary contract with it for that purpose.

It is perfectly evident, therefore, that neither such voting, nor such payment of taxes, as actually takes place, proves anybody's consent, or obligation, to support the Constitution. Consequently we have no evidence at all that the Constitution is binding upon anybody, or that anybody is under any contract or obligation whatever to support it. And nobody is under any obligation to support it.

IV.

The Constitution not only binds nobody now, but it never did bind anybody. It never bound anybody, because it was never agreed to by anybody in such a manner as to make it, on general principles of law and reason, binding upon him.

It is a general principle of law and reason, that a *written* instrument binds no one until he has signed it. This principle is so inflexible a one, that even though a man is unable to write his name, he must still "make his mark," before he is bound by a written contract. This custom was established ages ago, when few men could write their names; when a clerk—that is, a man who could write—was so rare and valuable a person, that even if he were guilty of high crimes, he was entitled to pardon, on the ground that the public could not afford to lose his services. Even at that time, a written contract must be signed; and men who could not write, either "made their mark," or signed their contracts by stamping their seals upon wax affixed to the parchment on which their contracts were written. Hence the custom of affixing seals, that has continued to this time.

The law holds, and reason declares, that if a written instrument is not signed, the presumption must be that the party to be bound by it, did not choose to sign it, or to bind himself by it. And law and reason both give him until the last moment, in which to decide whether he will sign it, or not. Neither law nor reason requires or expects a man to agree to an instrument, *until it is written;* for until it is written, he cannot know its precise legal meaning. And when it is written, and he has had the opportunity to satisfy himself of its precise legal meaning, he is then expected to decide, and not before, whether he will agree to it or not. And if he do not *then* sign it, his reason is supposed to be, that he does not choose to enter into such a contract. The fact that the instrument was written for him to sign, or with the hope that he would sign it, goes for nothing.

Where would be the end of fraud and litigation, if one party could bring into court a written instrument, without any signature, and claim to have it enforced, upon the ground that it was written for another man to sign? that this other man had promised to sign it? that he ought to have signed it? that he had had the opportunity to sign it, if he would? but that he had refused or neglected to do so? Yet that is the most that could ever be said of the Constitution.[c] The very judges, who profess to derive all their authority from the Constitution—from an instrument that nobody ever signed—would spurn any other instrument, not signed, that should be brought before them for adjudication.

Moreover, a written instrument must, in law and reason, not only be signed, but must also be delivered to the party (or to some one for him), in whose favor it is made, before it can bind the party making it. The signing is of no effect, unless the instrument be also delivered. And a party is at perfect liberty to refuse to deliver a written instrument, after he has signed it. He is as free to refuse to deliver it, as he is to refuse to sign it. The Constitution was not only never signed by anybody, but it was never delivered by anybody, or to anybody's agent or attorney. It can therefore be of no more validity as a contract, than can any other instrument, that was never signed or delivered.

V.

As further evidence of the general sense of mankind, as to the practical necessity there is that all men's *important* contracts, especially those of a permanent nature, should be both written and signed, the following facts are pertinent.

For nearly two hundred years — that is, since 1677 — there has been on the statute book of England, and the same, in substance, if not precisely in letter, has been re-enacted, and is now in force, in nearly or quite all the States of this Union, a statute, the general

---

[c]The very men who drafted it, never signed it in any way to bind themselves by it, *as a contract*. And not one of them probably ever would have signed it in any way to bind himself by it, *as a contract*.

object of which is to declare that no action shall be brought to enforce contracts of the more important class, *unless they are put in writing, and signed by the parties to be held chargeable upon them.*[d]

The principle of the statute, be it observed, is, not merely that written contracts shall be signed, but also that all contracts, except those specially exempted — generally those that are for small amounts, and are to remain in force but for a short time — *shall be both written and signed.*

The reason of the statute, on this point, is, that it is now so easy a thing for men to put their contracts in writing, and sign them, and their failure to do so opens the door to so much doubt, fraud, and litigation, that men who neglect to have their contracts — of any considerable importance — written and signed, ought not to have the benefit of courts of justice to enforce them. And this reason is a wise one; and that experience has confirmed its wisdom and necessity, is demonstrated by the fact that it has been acted upon in England for nearly two hundred years, and has been so nearly

---

[d] I have personally examined the statute books of the following States, viz.: Maine, New Hampshire, Vermont, Massachusetts, Rhode Island, Connecticut, New York, New Jersey, Pennsylvania, Delaware, Virginia, North Carolina, South Carolina, Georgia, Florida, Alabama, Mississippi, Tennessee, Kentucky, Ohio, Michigan, Indiana, Illinois, Wisconsin, Texas, Arkansas, Missouri, Iowa, Minnesota, Nebraska, Kansas, Nevada, California, and Oregon, and find that in all these States the English statute has been reenacted, sometimes with modifications, but generally enlarging its operations, and is now in force.

The following are some of the provisions of the Massachusetts statute:

"No action shall be brought in any of the following cases, that is to say: . . .

"To charge a person upon a special promise to answer for the debt, default, or misdoings of another: . . .

"Upon a contract for the sale of lands, tenements, hereditaments, or of any interest in, or concerning them; or

"Upon an agreement that is not to be performed within one year from the writing thereof:

"Unless the promise, contract, or agreement, upon which such action is brought, or some memorandum or note thereof, is in writing, and signed by the party to be charged therewith, or by some person thereunto by him lawfully authorized."

"No contract for the sale of goods, wares, or merchandise, for the price of fifty dollars or more, shall be good or valid, unless the purchaser accepts and receives part of the goods so sold, or gives something in earnest to bind the bargain, or in part payment; or unless some note or memorandum in writing of the bargain is made and signed by the party to be charged thereby, or by some person thereunto by him lawfully authorized."

universally adopted in this country, and that nobody thinks of repealing it.

We all know, too, how careful most men are to have their contracts written and signed, even when this statute does not require it. For example, most men, if they have money due them, of no larger amount than five or ten dollars, are careful to take a note for it. If they buy even a small bill of goods, paying for it at the time of delivery, they take a receipted bill for it. If they pay a small balance of a book account, or any other small debt previously contracted, they take a written receipt for it.

Furthermore, the law everywhere (probably) in our country, as well as in England, requires that a large class of contracts, such as wills, deeds, etc., shall not only be written and signed, but also sealed, witnessed, and acknowledged. And in the case of married women conveying their rights in real estate, the law, in many States, requires that the women shall be examined separate and apart from their husbands, and declare that they sign their contracts free of any fear or compulsion of their husbands.

Such are some of the precautions which the laws require, and which individuals — from motives of common prudence, even in cases not required by law — take, to put their contracts in writing, and have them signed, and, to guard against all uncertainties and controversies in regard to their meaning and validity. And yet we have what purports, or professes, or is claimed, to be a contract— the Constitution — made eighty years ago, by men who are now all dead, and who never had any power to bind *us*, but which (it is claimed) has nevertheless bound three generations of men, consisting of many millions, and which (it is claimed) will be binding upon all the millions that are to come; but which nobody ever signed, sealed, delivered, witnessed, or acknowledged; and which few persons, compared with the whole number that are claimed to be bound by it, have ever read, or even seen, or ever will read, or see. And of those who ever have read it, or ever will read it, scarcely any two, perhaps no two, have ever agreed, or ever will agree, as to what it means.

Moreover, this supposed contract, which would not be received in any court of justice sitting under its authority, if offered to prove a debt of five dollars, owing by one man to another, is one by which —*as it is generally interpreted by those who pretend to administer it*—all men, women and children throughout the country, and through all time, surrender not only all their property, but also their liberties, and even lives, into the hands of men who by this supposed contract, are expressly made wholly irresponsible for their disposal of them. And we are so insane, or so wicked, as to destroy property and lives without limit, in fighting to compel men to fulfill a supposed contract, which, inasmuch as it has never been signed by anybody, is, on general principles of law and reason — such principles as we are all governed by in regard to other contracts—the merest waste paper, binding upon nobody, fit only to be thrown into the fire; or, if preserved, preserved only to serve as a witness and a warning of the folly and wickedness of mankind.

VI.

It is no exaggeration, but a literal truth, to say that, by the Constitution—*not as I interpret it, but as it is interpreted by those who pretend to administer it*—the properties, liberties, and lives of the entire people of the United States are surrendered unreservedly into the hands of men who, it is provided by the Constitution itself, shall never be "questioned" as to any disposal they make of them.

Thus the Constitution (Art. I, Sec. 6) provides that, "for any speech or debate (or vote), in either house, they (the senators and representatives) shall not be questioned in any other place."

The whole law-making power is given to these senators and representatives (when acting by a two-thirds vote)[e]; and this provision protects them from all responsibility for the laws they make.

The Constitution also enables them to secure the execution of all their laws, by giving them power to withhold the salaries of, and to impeach and remove, all judicial and executive officers, who refuse to execute them.

Thus the whole power of the government is in their hands, and they are made utterly irresponsible for the use they make of it. What is this but absolute, irresponsible power?

It is no answer to this view of the case to say that these men are under oath to use their power only within certain limits; for

---

[e]And this two-thirds vote may be but two-thirds of a quorum—that is two-thirds of a majority—instead of two-thirds of the whole.

what care they, or what should they care, for oaths or limits, when it is expressly provided, by the Constitution itself, that they shall never be "questioned," or held to any responsibility whatever, for violating their oaths, or transgressing those limits?

Neither is it any answer to this view of the case to say that the particular individuals holding this power can be changed once in two or six years; for the power of each set of men is absolute during the term for which they hold it; and when they can hold it no longer, they are succeeded only by men whose power will be equally absolute and irresponsible.

Neither is it any answer to this view of the case to say that the men holding this absolute, irresponsible power, must be men chosen by the people (or portions of them) to hold it. A man is none the less a slave because he is allowed to choose a new master once in a term of years. Neither are a people any the less slaves because permitted periodically to choose new masters. What makes them slaves is the fact that they now are, and are always hereafter to be, in the hands of men whose power over them is, and always is to be, absolute and irresponsible.[f]

The right of absolute and irresponsible dominion is the right of property, and the right of property is the right of absolute, irresponsible dominion. The two are identical; the one necessarily implying the other. Neither can exist without the other. If, therefore, Congress have that absolute and irresponsible law-making power, which the Constitution — according to their interpretation of it — gives them, it can only be because they own us as property. If they own us as property, they are our masters, and their will is our law. If they do not own us as property, they are not our masters, and their will, as such, is of no authority over us.

But these men who claim and exercise this absolute and irresponsible dominion over us, dare not be consistent, and claim either to be our masters, or to own us as property. They say they are only our servants, agents, attorneys, and representatives. But this declaration involves an absurdity, a contradiction. No man can be my servant, agent, attorney, or representative, and be, at the same time, uncontrollable by me, and irresponsible to me for his acts. It is of no importance that I appointed him, and put all power

---

[f] Of what appreciable value is it to any man, as an individual, that he is allowed a voice in choosing these public masters? His voice is only one of several millions.

in his hands. If I made him uncontrollable by me, and irresponsible to me, he is no longer my servant, agent, attorney, or representative. If I gave him absolute, irresponsible power over my property, I gave him the property. If I gave him absolute, irresponsible power over myself, I made him my master, and gave myself to him as a slave. And it is of no importance whether I called him master or servant, agent or owner. The only question is, what power did I put into his hands? Was it an absolute and irresponsible one? or a limited and responsible one?

For still another reason they are neither our servants, agents, attorneys, nor representatives. And that reason is, that we do not make ourselves responsible for their acts. If a man is my servant, agent, or attorney, I necessarily make myself responsible for all his acts done within the limits of the power I have intrusted to him. If I have intrusted him, as my agent, with either absolute power, or any power at all, over the persons or properties of other men than myself, I thereby necessarily make myself responsible to those other persons for any injuries he may do them, so long as he acts within the limits of the power I have granted him. But no individual who may be injured in his person or property, by acts of Congress, can come to the individual electors, and hold them responsible for these acts of their so-called agents or representatives. This fact proves that these pretended agents of the people, of everybody, are really the agents of nobody.

If, then, nobody is individually responsible for the acts of Congress, the members of Congress are nobody's agents. And if they are nobody's agents, they are themselves individually responsible for their own acts, and for the acts of all whom they employ. And the authority they are exercising is simply their own individual authority; and, by the law of nature—the highest of all laws—anybody injured by their acts, anybody who is deprived by them of his property or his liberty, has the same right to hold them individually responsible, that he has to hold any other trespasser individually responsible. He has the same right to resist them, and their agents, that he has to resist any other trespassers.

VII.

It is plain, then, that on general principles of law and reason—such principles as we all act upon in courts of justice and in common life—the Constitution is no contract; that it binds nobody, and never did bind anybody; and that all those who pretend to act by its authority, are really acting without any legitimate authority at all; that, on general principles of law and reason, they are mere usurpers, and that everybody not only has the right, but is morally bound, to treat them as such.

If the people of this country wish to maintain such a government as the Constitution describes, there is no reason in the world why they should not sign the instrument itself, and thus make known their wishes in an open, authentic manner; in such manner as the common sense and experience of mankind have shown to be reasonable and necessary in such cases; *and in such manner as to make themselves (as they ought to do) individually responsible for the acts of the government.* But the people have never been asked to sign it. And the only reason why they have never been asked to sign it, has been that it has been known that they never would sign it; that they were neither such fools nor knaves as they must needs have been to be willing to sign it; that (at least as it has been practically interpreted) it is not what any sensible and honest man wants for himself; nor such as he has any right to impose upon others. It is, to all moral intents and purposes, as destitute of obligation as the compacts which robbers and thieves and pirates enter into with each other, but never sign.

If any considerable number of the people believe the Constitution to be good, why do they not sign it themselves, and make laws for, and administer them upon, each other; leaving all other persons (who do not interfere with them) in peace? Until they have tried the experiment for themselves, how can they have the face to impose the Constitution upon, or even to recommend it to, others? Plainly the reason for such absurd and inconsistent conduct is that they want the Constitution, not solely for any honest or legitimate use it can be of to themselves or others, but for the dishonest and illegitimate power it gives them over the persons and properties of others. But for this latter reason, all their eulogiums on the Constitution, all their exhortations, and all their expenditures of money and blood to sustain it, would be wanting.

VIII.

The Constitution itself, then, being of no authority, on what authority does our government practically rest? On what ground can those who pretend to administer it, claim the right to seize men's property, to restrain them of their natural liberty of action, industry, and trade, and to kill all who deny their authority to dispose of men's properties, liberties, and lives at their pleasure or discretion?

The most they can say, in answer to this question, is, that some half, two-thirds, or three-fourths, of the male adults of the country have a *tacit understanding* that they will maintain a government under the Constitution; that they will select, by ballot, the persons to administer it; and that those persons who may receive a majority, or a plurality, of their ballots, shall act as their representatives, and administer the Constitution in their name, and by their authority.

But this tacit understanding (admitting it to exist) cannot at all justify the conclusion drawn from it. A tacit understanding between A, B, and C, that they will, by ballot, depute D as their agent, to deprive me of my property, liberty, or life, cannot at all authorize D to do so. He is none the less a robber, tyrant, and murderer, because he claims to act as their agent, than he would be if he avowedly acted on his own responsibility alone.

Neither am I bound to recognize him as their agent, nor can he legitimately claim to be their agent, when he brings no *written* authority from them accrediting him as such. I am under no obligation to take his word as to who his principals may be, or whether he has any. Bringing no credentials, I have a right to say he has no such authority even as he claims to have: and that he is therefore intending to rob, enslave, or murder me on his own account.

This tacit understanding, therefore, among the voters of the country, amounts to nothing as an authority to their agents. Neither do the ballots by which they select their agents, avail any more than does their tacit understanding; for their ballots are given in secret, and therefore in a way to avoid any personal responsibility for the acts of their agents.

No body of men can be said to authorize a man to act as their agent, to the injury of a third person, unless they do it in so open and authentic a manner as to make themselves personally responsible for his acts. None of the voters in this country appoint their political agents in any open, authentic manner, or in any manner to make themselves responsible for their acts. Therefore these pretended agents cannot legitimately claim to be really agents. Somebody must be responsible for the acts of these pretended agents; and if they cannot show any open and authentic credentials from their principals, they cannot, in law or reason, be said to have any principals. The maxim applies here, that what does not appear, does not exist. If they can show no principals, they have none.

But even these pretended agents do not themselves know who their pretended principals are. These latter act in secret; for acting by secret ballot is acting in secret as much as if they were to meet in secret conclave in the darkness of the night. And they are personally as much unknown to the agents they select, as they are to others. No pretended agent therefore can ever know by whose ballots he is selected, or consequently who his real principals are. Not knowing who his principals are, he has no right to say that he has any. He can, at most, say only that he is the agent of a secret band of robbers and murderers, who are bound by that faith which prevails among confederates in crime, to stand by him, if his acts, done in their name, shall be resisted.

Men honestly engaged in attempting to establish justice in the world, have no occasion thus to act in secret; or to appoint agents to do acts for which they (the principals) are not willing to be responsible.

The secret ballot makes a secret government; and a secret government is a secret band of robbers and murderers. Open despotism is better than this. The single despot stands out in the face of all men, and says: I am the State: My will is law: I am your master: I take the responsibility of my acts: The only arbiter I acknowledge is the sword: If any one denies my right, let him try conclusions with me.

But a secret government is little less than a government of assassins. Under it, a man knows not who his tyrants are, until they have struck, and perhaps not then. He may *guess,* beforehand, as to some of his immediate neighbors. But he really knows nothing. The man to whom he would most naturally fly for protection, may prove an enemy, when the time of trial comes.

This is the kind of government we have; and it is the only one we are likely to have, until men are ready to say: We will consent to no Constitution, except such an one as we are neither ashamed nor afraid to sign; and we will authorize no government to do anything in our name which we are not willing to be personally responsible for.

IX.

What is the motive to the secret ballot? This, and only this: Like other confederates in crime, those who use it are not friends, but enemies; and they are afraid to be known, and to have their individual doings known, even to each other. They can contrive to bring about a sufficient understanding to enable them to act in concert against other persons; but beyond this they have no confidence, and no friendship, among themselves. In fact, they are engaged quite as much in schemes for plundering each other, as in plundering those who are not of them. And it is perfectly well understood among them that the strongest party among them will, in certain contingencies, murder each other by the hundreds of thousands (as they lately did do) to accomplish their purposes against each other. Hence they dare not be known, and have their individual doings known, even to each other. And this is avowedly the only reason for the ballot: for a secret government; a government by secret bands of robbers and murderers. And we are insane enough to call this liberty! To be a member of this secret band of robbers and murderers is esteemed a privilege and an honor! Without this privilege, a man is considered a slave; but with it a free man! With it he is considered a free man, because he has the same power to secretly (by secret ballot) procure the robbery, enslavement, and murder of another man, and that other man has to procure his robbery, enslavement, and murder. And this they call equal rights!

If any number of men, many or few, claim the right to govern the people of this country, let them make and sign an open compact with each other to do so. Let them thus make themselves individually known to those whom they propose to govern. And let them thus openly take the legitimate responsibility of their acts. How many of those who now support the Constitution, will ever do this? How many will ever dare openly proclaim their right to govern? or take the legitimate responsibility of their acts? Not one!

X.

It is obvious that, on general principles of law and reason, there exists no such thing as a government created by, or resting upon, any consent, compact, or agreement of "the people of the United States" with each other; that the only visible, tangible, responsible government that exists, is that of a few individuals only, who act in concert, and call themselves by the several names of senators, representatives, presidents, judges, marshals, treasurers, collectors, generals, colonels, captains, etc., etc.

On general principles of law and reason, it is of no importance whatever that those few individuals profess to be the agents and representatives of "the people of the United States"; since they can show no credentials from the people themselves; they were never appointed as agents or representatives in any open, authentic manner; they do not themselves know, and have no means of knowing, and cannot prove, who their principals (as they call them) are individually; and consequently cannot, in law or reason, be said to have any principals at all.

It is obvious, too, that if these alleged principals ever did appoint these pretended agents, or representatives, they appointed them secretly (by secret ballot), and in a way to avoid all personal responsibility for their acts; that, at most, these alleged principals put these pretended agents forward for the most criminal purposes, viz.: to plunder the people of their property, and restrain them of their liberty; and that the only authority that these alleged principals have for so doing, is simply a *tacit understanding* among themselves that they will imprison, shoot, or hang every man who resists the exactions and restraints which their agents or representatives may impose upon them.

Thus it is obvious that the only visible, tangible government we have is made up of these professed agents or representatives of a secret band of robbers and murderers, who, to cover up, or gloss over, their robberies and murders, have taken to themselves the title of "the people of the United States"; and who, on the pretense of being "the people of the United States," assert their right to subject to their dominion, and to control and dispose of at their pleasure, all property and persons found in the United States.

XI.

On general principles of law and reason, the oaths which these pretended agents of the people take "to support the Constitution," are of no validity or obligation. And why? For this, if for no other reason, viz., *that they are given to nobody*. There is no privity (as the lawyers say) — that is, no mutual recognition, consent, and agreement — between those who take these oaths, and any other persons.

If I go upon Boston Common, and in the presence of a hundred thousand people, men, women and children, with whom I have no contract on the subject, take an oath that I will enforce upon them the laws of Moses, of Lycurgus, of Solon, of Justinian, or of Alfred, that oath is, on general principles of law and reason, of no obligation. It is of no obligation, not merely because it is intrinsically a criminal one, *but also because it is given to nobody,* and consequently pledges my faith to nobody. It is merely given to the winds.

It would not alter the case at all to say that, among these hundred thousand persons, in whose presence the oath was taken, there were two, three, or five thousand male adults, who had *secretly—* by secret ballot, and in a way to avoid making themselves *individually* known to me, or to the remainder of the hundred thousand— designated me as their agent to rule, control, plunder, and, if need be, murder, these hundred thousand people. The fact that they had designated me secretly, and in a manner to prevent my knowing them individually, prevents all privity between them and me; and consequently makes it impossible that there can be any contract, or pledge of faith, on my part towards them; for it is impossible that I can pledge my faith, in any legal sense, to a man whom I neither know, nor have any means of knowing, individually.

So far as I am concerned, then, these two, three, or five thousand persons are a secret band of robbers and murderers, who have secretly, and in a way to save themselves from all responsibility for my acts, designated me as their agent; and have, through some other agent, or pretended agent, made their wishes known to me. But being, nevertheless, individually unknown to me, and having no open, authentic contract with me, my oath is, on general principles of law and reason, of no validity as a pledge of faith to them. And being no pledge of faith to them, it is no pledge of faith to anybody. It is mere idle wind. At most, it is only a pledge of faith to an unknown band of robbers and murderers, whose instrument for plundering and murdering other people, I thus publicly confess myself to be. And it has no other obligation than a similar oath given to any other unknown body of pirates, robbers, and murderers.

For these reasons the oaths taken by members of Congress, "to support the Constitution," are, on general principles of law and reason, of no validity. They are not only criminal in themselves, and therefore void; but they are also void for the further reason *that they are given to nobody.*

It cannot be said that, in any legitimate or legal sense, they are given to "the people of the United States"; because neither the whole, nor any large proportion of the whole, people of the United States ever, either openly or secretly, appointed or designated these men as their agents to carry the Constitution into effect. The great body of the people—that is, men, women and children—were never asked, or even permitted, to signify, in any *formal* manner, either openly or secretly, their choice or wish on the subject. The most that these members of Congress can say, in favor of their appointment, is simply this: Each one can say for himself:

I have evidence satisfactory to myself, that there exists, scattered throughout the country, a band of men, having a tacit understanding with each other, and calling themselves "the people of the United States," whose general purposes are to control and plunder each other, and all other persons in the country, and, so far as they can, even in neighboring countries; and to kill every man who shall attempt to defend his person and property against their schemes of plunder and dominion. Who these men are, *individually*, I have no certain means of knowing, for they sign no papers, and give no open, authentic evidence of their individual membership. They are not known individually even to each other. They are apparently as much afraid of being individually known to each other, as of being known to other persons. Hence they ordinarily have no mode either of exercising, or of making known, their individual membership, otherwise than by giving their votes secretly for certain agents to do their will. But although these men are individually unknown, both to each other and to other persons, it is generally understood in the country that none but male persons, of the age of twenty-one years and upwards, can be members. It is also generally understood that *all* male persons, born in the country, having certain complexions, and (in some localities) certain amounts of property, and (in certain cases) even persons of foreign birth, are *permitted* to be members. But it appears that usually not more than one half, two-thirds, or, in some cases, three-fourths, of all who are thus permitted to become members of the band, ever exercise, or consequently prove, their actual membership, in the only mode in which they ordinarily can exercise or prove it, viz., by giving their votes secretly for the officers or agents of the band. The number of these secret votes, so far as we have any account of them, varies greatly from year to year, thus tending to prove that the band, instead of being a permanent organization, is a merely *pro tempore* affair with those who choose to act with it for the time being. The gross number of these secret votes, or what purports to be their gross number, in different localities, is occasionally published. Whether these reports are accurate or not, we have no means of knowing. It is generally supposed that great frauds are often committed in depositing them. They are understood to be received and counted by certain men, who are themselves appointed for that purpose by the same secret process by which all other officers and agents of the band are selected. According to the reports of these receivers of votes (for whose accuracy or honesty, however, I cannot vouch), and according to my best knowledge of the whole number of male persons "in my district," who (it is supposed) were permitted to vote, it would appear that one-half, two-thirds or three-fourths actually did vote. Who the men were, individually, who cast these votes, I have no knowledge, for the whole thing was done secretly. But of the secret votes thus given for what they call a "member of Congress," the receivers reported that I had a majority, or at least a larger number than any other one person. And it is only by virtue of such a designation that I am now here to act in concert with other persons similarly selected in other parts of the country. It is understood among those who sent me here, that all the persons so selected, will, on coming together at the City of Washington, take an oath in each other's presence "to support the Constitution of the United States." By this is meant a certain paper that was drawn up eighty years ago. It was never signed by anybody, and apparently has no obligation, and never had any obligation, as a contract. In fact, few persons ever read it, and doubtless much the largest number of those who voted for me and the others, never even saw it, or now pretend to know what it means. Nevertheless, it is often spoken of in the country as "the Constitution of the United States"; and for some reason or another, the men who sent me here, seem to expect that I, and all with whom I act, will swear to carry this Constitution into effect. I am therefore ready to take this oath, and to co-operate with all others, similarly selected, who are ready to take the same oath.

This is the most that any member of Congress can say in proof that he has any constituency; that he represents anybody; that his oath "to support the Constitution," *is given to anybody,* or pledges his faith to *anybody.* He has no open, written, or other authentic evidence, such as is required in all other cases, that he was ever appointed the agent or representative of anybody. He has no written power of attorney from any single individual. He has no such legal knowledge as is required in all other cases, by which he can identify a single one of those who pretend to have appointed him to represent them.

Of course his oath, professedly given to them, "to support the Constitution," is, on general principles of law and reason, an oath given to nobody. It pledges his faith to nobody. If he fails to fulfil his oath, not a single person can come forward, and say to him, you have betrayed me, or broken faith with me.

No one can come forward and say to him: I appointed you my attorney to act for me. I required you to swear that, as my attorney, you would support the Constitution. You promised me that you would do so; and now you have forfeited the oath you gave to me. No single individual can say this.

No open, avowed, or responsible association, or body of men, can come forward and say to him: We appointed you our attorney, to act for us. We required you to swear that, as our attorney, you would support the Constitution. You promised us that you would do so; and now you have forfeited the oath you gave to us.

No open, avowed, or responsible association, or body of men, can say this to him; because there is no such association or body of men in existence. If any one should assert that there is such an association, let him prove, if he can, who compose it. Let him produce, if he can, any open, written, or other authentic contract, signed or agreed to by these men; forming themselves into an association; making themselves known as such to the world; appointing him as their agent; and making themselves individually, or as an association, responsible for his acts, done by their authority. Until all this can be shown, no one can say that, in any legitimate sense, there is any such association; or that he is their agent; or that he ever gave his oath to them; or ever pledged his faith to them.

On general principles of law and reason, it would be a sufficient answer for him to say, to all individuals, and all pretended associations of individuals, who should accuse him of a breach of faith to them:

I never knew you. Where is your evidence that you, either individually or collectively, ever appointed me your attorney? that you ever required me to swear to you, that, as your attorney, I would support the Constitution? or that I have now broken any faith I ever pledged to you? You may, or you may not, be members of that secret band of robbers and murderers, who act in secret; appoint their agents by a secret ballot; who keep themselves individually unknown even to the agents they thus appoint; and who, therefore, cannot claim that they have any agents; or that any of their pretended agents ever gave his oath, or pledged his faith, to them. I repudiate you altogether. My oath was given to others, with whom you have nothing to do; or it was idle wind, given only to the idle winds. Begone!

XII.

For the same reasons, the oaths of all the other pretended agents of this secret band of robbers and murderers are, on general principles of law and reason, equally destitute of obligation. They are given to nobody; but only to the winds.

The oaths of the tax-gatherers and treasurers of the band, are, on general principles of law and reason, of no validity. If any tax gatherer, for example, should put the money he receives into his own pocket, and refuse to part with it, the members of this band could not say to him: You collected that money as our agent, and for our uses; and you swore to pay it over to us, or to those we should appoint to receive it. You have betrayed us, and broken faith with us.

It would be a sufficient answer for him to say to them:

I never knew you. You never made yourselves individually known to me. I never gave my oath to you, as individuals. You may, or you may not, be members of that secret band, who appoint agents to rob and murder other people; but who are cautious not to make themselves individually known, either to such agents, or to those whom their agents are commissioned to rob. If you are members of that band, you have given me no proof that you ever commissioned me to rob others for your benefit. I never knew you, as individuals, and of course never promised you that I would pay over to you the proceeds of my robberies. I committed my robberies on my own account, and for my own profit. If you thought I was fool enough to allow you to keep yourselves concealed, and use me as your tool for robbing other persons; or that I would take all the personal risk of the robberies, and pay over the proceeds to you, you were particularly simple. As I took all the risk of my robberies, I propose to take all the profits. Begone! You are fools, as well as villains. If I gave my oath to anybody, I gave it to other persons than you. But I really gave it to nobody. I only gave it to the winds. It answered my purposes at the time. It enabled me to get the money I was after, and now I propose to keep it. If you expected me to pay it over to you, you relied only upon that honor that is said to prevail among thieves. You now understand that that is a very poor reliance. I trust you may become wise enough to never rely upon it again. If I have any duty in the matter, it is to give back the money to those from whom I took it; not to pay it over to such villains as you.

XIII.

On general principles of law and reason, the oaths which foreigners take, on coming here, and being "naturalized" (as it is called), are of no validity. They are necessarily given to nobody; because there is no open, authentic association, to which they can join themselves; or to whom, as individuals, they can pledge their faith. No such association, or organization, as "the people of the United States," having ever been formed by any open, written, authentic, or voluntary contract, there is, on general principles of law and reason, no such association, or organization, in existence. And all oaths that purport to be given to such an association are necessarily given only to the winds. They cannot be said to be given to any man, or body of men, as individuals, because no man, or body of men, can come forward *with any proof* that the oaths were given to them, as individuals, or to any association of which they are members. To say that there is a tacit understanding among a portion of the male adults of the country, that they will call themselves "the people of the United States," and that they will act in concert in subjecting the remainder of the people of the United States to their dominion; but that they will keep themselves personally concealed by doing all their acts secretly, is wholly insufficient, on general principles of law and reason, to prove the existence of any such association, or organization, as "the people of the United States"; or consequently to prove that the oaths of foreigners were given to any such association.

XIV.

On general principles of law and reason, all the oaths which, since the war, have been given by Southern men, that they will obey the laws of Congress, support the Union, and the like, are of no validity. Such oaths are invalid, not only because they were extorted by military power, and threats of confiscation, and because they are in contravention of men's natural right to do as they please about supporting the government, *but also because they were given to nobody.* They were nominally given to "the United States." But being nominally given to "the United States," they were necessarily given to nobody, because, on general principles of law and reason, there were no "United States," to whom the oaths could be given. That is to say, there was no open, authentic, avowed, legitimate association, corporation, or body of men, known as "the United States," or as "the people of the United States," to whom the oaths could have been given. If anybody says there was such a corporation, let him state who were the individuals that composed it, and how and when they became a corporation. Were Mr. A, Mr. B, and Mr. C members of it? If so, where are their signatures? Where the evidence of their membership? Where the record? Where the open, authentic proof? There is none. Therefore, in law and reason, there was no such corporation.

On general principles of law and reason, every corporation, association, or organized body of men, having a legitimate corporate existence, and legitimate corporate rights, must consist of certain known individuals, who can prove, by legitimate and reasonable evidence, their membership. But nothing of this kind can be proved in regard to the corporation, or body of men, who call themselves "the United States." Not a man of them, in all the Northern States, can prove by any legitimate evidence, such as is required to prove membership in other legal corporations, that he himself, or any other man whom he can name, is a member of any corporation or association called "the United States," or "the people of the United States," or, consequently, that there is any such corporation. And since no such corporation can be proved to exist, it cannot of course be proved that the oaths of Southern men were given to any such corporation. The most that can be claimed is that the oaths were given to a secret band of robbers and murderers, who called themselves "the United States," and extorted those oaths. But that certainly is not enough to prove that the oaths are of any obligation.

XV.

On general principles of law and reason, the oaths of soldiers, that they will serve a given number of years, that they will obey the orders of their superior officers, that they will bear true allegiance to the government, and so forth, are of no obligation. Independently of the criminality of an oath, that, for a given number of years, he will kill all whom he may be commanded to kill, without exercising his own judgment or conscience as to the justice or necessity of such killing, there is this further reason why a soldier's oath is of no obligation, viz., that, like all the other oaths that have now been mentioned, *it is given to nobody.* There being, in no legitimate sense, any such corporation, or nation, as "the United States," nor, consequently, in any legitimate sense, any such government as "the government of the United States," a soldier's oath given to, or contract made with, such nation or government, is necessarily an oath given to, or a contract made with, nobody. Consequently such oath or contract can be of no obligation.

XVI.

On general principles of law and reason, the treaties, so called, which purport to be entered into with other nations, by persons calling themselves ambassadors, secretaries, presidents, and senators of the United States, in the name, and in behalf, of "the people of the United States," are of no validity. These so-called ambassadors, secretaries, presidents, and senators, who claim to be the agents of "the people of the United States," for making these treaties, can show no open, written, or other authentic evidence that either the whole "people of the United States," or any other open, avowed, responsible body of men, calling themselves by that name, ever authorized these pretended ambassadors and others to make treaties in the name of, or binding upon any one of, "the people of the United States," or any other open, avowed, responsible body of men, calling themselves by that name, ever authorized these pretended ambassadors, secretaries, and others, in their name and behalf, to recognize certain other persons, calling themselves emperors, kings, queens, and the like, as the rightful rulers, sovereigns, masters, or representatives of the different peoples whom they assume to govern, to represent, and to bind.

The "nations," as they are called, with whom our pretended ambassadors, secretaries, presidents, and senators profess to make treaties, are as much myths as our own. On general principles of law and reason, there are no such "nations." That is to say, neither the whole people of England, for example, nor any open, avowed, responsible body of men, calling themselves by that name, ever, by any open, written, or other authentic contract with each other, formed themselves into any bona fide, legitimate association or organization, or authorized any king, queen, or other representative to make treaties in their name, or to bind them, either individually, or as an association, by such treaties.

Our pretended treaties, then, being made with no legitimate or bona fide nations, or representatives of nations, and being made, on our part, by persons who have no legitimate authority to act for us, have intrinsically no more validity than a pretended treaty made by the Man in the Moon with the king of the Pleiades.

XVII.

On general principles of law and reason, debts contracted in the name of "the United States," or of "the people of the United States," are of no validity. It is utterly absurd to pretend that debts to the amount of twenty-five hundred millions of dollars[5] are binding upon thirty-five or forty millions of people, when there is not a particle of legitimate evidence—such as would be required to prove a private debt—that can be produced against any one of them, that either he, or his properly authorized attorney, ever contracted to pay one cent.

Certainly, neither the whole people of the United States, nor any number of them, ever separately or individually contracted to pay a cent of these debts.

Certainly, also, neither the whole people of the United States, nor any number of them, ever, by any open, written, or other authentic and voluntary contract, united themselves as a firm, corporation, or association, by the name of "the United States," or "the people of the United States," and authorized their agents to contract debts in their name.

Certainly, too, there is in existence no such firm, corporation, or association as "the United States," or "the people of the United States," formed by any open, written, or other authentic and volun-

---

[5] [A reference to the national debt in December, 1869, which totaled $2,453,000,000 and the approximate population of the country, 39,818,449 people, according to the census the next year. A furious controversy was going on when this was written as to how this debt was to be paid. See James G. Randall, *The Civil War and Reconstruction* (Boston: D. C. Heath & Co., 1937), pp. 832-836.]

tary contract, and having corporate property with which to pay these debts.

How, then, is it possible, on any general principle of law or reason, that debts that are binding upon nobody individually, can be binding upon forty millions of people collectively, when, on general and legitimate principles of law and reason, these forty millions of people neither have, nor ever had, any corporate property? never made any corporate or individual contract? and neither have, nor ever had, any corporate existence?

Who, then, created these debts, in the name of "the United States"? Why, at most, only a few persons, calling themselves "members of Congress," etc., who pretended to represent "the people of the United States," but who really represented only a secret band of robbers and murderers, who wanted money to carry on the robberies and murders in which they were then engaged; and who intended to extort from the future people of the United States, by robbery and threats of murder (and real murder, if that should prove necessary), the means to pay these debts.

This band of robbers and murderers, who were the real principals in contracting these debts, is a secret one, because its members have never entered into any open, written, avowed, or authentic contract, by which they may be individually known to the world, or even to each other. Their real or pretended representatives, who contracted these debts in their name, were selected (if selected at all) for that purpose secretly (by secret ballot), and in a way to furnish evidence against none of the principals *individually;* and these principals were really known *individually* neither to their pretended representatives who contracted these debts in their behalf, nor to those who lent the money. The money, therefore, was all borrowed and lent in the dark; that is, by men who did not see each other's faces, or know each other's names; who could not then, and cannot now, identify each other as principals in the transactions; and who consequently can prove no contract with each other.

Furthermore, the money was all lent and borrowed for criminal purposes; that is, for purposes of robbery and murder; and for this reason the contracts were all intrinsically void; and would have been so, even though the real parties, borrowers and lenders, had come face to face, and made their contracts openly, in their own proper names.

Furthermore, this secret band of robbers and murderers, who were the real borrowers of this money, having no legitimate corporate existence, have no corporate property with which to pay these debts. They do indeed pretend to own large tracts of wild lands, lying between the Atlantic and Pacific Oceans, and between the Gulf of Mexico and the North Pole. But, on general principles of law and reason, they might as well pretend to own the Atlantic and Pacific Oceans themselves; or the atmosphere and the sunlight; and to hold them, and dispose of them, for the payment of these debts.

Having no corporate property with which to pay what purports to be their corporate debts, this secret band of robbers and murderers are really bankrupt. They have nothing to pay with. In fact, they do not propose to pay their debts otherwise than from the proceeds of their future robberies and murders. These are confessedly their sole reliance; and were known to be such by the lenders of the money, at the time the money was lent. And it was, therefore, virtually a part of the contract, that the money should be repaid only from the proceeds of these future robberies and murders. For this reason, if for no other, the contracts were void from the beginning.

In fact, these apparently two classes, borrowers and lenders, were really one and the same class. They borrowed and lent money from and to themselves. They themselves were not only part and parcel, but the very life and soul, of this secret band of robbers and murderers, who borrowed and spent the money. Individually they furnished money for a common enterprise; taking, in return, what purported to be corporate promises for individual loans. The only excuse they had for taking these so-called corporate promises of, for individual loans by, the same parties, was that they might have some apparent excuse for the future robberies of the band (that is, to pay the debts of the corporation), and that they might also know what shares they were to be respectively entitled to out of the proceeds of their future robberies.

Finally, if these debts had been created for the most innocent and honest purposes, and in the most open and honest manner, by the real parties to the contracts, these parties could thereby have bound nobody but themselves, and no property but their own. They could have bound nobody that should have come after them, and no property subsequently created by, or belonging to, other persons.

XVIII.

The Constitution having never been signed by anybody; and there being no other open, written, or authentic contract between any parties whatever, by virtue of which the United States government, so called, is maintained; and it being well known that none but male persons, of twenty-one years of age and upwards, are allowed any voice in the government; and it being also well known that a large number of these adult persons seldom or never vote at all; and that all those who do vote, do so secretly (by secret ballot), and in a way to prevent their individual votes being known, either to the world, or even to each other; and consequently in a way to make no one openly responsible for the acts of their agents, or representatives,—all these things being known, the questions arise: *Who* compose the real governing power in the country? Who are the men, *the responsible men,* who rob us of our property? Restrain us of our liberty? Subject us to their arbitrary dominion? And devastate our homes, and shoot us down by the hundreds of thousands, if we resist? How shall we find these men? How shall we know them from others? How shall we defend ourselves and our property against them? Who, of our neighbors, are members of this secret band of robbers and murderers? How can we know which are *their* houses, that we may burn or demolish them? Which *their* property, that we may destroy it? Which their persons, that we may kill them, and rid the world and ourselves of such tyrants and monsters?

These are questions that must be answered, before men can be free; before they can protect themselves against this secret band of robbers and murderers, who now plunder, enslave, and destroy them.

The answer to these questions is, that only those who have the will and the power to shoot down their fellow men, are the real rulers in this, as in all other (so-called) civilized countries; for by no others will civilized men be robbed, or enslaved.

Among savages, mere physical strength, on the part of one man, may enable him to rob, enslave, or kill another man. Among barbarians, mere physical strength, on the part of a body of men, disciplined, and acting in concert, though with very little money or other wealth, may, under some circumstances, enable them to rob, enslave, or kill another body of men, as numerous, or perhaps even more numerous, than themselves. And among both savages and barbarians, mere want may sometimes compel one man to sell himself as a slave to another. But with (so-called) civilized peoples, among whom knowledge, wealth, and the means of acting in concert, have become diffused; and who have invented such weapons and other means of defense as to render mere physical strength of less importance; and by whom soldiers in any requisite number, and other instrumentalities of war in any requisite amount, can always be had for money, the question of war, and consequently the question of power, is little else than a mere question of money. As a necessary consequence, those who stand ready to furnish this money, are the real rulers. It is so in Europe, and it is so in this country.

In Europe, the nominal rulers, the emperors and kings and parliaments, are anything but the real rulers of their respective countries. They are little or nothing else than mere tools, employed by the wealthy to rob, enslave, and (if need be) murder those who have less wealth, or none at all.

The Rothschilds,[6] and that class of money-lenders of whom they are the representatives and agents—men who never think of lending a shilling to their next-door neighbors, for purposes of honest industry, unless upon the most ample security, and at the highest

---

[6] [It is obvious from the context that Spooner intended no particular animus toward the Rothschilds by citing them in relation to the financing of various regimes in a number of military adventures in that time. They are mentioned mainly because of their greater familiarity among a number of such international financiers. One is reminded that not all the enterprises of these money lenders were necessarily successful, as there were losers as well as winners in these State combats; the loan of the French house of Erlanger to the Confederacy in the American Civil War, and that of the Austrian branch of the Rothschilds to the Austrian government and its swift defeat by Prussia in the Seven Weeks' War of 1866, may be cited as examples. And, of course, the Rothschilds met their match in such operations on more than one occasion; see, for example, the accounts in Otto Wolff's

Ouvrard: Speculator of Genius (New York: David McKay, 1962). There is a vast literature on this subject.

Spooner overlooked a striking development in this area, the discovery of the possibilities involved in fiat money operations by the State as an escape from the restraints imposed by a privately-controlled specie-backed money system. The Lincoln government's issuance of greenbacks was the most successful example of the moment when Spooner was writing. Of course, in modern times, with the evolution of managed money, the State no longer need depend on financial houses, but is limited only by the amount of paper and ink, and public confidence, insofar as it can manufacture claims on production and present them in the market place in competition with the citizenry for such goods and services as its objectives require.]

rate of interest — stand ready, at all times, to lend money in unlimited amounts to those robbers and murderers, who call themselves governments, to be expended in shooting down those who do not submit quietly to being robbed and enslaved.

They lend their money in this manner, knowing that it is to be expended in murdering their fellow men, for simply seeking their liberty and their rights; knowing also that neither the interest nor the principal will ever be paid, except as it will be extorted under terror of the repetition of such murders as those for which the money lent is to be expended.

These money-lenders, the Rothschilds, for example, say to themselves: If we lend a hundred millions sterling to the queen and parliament of England, it will enable them to murder twenty, fifty, or a hundred thousand people in England, Ireland, or India; and the terror inspired by such wholesale murder, will enable them to keep the whole people of those countries in subjection for twenty, or perhaps fifty, years to come; to control all their trade and industry; and to extort from them large amounts of money, under the name of taxes; and from the wealth thus extorted from them, they (the queen and parliament) can afford to pay us a higher rate of interest for our money than we can get in any other way. Or, if we lend this sum to the emperor of Austria, it will enable him to murder so many of his people as to strike terror into the rest, and thus enable him to keep them in subjection, and extort money from them, for twenty or fifty years to come. And they say the same in regard to the emperor of Russia, the king of Prussia, the emperor of France, or any other ruler, so called, who, in their judgment, will be able, by murdering a reasonable portion of his people, to keep the rest in subjection, and extort money from them, for a long time to come, to pay the interest and principal of the money lent him.

And why are these men so ready to lend money for murdering their fellow men? Solely for this reason, viz., that such loans are considered better investments than loans for purposes of honest industry. They pay higher rates of interest; and it is less trouble to look after them. This is the whole matter.

The question of making these loans is, with these lenders, a mere question of pecuniary profit. They lend money to be expended in robbing, enslaving, and murdering their fellow men, solely because, on the whole, such loans pay better than any others.

They are no respecters of persons, no superstitious fools, that reverence monarchs. They care no more for a king, or an emperor, than they do for a beggar, except as he is a better customer, and can pay them better interest for their money. If they doubt his ability to make his murders successful for maintaining his power, and thus extorting money from his people in future, they dismiss him as unceremoniously as they would dismiss any other hopeless bankrupt, who should want to borrow money to save himself from open insolvency.

When these great lenders of blood-money, like the Rothschilds, have loaned vast sums in this way, for purposes of murder, to an emperor or a king, they sell out the bonds taken by them, in small amounts, to anybody, and everybody, who are disposed to buy them at satisfactory prices, to hold as investments. They (the Rothschilds) thus soon get back their money, with great profits; and are now ready to lend money in the same way again to any other robber and murderer, called an emperor or a king, who, they think, is likely to be successful in his robberies and murders, and able to pay a good price for the money necessary to carry them on.

This business of lending blood-money is one of the most thoroughly sordid, cold-blooded, and criminal that was ever carried on, to any considerable extent, amongst human beings. It is like lending money to slave traders, or to common robbers and pirates, to be repaid out of their plunder. And the men who loan money to governments, so called, for the purpose of enabling the latter to rob, enslave, and murder their people, are among the greatest villains that the world has ever seen. And they as much deserve to be hunted and killed (if they cannot otherwise be got rid of) as any slave traders, robbers, or pirates that ever lived.

When these emperors and kings, so-called, have obtained their loans, they proceed to hire and train immense numbers of professional murderers, called soldiers, and employ them in shooting down all who resist their demands for money. In fact, most of them keep large bodies of these murderers constantly in their service, as their only means of enforcing their extortions. There are now, I think, four or five millions of these professional murderers constantly employed by the so-called sovereigns of Europe. The enslaved people are, of course, forced to support and pay all these murderers, as well as to submit to all the other extortions which these murderers are employed to enforce.

It is only in this way that most of the so-called governments of Europe are maintained. These so-called governments are in reality only great bands of robbers and murderers, organized, disciplined, and constantly on the alert. And the so-called sovereigns, in these different governments, are simply the heads, or chiefs, of different bands of robbers and murderers. And these heads or chiefs are dependent upon the lenders of blood-money for the means to carry on their robberies and murders. They could not sustain themselves a moment but for the loans made to them by these blood-money loan-mongers. And their first care is to maintain their credit with them; for they know their end is come, the instant their credit with them fails. Consequently the first proceeds of their extortions are scrupulously applied to the payment of the interest on their loans.

In addition to paying the interest on their bonds, they perhaps grant to the holders of them great monopolies in banking, like the Banks of England, of France, and of Vienna; with the agreement that these banks shall furnish money whenever, in sudden emergencies, it may be necessary to shoot down more of their people. Perhaps also, by means of tariffs on competing imports, they give great monopolies to certain branches of industry, in which these lenders of blood-money are engaged. They also, by unequal taxation, exempt wholly or partially the property of these loan-mongers, and throw corresponding burdens upon those who are too poor and weak to resist.

Thus it is evident that all these men, who call themselves by the high-sounding names of Emperors, Kings, Sovereigns, Monarchs, Most Christian Majesties, Most Catholic Majesties, High Mightinesses, Most Serene and Potent Princes, and the like, and who claim to rule "by the grace of God," by "Divine Right"—that is, by special authority from Heaven—are intrinsically not only the merest miscreants and wretches, engaged solely in plundering, enslaving, and murdering their fellow men, but that they are also the merest hangers on, the servile, obsequious, fawning dependents and tools of these blood-money loan-mongers, on whom they rely for the means to carry on their crimes. These loan-mongers, like the Rothschilds, laugh in their sleeves, and say to themselves: These despicable creatures, who call themselves emperors, and kings, and majesties, and most serene and potent princes; who profess to wear crowns, and sit on thrones; who deck themselves with ribbons, and feathers, and jewels; and surround themselves with hired flatterers and lickspittles; and whom we suffer to strut around, and palm themselves off, upon fools and slaves, as sovereigns and lawgivers specially appointed by Almighty God; and to hold themselves out as the sole fountains of honors, and dignities, and wealth, and power—all these miscreants and imposters know that we make them, and use them; that in us they live, move, and have their being; that we require them (as the price of their positions) to take upon themselves all the labor, all the danger, and all the odium of all the crimes they commit for our profit; and that we will unmake them, strip them of their gewgaws, and send them out into the world as beggars, or give them over to the vengeance of the people they have enslaved, the moment they refuse to commit any crime we require of them, or to pay over to us such share of the proceeds of their robberies as we see fit to demand.

XIX.

Now, what is true in Europe, is substantially true in this country. The difference is the immaterial one, that, in this country, there is no visible, permanent head, or chief, of these robbers and murderers, who call themselves "the government." That is to say, there is no *one man*, who calls himself the state, or even emperor, king, or sovereign; no one who claims that he and his children rule "by the Grace of God," by "Divine Right," or by special appointment from Heaven. There are only certain men, who call themselves presidents, senators, and representatives, and claim to be the authorized agents, *for the time being, or for certain short periods, of all* "the people of the United States"; but who can show no credentials, or powers of attorney, or any other open, authentic evidence that they are so; and who notoriously are not so; but are really only the agents of a secret band of robbers and murderers, whom they themselves do not know, and have no means of knowing, individually; but who, they trust, will openly or secretly, when the crisis comes, sustain them in all their usurpations and crimes.

What is important to be noticed is, that these so-called presidents, senators, and representatives, these pretended agents of all "the people of the United States," the moment their exactions meet with any formidable resistance from any portion of "the people" themselves, are obliged, like their co-robbers and murderers in Europe, to fly at once to the lenders of blood money, for the means to sustain their power. And they borrow their money on the same principle, and for the same purpose, viz., to be expended in shooting down all those "people of the United States"—their own constituents and principals, as they profess to call them—who resist the robberies and enslavement which these borrowers of the money are practising upon them. And they expect to repay the loans, if at all, only from the proceeds of the future robberies, which they anticipate it will be easy for them and their successors to perpetrate through a long series of years, upon their pretended principals, if they can but shoot down now some hundreds of thousands of them, and thus strike terror into the rest.

Perhaps the facts were never made more evident, in any country on the globe, than in our own, that these soulless blood-money loan-mongers are the real rulers; that they rule from the most sordid and mercenary motives; that the ostensible government, the presidents, senators, and representatives, so called, are merely their tools; and that no ideas of, or regard for, justice or liberty had anything to do in inducing them to lend their money for the war. In proof of all this, look at the following facts.

Nearly a hundred years ago we professed to have got rid of all that religious superstition, inculcated by a servile and corrupt priesthood in Europe, that rulers, so called, derived their authority directly from Heaven; and that it was consequently a religious duty on the part of the people to obey them. We professed long ago to have learned that governments could rightfully exist only by the free will, and on the voluntary support, of those who might choose to sustain them. We all professed to have known long ago, that the only legitimate objects of government were the maintenance of liberty and justice equally for all. All this we had professed for nearly a hundred years. And we professed to look with pity and contempt upon those ignorant, superstitious, and enslaved peoples of Europe, who were so easily kept in subjection by the frauds and force of priests and kings.

Notwithstanding all this, that we had learned, and known, and professed, for nearly a century, these lenders of blood money had, for a long series of years previous to the war, been the willing accomplices of the slave-holders in perverting the government from the purposes of liberty and justice, to the greatest of crimes. They had been such accomplices *for a purely pecuniary consideration,* to wit, a control of the markets in the South; in other words, the privilege of holding the slave-holders themselves in industrial and commercial subjection to the manufacturers and merchants of the North (who afterwards furnished the money for the war). And these Northern merchants and manufacturers, these lenders of blood-money, were willing to continue to be the accomplices of the slave-holders in the future, for the same pecuniary consideration. But the slave-holders, either doubting the fidelity of their Northern allies, or feeling themselves strong enough to keep their slaves in subjection without Northern assistance, would no longer pay the price which these Northern men demanded. And it was to enforce this price in the future—that is, to monopolize the Southern markets, to maintain their industrial and commercial control over the South—that these Northern manufacturers and merchants lent some of the profits of their former monopolies for the war, in order to secure to themselves the same, or greater, monopolies in the future. These — and not any love of liberty or justice — were the motives on which the money for the war was lent by the North. In short, the North said to the slave-holders: If you will not pay us our price (give us control of your markets) for our assistance against your slaves, we will secure the same price (keep control of your markets) by helping your slaves against you, and using them as our tools for maintaining dominion over you; for the control of your markets we will have, whether the tools we use for that purpose be black or white, and be the cost, in blood and money, what it may.

On this principle, and from this motive, and not from any love of liberty, or justice, the money was lent in enormous amounts, and at enormous rates of interest. And it was only by means of these loans that the objects of the war were accomplished.

And now these lenders of blood-money demand their pay; and the government, so called, becomes their tool, their servile, slavish, villainous tool, to extort it from the labor of the enslaved people both of the North and the South. It is to be extorted by every form of direct, and indirect, and unequal taxation. Not only the nominal debt and interest—enormous as the latter was—are to be paid in full; but these holders of the debt are to be paid still further—and perhaps doubly, triply, or quadruply paid—by such tariffs on imports as will enable our home manufacturers to realize enormous prices for their commodities; also by such monopolies in banking as will enable them to keep control of, and thus enslave and plunder, the industry and trade of the great body of the Northern people themselves. In short, the industrial and commercial slavery of the great body of the people, North and South, black and white, is the price which these lenders of blood money demand, and insist upon, and are determined to secure, in return for the money lent for the war.

This programme having been fully arranged and systematized, they put their sword into the hands of the chief murderer of the war,[7] and charge him to carry their scheme into effect. And now he, speaking as their organ, says: *"Let us have peace."*

The meaning of this is: Submit quietly to all the robbery and slavery we have arranged for you, and you can have "peace." But in case you resist, the same lenders of blood-money, who furnished the means to subdue the South, will furnish the means again to subdue you.

These are the terms on which alone this government, or, with few exceptions, any other, ever gives "peace" to its people.

The whole affair, on the part of those who furnished the money, has been, and now is, a deliberate scheme of robbery and murder; not merely to monopolize the markets of the South, but also to monopolize the currency, and thus control the industry and trade, and thus plunder and enslave the laborers, of both North and South. And Congress and the president are today the merest tools for these purposes. They are obliged to be, for they know that their own power, as rulers, so-called, is at an end, the moment their credit with the blood-money loan-mongers fails. They are like a bankrupt in the hands of an extortioner. They dare not say nay to any demand made upon them. And to hide at once, if possible, both their servility and their crimes, they attempt to divert public attention, by crying out that they have "Abolished Slavery!" That they have "Saved the Country!" That they have "Preserved our Glorious Union!" and that, in now paying the "National Debt," as they call it (as if the people themselves, *all of them who are to be taxed for its payment*, had really and voluntarily joined in contracting it), they are simply "Maintaining the National Honor!"

By "maintaining the national honor," they mean simply that they themselves, open robbers and murderers, assume to be the nation, and will keep faith with those who lend them the money necessary to enable them to crush the great body of the people under their

---

[7][Undoubtedly a reference to General Grant, who had just become president.]

feet; and will faithfully appropriate, from the proceeds of their future robberies and murders, enough to pay all their loans, principal and interest.

The pretense that the "abolition of slavery" was either a motive or justification for the war, is a fraud of the same character with that of "maintaining the national honor." Who, but such usurpers, robbers, and murderers as they, ever established slavery? Or what government, except one resting upon the sword, like the one we now have, was ever capable of maintaining slavery? And why did these men abolish slavery? Not from any love of liberty in general —not as an act of justice to the black man himself, but only "as a war measure," and because they wanted his assistance, and that of his friends, in carrying on the war they had undertaken for maintaining and intensifying that political, commercial, and industrial slavery, to which they have subjected the great body of the people, both white and black. And yet these imposters now cry out that they have abolished the chattel slavery of the black man —although that was not the motive of the war—as if they thought they could thereby conceal, atone for, or justify that other slavery which they were fighting to perpetuate, and to render more rigorous and inexorable than it ever was before. There was no difference of principle—but only of degree—between the slavery they boast they have abolished, and the slavery they were fighting to preserve; for all restraints upon men's natural liberty, not necessary for the simple maintenance of justice, are of the nature of slavery, and differ from each other only in degree.

If their object had really been to abolish slavery, or maintain liberty or justice generally, they had only to say: All, whether white or black, who want the protection of this government, shall have it; and all who do not want it, will be left in peace, so long as they leave us in peace. Had they said this, slavery would necessarily have been abolished at once; the war would have been saved; and a thousand times nobler union than we have ever had would have been the result. It would have been a voluntary union of free men; such a union as will one day exist among all men, the world over, if the several nations, so called, shall ever get rid of the usurpers, robbers, and murderers, called governments, that now plunder, enslave, and destroy them.

Still another of the frauds of these men is, that they are now establishing, and that the war was designed to establish, "a government of consent." The only idea they have ever manifested as to what is a government of consent, is this—that it is one to which everybody must consent, or be shot. This idea was the dominant one on which the war was carried on; and it is the dominant one, now that we have got what is called "peace."

Their pretenses that they have "Saved the Country," and "Preserved our Glorious Union," are frauds like all the rest of their pretenses. By them they mean simply that they have subjugated, and maintained their power over, an unwilling people. This they call "Saving the Country"; as if an enslaved and subjugated people— or as if any people kept in subjection by the sword (as it is intended that all of us shall be hereafter)—could be said to have any country. This, too, they call "Preserving our Glorious Union"; as if there could be said to be any Union, glorious or inglorious, that was not voluntary. Or as if there could be said to be any union between masters and slaves; between those who conquer, and those who are subjugated.

All these cries of having "abolished slavery," of having "saved the country," of having "preserved the union," of establishing "a government of consent," and of "maintaining the national honor," are all gross, shameless, transparent cheats—so transparent that they ought to deceive no one—when uttered as justifications for the war, or for the government that has succeeded the war, or for now compelling the people to pay the cost of the war, or for compelling anybody to support a government that he does not want.

The lesson taught by all these facts is this: As long as mankind continue to pay "national debts," so-called—that is, so long as they are such dupes and cowards as to pay for being cheated, plundered, enslaved, and murdered—so long there will be enough to lend the money for those purposes; and with that money a plenty of tools, called soldiers, can be hired to keep them in subjection. But when they refuse any longer to pay for being thus cheated, plundered, enslaved, and murdered, they will cease to have cheats, and usurpers, and robbers, and murderers and blood-money loan-mongers for masters.[8]

---

[8][Despite the severity of his language, Spooner deserves recognition as one of the few observers, in the period immediately after the Civil War, to dismiss the simple propaganda that the war was the consequence of the single-minded objective of abolishing chattel slavery, and to examine at least in part the deeper material factors involved.]

APPENDIX.

Inasmuch as the Constitution was never signed, nor agreed to, by anybody, as a contract, and therefore never bound anybody, and is now binding upon nobody; and is, moreover, such an one as no people can ever hereafter be expected to consent to, except as they may be forced to do so at the point of the bayonet, it is perhaps of no importance what its true legal meaning, as a contract, is. Nevertheless, the writer thinks it proper to say that, in his opinion, the Constitution is no such instrument as it has generally been assumed to be; but that by false interpretations, and naked usurpations, the government has been made in practice a very widely, and almost wholly, different thing from what the Constitution itself purports to authorize. He has heretofore written much, and could write much more, to prove that such is the truth. But whether the Constitution really be one thing, or another, this much is certain—that it has either authorized such a government as we have had, or has been powerless to prevent it. In either case, it is unfit to exist.

INTRODUCTION
by James J. Martin

The celebrated *Letter to Thomas F. Bayard* was a product of a coincidental triangular confrontation of Spooner, Senator Thomas F. Bayard (D., Del.) (1828-1898) and Lyman Abbott (1835-1922), the most eminent figure in the United States in the propagation of the theological tenets of Christian Evolution.[1] Abbott also was to establish a formidable reputation in journalism, in addition to taking over the pulpit of the famous Plymouth Church in Brooklyn upon the death of Henry Ward Beecher (1813-1887), the most famous Protestant clergyman in America in the post-Civil War generation.

Beecher founded a journal in 1870, *The Christian Union*, which became a significant voice in the country in the last decades of the nineteenth century.[2] Abbott joined him as co-editor in 1876, and became sole editor for a short span of years beginning in 1882. Abbott also wrote a department titled "The Outlook"[3] from the beginning of his association with Beecher in editing *The Christian Union*. This involved a weekly review of current events and politics quite apart from theology or religion, and gained the journal many readers and Abbott an increasingly influential status as a secular[4] commentator on the political and social scene.

---

[1] See in particular Abbott's books, *The Theology of an Evolutionist* (New York: The Outlook Co., 1897); *What Christianity Means to Me* (New York: Macmillan, 1921); *The Evolution of Christianity* (Boston: Houghton, Mifflin, 1896).

[2] *The Christian Union* began with the issue of January, 1870, and continued through the number for June, 1893, when the title was changed to *The Outlook*. It became increasingly prestigious thereafter, absorbing several other journals, suspending publication in May, 1932. It resumed as *The New Outlook* the following month, and suspended permanently in June, 1935.

[3] Abbott, *Silhouettes of My Contemporaries* (London: George Allen and Unwin, 1922), preface, p. v. The title of this department ultimately became the name of the journal itself.

[4] Abbott had no difficulty on the subject of conflict between Church and State; his strong patriotic and nationalist sentiments guaranteed this would not be a problem. On a trip to Europe in 1902 he commented favorably on the three-year period of compulsory military service in Italy, and considered it in importance "next to the school system" as a device through which the Italian State might have proper time to redirect young men from the influence of the Catholic Church to the State. Abbott, *Impressions of a Careless Traveler* (New York: The Outlook Co., 1909), pp. 182-183.

Abbott, once a member of the Republican Party, had severed his relations with it by this time, as had a number of other noted personalities, mainly because of unhappiness and revulsion over the conduct of the Reconstruction program in the South after the Civil War.[5] He relates in his memoirs that upon taking over editorial control of *The Christian Union* early in 1882, "I resolved to make it in politics independent of all party organization." A feature of the journal for some time thereafter was a series of fierce editorials which criticized politics and politicians unmercifully, including such sentiments as "Both parties are corpses; the country needs a live one."[6]

The immense increase in State intervention and concentration of power which resulted from the Civil War was still insufficient for Abbott. In this time of the innovation of centralized monopoly of money issue and the proliferation of federal interventions and controls[7] (which, incidentally, make a hash out of the easy and glib generalization that the 1865-1900 era was a time of runaway individualist "laissez faire"), Abbott wanted far more done in the

---

[5] It has been pointed out that Spooner also was a thunderous antagonist of Reconstruction as early as 1870. Perhaps a goodly majority of New England abolitionists were hostile to Reconstruction, a commentary on how badly askew the drive to end slavery had gone, though the Civil War was no more short of achieving "war aims" than any other martial enterprise accompanied by high and noble moral propaganda. Witness the "War to Make the World Safe for Democracy" and "Make This the Last War" slogans of World Wars I and II in this country. Spooner had been an active pamphleteer in the pre-Civil War attack on slavery, ironically enough fought from an argument based on the Constitution. (See his *Unconstitutionality of Slavery*, Boston, 1845). It may be that Spooner was subsequently influenced in his assaulting the validity of the Constitution by the pre-war condemnation by his fellow townsman William Lloyd Garrison, as "a convenant with death and an agreement with hell." Spooner also was not deficient in emotional content, but his approach was primarily logically analytic and not denunciatory.

[6] Abbott, *Reminiscences* (Boston: Houghton, Mifflin, 1915, 1923), Chapter 18, "A Political Revolution," pp. 430-431. Abbott, however, was an uncompromising enemy of individualism; as early as 1865 he had written, "Individualism is the characteristic of simple barbarism, not of republican civilization." *Ibid.*, p. 440.

[7] Those interested in searching out the origins of the ideology of State socialist propaganda and government ownership or control proposals might find it rewarding to divert their attention away from immigrant radicals of the 1849-1920 period and from native "proletarian" protagonists, and examine for a change the writings and thought of a generous band of native Anglo-Saxon figures of profoundly respectable reputation with an ancestry going back virtually to the Mayflower, if not before. The notion that such ideas are the product of recently arrived "subversives" dies hard, of course; it is one of the foundations of the "golden age" theory.

department of governmental direction, regulation, and control.[8] And it was in exasperation and discontent with the politicians of both parties that he condemned them all, although it was his reflection upon their moral character which drew a protesting letter from Senator Bayard.

And it was this objection from Bayard which provided Spooner the opportunity to introduce his argument, published separately, and directed solely to Bayard. Spooner's account of this is lost, since his papers and literary effects, in the possession of Benjamin R. Tucker, went up in flames when Tucker's publishing enterprise and its entire contents were destroyed by fire early in 1908.[9] But he was hardly a collaborator with Abbott; it probably would have been hard to find any two men in America as opposite as Abbott and Spooner. The two represented utterly divergent viewpoints and fundamental positions. They simply used Senator Bayard, each in his own way, to establish and further their views.

Bayard, if anything, though a United States Senator from Delaware for sixteen years (1869-1885), came closer to Spooner in overall ideological convictions, even if starting from quite different premises. William Alexander Robinson, in the *Dictionary of American Biography*,[10] characterized Bayard as having built a career upon defending "unpopular minorities and hopeless causes." A "Democrat of the old school," he was implacably opposed to Reconstruction policies as "harsh and impolitic," and because "they involved an undue centralization of federal power with a corresponding aggrandizement of the executive branch of that government."

Bayard is further described as having combated "anything else than a currency of value," namely, gold and silver, as "lawful or safe money." During his tenure, Bayard's party was almost con-

---

[8] "I have steadfastly advocated the doctrine that not only the railways, but the mines, the forests, the waterways—in short, the land and its contents—must be brought under government regulation, state or national, and that this regulation must be extended to all forms of business—including the regulation of food, beverages, and drugs—as fast and as far as is necessary to conserve the public welfare." *Reminiscences*, p. 441. Despite his enthusiasm for much of the foundation of nationalistic socialism, Abbott was hostile to Marxian communism. Abbott, *Silhouettes of My Contemporaries*, pp. 307-309.

[9] See this writer's account in the introduction to Paul Eltzbacher, *Anarchism* (New York: Libertarian Book Club, 1960).

[10] The excellent sketch by Robinson in DAB, Vol. 2, pp. 70-72. The definitive full-length account of Bayard's tenure in the Senate is Charles Callan Tansill, *The Congressional Career of Thomas Francis Bayard, 1869-1885* (Washington: Georgetown University Press, 1946).

tinuously in the minority, so the situation provided an almost endless opportunity to protest the employment of State power by the Republicans for the material enhancement of specific favored individuals or groups. Robinson declared that Bayard "hated class legislation of every sort, whether it took the form of ship subsidies, railroad land grants, or tariff protection," and that "militarism and socialism he considered equally inimical to freedom." But from the context of action, it appears that such public positions were matters of personal conviction, and not mere temporary political expediency or opportunistic harassment of the majority.

There is no direct evidence that Bayard was influenced by Spooner's *Letter*, an onslaught which dimmed the critical element in Abbott's position almost to the point of extinction. Nor is there verifiable documentation attesting to his having commented on Spooner's pamphlet, *Natural Law*, which Spooner sent Bayard and which undoubtedly contributed to further discomfort for the Senator. Of course, it was hardly possible to come to grips with Spooner and remain a politician. But Bayard's language in Senate debate two months after Spooner's *Letter* sounded almost as if it had been prepared by Spooner. In a speech on a proposed tax bill Bayard declared, "A tax, after all, is against natural right; it is a payment forced by the government for its use,"[11] and went on to criticize the internal revenue system in terms which read like yesterday's newspaper editorial,[12] though there is a vast difference between the tax jungle of today and the system Bayard found detestable.

Subsequent Senate exchanges reveal Bayard expressing other striking views concerning objections to the waxing power of Washington. In an attack on a bill in April, 1884, which proposed to transfer to the Congress the power to suppress and extirpate contagious diseases among domestic animals throughout the country, Bayard asserted opposition again in language which has a startling contemporary quality. "This constant intervention by government in tasks that belong to the individual must cease," he warned, "or ours will become as bureaucratic a government as that of Russia." [!] "This bill is nothing in the world but another illustration of the prin-

---

[11]*Congressional Record,* 47 Cong., 1 sess., Part 6, July 22, 1882, p. 6356.

[12]"There are many features of the internal revenue system which are to me most repulsive, most objectionable," Bayard declared, selecting for special criticism "their inquisitorial features and the manner in which they have been often-times conducted." *Congressional Record,* 47 Cong., 1 sess., Part 6, July 24, 1882, p. 6392.

ciple of socialism that is fast growing under our practices of legislation and penetrating every branch of this government and entering into almost every detail of our public expenditure. Day by day the doctrines and practices of a paternal government are speciously and tentatively expanding over the country, and the habit of popular thought is unhappily becoming accustomed to them."[13]

It is in the context of these factors and awareness of these background circumstances that one should read Spooner's letter of May 22, 1882. It is regrettable that Bayard's senatorial tenure ended in 1885 and that Spooner died in 1887. It would have been an exciting intellectual event had they and Abbott entered into an extended three-way public controversy and further explored the divergent positions they represented. It would also have been most useful for the illumination of the current day, three generations removed. The questions involved are still unresolved.

---

[13]*Congressional Record*, 48 Cong., 1 sess., April 28, 1884, pp. 3471-73. Bayard cited from Herbert Spencer's "Coming Slavery" article in the *Contemporary Review, above*, p. 3472.

A LETTER

TO

THOMAS F. BAYARD

CHALLENGING HIS RIGHT — AND THAT OF ALL THE OTHER SO-CALLED SENATORS AND REPRESENTATIVES IN CONGRESS —

TO EXERCISE ANY LEGISLATIVE POWER WHATEVER OVER THE PEOPLE OF THE UNITED STATES.

By LYSANDER SPOONER.

BOSTON, MASS.:
PUBLISHED BY THE AUTHOR.
1882.

A Letter to Thomas F. Bayard

"Challenging his right—and that of all the other so-called senators and representatives in Congress—to exercise any legislative power whatever over the people of the United States."

by Lysander Spooner

To Thomas F. Bayard, of Delaware:

Sir—I have read your letter to Rev. Lyman Abbott, in which you express the opinion that it is at least possible for a man to be a legislator (under the Constitution of the United States) and yet be an honest man.

This proposition implies that you hold it to be at least possible that some four hundred men should, by some process or other, become invested with the right to make laws of their own—that is, *laws wholly of their own device,* and therefore necessarily distinct from the law of nature, or the principles of natural justice; and that these laws of their own making shall be really and truly obligatory upon the people of the United States; and that, therefore, the people may rightfully be compelled to obey them.

All this implies that you are of the opinion that the Congress of the United States, of which you are a member, has, by some process or other, become possessed of some right *of arbitrary dominion* over the people of the United States; which right of arbitrary dominion is not given by, and is, therefore, necessarily in conflict with, the law of nature, the principles of natural justice, and the natural rights of men, as individuals. All this is necessarily implied in the idea that the Congress now possesses any right whatever to make any laws whatever, *of its own device*—that is, any laws that shall be either more, less, or other than that natural law, which it can neither make, unmake, nor alter—and cause them to be enforced upon the people of the United States, or any of them, against their will.

You assume that the right of arbitrary dominion—that is, the right of making laws of their own device, and compelling obedience to them—is a "trust" that has been delegated to those who now exercise that power. You call it "the trust of public power."

But, Sir, you are mistaken in supposing that any such power has ever been delegated, or ever can be delegated, by any body, to any body.

Any such delegation of power is naturally impossible, for these reasons, viz:

1. No man can delegate, or give to another, any right of arbitrary dominion over himself; for that would be giving himself away as a slave. And this no one can do. Any contract to do so is necessarily an absurd one, and has no validity. To call such a contract a "constitution," or by any other high-sounding name, does not alter its character as an absurd and void contract.

2. No man can delegate, or give to another, any right of arbitrary dominion over a third person; for that would imply a right in the first person, not only to make the third person his slave, but also a right to dispose of him as a slave to still other persons. Any contract to do this is necessarily a criminal one, and therefore invalid. To call such a contract a "constitution" does not at all lessen its criminality, or add to its validity.

These facts, that no man can delegate, or give away, his own natural right to liberty, nor any other man's natural right to liberty, prove that he can delegate no right of arbitrary dominion whatever—or, what is the same thing, no legislative power whatever—over himself or anybody else, to any man, or body of men.

This impossibility of any man's delegating any legislative power whatever, necessarily results from the fact that the law of nature has drawn the line, and the only line—and that, too, a line that can never be effaced nor removed—between each man's own interest and inalienable rights of person and property, and each and every other man's inherent and inalienable rights of person and property. It, therefore, necessarily fixes the unalterable limits, within which every man may rightfully seek his own happiness, in his own way, free from all responsibility to, or interference by, his fellow men, or any of them.

All this pretended delegation of legislative power—that is, of a power, on the part of the legislators, so-called, to make any laws of their own device, distinct from the law of nature—is therefore an entire falsehood; a falsehood whose only purpose is to cover and hide a pure usurpation, by one body of men, of arbitrary dominion over other men.

That this legislative power, or power of arbitrary dominion, is a pure usurpation, on the part of those who now exercise it, and not a "trust" delegated to them, is still further proved by the fact that the only delegation of power, that is even professed or pretended to be made, is made *secretly*—that is, by *secret ballot*—and not in any open and authentic manner; and therefore not by any men, or body of men, who make themselves personally responsible, as principals, for the acts of those to whom they profess to delegate the power.

All this pretended delegation of power having been made secretly—that is, only by secret ballot—not a single one of all the legislators, so-called, who profess to be exercising only a delegated power, has himself any legal knowledge, or can offer any legal proof, as to who the particular individuals were who delegated it to him. And having no power to identify the individuals who professed to delegate the power to him, he cannot show any legal proof that anybody ever even attempted or pretended to delegate it to him.

Plainly, a man who exercises any arbitrary dominion over other men and who claims to be exercising only a delegated power, but cannot show who his principals are, nor, consequently, prove that he has any principals, must be presumed, both in law and reason, to have no principals; and therefore to be exercising no power but his own. And having, of right, no such power of his own, he is, both in law and reason, a naked usurper.

Sir, a secret ballot makes a secret government; and a secret government is a government by conspiracy; in which the people at large can have no rights. And that is the only government we now have. It is the government of which you are a voluntary member and supporter, and yet you claim to be an honest man. If you are an honest man, is not your honesty that of a thoughtless, ignorant man, who merely drifts with the current, instead of exercising any judgment of his own?

For still another reason, all legislators, so-called, under the Constitution of the United States, are exercising simply an arbitrary and irresponsible dominion of their own; and not any authority that has been delegated, or pretended to have been delegated, to them.

And that reason is that the Constitution itself (Art. I, Sec. 6) prescribes that:

> "For any speech or debate (or vote) in either house, they (the Senators and Representatives) shall not be questioned (held to any legal responsibility) in any other place."

This provision makes the legislators constitutionally irresponsible to anybody; either to those on whom they exercise their power, or to those who may have, either openly or secretly, attempted or pretended to delegate power to them. And men who are legally responsible to nobody for their acts, cannot truly be said to be the agents of any body, or to be exercising any power but their own; for all real agents are necessarily responsible both to those *on* whom they act, and to those *for* whom they act.

To say that the people of this country ever have bound, or ever could bind, themselves by any contract whatever—the Constitution, or any other—to thus give away all their natural rights of property, liberty, and life, into the hands of a few men—a mere conclave—and that they should make it a part of the contract itself that these few men should be held legally irresponsible for the disposal they should make of those rights, is an utter absurdity. It is to say that they have bound themselves, and that they could bind themselves, by an utterly idiotic and suicidal contract.

If such a contract had ever been made by one private individual to another, and had been signed, sealed, witnessed, acknowledged, and delivered, with all possible legal formalities, no decent court on earth—certainly none in this country—would have regarded it, for a moment, as conveying any right, or delegating any power, or as having the slightest legal validity, or obligation.

For all the reasons now given, and for still others that might be given, the legislative power now exercised by Congress is, in both law and reason, a purely personal, arbitrary, irresponsible, usurped dominion on the part of the legislators themselves, and not a power delegated to them by anybody.

Yet under the pretense that this instrument gives them the right of an arbitrary and irresponsible dominion over the whole people of the United States, Congress has now gone on, for ninety years and more, filling great volumes with laws of their own device, which the people at large have never read, nor even seen, nor ever will read or see; and of whose legal meanings it is morally impossible that they should ever know anything. Congress has never dared to require the people even to read these laws. Had it done so, the oppression would have been an intolerable one; and the people, rather than endure it, would have either rebelled, and overthrown the government, or would have fled the country. Yet these laws, which Congress has not dared to require the people even to read, it has compelled them, at the point of the bayonet, to obey.

And this moral, and legal, and political monstrosity is the kind of government which Congress claims that the Constitution authorizes it to impose upon the people.

Sir, can you say that such an arbitrary and irresponsible dominion as this, over the properties, liberties, and lives of fifty millions of people—or even over the property, liberty, or life of any one of those fifty millions—can be justified on any reason whatever? If not, with what color of truth can you say that you yourself, or anybody else, can act as a legislator, under the Constitution of the United States, and yet be an honest man?

To say that the arbitrary and irresponsible dominion, that is exercised by Congress, has been delegated to it by the Constitution, *and not solely by the secret ballots of the voters for the time being,* is the height of absurdity; for what is the Constitution? It is, at best, a writing that was drawn up more than ninety years ago; was assented to at the time only by a small number of men; generally those few white male adults who had prescribed amounts of property; probably not more than two hundred thousand in all; or one in twenty of the whole population.

Those men have been long since dead. They never had any right of arbitrary dominion over even their contemporaries; and they never had any over us. Their wills or wishes have no more rightful authority over us, than have the wills or wishes of men who lived before the flood. They never personally signed, sealed, acknowledged, or delivered, or dared to sign, seal, acknowledge, or deliver, the instrument which they imposed upon the country as law. They never, in any open and authentic manner, bound even themselves to obey it, or made themselves personally responsible for the acts of their so-called agents under it. They had no natural right to impose it, as law, upon a single human being. The whole proceeding was a pure usurpation.

In practice, the Constitution has been an utter fraud from the beginning. Professing to have been "ordained and established" by "*we, the people of the United States,*" it has never been submitted to them, as individuals, for their voluntary acceptance or rejection. They have never been asked to sign, seal, acknowledge, or deliver it, as their free act and deed. They have never signed, sealed, acknowledged, or delivered it, or promised, or laid themselves under any kind of obligation, to obey it. Very few of them have ever read, or even seen it; or ever will read or see it. Of its legal meaning (if it can be said to have any) they really know nothing; and never did, nor ever will, know anything.

Why is it, Sir, that such an instrument as the Constitution, for which nobody has been responsible, and of which few persons have ever known anything, has been suffered to stand, for the last ninety years, and to be used for such audacious and criminal purposes? It is solely because it has been sustained by the same kind of conspiracy as that by which it was established; that is, by the wealth and the power of those few who were to profit by the arbitrary dominion it was assumed to give them over others. While the poor, the weak, and the ignorant, who were to be cheated, plundered, and enslaved by it, have been told, and some of them doubtless made to believe, that it is a sacred instrument, designed for the preservation of their rights.

These cheated, plundered, and enslaved persons have been made to feel, if not to believe, that the Constitution had such miraculous power, that it could authorize the majority (or even a plurality) of the male adults, for the time being—a majority numbering at this time, say, five millions in all—to exercise, through their agents, secretly appointed, an arbitrary and irresponsible dominion over the properties, liberties, and lives of the whole fifty millions; and that these fifty millions have no rightful alternative but to submit all their rights to this arbitrary dominion, or suffer such confiscation, imprisonment, or death as this secretly appointed, irresponsible cabal, of so-called legislators, should see fit to resort to for the maintenance of its power.

As might have been expected, and as was, to a large degree, at least, intended, this Constitution has been used from the beginning by ambitious, rapacious, and unprincipled men, to enable them to maintain, at the point of the bayonet, an arbitrary and irresponsible dominion over those who were too ignorant and too weak to protect themselves against the conspirators who had thus combined to deceive, plunder, and enslave them.

Do you really think, Sir, that such a constitution as this can avail to justify those who, like yourself, are engaged in enforcing it? Is it not plain, rather, that the members of Congress, as a legislative body, whether they are conscious of it or not, are, in reality, a mere cabal of swindlers, usurpers, tyrants and robbers? Is it not plain that they are stupendous blockheads, if they imagine that they are anything else than such a cabal? or that their so-called laws impose the least obligation upon anybody?

If you have never before looked at this matter in this light, I ask you to do so now. And in the hope to aid you in doing so candidly, and to some useful purpose, I take the liberty to mail for you a pamphlet entitled:

"NATURAL LAW; OR THE SCIENCE OF JUSTICE; a Treatise on Natural Law, Natural Justice, Natural Rights, Natural Liberty, and Natural Society; Showing That All Legislation Whatsoever Is an Absurdity, a Usurpation, and a Crime. Part I."

In this pamphlet, I have endeavored to controvert distinctly the proposition that, by any possible process whatever, any man, or body of men, can become possessed of any right of arbitrary dominion over other men, or other men's property; or, consequently, any right whatever to make any law whatever, of their own—distinct from the law of nature—and compel any other men to obey it.

I trust I need not suspect you, as a legislator under the Constitution, and claiming to be an honest man, of any desire to evade the issue presented in this pamphlet. If you shall see fit to meet it, I hope you will excuse me for suggesting that—to avoid verbiage, and everything indefinite—you give at least a single specimen of a law that either heretofore has been made, or that you conceive it possible for legislators to make—that is, some law of their own device—that either has been, or shall be, really and truly obligatory upon other persons, and which such other persons have been, or may be, rightfully compelled to obey.

If you can either find or devise any such law, I trust you will make it known, that it may be examined, and the question of its obligation be fairly settled in the popular mind.

But if it should happen that you can neither find such a law in the existing statute books of the United States, nor, in your own mind, conceive of such a law as possible under the Constitution, I give you leave to find it, if that be possible, in the constitution or statute book of any other people that now exist, or ever have existed, on the earth.

If, finally, you shall find no such law, anywhere, nor be able to conceive of any such law yourself, I take the liberty to suggest that it is your imperative duty to submit the question to your associate legislators; and, if they can give no light on the subject, that you call upon them to burn all the existing statute books of the United States, and then to go home and content themselves with the exercise of only such rights and powers as nature has given to them in common with the rest of mankind.

The American Letter Mail Company

Spooner's Private Post Office

Lysander Spooner appears at various times in American affairs of widely differing substance in the 19th century, with uniquely individual published contributions to legal, economic, political and even theological theory. The largest part of such activities is known only to a small number of students and researchers, and the history textbooks usually do not even mention his name. The best known venture of Spooner, which has been memorialized by several commentators, was his private mail business, the American Letter Mail Company. This was one of many such enterprises which competed successfully against the federal government's post office, but were driven out of business by an act of Congress which became effective July 1, 1845.

Spooner fought this in the courts and lost, but he always maintained that the government adopted his lower rates. (See his *The Unconstitutionality of the Laws of Congress Prohibiting Private Mails* [New York, 1944], and *Who Caused the Reduction in Postage?* [Boston, 1851].) He has been repeatedly described as "the father of cheap postage in America." Apparently Spooner's company handled a generous volume of business, because covers bearing its stamp and cancellation are not considered "of great rarity" even today, according to the specialist Donald S. Patton in *The Philatelist*. (One will find of considerable interest with reference to Spooner and his post the article by Ernest A. Kehn, Henry M. Goodkind and Elliott Perry, "Look Before You Lick," *Reader's Digest* [June, 1947], pp. 125-127, and Henry F. Unger's "Spooner and the Post Office," *Business Progress* [March-April, 1964], p. 16.)

Facing: one of the best-preserved covers of Spooner's American Letter Mail Company, from the Richard Schwartz collection. A particular thanks is extended to David L. Jarrett of the Postal History Society for making it available.

The Right Wing Individualist Tradition In America

An Arno Press/New York Times Collection

Bailie, William. **Josiah Warren:** The First American Anarchist. 1906.

Barber, Thomas H. **Where We Are At.** 1950.

Barnes, Harry Elmer. **Pearl Harbor After a Quarter of a Century.** Left and Right: A Journal of Libertarian Thought, Vol. IV. 1968.

Barnes, Harry Elmer. **In Quest of Truth and Justice:** De-Bunking the War Guilt Myth. 1928.

Barnes, Harry Elmer. **Selected Revisionist Pamphlets,** n.d. 1972.

Bromfield, Louis. **A New Pattern for a Tired World.** 1954.

Burgess, John W. **Recent Changes in American Constitutional Theory.** 1923.

Carroll, Charles Holt. **Organization of Debt into Currency:** and Other Papers. 1964.

Fleming, Harold M. **Ten Thousand Commandments:** A Story of the Antitrust Laws. 1951.

Flynn, John T. **As We Go Marching.** 1944.

Harris, George. **Inequality and Progress.** 1897.

Individualist Anarchist Pamphlets, 1867-1904. 1972.

Knight, Bruce Winton. **How to Run a War.** 1936. New Preface by Bruce Winton Knight.

Lane, Rose Wilder. **The Discovery of Freedom:** Man's Struggle Against Authority. 1943. New Foreword by Robert LeFevre. New Introduction by Roger Lea MacBride.

Left and Right: Selected Essays, 1954-1965. 1972.

The Libertarian Forum. 1969-1971. Murray N. Rothbard and Karl Hess, editors.

McGurrin, James. **Bourke Cockran:** A Free Lance in American Politics. 1948.

[La Monte, Robert Rives and H. L. Mencken.] **Men Versus The Man:** A Correspondence between Robert Rives La Monte, Socialist and H. L. Mencken, Individualist. 1910.

Montgomery, Zach[ariah], compiler. **The School Question:** From a Parental and Non-Sectarian Stand-Point. 1889.

Nock, Albert Jay. **Our Enemy, The State.** 1935.

Olds, Marshall. **Analysis of the Interchurch World Movement Report on the Steel Strike.** 1922.

Oppenheimer, Franz. **The State:** Its History and Development Viewed Sociologically. 1926.

Paterson, Isabel. **The God of the Machine.** 1943.

Phillips, C. A., T. F. McManus and R. W. Nelson. **Banking and the Business Cycle:** A Study of the Great Depression in the United States. 1937.

Schoeck, Helmut and James W. Wiggins, editors. **Scientism and Values.** 1960.

Scoville, John W. **Labor Monopolies or Freedom.** 1946.

Scoville, John and Noel Sargent, compilers. **Fact and Fancy in the T.N.E.C. Monographs.** 1942.

Snyder, Carl. **Capitalism The Creator:** The Economic Foundations of Modern Industrial Society. 1940.

Society Without Government: 1969-1970. 1972.
  Tannehill, Morris and Linda and Jarret B. Wollstein.

Spooner, Lysander. **Let's Abolish Government,** 1852-1886. 1972.

Sprading, Charles T., editor. **Liberty and the Great Libertarians.** 1913.

Sumner, William Graham. **What Social Classes Owe to Each Other.** 1883.

Tolles, Frederick B. **George Logan of Philadelphia.** 1953.

Tucker, Benj[amin] R. **Instead of a Book:** By a Man Too Busy to Write One. 1893.

Vreeland, Hamilton, Jr. **Twilight of Individual Liberty.** 1944.

What Is Money? 1884-1963. 1972. Rothbard, Murray N. and I[saiah] W. Sylvester.

Williamson, Harold Francis. **Edward Atkinson:** The Biography of an American Liberal, 1827-1905. 1934.

Winston, Ambrose Paré. **Judicial Economics:** The Doctrine of Monopoly as Set Forth by Judges of the U.S. Federal Courts in Suits under the Anti-Trust Laws. 1957.